MISTI MOMENTS

THE COLLECTION

Volume 1

Misti Rains

Jen Lee, I pray these words richly bless you! With love and appreciation! Misti Rains

MISTI RAINS
AUTHOR &
SPEAKER
#MISTIMOMENTS

Misti Moments: The Collection

Special discounts are available on quantity purchases by corporations, associations and others. For details, contact the publisher at the address below.

ISBN: 978-1-7340791-1-1 paperback
ISBN: 978-1-7340791-4-2 hardback

Printed in the United States of America

Misti Rains Publishing
300 Opelika Rd. #1844
Auburn, AL 36831
www.mistirains.com

Misti Moments

Misti Moments: The Collection can be read as a daily devotional
or as one continuous read.
It does not have to be read in chronological order.

I write these words for my children,
the great loves of my life.
May they serve as a lamppost
to help guide your way.

Contents

CONTENTS

INTRODUCTION

$\mathcal{L}$IFE IS A SERIES OF MOMENTS. Some you love. Some you wish you could forget. Some hold you down. Some lift you up. Some fight to keep you bound. Some arrive to set you free. There are defeating moments, heart-breaking moments, and moments that carry with them the sting of deep regret, guilt, and shame. There are moments of passion, moments of sheer rage, and moments of brokenness and great sorrow. You experience moments of rejection that appear to break you and moments of unconditional acceptance that serve to raise you. You suffer moments of unbearable loss, and you relish moments of profound gain. Moments bring you tears. Moments bring you laughter. Moments brings you folly and moments bring you wisdom.

Life is a collection of moments.
This book is a collection of what I have learned from mine,
my Misti Moments.

There are moments I wish I could take back, and moments I wish I could do over. But those moments were my teachers serving to make all the remaining moments more heart-piercingly beautiful. To mention but a few, my moments have consisted of an inoperable hemangioma bleeding inside my brain stem and the nerve damage that accompanied it, two divorces, and the unexpected death of my greatest love—my beloved best friend and mother. My moments have also consisted of authentic happiness, sheer bliss, and a spiritual journey that has taken my soul to heights of soaring growth beyond what I could ever have imagined.

Moments bring both love and loss, both hope and despair. They teach through both pain and pleasure, tears, and triumph. In the end, it's the wisdom, love, healing, release, and forgiveness our hearts and souls glean from this

1

array of moments that genuinely count. It's not the moment itself that leaves you forever changed. It's what the moment was there to teach you.

Moments are purposeful. I pray the moments you spend reading mine will help you better face all of yours. I pray you find healing, kindness, warmth, and a heart-gripping pull towards all that you truly are, towards your home, towards love.

These Misti Moments are my raindrops left for my children, Riley, Jack, and Kate. And just as I pray they fall as a refreshing rain to water the dry places of their souls, I pray if this book has found its way into your hands, it would also provide a fresh dew upon your heart. I pray that you would also feel the rain, relish in the morning mist, and dance beneath the raindrops you find drenching the pages of this book.

There's nothing like waking to the sound of rain falling.
Cheers to a glorious rising!

Dear Person Reading This Book

DEAR PERSON READING THIS BOOK,

Not too long ago, I was on the phone with a dear friend when I was distracted for a few moments by a car that had pulled into my driveway. I stopped our conversation and began talking to myself. I was reminding myself of who and why the person was there, which was to pick up a package I had left on our front porch. Afterward, my friend quickly replied, "Wait, do that again." "Do what again," I asked. "Talk to yourself." "Why?" I asked. "Because when you were talking to yourself, I could hear angels singing."

At that moment, I heard the Spirit loud and clear. I knew it was time to write for my children. There were things I needed to write to them from my heart to their hearts. I knew it was a prescription for my health. The following pages are a collection of those writings. At times it also felt like I was writing for the birds perched in the trees around me, for the villains of my past, for those I love and treasure, and for total strangers I would never know or meet.

I wrote in the forest nestled under a canopy of trees. I wrote swinging in my favorite hammock and nestled cozily on the back porch of my parents' lake cabin. I stared at the lake waters, and I wrote. I stared at the ocean, and I wrote. I stared at the butterflies, and I wrote. I gazed into the warm outdoor fire I would make for myself each morning, and I wrote. I wrote when I was happy, and I wrote when I was sad. Plain and simple, I wrote. And at the end of the day, I was writing for my precious three: Riley, Jack, and Kate.

I never stopped to ask if what I was writing made any sense. I didn't judge myself while I was writing, asking if I was writing from my ego or under the influence of the Divine. I didn't stop to ask myself if I was writing in order or with fluidity or if I had a topic or chapter heading. I just wrote. There were things that needed to be healed; things buried that needed to emerge, and things hidden and suppressed that needed to spring forth. There were conversations I needed to have with me and my infinite self without judgment, condemnation, or guilt. I needed to write and know there was nothing I could say, do, or ask that was off-limits or would lessen the space of unconditional love that was being held for me.

Why the incessant need to get a few things off my chest? A near-death experience seems to carry with it a tendency to purge, cleanse, and do whatever is necessary to get real and heal back to wholeness. There's nothing like a brush with death to make you realize the sacredness of life. It awakens you and tends to quickly prioritize the concerns of your life. There is a sudden lack of interest for continuing to spend time people-pleasing or chasing frivolous desires.

At least this is what happened to me when I was diagnosed with a hemangioma that was bleeding and growing in the middle of my brain stem. As the neurological effects began to sink in, I was gripped by the reality that was facing me. I was also keenly aware of the fact that something within me had created this illness that was drastically affecting my body and quality of life. I could either see this illness as a stumbling block or a stepping-stone. I could choose to respond in fear or faith. I chose to see my circumstances as my teachers and over time gradually stopped calling my imperfection a brain tumor and began to see it as a gift that had arrived to teach me and help release negative trapped energy within my body. My soul was crying out for truth, and the only way to progress was to boil all remaining impurities to the surface, expose them, and use a heavenly ladle to skim them off the top.

My path to healing has been one of significant personal development. It has required me to be the most authentic version of myself. I had to get real, get honest, and be prepared to release anything that stood in the way of walking in perfect divine health. Programs had to be deleted. Control systems had to vanish. Limiting beliefs were no longer allowed to linger. No matter how deeply programmed I had been, to truly live heaven on earth in the everyday functioning aspects of my life, I had to be prepared to release anything that no longer served my goal of living abundantly free. Philosophies, ideas, teachings, ways of thinking, and behaving, along with my entire religious upbringing, were called into question. I had arrived at a whole new level of walking the walk. Decisions had to be made as to what I truly believed and whether or not I could stand on those principles and live. I wanted eternal freedom, and I quickly learned that all beliefs rooted in fear had to be extinguished as they would most certainly create a stupor and sleep of the soul.

The following pages are those that depict my healing back to wholeness. My hope is that as you read, like my friend, you will also hear the angels sing. As I talk to myself, write letters that need to be penned, and leave words that hopefully will at some time be read by my children, my prayer is that the angels of God will awaken the truths lying dormant within you and fill you with a marvelous freeing light. May the soul that is touching these pages feel more divinely connected to the Source of your Being and the infinitely powerful force that exists within your own Spirit. May you feel lighter, freer, and more empowered to overcome any obstacle that may come towards you. May you be filled with the highest truths, the greatest compassion, an enduring and unconditional love, and strength and wisdom to forgive all those who have inflicted physical, emotional, or spiritual wounds. May these words help to release captives and set your soul abundantly free.

Glean the Field

ALL WE CAN DO IS SPEAK FROM OUR OWN EXPERIENCE, so it is with lessons learned that I pen these words to you. From these jottings, take what works for you and leave what doesn't. I've had many teachers and mentors in my life, and the wisest words pertaining to all of them came from the Spirit as I was reading the story of Ruth in the Bible. There is a part in the story where it mentions that Ruth was gleaning from the field. I didn't quite understand what the word glean meant, so I looked it up to which I read, "to collect gradually bit by bit."

At that moment I heard the Spirit say, "Glean, Misti, glean. You will enter many fields, and you are not to take everything that's made available to you. Only take what is needed for your journey. Leave what isn't for you. Collect what is for you. Gather bit by bit and make a feast for you and those who will come to glean from your field. They too, will take what is needed. Allow them to leave what does not serve their needs."

From that moment forward, I knew I would never fully absorb or need all the knowledge that would be made available to me. I certainly have not agreed with or adopted everything a mentor has shared with me, and I would strongly advise you along the same trajectory. I have been able to treasure bits of wisdom along the way, appreciating the message without glorifying the messenger. Although the answers to life's hurdles come from within, oftentimes we do get stuck and need the wisdom of one who has crossed the barrier we are currently facing to be the vessel through which a solution is given.

I believe everyone's life would flow much more effortlessly if they appreciated and acknowledged the dialog that is taking place all around them. This conversation is occurring at all times and through many different modalities. Your assistance may come from a person or through an animal. It may come on a billboard message or through a phrase typed upon the external wrapping of your lemonade bottle. Messages have come to me in the form of flowers, butterflies, fishes in the ocean, and trees, which have told me a story. Nature has brought me many divine messages as well as phrases and numbers and little reminders painted atop the canvas of my life and written into the fabric of my day. There is a beautiful, magical, and extremely helpful conversation occurring with a Divine Presence all throughout our day if we would but notice, tune ourselves to its wonder, and intuitively believe in its guidance.

There's nothing like a brush with death to make you realize the sacredness of life.

Whether you realize it or not your guides or angels as you may prefer to call them have guided you to the moment where you hold this book in your hands. As I open myself for the Holy Spirit to pour herself through my being and formulate these words to you, my prayer is that you would do as I do when listening to the channel of another. Ask yourself the question,

> *"Do these words help bring heaven to earth in any area of my life? Do they free me? Do they release a heavy yoke I am carrying? Do they help me become more loving, gracious, forgiving, and more closely connected to the truest version of myself? Do they connect me to a higher truth, a better way, and do they guide me to a deeper connection with the power of God at work in me?"*

If so, I encourage you to feast on these words. Dine well, absorbing all the nutrients. Glean from this field, leaving what does not serve you and taking what nourishes you. As you travel to other fields, remember to collect all that you need so that bit by bit you gather all you require for a bountiful harvest of your soul's ultimate desire.

A Divine Deposit

IT'S BEEN ALMOST THREE YEARS SINCE I WOKE unable to feel sensation in my mouth, tongue, and lips, and with the realization that the right side of my body was going numb. It's been almost three years since I woke from passing out on my hardwood kitchen floor unable to breathe, suffocating and gasping in a pool of blood from a cracked-open chin. It's been almost three years since I lay wondering if the ambulance would get me to the hospital in time to save my life. It's been almost three years since I was diagnosed with a brainstem hemangioma that was bleeding and causing miniature strokes in my brain. At one point, I was using a walker to get around, was forbidden to climb stairs, and had blurred vision in my right eye. It's been almost three years since I was told by my neurosurgeon that operating to remove the hemangioma could leave me brain dead. He wouldn't touch me. The gamma knife neurosurgeons wouldn't touch me. The hemangioma was in the center of my brain stem and to operate meant cutting through the healthy brain stem tissue I had, causing irreparable damage. I was left with only one plan of action from my doctor: to hope it wouldn't bleed again.

After the first brain bleed, the statistics showed I had a fifty percent greater chance of having future bleeds throughout my life. If my life eventually became severely compromised from future brain bleeds, the doctor told me he would

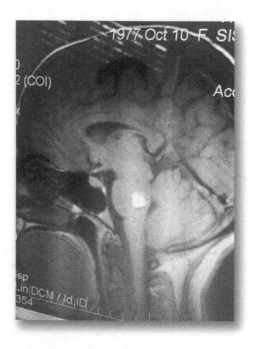

reevaluate the notion of operating in an attempt to remove the hemangioma. In the meantime, I was told I would have MRIs every six months to determine if the hemangioma had grown large enough to reach the edge of the brainstem where they could reach it. The neurosurgeon said if that occurred, he would then want to operate to try to remove it in hopes of preventing future bleeds. I was told to not lift heavy objects and to try to avoid stress or anything that could raise my blood pressure. It was suggested I connect with a pain clinic to help manage any ongoing nerve pain.

Have you ever been given a statistic,
and then the Spirit of God told you the truth?

That was the day I decided I would never live on pain meds.

That was the day I decided faith over fear.

That was the day I decided God could operate where man could not.

That was the day I decided God could touch what man could not, that God could heal what man could not.

That was the day I decided I would see dead nerves live again.

That was the day I decided God and I would supernaturally operate spiritually, removing the root of this benign tumor that had cultivated in the depths of my mind.

That was the day I decided I would learn mind over matter and live the rest of my life casting mountains into the sea.

That was the day I decided I would make something beautiful of any brokenness that still existed in my heart.

That was the day I decided I would free myself, truly free myself.

That was the day I decided when I figured all that out, I would write my heart out. I would write for strangers. I would write for friends. Most importantly and with laser focus, I would write for my children, the great loves of my life.

That was the day I decided that one day I would put my heart on paper—the pretty, the ugly, the whole pieces, the broken pieces, the parts that have been betrayed, the parts that have betrayed, the parts that have gleaned wisdom from playing all the roles—the healer, the wounded, the victim, the perpetrator, and the heroine.

Today I believe, with all my heart, God has granted me the time I need to write all the things I've held back, all the things I've shut up. I must. This season may last for the next thirty years, but there is nothing else to do, nothing more important but to leave a legacy of love notes to my children.

One of the last conversations I ever had with my mother before she tragically and unexpectedly died was about the book we were going to write together. That book has already turned into more books than I can count, deposited into my heart. I never thought we would write like this, Mom. Me sitting alone breathing you in—you and God, Spirits merged, at one with one another. With every whistle of the wind, with every bird that nestles beside me, with every leaf that sweetly falls, with every wave I feel crash over my feet, with every rainbow I admire—you are there. We will write together. I have a lifetime of deposits to pass down to the ones you treasured most.

None of us know how much time we have. It's been almost three years since experiencing one of the most painful memories I've ever had of seeing two ambulance doors open, being unable to talk, hooked up to wires, and seeing my mother, step-dad, and sister's face soaked in tears as they watched the gurney roll past them, rushing me into the emergency room. Everyone thought they were losing me. But today, I'm the one who has lost both my parents. I'm the one who ultimately found her face soaked in tears.

Life has her way of sending you curveballs. If you're here, there's a reason you're still here. Every day is a gift, an opportunity to live a life of contribution, to honor those we have deeply loved who have gone before us, to continue their mission, and to share their wisdom with our children. I understand the disciples of Christ more than ever now. Their tenacity and dedication weren't out of duty. It was in memory of a Great Love, their Christ, the one that was so meaningful and impactful to their heart that they wanted to share and continue His legacy, His life, and His ministry.

A great love never dies. That deposit you made, Mom—it's still with me. I'm pouring it into these pages. I'm pouring it into my children. I'm pouring it into everyone I see. You once wrote to me and said, "Misti, always remember this…fill your heart with God's love and give as much of it as you can to as many people as you can for as long as you can."

So, what more can I say, but as we say here in the South, "Yes, ma'am." I will do that, Mama. I will do that. I will do that for as long as I possibly can.

Let's begin.

SELF LOVE

Dearest Me

DEAREST ME,

Do you know how you love to listen to the birds sing their pretty songs? When you stand in the open places and release the contents of your heart, this is what I hear. I'm proud of the songs that you sing. I realize I haven't always spoken to you this way. I've criticized you, compared you, judged you, required unrealistic goals of you, and been a really horrible companion at times. I've tried to convince you of terrible things regarding yourself, and I've failed to really love you as you deserve to be loved. I've walked away from you, silenced you, and failed to believe in you. I've taken you places you should never have gone. However, today, I pen these words to you from the depths of my heart. Thank you for forgiving me. You have no idea how deeply my soul needed to hear those words and feel the genuine emotion of them.

Straight from myself to myself, I am so proud of you. Not because you've done everything right, but because you chose to be here. You chose to keep trying, to keep living, and to continue growing us. It's important for you to know that I genuinely love you.

I love you. I love you. I love you.
I love you like I have never loved you before.

No matter what happens as a result of you singing the song you are about to bellow forth, these pages will be golden to me. They are our story, and although some chapters of the journey may not be as delightful as others, they are a part of what has brought us to this place of deep love, understanding, forgiveness, and grace. For that, I give thanks for them. This journey has taken us to the heart of God and reunited us with the truest version of ourselves.

So, sing, pretty Songbird. Sing a song of your soul. May the world sit beneath the branches of your tree finding shade, comfort, and rest in your melody. May each note, each stroke of your pen, yield a symphony of healing, hope, and faith restored. May your songs be drenched in truth and the ringing of discovered freedom.

All my love,
Me

Perhaps there is a love letter inside of you that needs to be written to you. I would encourage you to pen it and carry it close to your heart. Some of us have waited far too long to say some things to ourselves. Begin today by saying the following words as an expression from your heart to your heart:

I love you.
Thank you for choosing to be here and fight for our growth.
I am proud of how far you've come.
You are really beautiful.

Happy Rising

THIS YEAR HAS BEEN MESSY. I have allowed myself to feel it all, and I've allowed myself to go completely numb. The rug was pulled out from underneath me one too many times. Maybe I even slipped a little and caused my own tumble. It all gets a little hazy when the tears cloud the lens. But it doesn't matter what caused the breaking when you're lying flat on the ground. Your focus is on one thing... the rising.

I have shared a lot this year, but for those who truly know me, I've been unusually quiet—quiet regarding all that matters. It's ok. I've needed this time. I've needed this phase. I've needed the search. I've felt quite lost at times, but also incredibly found, incredibly at home, incredibly experiencing everything I've needed to experience.

Healing is a process. Let it happen. Let it take its course.

I'm observing my journey more intently than anyone. I watch with critique. At times, I watch with disappointment. I've learned to respect those moments too. They help me know better and thus do better. I also watch with wonder and amazement. Sometimes we just need to tell ourselves, "I love you. I have compassion for you. Look at you, Girl. Look at how you're making it. Keep going. You'll work out the kinks. You've got God, Beautiful. You've got His Spirit. You're gonna come through this shining."

So, there've been a few nights I've allowed for one too many distractions or drank one too many sips of that wine, but I also danced a little longer and laughed a little more. And I really needed that. I also know full well I need more than that, a lot more. My soul knows it too. I've been learning how to love me, and it's taken me a while to really know how to do that. I'm gonna get there, fully. I know it. Keep going. You will too.

This journey has taught me grace not because I've read about it,
but because I'm having an experience with it.

My heart has gotten bigger. My capacity to love has increased beyond what I ever thought it could. My cloak now is mercy, and my face wears compassion. Failure has blessed me with these precious commodities.

My heart is light, but it also bleeds. My passion is still there. It's rising. In the craziest, darkest, most broken places, it's rising. In fact, it's rising stronger than ever before. My voice is building. It is coming back mightier in strength but laced with more potent pinches of love.

Your crazy is your catalyst. Be so freaking real that it shakes the souls of those around you. If you are lost, be lost. Stop pretending to have it more together than you do.

Authenticity is the gateway to freedom.
I personally believe God appreciates it.

You can't make yourself more mature than you are. You are where you are. Look at it. Really look at it. Look at you. Examine you. Let your heart feel the sting of all that is not in alignment with your highest and best self. Then give yourself a good check, bring yourself back into alignment with who God has ordained you to be, and offer yourself some ridiculously amazing compassion. You're the only one that knows your whole story. You know how hard it's been. You know what you've had to fight to overcome. You know what it's taken to get this far. Respect that.

The true friends, the anointed ones, the ones meant to last, will see your struggle. They will gaze upon it with endless love and patience and find beauty in your brokenness because they will never stop seeing your potential. These are the ones who will breathe on it when you feel you can't catch a breath for yourself.

Listen to me. You are going to rise! You are going to shed anything and everything that is holding you back. You will finish this race. Your passion is being ignited. You are walking your road to Golgotha, my Friend. You are dying. Isn't it blissful? Your resurrection is just around the corner. Keep climbing the hill. You will assimilate the crazy. All will come into balance. You will find your perspective. Your Compass is always there, guiding. Keep listening. He's whispering.

Trust who God says you are in the
moments where you have forgotten.

Time is short. Do your due diligence. Make these moments count. All of this has been building for what is to come. This is your Kairos moment. Recognize it. Embrace it. Let go of what is no longer serving you. You were meant for something sacred. Remember that. Do that. Live that.

Finally, sit with the sinner and call her a saint, pardon her with kind eyes, and break bread with her, laugh with her, get to know her, and tell her she is absolutely perfect. Dote over her. Give her undivided attention, uplift her, and then stand back to watch her complete metamorphosis. If you overtake her with that kind of goodness, you will be among the privileged to see her fly.

Love is the answer to everything.

At the end of the day, we all want to scream, "This is me!" The good, the bad, the ugly, and the crazy. We want to know we've got some solid souls in our lives that will love and embrace our scream, know what it means, and are prepared to walk a lifetime with us. Do someone a solid and be that for them. Be it well. Maybe if you do such unto others, others will do such unto you, and they'll do it when you need it most.

Spirit rising, soul shining, voice enlightening, love radiating, and a handful of humble tears always falling—these are your ingredients. Keep them boiling in the seat of your soul as a refining purifier. No need to fake it till you make it. God can handle your real. Your tribe can handle your real. Your messy beautiful is gonna rise strong and shine like the friggin' sun. You are powerful beyond measure. And those imperfections, they're only making you more stunning.

A true Queen and King of hearts have healed from a broken one and spend the remainder of their days healing the hearts of others. The seat of a sacred throne comes with a price, and the one that sits upon it will have stitches and scars. They will know what is holding them together, and they will remain committed to offering that blessed peace to the constituents of their kingdom forevermore—without question, without vetting, and without judgment of worthiness. For all are worthy of such healing.

Anyone willing to embark on a journey of looking inward, of fixing the broken places, of rising from the ash heap, of forgiving, of loving without boundaries, already wears the crown.

True, you may be messy, but never for a second doubt one simple truth—you are royalty. You are laced in the finest of all the land. Your garments are the fruit of a Great Spirit that is shining so brilliantly bright within you that it will be impossible for you to miss your destined mark.

You are the salt of the earth. You are a city on a hill that cannot be hidden. Now use that Light and walk ye in it. Your path is illuminated. Your promise is secure. Go be royal. Go be sparkly. Go be real and shiny. Give the world a refreshing bath of authenticity. It is desperately needed. You're here to water the dry places of the soul. Pour well. Seeds are shooting forth, ready to emerge from beneath the dirt. Give them your sunlight. There are many mighty oaks ready to stand tall.

Happy Rising!

Your Story

YOUR STORY IS PRETTY.
It's messy.
It's meaningful.
It's tragic.
It's triumphant.
It's significant.
Allow for your defeat.
Allow for your heartbreak.
Give yourself a moment to know grace.

Your story will disappoint.
Your story will inspire.
Your story is remarkable.

The broken pieces of your life are relatable.
They're real.
They are what is genuine and true.
Allow for your bruising.
Embrace and love it all.

Your story is you.
Don't delete parts of your journey.
Keep all of it.
It's making you so dang beautiful.
And someday the right people are going to see and appreciate that.

Hey, You!

YOU ARE DOING SO WELL. I mean, seriously...look how far you've come! You've survived things you never thought you could survive. Every day you hear more and more clearly. Every day you are discovering new truths, and most importantly, you are cultivating greater love for yourself and others. Your compassion is expanding. Your strength is increasing. Your authenticity is rising.

There is a humility about you that is rare and hard to come by. Your life experiences have gifted you with an ability to ask questions instead of needing to be the one who has all the answers.

Your actions and the way you carry yourself reveal your character to others. You no longer feel the need to tell people who you are. You allow people to discover that for themselves. You don't edify yourself. Others do that for you. You observe others around you who still find it necessary to explain how amazing they are. You listen to them articulating their various skill sets while observing their obvious need for validation and significance. They still have something to prove. You have outgrown those patterns of behavior. Knowing who you are intrinsically, in the silent recesses of your heart, is enough to validate your worth. You remain quiet while others speak for you.

You know what you need. You know what's best for you. You've taken your power back. You can stand up for yourself now. You can protect your values and beliefs without becoming uncentered by outside voices. Those days of trusting someone else to be more enlightened, have more wisdom, or have a better understanding of what is best for you are over. You now realize you have your own hotline to heaven, a direct link to your Source that is readily available for you at any time. It is speaking, and you have finally realized you have the ability to hear marvelously. You know who you are. You know where you are going. You may not know all the details, but you know better than anyone the trajectory of your destined path.

You've put in the time. You've put in the work, and now you are becoming. You are in the process of becoming the best version of you!

While on the journey, love yourself ridiculously. Surround yourself with voices that see you, edify you, and remind you of all the qualities you possess to shine like the Super Nova that you are! Life is too short to hang around people who attempt to limit you. There are no limitations except the ones you place upon yourself. Remove them. Your dream is as big as your imagination will allow it to be!

Romance yourself a little. When you find you, you will have struck gold!

You have everything you need...everything! It's inside of you! Keep pulling from that. Your answers aren't out there. They are in your heart. They abide in your Spirit. Take time to release them over yourself every day.

It is true I have found answers on the pages of a book, and I have found answers laced in the framework of the stars, but the true Logos is within the hearts of man. It is a breathing Word, a Divine Deposit that sits in the seat of the soul, alive and active and continuously speaking relevant, timely truth.

> *As above so below.*
> *As within so without.*
> *The Universe is inside of you.*
> *God is inside of you.*
> *Get still, and you will know this.*
> *You will know Him.*
> *You will know you.*

No one can know you more than you know you, so know thyself. Get busy with your love affair. Fall in love with you. Enjoy you. Fall head over heels. Make it a mad, affectionate love story to be etched in the history books of heaven.

Your search is being rewarded. Answers are being given. You are hearing wonderfully! Clear any doubt that would tell you otherwise. Keep listening. Keep swimming in your river. Stay in the flow! And while it's carrying you down the merry stream, live every moment as if you've already found paradise, because in all reality...you already have! Acknowledge that and be blissfully blessed.

Congratulations, you're finding yourself! You're finding more and more of you every single day! Keep falling in love with your discoveries! Just keep coming home to you! This is your pot of gold at the end of the rainbow. Bianca Sparacino once said,

"Be alone, take yourself on dates, sleep alone. In the midst of this you will learn about yourself. You will grow, you will figure out what inspires you, you will curate your own dreams, your own beliefs, your own stunning clarity, and when you do meet the person who makes your cells dance, you will be sure of it because you are sure of yourself."

So, take yourself to your favorite café and enjoy that yummy holiday-flavored latte. Sit at that fancy restaurant and delightfully sample the menu. Enjoy that stroll in nature and those nights on the back porch with just you and the crickets. Light a candle and play your favorite song. Romance yourself a little. When you find you, you will have struck gold!

You can't know what you need or
what you want until you know who you are.

And who are you? You are powerful beyond measure! You are your own game-changer! With a change of energy and focus, you can redirect any outcome! You can change the entire script of your life! You house the Creative Force that creates worlds. Utilize that!

Learn your lessons. Appreciate the classroom of life! And no matter how much you learn and grow along the way, please stay humble and grounded in the knowing that if you're in this world, you are still a student of it. If anyone tries to guide you from a place of an, "I've arrived," attitude, one word of advice: beware. Humility is a virtue. Wear it well. Make it a required fashion accessory for your daily wardrobe. Jesus Christ once said, "The least shall be the greatest." A true Guru or Master Teacher edifies you, not himself. He speaks to your greatness, not his own. He doesn't tell you he has transcended his ego, because he doesn't waste valuable time talking about and validating himself when instead he could be assisting you. Listen to yourself. Be willing to listen to others, but make sure others are also listening to you. If not, move on.

Do not pour your sunshine into someone
who does not think of you as their sky.
~ Gemma Troy

And lastly, laugh. Laugh a lot. Laugh at yourself. Laugh at life. Laugh at your joys and laugh at your failures. Author of the well-known series of novels, *Anne of Green Gables*, Laud Maud Montgomery said, "Laugh at your mistakes but learn from them. Joke over your troubles but gather strength from them. Have fun with your difficulties but overcome them." You grow up the first day you have your first real laugh at yourself. So, chuckle at your mistakes, pick up your peace, and keep marching forward! And just in case no one has told you today…

You're doing good, kiddo!
I believe in you!
The entire Universe is cheering for you!
~ Just a few essential statements everyone
should hear on a daily basis!

Wear your wisdom well, my friends.

You Are

YOU'RE A LITTLE BIT CRAZY, and a little bit cute.
A little bit healed, and a little bit bruised.

Your heart has bled, your tears how they fall.
You've been all alone, you've put up your walls.

You've cried for touch. You've cried for truth.
You've hungered for more. You want to be moved.

You're a little unsteady. You're a little undone.
But you're unique and quirky and a whole lot of fun.

You're meaningful. You're deep. You see more than most.
You've been strong. You've endured. You've continued to hope.

You fall apart. You fall together.
A hundred storms you've successfully weathered.

You're a mess. You're a message. You're both sides of the poles.
You are North. You are South. You're the part. You're the whole.

You've been good. You've been evil.
Both the Saint and the Sinner.
You've had losses, you've had gains.
You've been the failure. You've been the winner.

You've rushed, and you've waited.
You've been both sides of the storm.
Both the madness. Both the calm.
You've assumed every form.

The victim, the perpetrator, the heroine, the villain.
You've assumed all the roles.
But you never stopped swimmin'.

You've been misunderstood. You've put up a fight.
You were treated unjust. You walked away quiet.

You've wrestled against the current.
You've floated downstream.
You've protested. You've surrendered.
You've dreamed a million dreams.

You've imagined war. You've imagined hate.
You've fought for love and a better place.

You've cheated. You've been betrayed.
You've spoke truth, and you've lied to a thousand different ways.

You're the completion of the puzzle.
You're its many parts.
You're the all in all.
You are nothing. You are dark.

You are everything. You are light.
You have blinded. You have given sight.

You're the sun and the rain.
You're the one that has nourished.
You have taken away. You have depleted.
You have uplifted. You have discouraged.

You've been ugly. You've been beautiful.
You've been less. You've been more.
You've caused people to follow. You've made them walk out the door.

You're complex and simplistic.
You are everything, and you are nothing.
You are both the storm and the calm.
You're but a vapor. Yet your beauty is remarkably something.

You've been through what no one should have endured.
Yet you've been triumphant. You've risen solid and secure.

You've laughed and you've played.
You've cried, and you've run away.

You've been lost. You've found home.
You've wandered, but you were never truly gone.

Because you are love, you are light.
You are all that ever has been and could ever be.
You are Him. He is you.
The Christ that all are wanting to see.

You have lived. You have died. You have lived again.
You've been buried. You've been resurrected.
You've been brought low. You've been lifted.

You've crawled in the mud. You've soared upon the skies.
You've sat with the hurting. You've laughed with the ones who fly.

You've seen all the seasons.
You've traveled through the many houses.
You've healed. You've matured. You've broken all your curses.

You've circled that great wheel in the sky.
You've connected with the stars. You've figured out your why.

You've been confused, but you now know who you are.
The time has been short, and yet you've traveled so far.

You're here to lead. You're here to serve.
You're here to be stripped bare. You're here to discover your worth.

You're here to break. You're here to mend.
You're here to get mad. You're here to make anger your friend.

You're here to make war. You're here to make peace.
You're here to make what's on the inside be acknowledged and seen.

You are all of it and then some.
You're the great wonder of the world.
Make no mistake about it,
you are a Living Pearl.

You are the object of all awe.
You've risen from your fall.
You've turned your demons into angels.
You've shattered all your walls.

You've earned your wings.
No more back and forth.
No more time in the chrysalis,
it's time to soar.

Imperfectly You

1 SPENT MOST OF MY LIFE PERFORMING: performing for validation, performing to feel significant, performing to feel needed, and performing for love. I wasn't using my gifts and talents from a space of bliss and fulfillment. I was using them to feel worth. Until one day, my brain began to bleed. My hand and my mouth went numb. The two areas I used to express myself to this world began to fade on me. I was suffering from a brainstem hemangioma that was growing at a rapid pace and deemed inoperable by my neurosurgeon. My soul was literally bleeding out. It was tired. It was done exhausting itself for me to feel a sense of completion. It wanted to get my attention. It wanted me to know that I was already complete. I was already whole. I was significant. I was loved. It wanted me to understand I was all of those things, not because of my performance, but because of who I am.

My life circumstances let me know rather quickly that perfectionism was not in the cards for me. That glass house of appearing to have it all together eventually came crumbling down, and I've got to be honest with you, the glass-house-shattering moments of my life have been the most liberating and freeing moments of my life. They were uncomfortable. They were painful. They brought with them pressure, uncertainty, and a whole lot of embarrassment for feeling like I had failed.

But something else also happened. They also deposited things within me that I didn't previously have. They gave me courage. They helped me find my inner strength and worth. They taught me how to love myself. They taught me how to let go. They taught me how to forgive others. They taught me how to forgive myself. They taught me how to take risks, how to start over, and how to create something from nothing. They taught me how to change my story to how I wanted it to be written. That story was one of surrender.

When I let everything crumble, I found that things were actually coming together. I was coming together. I was finding authenticity, and I was attracting people into my life who could appreciate that. Mature friends don't need you to be perfect. They need you to be you, and they enjoy loving you not for your perfectionism but for the beauty of witnessing your progress.

My life has been a series of trial and error. It's how I learn. I would say it's how we all learn. Sometimes we get it right, and sometimes we get it wrong. But with every experience, we learn something that carries with it an opportunity to grow. Progress! I now believe that me not feeling like I have to be perfect is one of my greatest virtues. I emphasize progress versus perfectionism.

Perfectionism is suffocating. Perfectionism will exhaust you. Focusing on the progress you are making as a result of life's ups and downs will invigorate and inspire you. Perfection always wears a mask. Progress is transparent. Emancipate yourself from the unrealistic rat race of trying always to appear to have it together. None of us do. Perhaps that's why we're here: to be broken in the hands of the Divine and embark on the marvelous journey of experiencing the sheer bliss of all those pieces coming back together in perfect alignment. Yes, we are being ultimately perfected, but I can guarantee you that it will be the heated moments of your life that will make you, the priceless diamond, sparkle so beautifully in the light. Let it get a little messy. Every olive must experience a little crushing before producing its scared oil.

Speak to your life and your present circumstances in a loving way regardless of where you are on your journey.

Speak to your body in a loving way. It's the only one you've got.
It's your home, and it deserves your respect.
~ Iskra Lawrence

If you see anyone tearing themselves down, build them back up. Build yourself back up. Be kind to you. Watch your life positively grow when you give up the pursuit of perfection, because the real beauty ideal...

is being imperfectly you.

The Thief of All Joy

*H*AVE YOU EVER CAUGHT YOURSELF SAYING, "I've got a lot compared to other people" or "compared to a lot of other people I am doing pretty good." Whenever we do this, we should stop and ask ourselves, "Why are we comparing ourselves to people who have less than us?"

Some people cause themselves damage by comparing themselves to people who have more. Others cause themselves damage by comparing themselves to people who have less. If you are someone who is comparing yourself to people who have less, you are in essence looking for a way to feel better about your current situation. This is basically the ego's way of becoming superior. In trying to inflate itself, the ego will look for something smaller to compare itself against so it can feel bigger.

Comparing yourself to others is when you begin to lose confidence in yourself. Franklin Roosevelt said,

"Comparison is the thief of all joy."

Don't compare yourself with others. Instead, recognize what makes you happy and focus your energies on doing that well. Sow into your own garden. Water it, nourish it, and cherish it.

Why waste your time comparing yourself to others when in reality they could never be you?

Love Worthy

*Y*OU ARE WORTHY OF FORGIVENESS. You are worthy of grace. You are worthy of understanding and patience. You are worthy to be loved in the midst of your crazy and in the midst of your less than proud moments. You are worthy of being loved when you had to walk away because you couldn't hack it anymore. You are worthy of love when you win. You are worthy of love when you quit. You are worthy of love when you speak wrongly. You are worthy of love when you get it all right. You are worthy of love when you speak your truth, and you are worthy of love when you speak your misguided lies. You are worthy of love when you respond in faith, and you are worthy of love when you respond in fear. You are worthy of love when you love. You are worthy of love when you hate. You are worthy of love in your valleys, and you are worthy of love when you stand upon your mountain peaks.

Nothing can separate you from the love of God
Nothing
No fault
No error
No moment of getting off track

People may separate themselves from you. People may withdraw their love from you, but people can be frail and unaware of the Love within the temple of their being freely available to pour without measure. People may attempt to punish you by offering resentment, bitterness, or hatred instead of responding in love for you. Some people have not filled themselves with enough love to be a fully loaded vessel to coax your less than proud moments. They did not store in seasons of plenty to supply for your season of drought and disappointment. They are just people wrestling with their own demons. Don't put the responsibility upon them to offer grace and unconditional love for the off-course moments of your life. Perhaps you were meant to steer off the beaten path to learn how to find your way back home.

Maybe there is someone else out there who has also ventured far from their destination, and you are meant to be their heroine offering a guiding Light to show them the way home. You can acknowledge the purpose in your mishaps whether others do or not. See the meaning behind your madness and use such wisdom to build a solid and more enlightened future.

Fill yourself with the abundant never-ending love that God is capable of depositing in your life. Instead of relying on others to sooth you, pull from the wellspring of love from within your own inner fountain and as needed offer yourself a dose of unconditional, abounding love. You are worthy of this love offering whether others acknowledge this or not. Their inability to respond to your weakness with long-suffering, kindness, and with a higher spiritual perspective is a reflection of where they are on their journey and not an indicator of your life's current mile marker.

Sometimes what appears as our greatest moments of defeat are
actually opportunities for us to shine brighter than ever before.

For these are the moments God's Light shining from within us stands to receive the most glory. This is when we get to witness the strength of the Divine rise mighty within us making beauty from ashes and ugly ducklings into breathtakingly beautiful swans. You are worthy of love during your metamorphosis. You are worthy of love while you are no longer a caterpillar but also not yet soaring as a butterfly. You are worthy of love in the midst of your transformation.

Be nicer than most. Be more evolved than most. Be kinder than most. Someone very wise once said that it is easy to love someone who has done good to you, but true love reaches beyond this measure. To be filled and overflowing with Divine Love means to be infused with the capacity to love those who disappoint you. This is the way of the enlightened soul, the way of those who walk in the Light. This offering of love also includes a bestowing upon yourself when you find yourself amidst those still incapable of such a generous gift.

God is love. Fill yourself with this God—with this Love every day, so that if and when a moment of defeat finds its way into your life and no one is there who yet understands and can offer this Love, you have an unlimited storehouse to pour lavishly upon your deserving heart. This Love will revive you, inspire you, reaffirm you, and lift you to the place you were always destined to be.

Bloom, Baby, Bloom!

"Start over; my darling. Be brave enough to find the life you want and courageous enough to chase it. Then start over and love yourself the way you were always meant to."
~ Madalyn Beck

SOMETIMES THESE START-OVER MOMENTS in life can arrive unexpectedly and out of the blue. I think I could have a college degree in these "start-over moments." So, here's what I've learned from the do-overs. God has equipped you for any circumstance you may find yourself facing. There is a Divine Source within you that has an endless supply of unconditional love to offer you at any given moment for any given situation. Pull from it. People may be short of supply. It's ok. They are dealing with their own hurts, preconceived judgments, societal and religious conditioning. Your greatest enemy is just another broken soul trying to heal. Never forget that and offer compassion with this is mind.

In addition, never let someone else's beliefs determine what you believe about yourself. You can rest assured God isn't judging you. He is loving you. Ridiculously. Without measure. He is love. He embodies it. He is never without enough to offer you, and He does his best work with those in the biggest mess and most defeating circumstances. From life experience, I think I'm actually beginning to notice a pattern. He delights in the underdog's victory. He delights in taking the least likely of these and raising them up to be mighty and impactful for the inspiration and encouragement of many. Sometimes if we can only see someone else emerge from the crazy, we can believe that we can escape from it too. Again, God's desire was never to condemn you. God's desire is to free you. And I'm not convinced He doesn't like allowing us to feel that we had a part in our victory. He's kind of into giving out awards and crowns and allowing us to receive merit for our ability to utilize His power and the gifts He's uniquely hardwired in each person to provide that victorious ending to the wild adventure we call

Never let someone else's beliefs determine what you believe about yourself.

life. I think He enjoys seeing what we will do with all the amazingness He's placed within us. Maybe our societal defeats are setups for us to know what we're capable of when we utilize this amazing internal love.

Some of us just need to allow that God, that love, to be felt, to be applied, to be dispensed, and to be released lavishly upon others and upon ourselves. Don't wait for the world to do this for you. You may be allowing your worth to be determined by someone who's still locked in prison. They may have a lot of opinions, but have they ever been capable of allowing you to feel that kind of love? Why listen to someone who can't give you that? Why be attentive to someone who doesn't know that? A claim to know God is not the same as someone who embodies Him—who recognizes they are a temple of that love—who knows it's not out there but that it's within them—and they radiate pure unconditional God-force love over you at all times—in thoughts, in speech, and in non-judgment.

That kind of love is breathtaking because it is void of fear. It loves you without being afraid of anything you might be or become in detriment. That love is assured. That love just knows. That love can only relate to you as the person you are destined to become. It can only speak to you as the one who has fulfilled their ultimate purpose. That is all that love can see. It's the love that breathes life, that speaks life, and it's the love that awakens the seed of greatness within you. It's the love that even when you're still a seed buried deep beneath the surface of a hardened earth, can love the seed just as much as He loves the mighty oak. His love is no different for the seed than for the full-grown tree. His love is consistent. His love remains. In fact, it's the love and nourishment for the seed that allows the growth of the glorious oak. Don't waste your time on people who don't know how to love a seed. Certainly, don't waste your time listening to the opinions of those who can't even see you are a seed and that only have the capacity to love the full-grown oaks.

God made seasons for a reason. Start-over moments were written and laced into the very fabric of nature. Seasons are necessary for life to continue. Don't reject your Winter and Fall. Don't fight your pruning. There's a Spring awaiting you where you will blossom like the prettiest of all the flowers in the field. There's a Summer on the horizon where you are destined to bask in the Sunlight and sparkle like its glimmer upon the ocean waters. Stick with those who appreciate your Winter. Stick with those who understand restarts and do-overs. And if you find these people lacking in your life, God has placed an ample amount of love within you to fuel your new beginning, so release it like a rain shower all over yourself and bloom, Baby, bloom!

You Freaking Deserve It

TURN UP THE MUSIC IN YOUR EARS. Lie with a blanket beneath the stars. Daydream a little. No. Daydream a lot. Dream the biggest stories for yourself that you can possibly dream. Feel everything. Be wonderfully present.

Say something nice to yourself. Let your toes play in the dirt beneath your blanket. Light your favorite candle. Make the air smell especially sweet. Sip your tea.

Be romantic with yourself. Live beautifully. Feel crazy sexy. Fall in love with all that you have become and all that you are still becoming.

Kiss your mistakes. Extend an enormous amount of kindness and grace upon yourself. Smile as you reflect on the past and laugh an incessantly enormous amount when considering your stunningly, gorgeous future.

You freaking deserve it.

You Have Nothing to Prove

I STILL REMEMBER THE MOMENT WHILE DRIVING on the interstate in Dallas, Texas, when I heard the Holy Spirit say very clearly to me, "You have nothing to prove." Immediately I began to weep. Eventually, I exited the highway and parked my car at a park near my home. While watching children laugh and play on a Sunday afternoon, I cried and cried while letting the profoundness of that one statement settle deep into the fabric of my being. It has taken years for me to actually embrace and live its truth.

You don't have to prove who you are to anyone. You don't have to convince them of your goodness, your kind intent, or your reasons for doing something. You are going to make mistakes. You are going to have moments of utter failure. For those who haven't matured enough to see or recognize that this is part of growing, learning, and living, it is not worth your time and energy to explain it to them. You don't have to spend effort you could be putting into your self-betterment trying to prove your worth and value post a mistake that has only generated more wisdom for yourself going forward.

You don't have to prove or justify why you chose to walk away or why you may currently feel the need to stay. You don't have to prove or justify why you feel that decision was best for you or why you can't make it to that thing you were invited to or why you didn't reply to that message. You will never make it to a state of happiness, freedom, and peace if you care what people think.

Let go of all that need for validation.
Something beautiful is trying to grow in its place.

Make decisions based on what is best for you, your happiness, your sanity, and if you have children, their happiness, sanity, and well-being. After that, let what sticks stick. Let what falls off fall off. Your circle may get smaller, but the quality of it will be more excellent and profound. Trust me, you had rather be hated for who you are than loved for who you are not. You glow differently when you're actually happy. Break the cycle and realize genuinely...

You have nothing to prove.

You are ridiculously, eternally, abundantly loved.
Full stop.
No matter what.
Unconditionally.
Forever and always.

And no one should ever have to prove this to anyone.

Shine Anyway

OH, THE HEARTBREAK AND PAIN I HAVE CAUSED MYSELF searching and hungry for a validation that can only be obtained as a gift from myself to myself. No one is capable of filling that deep void inside of you, the one that gnaws and aches at you continuously.

You will never have enough of that guy you want to love you like you desperately need him to love you. He will never be divinely aligned enough to know exactly when to reassure you, or exactly when you need to be touched, or exactly when you need that much-desired verbal affirmation. He or she may satisfy for a moment, but they can never be there for every void-aching moment of your life. He or she was not designed to be your Internal Guidance System and Source of unconditional love and wisdom. There was an infinite Spirit placed within you to serve this auspicious role.

The ache for ultimate, divine fulfillment will never be satiated by another. One must learn to pull from within, to connect to their Source, to draw from His Light, to hear His voice of validation and higher wisdom in the face of the untruths we mentally feed ourselves.

Be brave.
Be confident.
Be free.
Validate yourself.

You have a Kingdom within you. Pull from it. Build upon it. The love and deep soul satisfaction you thirst for can satiate you there. And turn the Light on in there. The world wants to see you sparkle.

Oh, and one more thing…the world may not always validate your sparkle.

Shine anyway.

No More Compromise

IF YOU HAVEN'T EXPERIENCED IT YET, trust me, you're gonna want to. It's the moment where you can genuinely say with confidence, "I have compromised my standards for the very last time!"

This moment will generally be preceded with you finally getting ticked off enough at the circumstance you're in that you're able to see it for what it truly is. Allow that emotion to pass, and bow to the experience, thanking it for serving as a great teacher in your life. You will be richer. You will be freer. You will have established a greater sense of self-worth. You will have more clarity. You can thank the contrast for showing you with greater specifics and articulation exactly what you want and don't want in your life ever again!

Sure, you'll be angry at yourself
for allowing the circumstance,
but there is but one reason we are brought low,
and that is so that in due time we
may be exalted to higher ground!

Chin up. Keep it moving. We are the ones that set the limits for what is possible and what is not in our lives. Raise your standard. Know your worth. Don't limit yourself with less than what you deserve. Ever! What crap are you allowing for yourself that is causing you to create any form of compromise in your life? Clean house, friend.

And who cares if you may have lost your footing momentarily. Perhaps you lost your footing because your feet are no longer meant to remain on the ground.

That's right!
It's time for you to learn how to fly!

This Is Me

I LOVE THE TIME I HAVE WITH MYSELF.

It's my journey.

It's my strength.

It's my season of empowerment and becoming who I truly am.

I'm embracing me.

I'm believing in me.

I'm doing me,

and I'm loving me.

I'm done with fake.

I'm done with performance.

I'm stepping into my authentic self.

I'm feeling more powerful and confident in my skin.

I am worthy of the deepest love, the highest truths, and genuine liberation.

Love is freedom, freedom to be fully me and fully loved.

This is me, and I really love this girl.

Freedom Song

*T*HERE IS A PATH TO FREEDOM
A place we all want to go
It requires a bit of tenacity
It inspires a whole lot of letting go

It will take you low
and it will lift you up
It will mellow you out
And it will jazz you up

It requires a strength
A pulling from deep within
It warrants a rising
and a little fire to begin

You've got to know you are
You've got to know to whom you belong
You've got to beat to your own rhythm
You've got to sing your own song

For liberty to ring
You must find your good vibin' team
You must surround yourself with those
who appreciate and are never jealous of your bling

'Cause you are designed to sparkle
You are destined to be the Light
You must learn the lessons from the darkness
Yet not stay long, you're here to take flight

You must let go of the opinions of others
You must do your own thing
You must believe in yourself
And release what you came here to bring

Don't look back
Your future isn't there
Your freedom is already with you
Can't you feel the confidence in the air?

There's no one to compete with
Just be the best that you can be
Girl, do your cray cray
Come on, get liberated—Get ridiculously free

You will learn a whole lot of self-love
You will obtain a whole lot of grace from above

You will become a master of kindness
The Light in your eyes ridding others of their blindness

Your heart will wrap humanity like a perfectly, warmed glove
This is what happens when you fill it with love

It's an emancipation
It's a no turning back
It's a life full of colors
No darkness, no more black

But you must let go of any and all doubts
You must truly embrace a life of no droughts
You must believe you deserve no more strikes and no more outs

You were created to find life abundant and free
You were designed to be fierce, feisty, and sweet
You may at times feel like a plant in a desert
But you'll be as aloe vera that heals and converts

'Cause you'll be the ointment that soothes the hurts
You'll provoke change —You'll show others their worth

You can't find this space in the wide-open places
by comparing yourself to others
or by being judgmental or racist

You must find a way to see a Divine spark in all
See their seed of potential
Their rising and not their fall

Be love and light
Be joy and peace
Be happy and whole
You deserve to be free.

FORGIVENESS & LETTING GO

Forgive Them

*F*ORGIVE.

Forgive them for lying about you.

Forgive them for calling you names.

Forgive them for believing the rumors.

Forgive them for characterizing you without facts.

Forgive them for judging you.

Forgive them for talking about you instead of talking to you.

Forgive them for forgetting the kindness you always showed them.

Forgive them for betraying you.

Forgive them for blaming you.

Forgive them for demonizing you instead of accepting responsibility for their wrongdoing. Forgive them for their hypocrisy.

Forgive them for not telling the whole story.

Forgive them for making you look bad so they can look good.

Forgive them for making you the brunt of their anger and hurt.

Forgive them for all of it.

Forgive yourself when you have done the same.

Forgiveness is freedom.

Forgiveness is love.

Pray for those who have hurt you. There is a glorious plan mapped out in the heavens for you. It is complete. It's going to happen. All you must do is download it. Unforgiveness, bitterness, jealousy, and resentfulness are viruses blocking your download.

We have one mission on this earth: to love at the deepest levels of our being. Don't return evil for evil but repay evil with good. The more they spew hate, sow love in its place. Your harvest will serve you well.

Dear Body, Please Forgive Me

DEAR BODY, PLEASE FORGIVE ME.

One thing my spiritual journey has shown me is the truth regarding the consciousness living in each and every cell of my body. Every single cell is a living thing, a miniature living organism that is programmed with a specific function straight from the mind of God. Recently, I've come to think of these cells like the *Little People*, a cartoon I use to watch on Saturday mornings when I was a young girl. I imagine each of these cells having their own personality like the seven dwarfs in *Snow White*, yet so intelligent they function as a flock of birds flying as if governed by one mind.

There is something about giving a personality and a name to a specific part of the body that makes me see it with a new level of respect and admiration for how it's serving its God-designed purpose. Recently, as I held my hand upon my abdomen, I had a moment where I looked down upon these groups of cells. It was as if a whole village of thousands of tiny elves stopped their assignments momentarily and looked towards me. I had a chance to really look at them, and what I saw deeply saddened me. They were exhausted. I saw myself through their eyes, and I did not like what was there. They appeared in my mind as over-worked Egyptian slaves, and I was as Pharaoh, their hard taskmaster.

I felt as though at some point in times past we had been in unison and were companions, but I had lost my way in the world, forgotten about my true friends, and was living it up like a child wasting away her inheritance. I had forgotten about the ones that had gotten me where I was, the ones that had kept me alive. I felt like the evil villain of the fairytale story and knew this was not my true path. I was supposed to be the generous and benevolent Queen admired and loved by the people, not seen as governing them but viewed as one among them working together to accomplish a most noble mission.

With this awareness, I named the cells in my body the Keepers for they were the keepers of my body. My intention to place my gaze upon them caused them all to stop their assignments and pause in wonderment. This was the first time I had ever noticed them. It was an awe-inspiring, monumental moment. In their tired, weak, and frail state, they turned to face me as if stunned I had fixed my mind upon them. I began to address them with the respect and admiration they had always deserved. It was as poignant as any heart-quenching seen from any movie ever seen by the human gaze. They listened, and I spoke.

*D*EAREST *B*ODY AND ITS MANY *K*EEPERS,

Please forgive me. Please forgive me for not knowing then what I know now.

I came here today to tell you how much I love you. But first, I owe you a long-overdue apology. I haven't been kind to you. I've spoken negatively about you. I've called you names. I've belittled you. I've compared you. I've caused you great wounds, and I'm sure scars from repeated offenses leaving you to try and heal on your own. I've offered you no healing balm or soothing words to ease your aches and pains. I am a repeat offender, and I can't tell you how sorry I am for my misguided actions.

You know that old saying, "You don't know what you've got until it's gone." There's nothing like being left with numbness down the right side of my body from a bleeding hemangioma to wake me up to this significant truth. This is me realizing how truly precious you are. I was wrong. You were so right, and I want you back—all of you. I want to love, cherish, and nurture you like you should have been treated all along.

In 7th grade when that popular kid told me my legs were too white, and he laughed at us, I'm sorry I begged my mom to take me to the tanning bed and ultimately exposed you to harmful rays. I should have protected you, taken better care of you, defended you, and loved you exactly as you were. I love your beautiful skin. It's white and porcelain and reminds me of the pretty china dolls I see in those fancy cabinets. Sure, I think olive skin is pretty, but I want you to know that I wouldn't trade you for everything in the whole wide world. You are mine, and I want you. I've never told you that, and you need to know how I truly feel.

Those beauty pageants I entered . . . gosh, I'm so sorry I did that to you. I constantly critiqued you, criticized you, and compared you to all the other bodies. I stopped appreciating all you had given me and started wanting the other girl's hair, the other girl's smile, and the other girl's body. I even wanted to walk like someone else. I didn't know my comparison games were killing you.

I understand the consciousness that exists now in every cell of my body. How could I say those things to you? I know my words and how I felt about you affected your performance. And yet you loved me. You kept working for me. You kept helping me grow. I have given you such a beating.

I'm sorry I didn't believe in myself or accept my worth. I'm sorry I was too busy looking at everyone else's gifts that I could not see nor learn to appreciate my own. I wanted to sing, so I failed to see I could write. I wanted to dance, so I failed to see I could articulate my thoughts well. I wanted to be a cheerleader and an athlete to fit in with what was popular, so I failed to notice I was poetic and lyrical and a good storyteller. I wanted to say the cool things, so I failed to hear you speaking all the right things. I wanted to please everyone else, so I denied giving you what you truly needed.

I imagine each of these cells having their own personality like the seven dwarfs in Snow White, yet so intelligent they function as a flock of birds flying as if governed by one mind.

To my hair, I owe you the biggest apology. You originated wavy and beautiful, and when I wanted to follow the trends, I gave you the worst 80's perm ever. It took years for you to recover. You didn't know what to do. You were half straight and half curly. I can't imagine how confused you must have been. And if that wasn't bad enough, in 7th grade, I had my mom attempt to change the color you originally gave me. At this point, you were so distraught by the experience that it is no wonder the results came out multifaceted, with varying shades of yellow, black, brown, and white. The next day when I went to school my "friends" nicknamed me skunk. I went home and lay beneath my covers in a dark room with a hoody atop my head, hating myself. For what? Bad hair. Again, I'm sorry for not knowing then what I know now. I love my hair. I love how you grow it for me. It's perfect as is. There are those who have lost their hair that understands its value to them. May I never lose you in order to understand and appreciate your worth.

Body, there is one area I have been absolutely unmerciful to you about. I have been so unhappy with you in this regard, and I am deeply sorry. I have criticized your form, your shape, your size, your height, and your weight. I have held you to unrealistic standards and tortured you with unhealthy diets, pills, and vitamins from every diet program on the planet. I've made you eat weird combinations of food and restricted you in unhealthy ways all because of my lack of self-love, all because I didn't know how to love you, and to treat you with the kindness and respect you deserve. I was unappreciative and behaving like a spoiled brat. I now long to nourish you and feed you with pleasure and the best of all that you need and desire.

To my mouth and my hand, you gifted me well, yet I used you from a wrong space. My gifts were given to inspire and encourage, to help, and to teach. Yet, I used them as a means of performance to fulfill a need to be loved and accepted. I used them unconsciously as a means to feel significant. You went numb on me. My lack of being in alignment with how you were designed to function created nerve damage for you both. You were tired and unwilling to perform any longer. May you now feel the tremendous relief of me knowing I am loved and accepted simply because I am a beloved child of God. And may you heal more and more every day and awaken once again to life and vitality as I utilize you, not to heal something that is broken but as a means to celebrate that which is whole and well.

When I was pregnant with my three children, I was cruel to you. I'm so sorry that I judged you and compared you to standards set by others who were not me. I was so busy trying to fit a mold that I failed to see the beauty and wonderment of how you stretched and created the perfect form for the precious life within me. I was more concerned and ashamed of my growing body and change in appearance that I failed to appreciate the gift you were creating for me. I hurt you with my harsh critiques, and I'm sorry. You were not fat. You were bursting with life.

Whether it was needing glasses, having acne or a rash upon my skin, or any imperfection that arose from within you, I quickly turned on you and tried to hide, conceal, and cover you from being seen. I based your beauty on what was without instead of loving all that you had given me from within. The aggression within created the disturbances without. I'm sorry I made you feel shame. You were so perfect, and I was too wrapped up in everyone else's opinion to notice my true self. I should have been adoring you in all your beauty.

And finally, I'm sorry that I didn't accept what you were doing as holy, right, good, and true and perfect for me. I'm sorry that I tried to change you. I'm sorry that I tried to stop you from doing what you knew was best for me. I'm sorry that I undermined your authority, your position, and your place in my life and in my body. I'm sorry that I wished I had a different body. I'm sorry

I couldn't see that you were given to me for what I needed. I'm sorry that I haven't thought you were beautiful and wonderful, amazing and perfect just the way you are. I'm sorry that I've overworked you, overtired you, manipulated, and confused you. I've made you work harder than you should ever have had to work for me. And I'm sorry I did all of this because I didn't respect you. I didn't see your worth and your value.

And to my Body and all its Keepers, I just want you to know that I'm sorry from the bottom of my heart that I haven't cherished you, loved you, and honored you the way that I should have. Going forward, I want to work with you and not against you. I want to uphold you and the office that you carry within me. I want to treat you with love, compassion, respect, and integrity. I am proud of you, not ashamed of you. I'm sorry that in the past, I have put that shame and guilt upon you, because I wasn't willing to accept what you had given me or what you knew was best for me.

I want you to know that I love you, I am proud of you, and I thank you for all the hard work you've done for us. Thank you for keeping me here this long and for fighting for me when I was ignorant, stupid, prideful, and vain.

You are my Inner Wisdom given by God for my continual well-being. For this most ostentatious role, I humbly say how dearly I love you and ask for your forgiveness. Today I make a commitment to be in alignment with you instead of trying to be in opposition to you.

And I seal this declaration of intent with all my devotion,

Misti

I HAVE LEARNED IN MY LIFE THE VALUE of asking for forgiveness. It is so healing to the soul and releases the shame and guilt we carry with us for failures and mistakes. The faster we acknowledge where we've taken a wrong path and ask for forgiveness, the quicker we get back on the path we were meant to take. However, there is an important step I have learned that is invaluable to heal completely from such a mishap. We must forgive ourselves and receive that forgiveness into our spirit, heart, mind, and soul. That's what creates the shift in our lives and takes us out of the feelings of depression and unworthiness associated with guilt and shame.

So, in response to this plea to my body, my Body and its Keepers answered me back. With every cell turned towards me and with their utmost intention, they replied.

*D*EAREST MISTI,

We forgive you. Our mercy is extended to you. It wasn't your original intention when you came here to treat us this way. You simply lost your way. You forgot who you were, and now you have remembered. We know how to fix the problems existing within your body. We have been programmed by Divine Intelligence to function in your highest good and to keep you thriving at all times. We are eager to help you, and everything can be turned around. We ask that you only listen better. We *need* you to listen better. Love us by being attentive. Pay attention when we tell you what we need. The gateway to commune with us is love, and you found your way here by both loving us and loving yourself. We are energized and ready for the task at hand!

With great love,
Your Devoted Keepers

*W*ITH THIS RESPONSE SPOKEN, I saw the tired faces of these little people shift to ones of relief, glee, excitement, and joy! They began shouting and cheering and dancing amongst themselves! A divine light encapsulated the thousands of them and restored their life force with energy and vitality. No longer did they look tired, worn-down, confused, and misused. They were invigorated. They were happy! Their hope was restored, and they were more determined than ever to fix and mend all that was broken. Commands were being given, and parts were being repaired. I saw excitement, joy, exuberance, and the heart of thousands of cheerful givers working in unison to restore and repair all functioning systems.

Will some think I'm crazy because I talk to my body and these little people I have warranted as deserving of love, affection, a listening ear, and fellowship? Maybe. Who cares? We are reunited in the best possible way! We chat with one another, and every day I tell them that I love them, that I appreciate them, and that I am so glad they are mine. I know and can feel how much this invigorates them, how much they love my kindness towards them, and how much this blessed communion is helping me to heal and restore.

This one is for the Keepers! I choose you above all others. I love you! I love my body! I am listening to you. And I am thankful for each and every effort you put into making me…me.

Misti, from me to you, I love you, Beautiful One. You are lovely beyond measure. Keep shining, Bright Star! I love all that you are, and I'm really sorry it took me thirty-eight years to tell you that. Better late than never.

May this Misti Moment serve as a reminder to all that
how you speak to your body matters. Be kind.

Dear People from My Past

1 REMEMBER THE MOMENT SO WELL. It was so freeing! So, needed. My body needed to feel myself articulate the following words. Although I was saying them to thin air, my soul heard them and thanked me,

"Dear People from My Past,
If I had it to do over again, I would do exactly the same thing,
because that's where I was then, and I wouldn't have known to do
otherwise. And quite frankly, I'm sick and tired of beating up on
myself for not knowing then what I know now."

Condemnation for things you did in your past leads to such a negative vibrational state. Most of us did the best that we knew how to do in that moment, with that particular level of awareness. Instead of walking in condemnation and guilt, change how you view your past. Instead of allowing feelings of regret to plague you, arrive at a space of gratitude for how those mistakes, failures, and bad decisions helped you to grow and become who you are today. Be thankful for the contrast of those experiences and what they provided for your overall soul growth and expansion. Learn to appreciate the progress you are making and strive in every conscious moment to be in alignment with who you truly are and who you are destined to become.

There is beauty in your past because it helped
bring you to your present.

There is an anonymous quote that states,

"In your pursuit of happiness, don't forget to be happy."

Don't allow yourself to be entangled in needing more than what is available to you in your present moment to feel complete, happy, or to be in a state of health, life, and vitality. Appreciate and recognize the value of the moment you are currently experiencing and find ways to be grateful for what lessons are being learned from them that are positively affecting your soul's growth, purification, and expansion.

And when you fail in the present, don't look back and beat yourself up for not knowing then what you have now learned from those situations. Without the experience, we would not know a better way, a higher truth, and we would not be one step closer to the truest and most authentic version of ourselves.

Finding Success in Failure

ONE OF MY HARDEST PARTS OF MY JOURNEY has been overcoming the deep shame, guilt, and embarrassment that would cultivate within me whenever I exhibited the courage to face certain parts of my past. When reflecting on certain moments, great anger would rise within me. It was immense anger towards myself. How could I have been so weak, so ignorant, and so selfish? Why did I make that decision? Why did I give my power away so easily? How could I have ever allowed myself to be so manipulated? Why did I manipulate others? What was I thinking?! How un-classy! How immature! How could I?

The anger towards myself would build and build until, eventually, grief would begin to settle in as I thought about the consequences of past choices and how those actions had affected others. Yet, there was an underlying knowing in all that regret and disgust that there was no way I could have arrived at my current destination had one portion of my journey been any different.

One day while healing in bed from my brain aneurysm and while coping with the scary neurological effects associated with it, my mom asked me a question. "Misti, if you could change anything about your journey, would you?"

I paused. I pondered.

To my own surprise I looked into my mother's eyes and replied, "No, Mom. I can't believe I'm saying this, but no, I wouldn't." At that moment, I realized more than ever that it was those experiences that had shaped me into the woman of faith and strength I had become.

Your failures are your teachers.

Forgive them. Appreciate them and above all learn from them. Do not live the rest of your life punishing yourself because of them. Live in celebration for how they have directed you towards a wise, more glorious path. Do not silence them. Acknowledge them. Heal them. And by all means live in such a way that others may see the benefit of how even the worst of weaknesses can evolve into your greatest strengths.

You are not your failures and you are not your successes. You are God in action. You are infinitely beautiful. You are not simply here to please or displease a God sitting perched on a throne in the sky. You are here to express God through all that you are and all that you've learned. You are an extension of this goodness, and regardless of your pitfalls, this truth remains the light of your soul.

Sitting in a pile of tears due to past regrets will never liberate you. It will imprison you. Repentance doesn't mean to punish and condemn yourself. It means to turn, to know better, and to do better. Wash your face, wipe away your tears, stand tall again, and know that God is with you. God has not nor ever will He forsake you, because God is in you. The true Source of all life is omnipresent. There is no place His love cannot reach; this includes your darkest pits and the most hellish moments of your life.

"Where can I go from your Spirit? Where can I flee from your presence?

If I go up to the heavens, you are there; if I make my bed in the depths, you are there. If I rise on the wings of the dawn, if I settle on the far side of the sea, even there your hand will guide me, your right hand will hold me fast. If I say, 'Surely the darkness will hide me, and the light become night around me,' even the darkness will not be dark to you; the night will shine like the day, for darkness is as light to you."
(Psalm 139: 7-12)

God has a plan to work through you. Whether in your deepest valley or perched atop your highest mountain, God will ridiculously love you…forever.

Once in a moment of self-judgment, anger, embarrassment, and regret a dearly beloved friend said to me,

"Anger is just a cover for fear.
Misti, what are you afraid of?"

Ultimately, I discovered that I was afraid of being shamed, rejected, judged, or unloved based on various parts of my journey. To which he replied,

"Misti, repeat after me:
Once upon a time I appeared to live a perfect life.
I was beautiful, and everyone loved me.
And then I fell.
I no longer had a perfect life.
I was ugly and
everyone loved me
(he paused)
even more."

As I repeated these words with tears streaming down my face, I realized something that I will carry with me for the rest of my life.

Truth is always more beautiful than a lie. It stands alone
and is the key through which the soul finds its freedom.

So why am I writing about this particular Misti Moment? Perhaps there is someone out there who has suffered their fall and like me needs to know they are even more beautiful, more real, and more deserving than ever before. This is grace, and this is why I love it so. When applied during the least likely and least deserving of circumstances, there is no end to its transforming power.

Forgive to Live

MOST OF US WANT TO SEE THE EVIL IN THIS WORLD come to an end. Perhaps you've personally been affected it. Maybe you've lost a loved one. Perhaps you have suffered a personal injury by someone who caused you harm, and that incident has left you crippled physically or emotionally. Maybe you are living in fear, pain, anger, and heartbreak you never wanted to carry due to someone else's wrongdoings. I truly understand your anger. I believe Jesus Christ, of all people, understood it as well. He was also moved with compassion as He witnessed how lost those around Him were in their suffering. He desperately wanted to free them of their pain, and He offered solutions that can be hard to digest. His solutions taught us to love our enemies, to pray for those that persecute us, and to forgive without limit. He seemed to understand a powerful Universal truth His Father set in place:

That which we sow we shall also reap.

He knew that the path to change or end the evils of this world meant to fight evil with good. He knew that in offering love, love would be returned to us. He knew that in offering forgiveness, forgiveness would be offered to us. He even told us that He could not break these laws but must live according to them as well. He told us He could not forgive us unless we had forgiven others. He understood only love dispels hate and that only giving peace could ever end a war. He understood the truth: what we do to others, we ultimately do to ourselves.

Wayne Dyer once shared of the moment when he went to his father's grave and said, "Thank you for this experience. Without it, I wouldn't be the man I am today." Wayne had been abused as a child by his alcoholic father, but he became a teacher of love and kindness all over the world. His freedom came when he was able to feel gratitude and to "count it all joy," because he realized that even in his sufferings, he gained the wisdom of life. He was able to set himself free from bondage and what could have been a lifelong struggle with defeating strongholds.

Talk to someone that has freed themselves from years of carrying pain from housing feelings of hate for someone that hurt them. Ask anyone who has released hurt and forgiven someone that has stolen from them in any way, and they will tell you what that moment of release did for them. Whether it is difficult to digest or a hard pill to swallow, forgiveness for ourselves and others is still the way. It is still the truth. It is still the life. It is still the path to freedom.

Let Go!

"Getting over a painful experience is much like crossing monkey bars. You have to let go at some point in order to move forward."

~ C.S. Lewis

I once heard a quote that said, "Sometimes you don't realize the weight of something you've been carrying until you feel the weight of its release."

Some of us need to let go of those who are already gone. The secret to letting go is realizing you're worthy of the love they're incapable of providing. Others of us need to know what we could be if we stopped carrying the remains of who we were. Let go of the past, and the past will let go of you.

See, a funny thing happens when we finally let go; God intervenes. When you let go, you're clearing space for something better.

> *"We don't heal the past by dwelling there.*
> *We heal the past while living in the present."*
> ~ Marianne Williamson

Don't be afraid to let go of what wasn't meant to be. When crossing the monkey bars, did you know that it hurts more to hold on than to just let go and fly across them with a continuous steady rhythm of reaching for the next new grip? s

> *Close your eyes.*
> *Take a deep breath.*
> *Clear your heart.*
> *And just . . .*
> *let go.*

Let go of what was and have faith in what will be.

The Crossroads

WHEN I WAS A LITTLE GIRL, MY MOM WOULD OFTEN hold her fingers out in front of me, making a Y-shape with her pointer and index finger. In doing so, she created two roads, one which she called the "right" road and the other which she named the "wrong" road. With the pointer finger of her other hand, she would point to the space between her two fingers and tell me this was where I was standing, at the crossroad between the two roads. She told me all that was there were me and a choice. "Which path are you going to take?" she would ask. Sometimes it would take me longer to reply, especially if it involved an incident like my sister stealing my favorite blouse. Yet, somehow, I would ultimately feel that tug to "rise above," as my mom would call it, and seek to choose the better path. At times the "right" path didn't feel so right. In fact, more times than not, I felt it led to a no man's wilderness land instead of a blissful wonderland.

It appeared the "right" path should have been more appropriately titled, *The Road Less Traveled*. Each time a decision was made to chart its course, the terrain was never easy. Its pathways were narrow and rigid, yet oddly enough, I did come to discover the load was always much lighter. There was never as much baggage to carry on its route, and each time I chose to step upon it, there was a peace that permeated the ground on which I walked.

Mom would also tell me that even if I selected the wrong road, I always had a choice to turn around and make my way back to the crossroads, in the middle of the two fingers, and choose again. These two roads have constantly presented themselves to me throughout my life, appearing and reappearing time and time again. Life has shown me there is always a right road, and there is always a wrong road. They never change. There is always a choice: judgment or forgiveness, mercy or intolerance, greed or generosity, peace or war, bitterness or sweetness, hang on or let go, fear or faith, hatred or love.

With both roads, there are lessons to be learned, teachers to be found, and opportunities to be either gained or lost. Either way, there is grace to be granted upon both paths, and there is a Master Guide whose love is not limited by a wrong choice. He has traveled from afar and met me on the wrong road more than once. Some call Him a Shepherd in search of His lost sheep, one willing to sink into the deepest pit of the most darkened wayward road. I call him a Savior, one willing to give His life that I may live. His name is Christ. His name is Emmanuel, God with us. I have found if you call to Him on either path, He will make a way where there seemed to be no way. His path of redemption leads to a higher road, one we all inwardly seek to walk upon whether we realize it yet or not. He has ordained a path for us all, and He stands upon it, saying, "Come follow me."

How do we discern the inner voice of our Shepherd? How do we determine which path is the "right" one? When standing at the crossroads between the two paths, I close my eyes, still myself from within, and wait till I clearly see both roads before me. I'll imagine both paths in my hands, one in my right hand and one in my left. I'll then ask myself, "Where is my peace?" There have been paths I have desperately wanted to take, and yet there was no peace when I looked upon them. There have been paths that seemed hard and difficult to follow, and yet peace hovered their grounds. Often, I have looked ahead and seen the course of a path only to find no peace at its end.

I've discovered there is a peace that guides me. It is given by the Master Guide. Follow it. Allow it to govern you. Peace is something we have all been given lavishly without measure; however, our choices determine how much of it we experience. Choose your path wisely. Choose life. Choose love. Choose forgiveness. Choose the mind of Christ. Choose the path of the Divine. And if by chance you find yourself standing upon a path and realize you have lost your peace, go back to crossroads between the two fingers and choose again. Grace will meet you there, and God's peace will once again chart a new course for you to travel upon.

Why must you travel back to the crossroads between the two roads? Why can't you simply begin anew from the place you currently stand upon on your path? Because in order to find your destined course, you must carry with you a repentant heart. In Hebrew, the word repentance means to turn, to turn back, or to return. I believe to find your true, God-ordained destination, you must feel sorrow or remorse for choosing the "wrong" road, or for any way in which you have harmed another, including yourself. You must turn around and begin making the authentic changes and steps required to see your way through the wayward path you have found yourself traveling upon.

Repentance is a beautiful mile marker. It tells you that you've come closer to finding the place you desire to be. It's a beacon of hope to remind you of the power of redemption and how far you can travel when you allow her to assist you on your journey. Repentance ushers in your Master Guide and when He appears, you can rest assured He holds the key to a life-giving map specifically designed for you to finish well.

The Phoenix

YOU HURT THEM. YOU HURT THEM BADLY. But they hurt you too, and you know what they say, hurting people hurt people. So, you made some bad choices. But regardless of some wrong turns on the highways of life, your heart remained pretty. It had to sparkle. It was destined to shine like a city upon a hill. And despite your wayward path, it had always been coated with humility and love. All who carried a genuine Light would have no other choice but to recognize this blatant and undeniable truth.

Maybe the ones who should have remained to nurse you back to health scattered. Perhaps your friends abandoned you. Maybe you were weak. You were down, and they left you to try and heal by yourself. The ones you had loved, the ones you had journeyed with, choosing self over service. Jesus understands. His brothers deserted and denied Him as well. There are many who choose the limelight and self-preservation instead of fighting to help restore the Light that has temporarily dimmed inside of another. Most walked past the Samaritan beaten, desolate, and bruised on the side of the road. Only one stopped to offer ointment to mend the wounds.

Be grateful.

The Phoenix is said to be a unique bird that lived for five or six centuries in the Arabian Desert, and after its time burning itself on a funeral pyre, it rose from the ashes with renewed youth to live through another cycle. You have transitioned from the scorpion stinging itself to death in a darkened corner to the Phoenix soaring high above the world below you. You have emerged from the ashes of your refiner's fire. You're soaring now.

Be grateful because you have been granted a great and sacred gift from the Divine. You've learned how to stand alone. You've learned how to rise from the power at work within your own soul. Your soul has been strengthened. Your heart has found its restoration. Your Light has grown brighter.

You had to make your solo journey through the dark night of the soul. You had to have your time in the shadows to learn to appreciate the Light.

While others gossiped and critiqued your demise, heaven was applauding you. They were celebrating what they knew to be true of you. They knew you would find your path to healing, to authenticity, to the treasure box of all that mattered in this world.

And you did.

Your soul has embarked on a profound journey. You showed others mercy, and God bestowed mercy upon you. You obtained forgiveness, and you gave it lavishly to others. You made peace and pardoned those who forsook you when the chips were down. You loved in the face of anger, bitterness, and hate. You've been faithful. Your heart radiates goodness, light, and love.

You found the treasure in a field. That is a true and lasting story to be etched in the books of heaven. You came home to yourself. You found you. You found God within you. You release Him every day of your life. This is the ultimate fairytale. You were blessed enough to obtain it, and now you have been given the eternal award of living happily ever after.

APPRECIATING THE DARKNESS

Dearest Villains

DEAREST VILLAINS,

To one who lied to me, you helped me identify the truth

To the one who used me, you helped me to discover my value

To the one who walked away from me, you helped me to let go of what was no longer needed in my life

To the one who betrayed me, you helped teach me how to be loyal to myself and to others

To the one who judged me, you taught me how to be merciful

To the one I couldn't please, you helped me accept myself and say goodbye to a lifetime of people-pleasing confinement that had me bound

To the one who sowed chaos, you taught me how to release peace

To the one who hurt me, you taught me how to forgive

To the those who were jealous and compared themselves to me, you helped me find more compassion and understanding

For the one who hated me, you helped me understand love for others and myself

To the one who wouldn't speak up for me, you helped me discover my voice

To the one that was hard on me, you helped give me a softer heart

To the one who provoked fear in me, you taught me how to walk atop the waters amidst any raging storm

To the one who made me anxious, you helped me find my inner calm

To the one who didn't want me, you helped me discover how desirable I am

To the one who confused me, you helped me find my balance

To the one who condemned me, you helped me embrace a saving grace

To the one who left me, you helped me find myself

To the one who was disappointed in me, you taught me that my failures were the building blocks for my success

To the one who controlled me, you taught me how to free myself

To the one who stole from me, you showed me where my treasure lied

To the one who oppressed me, you showed me how powerful I am

To the one who blinded me, you taught me how to see

To the one who made me feel insecure, you gave me the gift of confidence

To the one who tried to keep me in the dark, you taught me how to walk in the Light

And to the one who tried to kill me, your disease and near-death experience helped me choose life.

Dearest Villains, thank you for your roles played well in my life. You served as a wonderful mirror for all that lied within. Thank you for being the heat and the pressure that sculpted me into the diamond I was destined to become. Without you, I wouldn't be me.

Thank you for staying when I tried to pray you away. I needed your darkness to help me understand I was the Light. I needed your hatred to help me be love. You took me to the edge of death and taught me the value of life. Every sensation you produced in me was a fire cultivating liquid gold. You boiled all impurities to the surface. You made waking up to the truth of whom I am so delightfully rewarding.

I understand Jesus so clearly now as He said,

"Pray for your enemies. Bless those who persecute you."

So Dearest Villains, with deep gratitude and immense love, I thank you from the depth of my heart for sacrificing your time to aid my journey. To those who were up close and personal to those who were opposing on a worldwide scale, congratulations for your roles played well on my soul journey. The evolution of one is the evolution of many, and my ripple effect is touching the world.

Oh Father, great God that You are, I see it now. I know why you created the darkness. Thank you for the contrast. I learned to see in the darkness with my eyes closed. You taught me that. And now I stand in the Light unafraid of the darkness and all its beautiful gifts. For choosing this for me, for choosing this for us—thank you with all that I am. I understand why we rest in the heavens and laugh in joy together as One. This has been the greatest game of hide-'n'-seek ever. I found you. I found me. Reunited and it truly feels so good. Jesus, you knew it all along, and your words are oh so pretty as I recall them now,

"On that day you will know that I am the Father,
and you in me, and I in you."

This *Misti Moment* was dedicated to the villains in my life but to the one reading this, remember this . . .

You are allowed to have a villain in your story. "Why?"
you might ask. Because without a villain in your story,
you would not have the hero's journey.

Often times, situations occur in our lives that we feel we need to pray away. It may be an illness or a near-death experience. It could come in the form of someone hating, condemning, or challenging you. It could be the person that is angry with you, jealous of you, or misunderstanding you. Perhaps they have stolen or taken something very precious from you. I wrote "Dearest Villains" to help others understand that these people and circumstances are the greatest teachers of their lives. Embrace them for their duration. Celebrate the gift they bring to your heart, mind, and soul. Appreciate the classroom. Allow your character to make the honor roll in the classroom of life.

"Nothing ever goes away until it teaches us what we need to know."
~ Pema Chodron

Allow the graduates of this experience called life to imprint their legacies of wisdom and truth into your journey. Learn from them. Implement their teachings into your current circumstances. Remain for as long as needed. Allow the cycle to complete itself that you may emerge strong and ready for your new beginnings—some of which come in a physical sense and some in a mental and more spiritual sense. Nonetheless, celebrate your breakthroughs and show immense gratitude for the circumstances that create them.

Life is not about praying away the storm. It's about praying that you be strengthened in the storm. It's about realizing what your experiences are here to teach you because the gold that comes forth from them is so much more rewarding to the soul than the temporary circumstance you may find yourself in while you are experiencing them.

I'm guessing you might have your own lines to write and add to this poem. Start writing your thank you letter to your villains. Acknowledge the gifts awarded your soul from all your experiences with some of your life's greatest teachers.

Big Bad Wolf

FOR MY ENTIRE LIFE, I'VE HAD A FEAR OF WOLVES. From images placed in my imagination from stories like the *Big Bad Wolf* and *Little Red Riding Hood*, I envisioned wolves to be terrible, evil creatures that serve one purpose, to devour the sweet innocent sheep. I've also carried a fear of certain people who entered my life, wondering if they were actually wolves in sheep's clothing. This fear undoubtedly kept me separated from certain experiences and people who seemed different than my customs or beliefs.

Yesterday my son, Jack, had to complete a school project where he was told to choose an animal from the northern region and write a report about it. He chose the arctic wolf. In preparation for his report, we went to YouTube to learn more about these animals, their habitat, and their way of life. We came across a documentary of a husband and wife who raised a pack of wolves and lived with them for almost ten years. I sat in awe and wonder as I observed they had filmed and documented. By the end of the documentary, Jack and I had tears in our eyes as they had to say goodbye to this beautiful pack of wolves. Something I had thought was so evil had shown me another side to its purpose and design. I had a new appreciation for this fellow-creature that stemmed from the same Creative Power that sculpted all life.

As I watched the wolves interact, I saw them display compassion, protection, support, playfulness, love, honor, and respect. The Alpha wolf was there to determine the order of things. He was the leader, the dominant one. I saw distinct personalities in each wolf: the protector, the peacemaker, the playful and joyful soul given to lighten the mood, and the weak and submissive one labeled the Omega. I thought to myself, "Is there not the polarities of both the Alpha and the Omega within us all?" Perhaps this is one reason God named Himself both the Alpha and the Omega, and I imagine He would also represent every multi-layered facet of characteristics between the two.

I watched as this tribe, this pack, fought for one another, showed compassion, cared for their pups, and mourned in deep sorrow when one of their own died. I watched them howl in moments of frustration and pain. I watched them wander off when they felt they were not wanted or included in the pack. I watched as a lowly and submissive Omega was ultimately chosen as the wife and lifelong mate of the Alpha King. Joy filled my heart to see nature play out a Cinderella story of the least likely rising from a pit to a palace and being crowned as Queen. I saw her finally receiving honor and respect after years of pleading to the skies above with continuous cries and howls.

It was the darkness that helped me see and value the Light.

Could the wolf I had feared all these years been a figment of my own imagination? I watched the bond between the husband and wife filming the documentary and the wolf pack. They played with them, and the wolves licked their faces. The husband and wife became part of the pack, part of their family.

Jack, my ten-year-old, turned to me during the film and asked, "Mom, does bad and good make peace?"

I asked, "Why did you just ask me that, Jack?"

He replied, "I don't know. It just came to me."

I felt the chills emerge throughout my body, like when I hear the sound of truth. The Voice said, "Be still. Listen. Absorb that."

God was showing me that even in the things we fear the most, there is purpose, protection, love, and a place to live in unity and peace with all. The compassion I grew for the wolves helped me understand their purpose in the universe.

Perhaps it is time to lay aside our fears and to learn to coexist in peace. Is not both good and evil residing in us all? Has not one taught us to appreciate the other? There is an anonymous quote that says, "It takes sadness to know what happiness is, noise to appreciate silence, and absence to appreciate presence." It was the darkness that helped me see and value the Light. It was in being lost that ultimately helped me recognize when I was finally home and found.

Could the labels of good or bad, wolf or sheep, Muslim or Christian, gay or straight, vegan or not vegan, breast-feeder or formula feeder, Jew or non-Jew, black or white, educated or not educated, Republican or Democrat, saved or not saved, be judgments made due to our own fears of something we simply do not understand, perhaps of someone we do not understand? Are our definitions of good or bad only labels defining separation within us all? Yesterday as I shared these thoughts, a wise friend told me, "Both wolves will be fed in the end. They teach us nature's balance."

As the wise Cherokee once told his grandson, "My son, there's a battle between two wolves inside us all. One is Evil. It's anger, jealousy, greed, resentment, inferiority, lies, and ego. The other is Good. It's joy, peace, love, hope, humility, kindness, and truth." The boy thought about it, and asked: "Grandfather, which wolf wins?" The old man quietly replied: "The one you feed."

Perhaps instead of trying to pray our wolves away, we learn to embrace them. Not kill them, not blow them up, not make war with them, not fight against them, and not speak badly of them. Maybe instead of making war with them, we simply stop feeding them. Maybe it's time we recognize there is a wolf inside us all and begin to accept the similarities in all life forms instead of highlighting the differences. Maybe we should begin to feed that which is good, lovely, virtuous, just, pure, and of a good report.

Let us not be so focused on the obliteration of all evil in our lives and all storms from our path. Perhaps the problem has been sent to help us find a solution. Perhaps we attracted the problem so we could be given the gift of overcoming it. Perhaps learning to be strengthened in the midst of evil is what is truly in our highest good.

> *"Yea, though I walk through the valley of the*
> *shadow of death, I will fear no evil."*
> (Psalms 23:4)

Embrace the polarities, and the imbalances in the world around you. Embrace the dual nature within yourself. Stop trying to expel the wolf. Just focus on feeding the correct one.

Appreciating the Contrast

THE SHORTEST PATH TO KNOWING WHO YOU ARE IS TO KNOW who you are not. Appreciate the contrast you are experiencing. If you are not where you want to be, allow the place you are to help you identify where it is you do not want to be in your future. Be able to appreciate the knowledge you are gleaning from your experience. It is allowing you to more clearly identify what it is you do want.

It's very difficult to truly appreciate the light for all it gives to us without experiencing the blackening darkness of night. Use this period of your life to say,

> "Well, I know I am not this, and I've discovered that does not
> work for me. I don't enjoy how I feel when I am around this,
> and I don't like who I am when I believe that. I don't want to
> make the compromises I'm allowing by doing this. I am not
> happy with the feeling I'm experiencing by agreeing to that."

As you have more circumstances that are contrasting where it is you ultimately want to be, learn to walk away from those experiences with a grateful bow. Each one of them has helped mold and shape you into discovering who you genuinely are, what you genuinely want for yourself, and each circumstance will have helped you clearly define your ultimate value and worth. And if you are experiencing something unwanted, say to yourself,

> "Since things are always working out for my good,
> there must be value in this."

And then, look for it. Look for the value. I can guarantee you that you will have discovered more of who you truly are.

From Broken to Beautiful

TODAY WHILE SEASHELL HUNTING, I began to notice a common theme amongst them all. Through all the many different variations of shells, brokenness seemed to have touched them all. Some had scrapes, some had chips, others had ridges, bumps, and many were left with their insides exposed. All the shells were different sizes, shapes, and were an assortment of colors. Some were found to be as black as the night sky. All of them had layers showing their growth and phases of development. However, despite the brokenness of the shells, there was no denying their beauty. Perhaps that is why God is close to the brokenhearted.

Beauty is in the eye of the beholder.
Perhaps your beauty lies in your brokenness.

I noticed this one shell that was set apart and washed far away from the others. I picked it up and observed it to be a lovely shell delightful in color with only one defect, a small hole at the top-center of the shell. Joy flooded my heart. My mind immediately thought of a long gold chain in my closet and how gorgeous this little shell would be, daintily hanging upon it. I wondered how far this shell had traveled on its journey to serve such a sweet purpose, to bless me and be an object of value worn around my neck. Did the little shell know it would forever serve as a daily reminder of the powerful message God spoke to my heart that day about brokenness? When its hole was being formed by the massive beating of the violent waves, did the shell feel the pain from this etched void in its structure? Was it unaware of the purpose its hole would one day serve for another?

God is a healing power that lives within you and is continually
falling in love with you. He sees value in your brokenness and
wants to utilize it for something glorious.

Broken shells have been used to make necklaces, lampshades, works of framed art, furniture, and much more. Sometimes we just need a change of environment and what was broken in one place becomes something of beauty in another. Whatever condition your outward "shell" is in today, God has a purpose for your brokenness. Like the shell, many of you have traveled a long journey to serve a purpose, to be a blessing to someone else in need, to be an object of value and adornment to another. That empty void, the hole carved into your frame via the weathering of life's circumstances, will serve as something useful. It will be laced with a gold chain linking you to the hearts of those you are destined to serve. Your brokenness will someday serve as a shimmering ornament worn as a display of beauty for the world around you.

God stands upon the waters seeing us all, those hidden, those exposed, those broken, and those set apart and ready for display. You have been crafted with a glorious plan, with a precious promise, and with a productive purpose.

Allow for the breaking. Allow for the weathering. Allow for the sifting.
Allow for the emptying and allow for the filling
Allow for the molding and allow for the unraveling
Allow for the withdrawals and allow for the deposits
Allow things to be added and allow things to be taken away
Allow for the exposing. Allow for the covering.
Allow for pulling down. Allow for the lifting up.
Allow for the surrender.
Thy will be done.

The Pink Diamond

1 WAS DOWNSTAIRS YESTERDAY WHEN I HEARD KATE CALLING ME with excitement, "Mommy! Come here! You have to see this!"

I entered Kate's room to see a rainbow of colors dancing on her ceiling. She was mesmerized and had no idea where they came from. She just kept saying with joy as she pounced on her bed, "Mommy, it's God!"

I began to explain to her that the rainbows were coming from a pink crystal in the shape of a diamond that was sitting next to her window. It had created a prism as the light rays from the sun were striking it. I explained to her that a prism is a transparent object with a flat, polished surface that refracts light.

And then, unexpectedly, the Spirit rose within me and I knew I must speak the message the Spirit had given to the heart of this precious little girl.

"Kate, we are the pink crystal. Christ is the sun that shines through us and makes us sparkle. His spirit is what purifies us and makes us transparent, removing all the yucky stuff in our hearts so we can make rainbows in the world around us. Do you see all the beautiful pictures created when we position ourselves to receive the light of the sun?

"There's also something very important I want you to pay close attention to when you look at the pink crystal. Do you notice all the cuts and edges chiseled in it to make it the shape of a diamond? Those edges make it so the light can refract, which is what is making the rainbows sparkle on your ceiling. Refract means to make the light change direction when it goes through at an angle.

"The sharp edges are often the difficulties and the struggles we experience in life. Yet, without them, we could not be molded into the shape of this beautiful diamond. Without them, we wouldn't be able to change direction in such a way that would allow the Light to come through us. It's the sharp edges and cuts in our lives that allow us to change directions and that position us to fully receive the Light that makes us create the sparkles."

The message: Be transparent. Allow the Son to remove the impurities so you can reflect the Light. Appreciate the cuts and the sharp corners, the difficulties, and the trials. Cuts cause suffering, but they also provide an opportunity to heal. Allow them to be polished so they can reflect a glorious Light that makes rainbows of beauty surround you. The more transparent and authentic you become and the more cuts that are etched into your mold, the more you are being shaped into a gorgeous, priceless diamond. Diamonds are made from pressure and heat, but when the process of purification is complete, they become objects of great value. Once the Light penetrates through them, they become wonderful reflectors with an ability to make everything around them sparkle. They may even become a prism to create the colors of a rainbow where there was once a seemingly plain existence.

The best part of this story is that once the process of evolving from charcoal to a diamond is complete, like Kate, you will be left saying, "Everyone, come quick. Come and see! It's God." To which my reply was, "Yes, Sweetie. That is most definitely the touch of God."

Built to Last

WHEN YOU ARE BORN, YOU BEGIN A JOURNEY OF SPIRITUAL DEVELOPMENT. While you are here, you learn valuable lessons that help you on your journey and go on to make you the remarkable individual you are. It's a bit like being in school. Sometimes the lessons you face are painless, and you can sail through them with ease. At other times, they can be hard-hitting and difficult, making you face arduous challenges head-on.

For example, consider the person who seems to constantly experience trials and tribulations. From a spiritual perspective, what is this all about? Once you have undergone a lesson and have learned it properly, you won't have to go through it again. That chapter of your life will be over, and you will move on to other lessons. You might think that it's unfair to have to go through problematic situations, especially if others around you seem to have it easier, but each lesson you face gives you an internal strength that can never be taken away from you. Call it character-building. These lessons enhance your inner wisdom, which is what your soul is ultimately striving to obtain.

In this world, you will have trouble BUT...

"Consider it pure joy, my brothers and sisters, whenever you face
trials of many kinds, because you know that the testing of your
faith produces perseverance. Let perseverance finish its work so
that you may be mature and complete, not lacking anything."
(James 1:2-4)

Don't Pray Away Your Heat

THERE'S ONLY ONE WAY TO BOIL AWAY IMPURITIES IN WATER. Apply heat. You are made of over 70% water. Could it be that your problems and your pressures are your means to perfection? Is this the wisdom behind such statements as, "In this world, you will have trouble."

Some food is only fit to be eaten once the heat has been applied. If the temperature of your life's circumstances is heating up, might you consider, like the food you eat, your life is being prepared for the dispersion, nourishment, and enjoyment of others? Might you be the "food" or sustenance for those your soul longs to feed?

A delicacy worthy of admiration, savoring, and appreciating requires attention to detail and a process of refinement to be considered incredibly valuable. Pearls endure much irritation by the sand before they shine so pretty. They also require a fervent search by someone who is diligent enough to seek out their beauty, uncover them, and bring them to the surface to shimmer in the Light.

Diamonds undergo their journey though darkened buried crevasses and intense heat before preparing to shine in the hand of the one committed enough to search for their beauty. Yet, once discovered and brought into the sun, they produce a sparkle and a reflection of Light, second to none.

Don't pray away your heat. The purpose of a pressure cooker is to reduce cooking time. Perhaps God is allowing the pressure you are undergoing, because He wants to quickly prepare you for service. You are a delicacy. Your soul came here that it might ultimately be perfected and glisten like the stars or angels that twinkle above us. Be committed to your sparkle. Transformation is a worthy cause. Your troubled circumstance was destined to be your ultimate celebration.

Dearest Nature

DEAREST NATURE,

Thank you from the depths of my heart for being such a wonderful teacher to me. I see you. I feel God in you. Thank you for all the kind, loving, and healing whispers carried by your refreshing winds and magnificent skies. As I type these words sitting on the dock and listening to the soothing flap of the waters against the shoreline, I notice the post of wood at my feet. Hundreds of circles ripple out from its center, and I am reminded I am the ripple echoing throughout time and space having been derived from you, the core of who I truly am.

Oh nature, the beauty of God is displayed so well in and through you. Indeed, you wear Divinity so well. Every day you remind me of the true nature of God's love. When I see the sun never fail to rise and bring warmth, when I see the rain never fail to replenish and revive, I am reminded of the abundant storehouse of loving energy that is given to us all. The sun helps to grow the good man's crops. The sun helps to grow the evildoer's crops. It shines without judgment. It simply is. It simply shines. The sun demonstrates how I have come to know the love of God. Electricity has been used to light a brothel, and electricity has been used to light a nursery. It never judges which one is worthy or deserving of its light. It simply shines for anyone that is aware of it and uses it. Nature, you lovingly serve us all and provide to anyone who is in need. Thank you for your daily analogy of this picture-perfect love granted us by the true Source of all things.

To Mother Nature and her dark side, the moments when you are cruel and unkind, when the tornadoes swirl and the waters flood, when your heat is unbearable, and your cold is frigid and harsh, is it you that we should blame or has our land simply responded to the rage and turmoil that stirs within the people? James, the brother of Jesus said,

> "What causes fights and quarrels among you? Don't they come
> from your desires that battle within you?"
> (James 4:1)

Has Mother Nature responded the same? Have we rattled her to quake or enticed her to explode? Will she not be at peace until we make peace within ourselves? Perhaps she will still herself when we find the path to stillness. Perhaps we are more connected to the environment than we have previously thought ourselves to be.

Ahhhh, the great error of the human soul, seeing all that happens without as no indication of what is occurring within. Perhaps the illness is a reflection of something inwardly out of emotional alignment. Perhaps it emerged as a result of misaligned beliefs rooted in falsehoods and opposition to genuine truth regarding ourselves, others, and potentially even God. Maybe the weather has everything to do with our internal emotional climate. Maybe the angry man who threatened you is the manifestation of an angry threat your subconscious mind holds against you.

When we learn to see ourselves as one with our environment and
not separate from it, we spiritually position ourselves for progress.

There is a consciousness within you affecting everything around you. The consciousness of your city is affecting how it functions and operates. The consciousness of your nation impacts what transpires and occurs within it. The collective consciousness of this Earth is affecting the outcome and status of our existing world. Don't play victim to the kings and queens of this world or allow anything to distract and disempower you. How you feel right now is affecting the consciousness of the entire world. Your energy, your Spirit, and your thoughts are part of a giant whole.

Recently, my son brought home a math lesson in which all the problems were based on the equation, part = percent x whole. How much your part contributes depends on what percentage of yourself is affecting the whole. How strong is your frequency? Are you omitting a vibration of love, kindness, healing, and hope? What percentage of enlightened souls on this planet are touching the whole? The conditions of the world will showcase the condition of the majority of earthly souls. It takes a very small number to impact a great many. Less in some cases is more than enough.

Don't be manipulated by the media, television, radio, internet, or any other form of technological mind control. It takes very few people who own these vehicles of mass hypnosis to control and lead large numbers of people to do as they will. Thus, the power that is unleashed when two or more gather together to petition God or more importantly release the power of God housed within them, can accomplish mind-blowing, miraculous things. Never underestimate the power of one, much less a handful of people who radiate a vibration of love and peace. One person can affect millions of people. We see it all the time. You could name several people whose lives have impacted the masses. Your ripple effect begins with you.

Sweet Mother Nature, there is one more thing I must express my gratitude to you about. For the times when you did replace the crisp, relaxing breeze with the violent winds of a twisting tornado or raging storm, I offer you my sincerest thanks. Once again, you taught me something I must learn to master within myself. You proved yourself a magnificent Teacher once more by illustrating the perfect analogy of how the storms of life allow us to see what we are truly made of. They cause heroes to emerge. They rally us together to serve, protect, uplift, and guide. Could it be that evil has her purpose to serve as well? Is the force that pushes against a soul what causes the victor to rise?

> *Everyone has their role to play in the path of evolution. Perhaps we must play all sides of the coin before we can appreciate the value of the currency. It was experiencing the contrast of all that I desired that helped me discover what I authentically longed to obtain.*

You may feel anger against the corruption being exposed in the governments of our world. You may be shocked to learn those you trusted have deceived you. You may have even played into their hands and drank their Kool-Aid for most of your life. Yet, it was the recognition of all that was wrong for you that allowed you to discover all that was right for you. Sometimes we have to see it done wrong to know how we should do it right, to orchestrate a system of justice for ourselves and the world at large. All has a purpose. Trust the process. Before you know it, you'll be speaking to the storms and releasing peace wherever you go.

Significance in the Suffering

WHAT IS THIS MIGRAINE TEACHING ME? What am I learning from the sleepiness? What has the weakness and numbness shown me? Why did I have an aneurysm in my brain stem? What is the purpose of my suffering? What is this experience here to teach me?

> *The difficulties and hardships I have encountered in my life are what have generated the most meaning and depth.*

The reality of life is that none of us can escape suffering. If you live long enough, you will encounter disappointment, heartbreak, loss, and eventually, death. All of these things will be just a sliver of what we will encounter in this life. These experiences have the potential to shake us and test our resolve. However, good can come from suffering and perhaps even begin the journey to wisdom.

These moments serve to awaken us. They help us find meaning and answer purposeful questions regarding who we are and why we are here. These experiences fill our hearts with greater compassion and love for others. They inspire and provoke newfound creativity and passion. Your current suffering might turn out to be a blessing in disguise, providing the most significant contribution to your overall successes and soul growth.

I love my journey. My head may hurt but my heart now knows compassion in a realm I had not previously known. The illness may be affecting my head, but the result has touched my heart. I'll take the latter.

This Year

THIS YEAR I HAVE BEEN UP AND DOWN. I have pushed and pulled.

I have fought. I have surrendered.

I've been ready for war. I've heralded peace.

I've been loud, and I've been quiet.

I've been sad. I've been mad. I've been happy. I've been glad.

I've laughed. I've cried.

I've been frustrated. I've been at peace.

I've been angry. I've been calm.

I've been judgmental. I've been compassionate.

I've been right. I've been wrong.

I've been persuaded, and I've also stood my ground.

I've pleased, and I've disappointed.

I've been weak, and I've been strong.

I've been gentle. I've been bold.

I've been inclusive. I've been restrictive.

I've wanted justice. I've wanted mercy.

I've been overwhelmed. I've been empowered.

I've been unifying, and I've been divisive.

I've been in the flesh. I've been in the Spirit.

I've spoken with my ego. I've spoken with a Divine Voice.

I've fought death. I've embraced life.

I have experienced many paths.

I have loved.

I have lost.

But most of all

I have learned.

This year.

Count It All Joy

I BELIEVE OUR UNIVERSE IS GOVERNED BY A RESTORATIVE GOD who is committed to the triumph of His people. The will of God is for you to finish your journey here with excellence. If only mankind could learn from this intention and cheer for others with this never-giving-up kind of love. It is exemplified in the hosts of heaven and their commitment to continually serve and aid us as well as in the depths Christ was willing to go to herald His message, a message designed to take you from darkness to light and help you enter this glorious inner kingdom of heaven that He spoke of with such fondness and affection.

You may go through different times in your life where things feel broken. This can be the result of many different kinds of circumstances. Sometimes we are to blame for them, and sometimes it's just a result of the rain falling on the just and the unjust. Regardless of the root cause, the goal of your Heavenly Parent is to see you completely restored. It is in feeling everything has fallen apart that we learn to cry out for help to put the pieces back together. In our weakness, His strength is made perfect. There is great reward and beauty to come from bended knees, humbled hearts, and quiet confessions. Desperation teaches surrender and dependence upon God to lift your burdens and allow for His help and guidance in your life. Doing life alone without feeling the love and support of a loving Father that has your back and wants you to succeed is beyond depressing. Regardless of how lost or how found you might currently be at the present moment; I believe in a God who is sincerely committed to moving heaven and earth to see you triumph.

A wayward son is still loved and dearly held
in the mind of a committed Father whose
affections are unconditionally upon his child.

Difficult seasons, trials, and tests are generally the greatest catalyst for genuine transformation as well as an opportunity for God to instill within us strength, confidence, and resolve we otherwise would not have had were we not pushed to discover and release it. Allow the Winter season to prepare you for Spring. Ask, "What is this experience here to teach me?" If restoration and wholeness is our Father's ultimate goal, perhaps we must endure some circumstances that would boil any impurities to the surface. If you are in one of these seasons, allow a heavenly ladle dipped by the hand of God to skim across the surface of your heart, collecting any impurities that need to be removed. May the aroma be fragrant in the nostrils of God and may the aftertaste of such an experience leave a blessed sweetness in your life. There is great hope in knowing all things are working together for good for those who love God and are called according to His purpose.

Count it all joy.

Resistance

"The flower that blooms in adversity is the rarest and most
beautiful of all."
~ Walt Disney

SCIENTISTS CREATED AN EXPERIMENT FOR GROWING TREES IN CAVES. They brought in the proper, nutrient-rich soil as well as good water and artificial sunlight. The trees grew and seemed like they were thriving for some time. Then without warning, they began to die. It was diagnosed that the trees were weak and could not support their own weight. The scientist on the project concluded that the reason for the death of the trees was the lack of wind resistance. Trees that grow in their natural environment regularly sustain an internal strength as a result of growing up with resistance. The trees in the cave had everything they needed to thrive, except natural resistance.

If olives need the crushing to produce the oil,

If diamonds need the heat and the pressure to make them sparkle,

If pearls need the irritation of the sand to make them valuable,

If trees need high-powered winds to make them grow,

then perhaps your adversity is the catalyst to you thriving.

When we avoid adversity, we are avoiding success.
Mother Nature has shown us that success is made out of the
struggle.
Resistance qualifies us to thrive.
Trust the process.

Stirring Waters

"For an angel went down at a certain season into the pool,
and troubled the water:
whosoever then first after the troubling of the water
stepped in was made whole of whatsoever disease he had."
(John 5:4)

IF WE ARE MADE OF 70% WATER, PERHAPS WE NEED TO BE STIRRED or troubled before healing can arise. Water, when left sitting for too long unstirred or "troubled," can become stagnant and grow bacteria.

Today, if you are experiencing a stirring or troubling in your circumstances and in your life, perhaps it is an indicator that you are about to receive the most miraculous healing of your life.

I believe the "stirring of your waters" could indicate an opportunity for healing and wholeness. However, keep in mind the people in this story had to step into the waters in order to be healed. Don't be afraid to step into troubled waters. Instead, acknowledge that you know the One who walks upon them. Recognize the same power to stand atop the turbulent seas of your life abides in you. Speak peace into the storms of your life and feel the calmness encapsulate you. Arise from the stirring of your waters with the healing and wholeness your soul so desperately longs to obtain.

For Our Good

I DON'T NECESSARILY BELIEVE THAT GOD ORCHESTRATED the circumstances of my life without my consent. When in the higher wisdom of my Spirit form, I would imagine that I was quite aware I needed this pilgrimage. My soul needed this journey, and those who are walking it with me chose it too. I could not see what I see now had I not selected certain hardships.

The God part of you has always been working everything for your good. He will even allow you to believe a lie if the lie will one day serve to help you find the truth. For without darkness, the seed cannot grow. Without darkness none us would understand or know how to enjoy and appreciate the Light as we do. I wanted to see the darkness. My soul wanted to see it. It was in the darkness that I learned how to seek for and become the Light.

As deep darkness rises upon a land, so too can the Light of God be rising from within the hearts of its people. There is goodness in there. There is Light in there. There is truth in there. There is healing there for the world. All is well. All is as it should be.

Often, the so-called bad guys in the story are also serving an important role. Evil is used to perfect and heal, much like the fire purifies the gold. If we are brave enough to acknowledge this, these so-called evil monsters that cross our paths can serve as mirrors for what God is so lovingly trying to show us is dwelling within our hearts. Like the sand to the pearl, we often need an irritant to purify our souls and make us shine.

Jesus Christ told us that in the current realm we live in, we would have trouble. He wanted to teach us how to walk upon the waters in the midst of our storms. He wanted us to cheer up, to step out of the boat, and to know He had already overcome the fears, the death, the diseases, and the wars. And He wanted us to know that we could too.

Take a moment to breathe deeply and step atop the waters. Go outside. Allow nature to teach you once more. Let God's love consume you, fill you, and overflow from you in such a way that you gain compassion for even those who wish to harm you. For without the contrast of evil, we wouldn't know the delight our soul receives from choosing good.

Life Schooled

I USED TO WANT MY CHILDREN HOMESCHOOLED, but now I want them life schooled.

May their failures teach them

May that which they fear become that which they love

May their regrets be their steppingstones to a better way

May they be in this world but not of it, schooled by the Spirit of Life, the greatest teacher of all

May they learn that the Voice they carry within is greater than any voice they could ever hear outside of them

And may the Light of God shine through them each and every day of their beautiful lives.

Happy Beginnings, Little Ones. May we learn all you came here to teach us.

To my children ~ I love you.
Always have. Always will. Unconditionally.
From your mom, your sister, and your soulmate

HEALING BACK
TO WHOLENESS

Do You Want to Be Here?

SOON AFTER I HAD MY BRAIN ANEURYSM, I reached out to a spiritually-based guidance counselor to assist in my healing journey. Immediately upon returning my phone call, he said, "Before I can determine if this is going to be a good fit for us to work together, I need to ask you one important question. Do you want to be here?"

I knew the Holy Spirit had chosen these words, and they pierced deeply. Instantly it reminded me of when someone sick would approach Jesus Christ in need of miraculous healing. The first question he often asked them was, "Do you want to be healed?" There was a part of me that wanted to snap back at him and say, "Of course I want to be here! What do you mean, do I want to be here?! Do you think I want to die?! What a ridiculous question to ask someone that is sick!" Yet, instead of responding in this manner, I noticed a tear began to fall down my cheeks and a tightness began to grip my chest. The question had reached into the deepest crevices of my heart. I heard so much more underlying his question to me. I heard,

> *"Misti, do you want to finish this? Do you want to face whatever you need to face to overcome your fears and obstacles once and for all? Do you want to heal 100% back to wholeness, because in order to do that, you must face yourself like never before. You must learn to stand atop the waves unmoved by the storms around you. You must also learn to quiet the storms within you. Not everyone wants to heal, Misti. Not everyone wants to stop blaming others*

and looking outside of themselves for answers and causes for their
pain. Not everyone is prepared to look within and accept
responsibility. Not everyone can accept they have the power to
change the tide. You chose to come here, Misti. In our blessed
oneness, we chose together a perfect divine will for your soul. You
came with intention. You came with purpose. You came to
overcome this world, but you are not required to be here against
your will. Your will to live is essential to your survival.
Do you want to be here?"

I didn't think it was a coincidence that this question was asked directly after being confronted with a circumstance that would require an answer. My mind drifted to earlier in the week when I had come face to face with a choice of life or death. Days prior, I had awakened from a deep sleep unable to breathe, unable to see, and unable to hear. While attempting to place me in the car and get me to the emergency room, I passed out, which left me covered in blood having split my chin apart on our hardwood floors.

My mind began to refocus as the counselor says, "Misti, you have sent forth a death wish. It's up to you whether or not you will choose to reverse it; however, if you do choose to do so, it will take a strong act of your will and a renewed commitment to being here."

His words were gripping. I had just recently emerged from years where I had engaged in the hardest battles I had ever faced. More times than not, I had wanted to quit, not just the situation I was in, but life in general. My soul felt like it had been crushed and perplexed on all sides. I was fortunate in that I never had thoughts of suicide, but I had cried out in desperation many times for God to take me home. I was tired. I had moments of deep defeat and mental exhaustion, where I just wanted the whole experience called life to be over. My endless love for my children, coupled with the immense power of the Holy Spirit enabled me to plunge forward and push through the seemingly hopeless moments. The Holy Spirit had empowered me with a continuous faith and overall feeling that no matter how dark things appeared, my life had meaning and purpose. It was impossible to escape the pull of the Spirit, guiding me towards higher thoughts. At times I fought hard against the current, but the flow of the Spirit would overpower me, and I would gently surrender to her nurturing stream of life.

Yet, all those moments of holding a strong intention of defeat and wanting escape had finally caught up with me. I was realizing how powerful we are as spiritual beings to manifest the dominant thoughts we hold in our hearts. We are creative because we were created in the likeness of a Creator. Our creations can either bring life or death, blessings or curses. We have been given free will. Based on what my experiences have taught me, I believe that will is so powerful that if we don't want to be here, we can most definitely manifest a circumstance that will allow for our exit. I do not believe all traumatic incidences are related to this, but I have often wondered if many cancers, fatal car accidents, or other close calls have been linked to an underlying desire held too long

Can our commitment and desire to complete our life's mission or our surrender under the weight of it determine the outcome of our fate?

within the heart and mind of an individual that they don't want to be here anymore.

Jesus once said that unless he laid down his life, no one could take it from him. Are we truly as He was in this world? Are we that powerful that by sheer will and determination we can overcome death's grip? Can our commitment and desire to complete our life's mission or our surrender under the weight of it determine the outcome of our fate? There is a story in the Bible about a man named Hezekiah who prayed and asked God to extend his life. God replied to him and told him that He had heard Hezekiah's prayers and seen his tears, and as a result, He was going to add fifteen additional years to Hezekiah's life. (Isaiah 38:5) Does our desire to live touch the heart of God? Does our commitment to our journey resonate in the courts of heaven? Are we the directors of our life's play? Like Christ, have we been given the power and dominion to determine when that final curtain call will be?

I reflected on the many miniature moments though small and random, where I chose to escape. Perhaps it was a bad day, a moment where someone misunderstood my intentions or a moment I felt judged. Maybe it was as a result of my failure, a moment when someone was angry or disappointed in me, or a moment of hurt or of dealing with an unfair situation. Instead of facing those moments with courage and strength, I would crumble under the weight of them. For some people, these moments can arise from a financial crisis, a divorce, a betrayal, rejection, or the loss of someone they dearly love.

For far too long instead of keeping my head above the waters, I sank under the weight of them. There were many days of turning off the lights, pulling the covers over my head, and crying myself to sleep. In those moments, I would think of how exhausting and challenging life can be and would wish to be free from its shackles. Yet, without fail, the following morning, the sun would rise again, and I would once again begin to count my blessings. My children would inspire me, nature would heal me, and most often, God would provide an angelic voice to encourage me to keep going and to keep growing.

However, these brief moments of utter defeat collected over a lifetime and began to take their toll. They left stains of unresolved issues and beliefs about myself and others that were misaligned with God's divine wisdom and truth. I now know it is foolish to think we are not affected when we view life as something that is merely happening to us. I had a victim mentality that kept me feeling powerless. I had yet to realize the power I possessed to choose a different life. For me, this began by choosing a different response to the life I currently had. It began with the renewing of my own mind. There were lingering habits and patterns that were no longer serving me and needed to die. I was faced with a choice. It was life or death for me. I could no longer continue to thrive responding to life the way I had in the past. I could no longer perform, or people-please for approval, acceptance, and love. I could no longer suppress my feelings to avoid confrontation. I could no longer hide parts of my journey for fear of judgment. I could no longer allow the environment around me to direct my emotions.

As the paramedics were placing the oxygen mask on my face, I began to use what breath I had to cry out, "I choose life! I choose Christ!"

> I made a statement to God with all my might and will. I was choosing to be here, to face my demons, and to overcome this world. I had come here to bring the Light, not run from the darkness. It would no longer influence me. I would influence it. It was a definitive moment in my life. I made a decision that day that no matter how difficult life might present itself at times, I would cherish her forever. Never again would I wish to escape her. Never again would I spend more time wishing for Jesus to come get me than I was releasing Jesus from within me. I would do my part to bring heaven here, to focus on God's will on earth as it is in heaven. I would treasure life as the miraculous, marvelous gift that she was and would commit to embracing and learning all she was here to teach me.

As I chose faith over fear, and as I chose a commitment to life versus a hidden desire to escape from it, my health diagnosis was miraculously lessened

from the neurologist's original diagnosis of an AVM, arteriovenous malformation, to the neurosurgeon's diagnosis of a lesser aggressive hemangioma called
a CCM, cerebral cavernous malformation. A CCM bleeds more slowly than the
massive eruptions that occur with an AVM.

Most importantly, I began to notice a pattern in my recovery. The more I
began to take control over my responses to life's circumstances, the more physical improvement I began to see. I began to change the way I looked at what
was happening to me. If I had a bad day or something physically scared me
due to the neurological damage I was suffering, I began to train my mind to
turn the negatives into positive statements of affirmation.

Being committed to your wholeness requires being honest with
yourself. When you get serious about wanting to live, you
quickly begin to identify the things that are causing you to die. If
I wanted to change my future, I had to stop telling a story that I
didn't want to be a part of it.

Every time I spoke about my brain aneurysm, I was acknowledging it once
more. I was giving life to it all over again. I had to be willing to tell a different
story, and I had to be willing to let go of the attention my ego was receiving
from playing the role of victim. I've never been more loved and supported in
my entire life than when everyone thought I was dying. A part of me didn't
want to give up that attention. I had to be willing to desire to be healthy and
strong more than the recognition I was receiving from being weak.

I also had to learn how to protect and conserve my energy. I had dispersed
my energy to anyone and everything in an attempt to people-please for love and
validation. And I had done it for so long that I had very little life-force energy
remaining to help me heal. I had to learn self-care, self-love, and how to emotionally and spiritually put my oxygen mask on first. I stored my energy, and I
began to apply that to loving and nurturing myself in thought, word, and deed.

It was a gradual process of progressing as often on a healing journey
things can get worse before getting better; however, the more emotional and
spiritual healing I received, the more my physical body responded positively.
Like a computer program, there were many programs running in the background of my subconscious mind that had to be deleted. The more clearing I
did, the more healing occurred. It was as if every program or perhaps limiting
belief was linked to a portion of my body. One by one, as I healed my mind,
heart, and emotions, my body followed suit. Previously, this inoperable brain

tumor had been rapidly growing within my brain stem. In fact, the neurosurgeon told me that in one month, it had grown beyond what they had expected it to grow for an entire year. This, of course, was during the time I was focusing all my attention on the problem instead of the solution.

When I began to change, so did my tumor. I began doing daily visual exercises where I vividly imagined walking into my neurosurgeon's office and him telling me the tumor was gone. I stayed in that imaginary space until it was so real to me that it was gone that I was crying tears of joy and jumping up and down with excitement over what God and I working together had been able to accomplish and heal! I began to no longer talk about my tumor because in my mind, it was gone.

Six months later, I walked into the neurosurgeon's office and listened as he said, "Hang on a minute. I want to go back and look at this current MRI once more." He left the office and came back once more, "Misti, the hemangioma is less pronounced. Not only has it stopped growing. It is shrinking!" The tears flooded my eyes with gratitude just as they had done time and time again alone in my bedroom, imagining the day I would hear those beautiful words.

Herein lies the message: You are powerful beyond measure. You are the earthen vessel by which all the treasure of heaven is stored. You can create miracles. You are the miracle! With an adjustment of your mind and heart, you can change any situation or circumstance in your life. Ancient scriptures teach that all wars and conflicts come from within the hearts of humanity. I believe when we heal the heart, we can heal anything, including the body.

How We Feel
Determines How We Heal

THIS WEEK HAS BEEN A PIVOTAL ONE FOR ME. I have quietly been pondering the turbulent conditions surrounding us in our country, and I have considered the way in which I am accustomed to responding to them. There has and will always be an activist spirit in me, one seeking justice and wanting to expose the truth and silence lies. However, this week there was a shift that took place in me. I will no longer go about expressing my views or doing my part to heal the world the same way in which I have done in the past. The Spirit took me on a profound journey the past few days, and as always when the Spirit speaks, I was left with a new perspective.

Last week I posted on my Facebook wall expressing my agitation with our nation's current state of being. Although I gave the solution to look within and seek the counsel of the Spirit instead of following after corrupt politicians or the mainstream media that propagates division and separation, I was still giving attention to the problem instead of being the solution I want to see transpire. Whenever we focus on a problem, we only get more of it. Was I really promoting peace by raising more awareness of how twisted and messed up things have become?

The following morning after I made the post, I received a phone call from my cousin and dear friend, Melanie. As we began to chat, I gave her an open invitation to share what was on her heart. In her wisdom, she replied,

"Misti, I want you here. You are supposed to be here. You have a wonderful calling and message to share with the world, but the way to ensure that happens is by you reading and ingesting only positivity. Feeling good is what is going to untwist that hemangioma in your brain stem. You are a Way-shower, a Healer, and a Light-worker brought here to stand for justice and to teach spiritual truth. With that said, I understand it is hard not to participate in activism and speaking against wrongdoing. However, just for now, you must focus on your healing. You must heal before you can do all those things. Just until this tumor straightens up, look away from politics and from anything that is not pleasing to you. Focus your heart, mind, and attention on everything that is good, true, and beautiful to you. Write about your children and sit in nature and ponder the works of God as you love to do. Cook those beautiful vegan meals you enjoy blogging about. How you spend your time is important to your healing. Focus intently on what makes you happy. If you find yourself in a conversation where you feel like it's work, stop. Explain to the person talking that you need to kindly bow out and step away because you have made a commitment to yourself to only focus on what is life-giving to you. Protect yourself, Misti. Follow good. How you feel is going to determine how you heal. For now, only focus on your favorite things. Run fast from anything that isn't making you feel good."

Melanie's words fell like a fresh rain. I felt my soul was watered and a thirst I had not realized existed was quenched and nourished. She was right. She was so right! As the day progressed, I could not get her words out of my mind. I pondered them. I chewed over them. I was deeply moved and touched by them. I began to realize that a key component to my healing was connected to how I feel: how I feel about myself, how I feel about others, and how I feel about God. I realized that if I was unbalanced in my beliefs in any of those areas, there was an imbalance in my body and in my environment. I also realized what she had spoken was the key to much more. Her words carried wisdom and truth to unlock unrest, wars, and lack of peace on a worldwide scale.

I have been diagnosed with a physical brain tumor, but all of us have our "tumors" so to speak. We all have those things in our lives that are threatening our lives or the quality of them. For some, it is hatred, bitterness, un-forgiveness, or pride. For others, it's a lack of understanding, knowledge, and love and acceptance for all created beings. For myself and many others, it may be a physical issue that is affecting our health, vitality, and quality of life. How can we expect to change what is taking place in our environment without first focusing on ridding ourselves of the "tumors" we carry within us? It reminds me of the words of Christ when he taught us to remove the plank in our own eye before trying to remove one in the eye of another.

My brain tumor has been placed where no man can touch it, because this struggle is one I must win internally. Man cannot fix it. It has been surrounded by healthy brain stem tissue and to operate would mean cutting through the healthy tissue, causing more damage. Only the work of the Spirit with my participation is going to heal it. Isn't this simply a physical manifestation of what is true of all disease, sickness, and wars? We can never obtain peace in the outer world until we make peace within ourselves. When we try to forge ahead or place more attention on an issue or when we try to operate with physical weapons, we only cause more damage than what previously existed.

If we want to shrink the tumor of racism, hatred, separation, and injustice, we must begin by looking within our hearts, not criticizing or judging the hearts of others.

This fight cannot be one of the flesh. It must be one of the Spirit. We do not need guns and bombs to bring peace. We need love and compassion. Today I made a decision to lay down my sword. War is the fruit of corrupted politics, and so I won't involve myself any longer. If I am working for peace, that peace will lessen the war that rages amongst us.

If I am focused on my healing, on what is beautiful, good, and true, and if I am focused on my favorite things as Melanie explained to me, I am becoming well. I am healing my tumor. I am promoting peace within myself. If this is the path to healing my inoperable brain tumor, is this not the path to healing us all? If we are to have peace on earth, our loyalties must ultimately transcend our race, our tribe, our class, our nation, and yes, even our religions, which have created much division and separation. We must develop a world perspective that warrants love and compassion for all. We must love one another without boundaries and conditions.

We can never obtain peace in the outer world until we make peace within ourselves.

It's interesting to me that when Mother Teresa was invited to participate in anti-war demonstrations, she responded, "I will not do that but as soon as you have a pro-peace rally, I'll come to that." I suppose Mother Teresa already knew what I had yet to learn. She was protecting her consciousness from being affected by the spiritual and political diseases running rampant in the world. The protests, the rants on our Facebook walls, the hours of watching people argue, discuss and debate the issues on television and social media—none of this is what will heal the worldwide tumor we all share. The attention we are giving towards fighting issues is only making them bigger. Is it not true we become that which we focus our minds upon? Most headlines in today's papers are only throwing another round of gasoline on the fire. Is this what the media wants to propagate? More anger, more hate, more frustration, more fear, and more hopelessness? The more we talk about it and give focus to it, the more we feel angry, bitter, and disturbed. If feeling good is what warrants my healing, why does feeling good not warrant healing for the whole world? Melanie's words were not just for right now until my tumor heals. They are forever. They are to keep more "tumors" from appearing.

How are the activities you are participating in making you feel? How are your thoughts and beliefs making you feel? How do you feel when you look upon the problems of your life or dwell upon the issues you take offense to? How do you feel when you read that political article? How do you feel when you watch the news? Is it making you feel more peaceful, joyful, content, and happy? Or is it making you feel angry, resentful, defeated, and more separated from others? As Melanie said to me, "How you feel determines how you heal." Your emotions are affecting the outcome of your life and the world around you. Keeping this in mind, I would like to make a suggestion:

"Whatsoever things are true. Whatsoever things are honest. Whatsoever things are just. Whatsoever things are pure and lovely. Whatsoever things are of a good report. If there be any virtue, and if there be any praise, think on these things. Think upon these things."
(Philippians 4:8)

We must feel something different before we can see something different. We must love our enemies before they will learn to love us. We must pray for our opponents before we can make peace with them. How can we believe and hope for a world without weapons when we refuse to control the deadliest weapon of all, our own tongues? How can we bring peace when we are still engaged in the fight? Do we truly want a golden age? How can we hope for a Millennium Kingdom that we are not prepared to help create? Should not the hearts of the constituents of a kingdom match its glory?

Today I made a decision to stop worrying and constantly looking at what was wrong with our world. I made a decision to stop talking about what was broken, to stop giving attention to it, and to simply start being what I want to be right in this world! I chose to see my brain tumor as a possibility for something more divine. This is how I will heal it, and this is how we must heal our international tumor. How we all feel is affecting our worldwide healing as a whole. How much better would we feel if we focused on the good, and if we placed our attention upon being what is good about our world? If each person did that, where could we be as a society?

A Prayer by St. Francis of Assisi:

Lord, make me a channel of thy peace,
that where there is hatred, I may bring love;
that where there is wrong,
I may bring the spirit of forgiveness;
that where there is discord, I may bring harmony;
that where there is error, I may bring truth;
that where there is doubt, I may bring faith;

that where there is despair, I may bring hope;
that where there are shadows, I may bring light;
that where there is sadness, I may bring joy.
Lord, grant that I may seek rather to
comfort than to be comforted;
to understand, than to be understood;
to love, than to be loved.
For it is by self-forgetting that one finds.
It is by forgiving that one is forgiven.
It is by dying that one awakens to Eternal Life.

You Are Not a Victim

I ONCE HEARD GREGG BRADEN GIVING A LECTURE in which he described a particular experiment. In the 1980's Israel and Lebanon were in the first Israeli and Lebanon War. Researchers from the United States performed an experiment in the Middle East where they trained individuals to feel the feeling of peace as if it had already happened. This was a famous experiment called the International Peace Project of the Middle East. The results of this experiment were so profound that they were eventually published in the Journal of Conflict Resolution, Volume 32, in 1988. Here's what happened. They trained individuals to go into the war-torn areas and feel the feeling of peace as if peace had already happened there. They did not judge the war. They did not judge the Israeli's good or bad, the Palestinians good or bad, or the Lebanese good or bad. They removed all judgment and all ego. Each time the practitioners performed the experiment, peace happened. The terrorist activity stopped altogether. Crimes against people declined. Emergency room and hospital visits declined. Automobile accidents declined.

What they also discovered is that when the practitioners stopped their experiment, all of the above statistics reversed, and everything went back to normal. The researchers thought maybe it was a coincidence, or maybe it was because of a holiday, or full moon, or maybe because there were more people on the streets on one day versus another. So, they performed the experiment over and over again. Every time the results were the same. In fact, they were able to determine how many people it would take to feel peace for peace to happen in a particular area. Surprisingly, they found it to be a very small number.

They discovered that if you can get the square root of 1% of your population to feel peace, peace will happen. The number required to create peace globally is 9,000, which is approximately the square root of 1% of the world's population of seven billion. How many of us have a Facebook page with a minimum of 1,000 friends? Nine Facebook pages communicating and radiating a message of peace could literally change the world.

We have the ability to speak peace to the elements around us and create peace. We can speak peace to our bodies, and we can speak peace to the world. It begins with what we are holding in our thoughts and in our emotions. It begins with our hearts. We live our lives based on what we believe about our world. How we feel is affecting whether or not we are experiencing peace in this world. Should our concern be what is going on around us or what emotions we are carrying within us? Do you believe you're a victim, or do you believe you are victorious? Do you respond with fear, or do you respond with faith?

If you want this world to heal, heal you.

Perhaps looking around at the condition of our country is like being told our nation has a brain tumor. We could choose to look at the situation like it will continue to grow and bleed. For me, this was the path of fear, not faith, not hope, and not belief. It was not a path of acknowledging that I housed the treasure of heaven within my heart. It was not a path of acknowledging I was Christ and Christ was me, and that as One we were capable of healing or accomplishing anything. It was not a path of acknowledging that I could do a new thing with what God had already given me, with what had always been with me.

You can't heal with a mindset that a devil is attacking you, or that a God is punishing you. You must respond in truth. You must respond in faith. You must respond with a belief in your ability to change the outcome of your life with the power God has placed within you. Look deep within your own heart. Ask yourself the hard questions. Ancient wisdom teaches that we reap as we have sown. What seeds of untruth have you sown in your mind that is harming you? What thoughts have you planted that are no longer serving you?

God is the force within you guiding you towards the truth, ushering you away from the lies that have ensnared you from the beginning. Ask God to help you eliminate the mindset that He is outside of you, above you, or removed from you. Start with the mindset that God is the one loving you and willing to help you find this inward treasure called the kingdom of heaven, a place where one is at peace amidst a raging storm—a place from which you can release peace to both yourself, your friends, your enemies, and to the world.

You see, it is not hopeless. The story of your life has not been written for you, at least not without your consent. I believe in free will. I believe in freedom. I believe the *true* Spirit of Christ will set you free. It will set you free from yourself, free from what is harming you, free from the lies you've believed about yourself, about God, about your enemies, and about the world.

Does Jesus want us to wait for Him or *be* Him? And how can we long for Him, miss Him, mourn Him, or be awaiting Him when we are already together? We share the same Spirit. He hasn't left us or forsaken us. He is with us. You can feel Him. You can know Him. He's your best friend. You can talk to Him every day.

You must respond with a belief in your ability to change the outcome of your life with the power God has placed within you.

Here is the question I would like to pose. Do you or do you not believe that God lives in you? Is it truly no longer you who live but Christ who lives in you? Do you really believe you carry the same Spirit, the same power, and the same strength? I have heard a lot of people that say God is the only one that can fix our country. Again I ask, where is God? Where does He live? If I am to believe that God is the only one that can fix the problem, and I believe that Christ abides in me, then I am going to look inward for strength, for answers, for hope, and for a way out of the darkness.

I believe God has placed His Spirit in us, His ultimate treasure in each of us. It is there when we breathe. If we would listen to its guidance, we would all have a compass for our souls that would guide us to the kingdom we have all been seeking. I have learned in my life I am not here to simply please God. I'm here to express God. I'm here to release God. I am here to be God. I'm here to be Christ. I'm here to do greater things than He did if I can believe I can do them. I'm here to know I have the same mind, the same truth, and the same power. And so do you. We are not victims to our circumstances. They are but one possibility. We have the power to create something new. Christ in you and me, the hope of glory!

When healing people, Jesus would tell them that it was *their* faith that had made them well. He did not claim to be the miracle worker. He simply wanted people to know they had the power to heal themselves. He wanted people to know that nothing on this earth could disempower them lest they yielded their power to it. He wanted them to know they had the power to change their lives and thus the world around them. He wasn't seeking to escape this world. He was willing to be in it, to bring forth hope and a better way to exist here, now, in this moment. He wanted what He found in this beautiful kingdom of heaven that he carried in His heart to be discovered on this earth, in our hearts.

Choose Life

YOUR CONDEMNATION, THE GUILT YOU CARRY, the feeling of being trapped, the comparison games you play, the insecurities you allow to plague you, the way you allow yourself to feel there is no hope and that no one is listening to you, is not serving you. It's killing you a slow death. Those moments when you wish you could check out, those moments you want Jesus to come and get you but for all the wrong reasons, those moments when you want to avoid the mess of your difficult circumstances, your marriage, and your battle with your children, are hurting you. I beckon you. Please stop. You are choosing death. I say to you, choose life! It's not just a choice you make every day. It's a choice you make every moment. With every circumstance, you are being given an opportunity to choose anxiety, fear, defeat, and despair, which will lead to sickness, disease, premature aging, and ultimately death. I say again, choose life! Moment by moment, choose love. Choose forgiveness. This road leads to life abundant. Sow well that you may reap well. Don't do as I once did and deplete yourself of two of the most essential ingredients for the human soul, self-love, and self-belief. Insecurity, doubt, and fear are emotions no one should carry around with them, not for a moment, not at all.

It took time for me to manifest a serious illness in my body. It came about as a result of years of thinking in patterns that were not serving my highest and best good. I had to learn to hold the feelings of health and abundant life in the midst of the suffering long enough to begin changing and redirecting the cells in my body towards a different outcome. It may take time to completely heal my body, but the saving grace for us all lies in the fact that our Creator designed the human body with an ability to recover and heal itself. Often, the rate at which this occurs is largely connected to the degree by which the human soul is healing itself. The blessing is in the fact that you can change your life with a change of mind. Healing can spring forth rapidly when the heart and mind come into proper alignment.

God is not to blame. Quite frankly neither is some big bad Satanic enemy. The truth is that I did not choose wisely because I allowed the storms of my life to distract my eyes from seeing the truth. I lost my focus, and I sank into the waters. But this is ok. It has all been significant to the magnificent journey my soul came here to embark upon.

Not all who wander are lost. Sometimes it takes getting lost in order to be found. Sometimes it takes being blind in order to see. Sometimes it takes being buried before you can rise. Sometimes it takes being lost in the darkness in order to appreciate the light.

God will lift you from the waters. He will restore your soul. He will put a new song in your heart. You have everything you need to turn your situation into a marvelous testimony of what can happen when you utilize the power God has placed within you, and when you absorb the power offered to you by those standing in the gap holding a space for your healing and your peace.

Your circumstance does not have to be a mountain lest you make it into one. Your situation does not have to be a massive struggle lest you mentally agree that it will be. It is hard, yet it is also incredibly easy. The yoke is easy. The burden is light. Again, it's just a choice. Your emotions will tell you the battle is hard. Your Spirit will tell you that difficulty is a choice. You can wrestle with your circumstances or surrender to them and approach each situation with grace and ease. By surrendering to it, you're not condoning it. You're not agreeing to your unfavorable circumstance or illness. You're simply opening yourself to accepting what it is temporarily there to teach you.

We all came here to face a battle, to master thyself. When your body is saying one thing, but your Spirit is saying another, will you choose life? When your reality is saying one thing, but your Spirit is saying another, will you position yourself in the spiritual kingdom of heaven that exists here on this earth?

One week ago, I thought I was dying. I could not breathe. The fear that rose mightily within my body was fierce and did not want to leave. So, what was there left to do? I made a decision to love the fear. Perfect love casts out all fear. Love dispels all hate. Love conquers all. I thanked the fear of death for showing me how desperately I wanted to live. I chose life. When I embraced the fear, loved it for what it was there to teach me, it no longer had a purpose through which to serve. It no longer needed to maintain its grip.

Stop fighting the enemy. You're giving away valuable life force energy to help you heal. Do as Christ said to do. Love that which opposes you. Once the resistance has served its purpose, you embrace it, and you understand why it is there, it will no longer need to push against you. Look to the pearl or the diamond for understanding for these are what you are destined to become. Don't hate the fire or the pressure that has been provided so that you may sparkle in the light of the sun. Embrace all that is there to help make you a pearl of great worth. Perhaps if we would but thank the problem for what it is there to offer us, the problem would dismiss itself in light of the acknowledgment of a more enlightened solution.

You must become a match to that which you have asked God to provide for you. If your focus becomes the lack of health or upon that which you are losing, it will only attract more of the same. Jesus understood this when he said,

> *"For to the one who has, more will be given,*
> *and he will have an abundance, but from the one*
> *who has not, even what he has will be taken away."*
> (Matthew 13:12)

The journey to master thyself is a most noble feat. Attempt it with grace, ease, and an ample supply of self-love. When you see and feel defeat in your body, remind yourself this is just the physical realm. Bring that which you hold in your heart and feel in your Spirit forth. Make it your most dominant vibration. Create a new reality with new possibilities. Silence the fears and self-doubt and rise with the Light of God as your strength.

I wish to live to tell my story. I wish for you to live and tell yours. Do not let that which you see affect that which you know to be true. The lies you carry in your body distort it from functioning properly. Immerse yourself in the truth. Clear the limiting programs and beliefs that have hacked your system and been a fog diluting your ability to see clearly the truth that will set you free.

You are full of power, love, and a sound mind. You are mighty for the pulling down of strongholds. You may be a drop to the wave, but you are still a part of the wave. You still hold the same properties, created in the same image, carrying the same capabilities of the Source from which you came forth. Little Drop, do not limit what you can achieve. A waterfall begins with only one drop of water.

I pray these words arrive in your heart as a blessed hope because the truth is that you have been given all you need to change any circumstance in your life. Release the beauty of the glorious kingdom of God living within your soul. Fix your eyes on that which is good, true, lovely, and of a good report. This is your path to the happiness, joy, and peace you seek. Stop waiting on God. God is waiting on you. Choose life.

No More Weeds

THERE IS A QUOTE THAT SAYS:

How did you know you were meant to be a healer?
Because I kept falling in love with broken people.
Then why are you alone?
Because I'm broken too, so I'm falling in love with myself
to get a taste of my own medicine.
~ Kwabena Foli

I FEEL LIKE THIS QUOTE COULD BE MY MANTRA for this stage of my life: still learning to love myself, still needing a dose of my own medicine, and still carrying this deep, burning passion for healing others. Although I was the queen of preaching, "You can't take someone somewhere you haven't been," I wasn't expecting to go where my current circumstances have taken me. I wasn't prepared to literally endure my life being threatened with a disease in order to discover the path to overcoming it. Yet, this is what I came to face, and I was determined to learn everything the experience was there to teach me.

I decided to start writing a journal depicting my journey from broken to beautiful. However, a more accurate truth would be to untangle the misconceptions attached to not believing I was already a priceless gem.

We don't truly transform from broken to beautiful until
we are able to recognize and appreciate the beauty
that exists in our broken place.

The feelings of inadequacy, fear, doubt, rejection, and unworthiness are just as important as our feelings of worth, belonging, love, belief, and acceptance. They are both given as gifts to teach us something about ourselves.

I happen to believe in what Jesus spoke regarding what brings harm upon someone. He said,

> *"There is nothing that enters a man from outside*
> *which can defile him; but the things which come out of him,*
> *those are the things that defile man."*
> (Mark 7:15-16)

Buddha articulated the same truth by saying,

> *"What we are today comes from our thoughts yesterday,*
> *and our present thoughts build our life tomorrow:*
> *our life is the creation of our mind."*

In ancient traditions, the shaman, medicine man, or healer of the village would isolate people deep in the forest when they were sick be that emotional, spiritual, or physical illness. They believed when you place someone in solitude surrounded only by nature, the person had no way to hide from himself or to avoid different, uncomfortable sensations and unpleasant emotions. In today's modern world, many of us are so separated from nature and locked into technology that stepping into a rainforest would feel like being castaway on a deserted island. If you take today's generation away from their cell phones, social media, television, computers, books, movies, toys, games, and the constant sources of entertainment distracting them and place them in a quiet spot in nature, most people would have a challenging time staying for any length of time. How many of us could last a few minutes much less hours, days, or weeks alone in the wilderness? I suppose it would be quite uncomfortable in the beginning. One of the reasons and profound significance behind doing this was to break any patterns, be them social, emotional, or mental that someone had previously established as a way of life. The time away in isolation would give those patterns time to die.

In a sense, people would go into the wilderness or the jungle to die and be reborn. This time in solitude would allow them to feel again, to feel everything: sadness, anger, confusion, or perhaps self-pity. There was nothing to distract them from facing themselves and the issues that were weighing them down and prohibiting their spiritual, mental, and physical progress. There wasn't a song to listen to or a Facebook status update to read. There was no "checking out" or turning on a motivational YouTube video to help them out of a slump. There were no phones to dial a friend and no business or workload responsibilities to busy their minds. They had only one option: to acknowledge and face what they were feeling...alone...in the stillness...in the black of night— just them, their thoughts, and the sounds of crickets or the pitter-patter of rain falling on their tent. Naturally, as the process unravels, breakthroughs, and often breakdowns would happen. People would go deeper into themselves where they would uncover different layers and negative seeds that had been planted. Being with ourselves for a prolonged period of time allows us to recognize those things. In this way, we can deal with a lot of repressed emotions and feelings within ourselves.

Although I did not track into a rainforest, I was able to experience the above process during meditation and embraced a mental wilderness of sorts. The quiet moments of pondering and listening to my Spirit and soul revealed deep layers of unconsciously sown negative seeds. Layer by layer, I began to uproot each one on my path to healing.

Every flourishing garden must be cultivated by a gardener who is willing to remove the weeds. I suppose being diagnosed with an inoperable tumor in my brain stem that was wreaking havoc on my nervous system made me more than willing to remove mine. It did more than gently nudge me into a place of deep meditation and isolation. That time of pondering, asking the tough questions, connecting to the Source of the Universe, and facing myself accomplished so much more than just healing my body. It proved to be the greatest experience of my life. It became a gift that served to launch me into a

The feelings of inadequacy, fear, doubt, rejection, and unworthiness are just as important as our feelings of worth, belonging, love, belief, and acceptance. They are both given as gifts to teach us something about ourselves.

pivotal life-awakening journey that produced tremendous spiritual growth and ultimately helped bring authentic freedom to my heart. It also helped further connect to me to my purpose and destined life path.

If only everyone would spiritualize their ailments, face them head-on, and be willing to enter the wilderness and die a joyous death to that which no longer serves them. It's long past time for some of us to remove the unfruitful beliefs that we've allowed to be planted either consciously or subconsciously into the recesses of our hearts and minds. If these weeds are not removed from the garden of our soul, they will cause disease, first to the Spirit and then to the body.

Rebirth is an essential part of the healing process. As a man thinketh in his heart, so is he. Our consciousness towards ourselves, towards the Source of Life, and towards others, matters. It is affecting us. When you believe wrongly in any of these areas, ultimately these negative thoughts will move from the energetic field surrounding you and take up residence within you. If they are not cast down or cast aside, the negative energy emanating from these destructive thought patterns will begin to affect your physical body. This is where disease comes from. It is not a punishment from an angry, condemning God perched on a cloud in the sky.

If you sow poison into a field, you reap poison for a harvest. If you believe you are a wretched, filthy rag who will continue to sin and mess up, I guarantee that not only will you continue in this behavior,

Before a new mind can emerge, an untangling of old patterns must occur.

but you will also physically look the part. You will never find the rich, abundant, fruitful, righteous, life you are seeking to obtain. This is why there are passages in almost every religion urging us to take every thought captive that sets itself against the knowledge of Christ, or the knowledge of the truth. You are not just fed via physical nourishment. You are also taking in spiritual nourishment, spiritual energy, based on what you believe. If you don't believe as Jesus taught that the kingdom of God is in your midst or as other interpretations read that it is within you, then you will never believe it is possible to obtain a state of heavenly bliss here on this earth.

When you remove the distractions and are brave enough to face the journey within yourself, the truth regarding the spiritual state of your inner man will be revealed. This will lay a foundation for the necessary spiritual instructions to be given and the meditative, mental work to be done, which will enable you to regain health, vitality, new perspectives and goals. It will also deepen your capacity for unconditional love both for yourself and others.

I believe my Higher Self, the God part of me, knew what I truly desired. I don't believe it was an accident that this area of twisted blood vessels was positioned in an area of my brain where doctors could not physically operate. It forced me to spiritually operate and remove the disease.

You are in God. God is in you. You are one flesh,
one Spirit, and one unit.
Together you can mold and shape a new possibility.

I did not need to wait for the mercy of God to heal me. God always wills healing and life. I was not waiting on God. God was waiting patiently and with unconditional love for me! However, before a new mind can emerge, an untangling of old patterns must occur. For me this meant no more toxic thoughts, no more being afraid to express my thoughts or opinions for fear of rejection or abandonment, and no more believing I had to be contributing something valuable to feel valuable. My hands and mouth were numb from performing, and my body was saying, "No more." My muscles were tired of fighting to belong. They wanted me to relax and remove the pressure that I had placed upon them. My nerves were tired of transmitting a message through my body that wasn't true. They wanted to send me a message of sincerity and honesty. They were tired of me seeking for significance externally instead of resting in the knowledge of the truth, a truth that had always been. This life-giving truth was not based on what I had done, what I was doing, or what I would do in the future. It was a truth that existed as a result of who I am. It was a truth that declared I was already valuable.

I am loved. I am needed. I am wanted.
And so are you.

Somewhere along my journey, I had begun to adopt a belief that people did not enjoy spending time with me unless I was constantly pleasing and holding their attention. Perhaps it was a result of the hours I had spent at business conferences listening to the repetitive significance placed upon the need to capture an audience, establish a following, and build your brand. Each voice had a different opinion about how long you should talk, how much you should write, and how you should go about grabbing the attention of others. My desire to share and contribute the gifts God has so graciously given me was stifled by the idea that they had to be packaged in a way that would be warmly received by others. I let the people-pleasing spirit take hold of me, and it began to affect me greatly.

I felt like the child trapped playing with the dominant kid who only wanted to play if things were on their terms. They had to be the teacher. I had to be the student, and they only played a selected game if they were the one winning. I cowed to the notion that if I won, or if I got to play on my terms, my playmate would leave and abandon me. To avoid this horrific withdrawal of time and attention, I continued to make my playmate happy. The idea was that if I continued to make him or her feel special and placed all the attention and focus on him or her, I would, in turn, be included and loved. If I continued to lift up others and helped them shine, always making it about them, others would stay and want to play with me. Then and only then would I receive the love and appreciation I was craving.

What causes a mindset like this to emerge in the human psyche? Without even realizing it, I had adopted the mindset that no one could possibly be interested in just me. I had concluded that inevitably, at some point after failing to win their approval, they would become disinterested and leave me. I had become prey to the idea the world had fed me that I must have some special gift that is rare and unique. I must possess something that people need and want so I can serve them, so they will want me, so they will want to spend time with me, so they will want to love me. I needed to stand out and compete so I would be chosen over the others. Subconsciously, this is what I believed I must do if I wanted to obtain affection, love, and admiration.

Enough with the hogwash. You get the point. No wonder my brain got twisted into a mess! Isn't all that mental rhetoric exhausting? Yet, so many of us have been slowly seduced into this trap of lies. Here is the truth, one the Spirit has had to work hard to impress upon me due to years of wrongful programming:

You were born to collaborate not compete. You are designed to serve and assist others from a place of fulfillment not to satisfy a need for acceptance or significance.

In moments of stillness and in having the courage to face myself, the Spirit showed me that I did not know how to be loved unless I was contributing something to someone in an attempt to "earn my place" of feeling valued. In fact, I used to advise people who wanted to build a following on their Facebook wall to not talk about themselves. I told them they should only ever speak of themselves if it was in the context of helping someone else. I can literally remember telling someone, "No one wants to hear about you. They are only interested in themselves. Speak to their needs and wants, and they will have a reason to follow you." How backward and messed up was that advice?! I shared that because it was what I believed to be true. It's how I saw the world.

I believed that way because I did not know how to receive love. I didn't know how to receive it from others, and I didn't know how to give it properly to myself. You can't give someone else what you don't have. A more enlightened way to advise others would have been to tell them to follow their intuition, build their Light, and shine it brightly. I would have better served them had I told them to care less about what others think and to share from a place of fulfillment and not performance. I should have told them to focus on what makes them happy and to begin by talking about that instead of trying to figure out what interests and pleases everyone else. The best way to serve others is first to learn how to serve yourself. You can't steward others until you first learn to steward yourself. Be faithful with what you have, *you*, and you will prove that you can be trusted with more, *others*. The ancient scriptures say to love others as thyself. It's really hard to know how to love and serve others until we first know how to love and respect ourselves. Happiness begins with you! When you have your oxygen mask on, you can then proceed to be a life-giver by serving others in helping them put on theirs.

Before happiness can come to you or from you, it must be in you. I needed something to get my attention and redirect me towards the path of truth. I asked the Spirit how I was to help my body heal, and she replied, "Stop writing, speaking, teaching, serving, and giving to make yourself feel valuable. You must come to the realization that you already are valuable. The way you have been living is out of balance and alignment, and your body

It's long past time for some of us to remove the unfruitful beliefs which we've allowed to be planted either consciously or subconsciously into the recesses of our hearts and minds.

is responding to it. Your mouth and your hand are shutting down. Your gifts are literally going numb because they don't want to perform any longer. They are being used wrongly. They are being used to satisfy something that is broken and needs repairing. By continuing like this, you are growing disease in your body. Your body is alerting you to stop and fix the imbalance."

I wasn't expecting this response from the Spirit, although I was ready, willing, and desperate enough to listen without arguing. I truly thought all I was doing was because I loved sharing, inspiring, and encouraging others. While this is true, and while it is also my purpose for being here, when I was brave enough to look deeper, it had been coming from the wrong place. I was using my gifts to feel validated and to earn acceptance and love. The Spirit was showing me this was a weed in my garden that must be removed as it was now affecting my body.

While meditating, the Spirit showed me an image of me playing in my basement as a little girl. I used to spend hours teaching school to my imaginary dolls. I couldn't wait to get home from school, so I could finally be the teacher and share what I had learned that day. The Spirit asked me what I noticed about the scene I was shown. What was immediately impressed upon my heart was how happy I was in this particular memory. The other thing I noticed, and that was of utmost significance, was that I was all alone with my imaginary students. I didn't need anyone there to validate me. I was in my own little, happy world, and I was teaching for love of the game—because I delighted in it and passionately enjoyed teaching what I had learned. It didn't matter if anyone was there or not. The Spirit showed me that I needed to write or speak from this place and with this imagery. I needed to do it because it was fulfilling for me and because it makes me happy. I needed to detach from how I was being received, whether or not the audience was cheering, or whether or not someone unfollowed or disapproved of me. That mindset was feeding the disease of needing someone to "play with me" in order to feel loved and cherished. I needed to relax and let my nervous system heal. I had to realize that I was loved, wanted, and included simply by choosing to be here and be a part of God's plan for this time.

Why am I being so vulnerable, sharing such personal and intimate moments of my journey with you? Why am I exposing my life-long battle of people-pleasing? Because I've learned to come from a space of writing from fulfillment. Because it makes me happy. It gives me joy to know that someone may be reading this who has failed to acknowledge that they are doing the exact same thing. Perhaps God will use this as their "aha" moment to unlock them from traveling as far down the path of this mind lie as I once did. And if that is the case, here is what I would say to you and here is what I would say to a much younger version of myself.

God loves everything about you. There is no displeasure or withdrawal from Him. He is a part of you and your expression. He delights in watching you learn, explore, try new things, adventure, and discover what you love and what motivates you. Allow what will come to come. The pain you often experience is from a deep longing to be special and significant so that you will be sought after and needed, and so that you will feel loved. This mindset is a lie, a distortion of truth, as you possess everything you need and are already being pursued and are greatly desired by the Creator of the Universe. The lies you are carrying are creating a burden for you as you compete with others to stand out and be special.

The truth is that you are special—as is! You are a pearl of great worth. It's fulfilling to relax in the knowing that you belong simply because you are here. You were destined to be here at this moment in time to fulfill a purpose your soul came here to

*experience. If you are alive and breathing and reading this
message, there is a reason you are still here. Your beliefs are
affecting the world. Heal them, and you will make a
difference in the consciousness of all humankind.*

The Spirit gave me one final imagery or prescription for my healing journey with a precise understanding of how perfectly it was suited for my heart. She chose to show me the unconditional love and bond between a mother and a child, something Spirit knew would be meaningful to me.

She said,

*"I want you to learn to love yourself in the way one loves a baby.
A baby is cared for expecting nothing in return. The mother is
fulfilled simply by holding the baby. The mother is fascinated by
the baby. The mother doesn't get angry when the baby cries. She
feeds it. She doesn't get angry when the baby poops. She simply
changes her child's diaper. Her reward is in delighting in
everything the baby does and watching the baby grow and learn.
To the mother, everything about the baby is adorable: how the
baby eats, how the baby rolls over, and even how the baby cries. I
want you to learn to accept yourself in this way. I want you to
see God loving you in this way. You seem to think that if you
poop on yourself and make a mess of things, it changes God's
willful desire to be there for you, to love you, to heal you, and to
adore you. Change the way you view God's love for you and
change the way you love yourself."*

When we program ourselves with the wrong information, our body eventually responds by not functioning properly. Lies make everything work backward. It can cause a perfectly functioning immune system given to protect you, to turn and work against you. The very thing that was given to support you, when fed untruths, can fight and work against you. With that said, here's the good news:

Although damage may have occurred in your life or even perhaps in your body, it can be repaired. It can be perfectly healed. For me, that journey to wholeness began with loving myself, finding fulfillment without competition or comparisons, replacing lies with truths, and holding myself like the baby mentioned above. Perhaps you have read this far because God wants to hold you like a baby. Perhaps He knows your view of His love needs to change to one of unconditional love and acceptance. Perhaps He knows you need to know you are loved and wanted right now in what you believe to be your broken place. Perhaps we all need a reminder of the importance of doing all things from a place of fulfillment and not performance.

You are amazing exactly where you are! Keep shining! Amazing truths await you on your journey of discovery! The failure you are currently experiencing has the potential to be the catalysts for your greatest breakthrough yet!

P.S. In my mind, I wrote this as a seven-year-old little girl in my parent's basement teaching my imaginary dolls while being 100% unequivocally, blissfully happy! Fulfillment never felt so good! I just felt my brain tumor shrink a little bit more!

The Building Blocks of Life

WHEN WAS THE LAST TIME YOU SAID these three words to yourself?

I love you.

A cell is defined as the basic structural, functional, and biological unit of all known living organisms. Cells are so important that they have been named "the building blocks of life." If your body is made up of these living components, what are you speaking to them on a daily basis? Could the thoughts and words you are communicating to these cells literally be building your life?

Your brain governs your body. If your brain thinks the thought "move your arm," your arm moves. If your brain thinks to walk a certain distance, your body obeys the thought and begins to walk. What are your thoughts about yourself telling your cells to do?

Could many diseases and illnesses potentially be the direct effect of what we believe about ourselves? To take it a step farther and moving beyond our bodies, could our external environments be a direct result of our perception of the world around us?

As so many great spiritual teachers have previously instructed, when you change your thoughts, you change your life. Start today by telling your mind, body, and soul, "I love you." Speak a blessing over the precious vessel that has been explicitly gifted to you.

You can get a chance to begin anew. Did you know that your body is continually replacing itself? Cells are dying and being replaced all the time. Individual cells have a finite life span, and when they die off, they are replaced with new ones. God has literally hard-wired us with a way to shed our past and emerge not just with new skin but with a new cellular makeup!

God does not just repair or renovate you.
He creates a whole new you!

You can experience a replacement of new cells that are so uniquely you that they are unlike any other human who has or ever will live on this earth. You have the ability to literally have nothing in common with the former version of yourself.

"There is hope in the darkness for all things will be made new."
(Revelation 21:5)

Two Main Ingredients

"Inner peace begins the moment you decide not to allow another
person or event to control your emotions."
~ unknown

YOU CAN NEVER OBTAIN PEACE IN THE OUTER WORLD until you first obtain peace within yourself. You have an Internal Guidance System freely providing up–to-the-minute help for you to achieve this. You will be told what to release, what to adjust, and what mindset or limiting belief needs to change. You will be told that *forgiveness* and *love* are the true miracles, and no matter how badly you've stuffed up your circumstances or relationships, those two main ingredients are all you need to give your heart and others what they need to obtain that glorious inner kingdom of peace. Take a moment and ask the Holy Spirit to help you with this.

"I am able to keep you from stumbling."
(Jude 1:24)

"I will never fail you. I will never abandon you."
(Hebrews 13:5)

God's Prescription

WRITING IS MY PRESCRIPTION FROM GOD, a healing tool for the collected mass of painful emotions that became trapped within my body. As I write and share my Misti Moments, it allows me to be the observer of my life experiences and look intently at what incidences can still trigger and create grief or heartbreak within me.

Although difficult to endure, I have learned to appreciate even when my physical body goes through any form of discomfort. These incidences have allowed me to see what has been buried beneath the surface in need of exposure and release. I have come to see these occurrences as a means to alert me that something is not in spiritual alignment, which is of much greater importance.

It is not what harms the body that is of utmost significance but that which harms the soul. The scars upon the soul create the aches and diseases of the body. Therefore, go to the root of the pain. Look upon the soul. Heal that which is broken in spirit, and that which has broken the body will mend itself. A prescription from a doctor can treat your symptoms. Healing the soul will pluck up and remove the root that created them and will ensure they never return.

PATIENCE WITH THE PROCESS

The Chinese Bamboo Tree

ZIG ZIGLAR TELLS THE STORY OF A CHINESE BAMBOO TREE. When the seed of a Chinese Bamboo tree is planted, watered, and nurtured, nothing happens for the first year. There is no sign of growth, not even a hint. The same thing happens in the second year. And then the third year comes along but still nothing. The tree is carefully watered and fertilized each year, but nothing shows. There is no growth, no anything. And so it goes as the sun rises and sets for four solid years. The farmer and his wife have nothing tangible to show for their labor and effort. After many years of care, the bamboo tree still only yields an outward growth of one inch. However, after five years of fertilizing and watering have passed, with nothing to show for it, the bamboo tree suddenly sprouts and grows over ninety feet in just six weeks!

Did the little tree lie dormant for four years only to grow exponentially in the fifth year? Or, was the little tree growing underground, developing a root system strong enough to support its upcoming outward growth in the fifth year and beyond? The answer is obvious.

Had the tree not developed a strong unseen foundation, it could
not have sustained its life as it rapidly grew.

The story of the Chinese Bamboo Tree lays out the period of time that seems to delay the appearance of success. However, the delay is just an illusion. There is an underground success story being cultivated in the roots of the tree to make it grow exponentially and with rapid success.

Keep watering your life. Nurture well. I understand it may take a while for you to grow as high as you are destined to grow. However, I also understand that while most trees are easily cracked, the Chinese Bamboo Tree survives in the midst of terrible storms with a capacity and strength to bend with the wind.

"The bamboo that bends is stronger than the oak that resists."
~ Japanese Proverb

Too Much Too Soon

YESTERDAY I SPENT THE DAY AT THE BEACH, and I spent way too much time in the sun. Today although still at the beach, I'm spending my time in the shadows allowing myself time to heal and for my skin to adjust to the light it absorbed. It is red, tender, and sore. As I rest here in the shade shielding myself from the sun, the Holy Spirit is gently teaching and nudging my heart towards something She wants me to understand from this experience. As much as I love the light, and as much as I'm drawn to bask in the sun, there is a great need for time spent in the shadows.

There are times in my life when I have desperately wanted to know the truth and the answer to my questions regarding my life. I have cried out to God many times saying, "Father, please give it to me! I can take it! I want to know the whole truth!"

Sometimes it's gone beyond wanting to know the truth or understand the entire picture, and I progressed into wanting to know why the breakthrough hadn't come, the healing hadn't happened, or the financial outpour hadn't hit. I would cry, "Father, don't you trust me? I can handle the position. I can handle the platform. I can handle stewarding of more abundance, of more favor, and of more knowledge. Give me the answers, God. Trust me to steward your wealth. Pick me!"

And as much as I would love the destination to magically appear or the answers to all of life's questions and my present circumstances to be granted, as a parent, I can understand the significance of lessons that need to be learned over time. There have been moments, hard as they may be, when I have had to let my children take the journey, walk through the trial, and discover for themselves the answers to what their experiences were trying to teach them. There are some things in life that we can't learn until we experience them for ourselves.

I can remember my mother giving me the answers to so many problems when I was younger. She had already discovered many truths from both her successes and her failures and wished more than anything to spare me hard lessons learned. Yet, even though she housed great wisdom for me, more times than I would like to admit, I was stubbornly determined to take the hard path of discovering the truth for myself. My mom had to learn to listen, ask the right questions, provoke thought, be patient, and wait for me to absorb what I was capable and mature enough to handle at each particular phase of my life. Often, I was too immature to receive precisely what she was saying to me. This wasn't because I couldn't understand it, but because I thought I knew better and wasn't mentally and emotionally in a place to handle or absorb the "sunlight."

I know God wants me to reach my destination. There is no doubt in my heart that He wills that I find, live, and relish in my life's purpose. I know He wills that I discover the answers to my fervent prayers. I also realize He wants my soul to experience the growth required to sustain the answer, the promise, and the ultimate destination.

No matter how much I think I can handle,
God knows how much I can absorb.

With this knowledge, I am left with a decision. Do I trust He is giving me exactly what I need at each step of the journey? I've lived my life long enough to see people's talents and abilities carry them beyond what their character and integrity had matured enough to support. I've seen how people with tremendous talent step onto the stages of life and are given positions of influence well before God has cultivated within them the character to handle the light shining upon them. I have been there myself and do not wish to learn those lessons again. As a result, a continuous prayer in my life is that God would not elevate me or take me farther than I am spiritually mature enough to handle.

In the Bible, the story of King David's life articulated that there was a fifteen-year gap between when he was chosen and anointed as King and when he was ultimately appointed King of God's kingdom. I see a similar example given in the life and story of Joseph. There is a profound passage in this ancient text that yields a pearl of deep wisdom for our lives. It reads,

> *"And the Lord was with Joseph, and he was a prosperous man; and*
> *he was in the house of his master the Egyptian. And his master*
> *saw that the Lord was with him, and that the Lord made all that he*
> *did to prosper in his hand. And Joseph found grace in his sight,*
> *and he served him: and he made him overseer over his house, and*
> *all that he had he put into his hand."*
> (Genesis 39:2-4 KJV)

Joseph's promotion to be the second in command of all of Egypt came through serving. The text says that he prospered as he served. What's interesting to me is that Joseph was in a foreign land, serving a foreign king and belief system that was completely opposing to his. Yet, he served his Pharaoh with all his heart. And something about this was seen to be so good that it got heaven's attention and brought goodness, wealth, and prosperity to not only Joseph but all within his house. Perhaps Joseph found grace in the eyes of God, causing every single thing he touched to prosper simply because he served well.

Like King David and Joseph, we can be anointed and dripping with God's favor, talents, and creativity and yet we may have not yet learned our lessons and walked through life's experiences long enough to be seasoned for our appointed roles. Preparation and equipping to rule a kingdom are as important as the original call to service. We all have seeds of greatness within us, but a mighty oak still requires the proper environment and nourishment to grow into all God intends it to be. I am finding this includes time spent in the shade.

No matter how much I think I can handle, God knows how much I can absorb.

My skin is only capable of absorbing so much light at one time. No matter how much I enjoy being in the sun, I must learn the significance of the shade. Perhaps this is why God made so many promises to those who abide under the shadow of the Almighty. He told them this was the secret place of the Most High where they would find a fortress, refuge, and deliverance from the snare of the fowler. He told us that in the shadow we would not fear the terror by night nor would evil befall us nor come near our dwelling place. In the shadows is where we find ourselves resting beneath His wings and covered by His feathers. It is there He promises to bear us in His hands and place His angels in charge over us to keep us in all our ways. (Psalms 91)

The shadow is the secret place. A secret is something that is not known or seen or meant to be known or seen by others. Perhaps this is where we are designed to be still and process the light we have absorbed. A secret is a confidential matter. It is an intimate place reserved for you and God where He protects and shields you from exposure. Have you ever been there? I have. Things happen in the secret place when God hems you in and removes the distractions. This isn't a place where the light should shine. It is a place of formation, much like in the womb where things are hidden from the outside world. It is a place for knitting together and growth. It is a place where you can be exposed before God but hidden from the outside world. The greatest surgical operations I have ever undergone have occurred in the darkest places, in the shadow of the Almighty. This is where God has done the most delicate and intricate work in my life.

Today as I sit in the shadows, I am reminded of the significance of the moments of my life where I have found myself here. I have contemplated the tremendous value I have gleaned from the dark places. Indeed, it was here I learned to sing, "It Is Well with My Soul." It is here I learned to be content without the answer I was seeking. It is here I learned unspeakable joy and the peace that passes all understanding.

Too much light can burn the skin. It takes time to absorb the Light of God, to allow His truth to sink in, and to build resistance to the sun. My skin needs time to process the light it received yesterday. As much as I would love to sit in the sunshine today, I couldn't handle it. Perhaps this is why only the pure in heart can see God. The light of His brilliance is simply too much for the wayward, downtrodden, or young soul to absorb. However, there is great reassurance in knowing that the more sun we absorb, the more resilient our skin becomes, and we are capable of taking in more and more sunlight. We even begin to glow with a beautiful, bronzed suntan. It reminds me of the diamond. The more pressure and heat the diamond can absorb, the greater its brilliance and shine.

Take time to process the moments you are granted by God. Trust that when you are ready for more, more will be given. Until then, chew on the food that is currently nourishing you. Don't skip steps lest you fall and are required to repeat them. Don't be in a rush to step on a stage that places you in a spotlight you aren't prepared to absorb. Just like acquiring the perfect suntan, don't fall victim to too much too soon. Allow truth to come in doses, and may it perfectly fall upon you engrafted into your skin with a radiant, glorifying glow.

Pour Well

DID YOU KNOW THAT WHEN BUYING A FULL-GROWN OLIVE TREE, you are paying for the time it takes for it to mature? It takes twenty plus years for an olive tree to form bark. It can take twenty-five to fifty-plus years for them to become gnarly (bumpy/rutted) with nooks and crannies that make them so distinct and full of character. In fact, when looking for an olive tree, you aren't supposed to focus on or worry about the amount of foliage on the tree but instead, look at the burling, shape, and structure of the tree.

The bumps, bruises, and possibly even scars life has yielded you is what has made you so distinctly unique and gnarly. These moments are the catalyst for your maturity and growth. These are the moments of soul cultivation. The crushing you are undergoing during these times is what produces the anointed, sacred oil, which will pour from your heart with an ability to heal both yourself and those around you.

When the olive tree does eventually grow an abundance of foliage, it comes as a benefit of years of trimming it back. It can also develop suckers and deadwood that require a thorough thinning-out. Can you relate to needing to get rid of some suckers and deadwood? Every now and then a healthy thinning-out might leave us feeling stripped and bare, but it is also the pruning that enables a future of endless flourishing.

For maturity and growth to take place, you will experience your own trimmings and moments that seem to take you back a few steps. No one goes through life without struggle. The question is, "What can we learn when we fall, and how do we find the strength to get back up?" Failure, disappointment, heartbreak: these moments can expand our souls and create beautiful foliage if we are willing to face our real truth.

After an olive tree is replanted, it has to be watered thoroughly, and then it should not be watered again for two to three weeks until the tree has time to re-root. If over-watered in the beginning, there is a risk of rotting the old roots, and the tree will suffer, maybe even die.

After being replanted, don't be bothered by the seasons of your life that feel like drought. You're just being re-rooted. Perhaps, like the olive tree teaches us, too much water can choke the seed. The complexities of life are mysterious, but without question, nature teaches us that adversity is an incubator for greatness. The very process of bringing forth the greatest miracle of all time, a human life, demonstrates the value of time spent in the darkness of the womb. Every butterfly needs her time in the cocoon. Every eagle needs her time spent in the cleft of the rock. And every seed needs her time beneath layers of blackened dirt.

Surrender to the flow of life. Get in the current. Let the waters carry you. Trust the process by which you emerge from the sediment of your life and stand tall and rooted amidst the field of this world. For the olive tree, there is a season of its growth by which withholding the nourishing waters was saving its life. Trust that when the water isn't provided for you that everything is working together for your good. You are learning to pull from a supply that is not of this world. You are learning you can rely upon what has been placed within you. You are also learning how to release it.

Did you know the root system of a tree can be the same size as the tree? That is such an amazing metaphor for me! It reminds me of the story in the Bible about a man named Moses who spent forty years in a wilderness before being equipped to spend the following forty years leading people out of one. True maturity requires seasons. It requires time for growth. The stronger the tree, the deeper the roots. The same measure by which you are gifted for a task may require the same amount of time in preparation for it. The greater the assignment, the more patience you will need to endure for the equipping of it. Don't be rushed. Let those roots grow wide and deep.

Embrace the planting and wilderness seasons of your life. Embrace the time spent beneath the soil. A sprout may not yet be seen, but I can guarantee you there is cultivation and growth taking place in the darkness. You are being prepared to rise strong and stand in the light, able to withstand decades of howling winds and ferocious storms. You're being prepared to provide shade to the wayward traveler needing rest from the scorching heat that has made him weary. You are being conditioned to be a life-giving safe haven to the world around you. Your twists and turns and your nooks and crannies are developing the glorious character that will become a part of what makes you so awe-inspiring and uniquely wonderful.

Given time and patience, the foliage will emerge, and the olives will appear. Any seed placed in fertile soil and given enough time and the appropriate nourishment will flourish. After all, it's a tree. All it knows how to do is grow!

You, too, are like a tree planted by streams of living water. Do you feel the rising? Do you feel the waters bubbling within you? Don't be afraid of the pounding rain that occasionally falls upon you. It's clearing away the debris of your life. Do not shy away from the sun that is scorching its rays upon your leaves. It's burning away impurities. It's filling you with the newness of life. It's establishing your root system.

Your season is coming. You're emerging now. It's time to prosper. Your leaf does not wither, and you have fruit to bear. Others want to pluck from your branches and extract your rich, favorable oil. You are a storehouse of seasoning for the world around you.

Pour well.

A Tree Called Hope

I WAS AT MY PARENTS' LAKE CABIN TODAY enjoying the gorgeous sunshine and the sweet presence of God. Immersion in nature is a must for me. Relaxing upon the waters or sitting under the shade of the trees has provided some of the most intimate and divine moments of my life.

Today as I arrived, Mom grabbed my hand and said, "Come here. I want to show you something. Do you see this tree? Do you see the scars on it? The men

that were here working this week stood in amazement of it. They told me that the markings are from where it has been hit by lightning twice, and yet the tree healed and repaired itself both times and in both places. I've named this tree Hope, and I wanted you to meet her."

Everyone who reads this story will interpret it in different ways. I don't know what your scars are or what has hit you like a bolt of lightning. What I do know is that there is a Divine Life Source flowing through you that wills you to live, that wills you to repair, and that wills you to heal.

Miracles happen every day. Notice them. Perhaps you'll even find them spoken through a tree called Hope.

Fall Pretty

I'VE BEGUN TO NOTICE THIS LITTLE TREE ON MY MORNING WALK. A section of the tree was the first to begin changing her colors, and every morning I have watched her. Her little leaves called to me. There was something similar between us that I could identify. I witnessed her be the first to die. She stood alone. She was the only one of her close companions to look different. She went first. And yet, she was the first to shine, the first to be noticed, the first to add a touch of color to the world. I watched her leaves dancing wildly yet gracefully in the wind while facing her future with boldness, knowing she would be the first to fall. It appeared as if she was maintaining unwavering confidence and an intuitive knowing that her upcoming fall would ultimately be her glorious rise. She would be the first to bloom when Spring yielded her new life-giving buds.

As my morning walks have continued, I have watched as more trees begin to showcase a new, brave patch of colors shining boldly as the first of their friends to step forth and face the music of their upcoming Winter season. I've wondered if my little beloved tree knows there are others that she can't see but that are also facing the dark night of their soul with brave intent. Does she know she is not alone? I am reminded of when my Great Source once spoke to a fellow Seer,

"Elijah, Elijah. You are not alone. There are many more, my son. I've raised up an army of brethren, seventy more glorious prophets just like you. Now allow my angels to strengthen you. Break your bread and be filled."

I've been comforted by these little leaves dancing in their beautiful shining colors. I notice how they look the most glorious just before they make their moment of great surrender, falling to the ground to nourish the soil beneath them. Are we like these sweetly colored leaves, at our most beautiful in a place of utter surrender to nature's course and being guided by the hand of the Great Divine? I like to think these leaves, draped in their rich colors of Solomon's glory, must know deep down that they are not alone. They know there is a time to shine, a time to fall, and a time to rise victorious all over again and again and again.

I love you, my brave little leaves. Thank you for being the first to fall. You made me happy. You shined so pretty. You taught me something about myself. I said goodbye to one of you today as I watched you fall to the ground, and I will be the first to

Sometimes we go through things, and they make us feel like we are dying like these little leaves.

look for you and welcome you again when it's time to watch you bloom again in your life-giving Spring season. I am you. You are me. So, let us color our world. Let's surrender in the midst of it. Let's die to what was and let's live to the possibility of what is coming—to what will be—to newness of life—to the richness of summer. May we take our scorching heated season of the harsh summer burn, when life applies the pressure to our delicate skin, knowing with full assurance that the rain will fall again. It will wash away the hurt, the relentless heat, and the scorching sun. It will replenish. It will bring new growth. The sun will shine. The wind will blow the seeds of possibility and new beginnings. The cold will rid us of everything that needs to die, and the seasons of our life will purge and perfect us to stand as the mighty oaks we are destined to become. For the soul carries with it an innate strength interlaced by the hand of God to endure the elements of life's many seasons.

Sometimes we go through things, and they make us feel like we are dying like these little leaves. They may make us feel very isolated and all alone. But they are just the rose bush being pruned to spring forth with greater glory and splendor. And when we feel we are preparing for our greatest surrender, it is often then when we are sparkling the brightest and adding the most unique colors to the world around us.

Just as I have enjoyed watching these brave little leaves, someone is watching and appreciating your season of transformation. The leaves have to change and experience a certain death before they can sprout, soak in more light from the sun, and spring forth into a new cycle of life.

And so do you.

Allow your new beginning to come about as nature has intended. Your leaves are changing. You are surrendering. You may be experiencing a pruning of your soul. You may even suffer a fall. Oh, but Darling, this is only half of the story! Soon, the cycle will continue. You will live again! You will have grown more brilliant! The tree by which you are attached will have grown stronger. Its roots will have become anchored deeper. Its foundation will have become more secure, and your tree will carry with it greater wisdom as a result of one more journey through life's glorious transformative seasons.

So yes, the breaking is constant, and the leaves suffer repeated falls along with a continuous cycle of death and rebirth. Yet, with every fall, the tree's roots grow deeper, and the tree herself grows stronger. She is able to stand amidst any storm and is filled with deep wisdom and an unwavering ability to position herself unshakable throughout the ages of time. A tree that has weathered many cycles it not easy to chop down. Therefore, it's a beautiful "Fall," my beloved friends.

Fall pretty.

This particular Misti Moment is sacred to me. I felt led to write it and post it on social media one morning after arriving home from a morning walk. It was November 6th, 2018. Little did I know after posting it, a few hours later, I would discover my mother in her bed having passed away from an unexpected heart attack.

I dedicate this entry to the most beautiful Leaf I have ever known, my mother, Diann Weaver Cruickshank.

I now know full well why the Spirit prompted my heart to notice the leaves and pen these words. You fell pretty, Mama. I'll see you in the Spring when it's time for you to bloom again. Rise strong. Thank you for the deep roots. I am me because of you.

It's on the Way!

THIS MORNING I SAW A CARGO SHIP PASSING IN FRONT OF ME. There may come a point someday where you find yourself waiting for an answer to your prayers. I believe God sent this mighty ship loaded with supplies as a picture for you. It is so large that it covers the majority of the shoreline, full of an abundant supply of all you have asked for in your prayers. It's exceedingly, abundantly, above and beyond all that you could have thought or imagined! Due to its weight and the richness of its value, it's moving slower, but the fact remains, it's on the way!

As I was typing the above sentiments, another boat appeared. This boat was a speedboat. I've included a picture of them both. The speedboat is moving fast, like lightning across the waters; however, it is so tiny you can hardly see it in the picture. Good things take time. The larger the load, the bigger the ship needed to contain it.

When you look at the cargo ship stretching across the sea, moving closer to its destination, see it as a representation of all that is coming for you. It is full of the promises of God stored in precious containers. Every prayer has been remembered, a container for every cry of your heart. A large ship takes time to make its way across the vast ocean. But when carrying your destiny, is it not worth the wait?

The best part of this story is the Light of the Sun shining upon the carrier of your treasures guiding its journey. A voyage that is so precious to God that He's made a way to shine a Light even in the darkest of nights to ensure your blessings arrive safely and on time.

And lastly, you are God's precious cargo. You are his treasure. He is carrying you on a long journey, guiding you by His Light, taking you atop the waters, and filling you full of his abundant promises and supply. He's guiding you to a place beyond the seas, beyond the heavens, to an eternal home he has lovingly prepared for you. You are destined to sit at his table, dine from the finest of the land, and dwell amongst royal saints. Your house will be flooded with His magnificent glory. Your eternal days will be spent immersed in His goodness and mercy, which endureth forever. Don't wait for this kingdom. Look within and enter it now.

Eternity awaits in the hearts of mankind. Enjoy the journey. Make sure upon arrival your cargo vessel is filled with light and precious oil. And don't forget, "It's on the way!"

Happy Sailing!

But on the Way Back

SOME OF US SPEAK TO OUR MOUNTAINS, but when we turn around, they are still there. There is a story in the Bible about an incident where Jesus was walking to the city of Jerusalem, and He cursed a fig tree because it wasn't bearing any fruit.

> *The next day as they were leaving Bethany, Jesus was hungry.*
> *Seeing in the distance a fig tree in leaf, he went to find out if it had*
> *any fruit. When he reached it, he found nothing but leaves, because*
> *it was not the season for figs. Then he said to the tree, "May no one*
> *ever eat fruit from you again. And his disciples heard him say it."*
> (Mark 11: 12-14)

It says in the passage that Jesus was hungry. He was in need and yet the tree He needed to feed him was barren. I can relate to this feeling. I know what it's like to be hungry, and nothing is there to satiate the ache. I'm not just speaking of physical hunger, but emotional and spiritual hunger as well. Often, it's when we are in a state of inward emotional hunger for our delayed, desired outcome that we end up cursing our awaited blessings prematurely.

It says that the reason the tree was barren was because it wasn't the season for the tree to bear fruit. Maybe there is a sacred, special reason for why this made Jesus so mad that he caused the tree to wither. Perhaps it irritates the Universe when we fail to produce the fruit we should during our season to bloom and grow. I'm also quite certain there is a more esoteric meaning to what lies beneath the surface as the obvious meanings for this text. My focus today, however, is the reminder that sometimes we aren't seeing a result because it's not the season for it. There is more growth needed before the fig is ripe and ready to pluck!

I don't know what the so-called "fig" is you want to see sprouting on your tree. I don't know what it is you are speaking into existence that you have yet to see emerge in your current reality. What I do know is that if you curse your tree for not producing before it is in its season to supply, you can wither your tree from delivering that which you were hoping to see sprout. Don't get bitter with the wait. Let things mature. Give your tree time to bloom. Give yourself time to bloom. Speak life into the things you want to see produce for you, and they will yield a sweet fruit for your consumption.

What's also interesting in this passage is that nothing happened to the fig tree until they were on their way back from their journey. The passage says that it wasn't until on the way back from the city that they looked at the fig tree and saw that it had withered and died. It had dried up from its roots.

When evening came, Jesus and his disciples went out of the city. In
the morning, as they went along, they saw the fig tree withered
from the roots. Peter remembered and said to Jesus, "Rabbi, look!
The fig tree you cursed has withered!"
(Mark 11: 19-20)

If you speak to your mountain, and you don't see a change, still confess what you believe. Keep walking on your journey, and you may notice as you are traveling down your path, the things that you once spoke to have completely transformed.

Jesus didn't stand there and wait for his words to happen on the way to the city. He kept moving. He stayed focused on his mission for the day. He knew what had just taken place by the word of his mouth would come to fruition.

It can take time for the physical realm to catch up with the spiritual realm, for you to come into alignment inwardly with that which you desire. Stay patient. Keep journeying on the path the Father has laid before you, and one day you will be traveling on your way and notice the mountain that once stood as opposition to your path is no longer there. By faith, you will have moved your mountain.

Do you have a mustard seed of faith? This is all you need to overcome the difficult circumstances of your life. By faith, Enoch walked with God and was taken up so that he did not see death. By faith, Noah worked for God building an ark to save his family from a flood. Because of faith, Abraham was considered righteous before God. By faith, we obtain the most precious gift ever offered, salvation unto eternal life.

Everything begins with faith. As Zig Ziglar once said, "You don't have to be great to get started, but you have to get started to be great." Become great at moving your mountains by starting afresh today with planting a seed of faith.

To Those Who Wait

ALL THREE OF MY CHILDREN WERE BORN PREMATURELY. I suffered bed rest with them all, including a total of seven months with my little girl, Kate. The doctor said my body just didn't seem to want to carry them full term. In every pregnancy, I would begin to contract prematurely or bleed without cause. In hindsight, the doctors were correct. Both my body and my mind were too impatient to wait for them.

Impatience has always been a struggle for me. My mind was having a direct effect on my body. Nine months seemed much too long to wait to hold my precious awaited Treasures. The longing to behold the creation within me was manifesting my desire prematurely. Jack, my second child, was born six weeks early and was taken from my arms directly after birth. That moment of beholding him was interrupted by his nonfunctioning lungs and an ambulance ride to the neonatal care unit at a larger hospital in the city.

Life is teaching me the value of waiting until something is fully developed. We must give our creations and our dreams time to form. Impatience can create imperfections and underdevelopment in what could have been a healthy living organism. We often want our prayers answered immediately. We must remember that fascinating and imperative pieces to the formation of our requests are being developed and cultivated in the waiting. Like a child within a womb, time is needed to ensure all is formed exactly as it should be. Don't give birth prematurely. The wait will be worth it when you hold your dream in your arms and behold all the intricate details that were being developed while you waited in anticipation.

A photograph must not be exposed before it has been fully developed or it will ruin the picture. A premature birth has the potential to kill a child. Allow "mother nature" to complete her perfect work. Trust the process. The more precious the creation, the more time is needed to ensure its perfection. And you know what they say, "Good things come to those who wait."

Trust the Process

STAY PATIENT A LITTLE LONGER AS DETAILS are being worked out behind the scenes and are not quite ready. In divine timing, everything will fall into place. Your prayers are granted the moment you receive the answers for them into your Spirit. Await the manifestations of them with expectant glee.

The hard work and effort you have put into your circumstances will reap abundance, and you will be recognized for a job well done. Maintain faith, trust, a positive attitude and outlook, and expect the best results. Your patience will be rewarded.

Foster passion and enthusiasm as you travel your current path. Believe in yourself and the inner talents and abilities God has given you to obtain success and achieve your desires. Trust that achieving your goals is within sight. Begin to cultivate a feeling within yourself that aligns with the knowing that your prayers have been answered.

Your angels are always there to encourage you and remind you of your ability to hear and connect with the voice of God, with the highest truths, and with the Holy Spirit that is abiding within you. Begin today feeling as much joy, bliss, and peace while traveling your journey, as you would expect to feel once you've arrived at your destination. This is the key to ensure your arrival.

As you learn to live more and love more,
so you will grow and prosper.

FINDING HAPPINESS

Finding Happy

RECENTLY, A SWEET LADY LEFT A COMMENT ON MY FACEBOOK WALL in which she said, "Misti, I love how no matter what life throws at you or how your life circumstances have changed, you always find your happy." Her comment really resonated with me deeply and inspired me to pen some thoughts regarding how I found "my happy."

First up, life hasn't always been this way for me. I haven't always been happy. I spent a lot of my life feeling like I was in a desert wasteland not really knowing what it was that fulfilled me or made me happy. It has been a journey of me discovering that for myself by having to learn who I am, what my values truly are, and what is important for me to do in order to protect that happiness. I have now learned how to ensure my happiness, but it hasn't always come easy. It's come through a sincere spiritual search accompanied by a lot of mistakes and some broken relationships along the way. Today I have grown to respect my happy bubble and have learned how to protect it physically, emotionally, mentally, and spiritually.

Happiness comes as a result of protecting that which we value, primarily our minds and our hearts. We guard our happiness by monitoring what we allow ourselves to think about and what emotions we allow into our hearts. I've trained myself through spiritual discipline to meticulously filter the voices that I allow inside my head. I renew my mind daily and take thoughts captive that aren't in alignment with the highest truths. It's amazing how quickly wrong mindsets can seep through the crevices of our mind. Guarding the heart and mind is a daily routine, much like taking a bath. Depending on how dirty we get depends on how often we need to cleanse our bodies. In

113

the same way, depending on how much junk has attached itself to us throughout the day guides how often we need a spiritual cleansing and renewing of the mind and heart to cleanse away debris. Toxic thoughts or emotions if allowed to sit with us too long create depression, defeat, disease, and ultimately death.

Heal your mind.
Heal your heart.
Heal your soul.
Heal your body.
This is the progression of truth.

Emotions are just as harmful as misaligned thoughts. Thoughts that are opposing to divine truths such as ones that limit you, entrap you, diminish your value, or move you away from a heart full of love and forgiveness will always lead to suffering. Emotions are the same. If you allow yourself to carry emotions of sadness, grief, guilt, anger, defeat, entrapment, insecurity, shame, separation, judgment, or fear, your body will eventually try to get your attention. Your body most often serves as a code-red alert that something within you is being suppressed or has moved out of spiritual alignment with love and truth. Nothing can get your attention faster than pain or discomfort. As pleasure-seeking human beings, when all else failures, Divine Intelligence knows full well that a brush with discomfort will most likely work to grab our focus. Thus, count your sufferings as joy because, ultimately, if you will get still and listen, they will teach you something valuable for your soul journey. Doctors write prescriptions to treat symptoms. The Divine Voice within your soul will show you what created your illness or unpleasant circumstance. It will take you to the source or root that caused it to emerge in the first place. It will also lovingly show you how to pluck it out and replace it with wisdom and truth that will forbid its return.

Happiness is not a destination. It is a state of being that you cultivate within yourself. Happiness is a choice you have to make continuously throughout your day as various moments and circumstances present themselves to you. Happiness requires action. At times it will require holding on tightly to something you treasure, and at times it may require letting it go. But make no mistake. Your happiness is everything. If you have children, your happiness is ultimately everything to them as well. It affects your parenting, your mood, your productivity, your creativity, and even your health.

Never make the mistake of equating happiness to worldly success or how well you fit the mold of what society tells you that you should be. Authentic happiness is not based on the amount of money in your bank account or the level of status you have achieved among your peers. For the genuinely happy souls, these things stem as a result of the abundance they carry within their hearts. The true happy campers didn't wait for the world to make them happy. They made a decision to be happy in the midst of their world.

Happiness comes as a result of surrender. It is a detachment from the emotional entanglement of life. It's an acceptance and contentment for what your circumstances are there to teach you. It's placing yourself in a river trusting it will carry you exactly where you need to go. Happiness is trust in the Divine. Happiness is willing to be buried in order that you might grow some roots, make your way through the blackness of dirt that has encased you, and rise through the obstacles to find your place in the sun. Your dirt and darkness also provided the nourishment for your growth. Surrender to the process, Little Seedling, and you will emerge as the mighty oak you are destined to become. You will sprout into a tree of life-bearing fruit that will never be barren again.

In my life, I have experienced three near-fatal car accidents and a serious cancer scare that caused me to endure an incredibly painful bone marrow biopsy coupled with a hospital stay that lasted for weeks on an oncology floor. I've been through two divorces, a brain aneurysm that left me with neurological damage and an inoperable benign tumor unreachable in the center of my brainstem. I've been to the heights of tremendous worldly success, and I've been to the utter depths of loss and despair. I've walked in on my mother, lifeless in her bed, having fallen into her final sleep as a result of a tragic and unexpected heart attack. The latter of all these experiences was by far the most significant blow of my life. My mother was my best friend and the greatest love of my heart, and it was my precious mother who taught me that happiness was a choice. She taught me how to rise. She also taught me that there would be times I would have to put up a sincere fight for my happiness. After her death, I learned that by my surrender to what the Divine had mapped out for my life, I was making a declaration for my ultimate peace and contentment. I decided to allow for my breaking and to place myself in the hands of God committed to the journey that was ordained for the cultivation of my soul. My surrender was my fight for something real. Soul prosperity became my ultimate destination, and my happiness is a result of this noble quest.

You can be happy when your circumstances tell you that you should be sad. You can experience contentment and even joy when your journey is giving you loss and defeat. It takes higher wisdom, a spiritual strength, and an eagle's eye view—something available to us all. It requires appreciating that our circumstances are in our lives to teach us valuable lessons that are of great worth to the soul. It takes a sincere cry of the soul for help. I cried for something bigger than me to help me. My cry wasn't for fame, fortune, a career, or success. My cry was to feel God, to be close to His heart, to be free of pain, to feel loved, and to become as much of that love as I possibly could become in this life. I knew in my soul this would be my ultimate happy place, and it is. Arriving at genuine happiness required a realization that this God I was crying out to touch me was within my own heart, and I could feel Him continuously and endlessly.

You may go through things that are simply awful, but the more you rise and wash your face from the heartbreaking moments of your life, and you pull from the Divine Source within you, you will be empowered and strengthened to keep going. You will keep standing. You will even find yourself sprinting, and at times, you will even soar! That Source is as a life-giving Fountain that can nourish and strengthen you to endure whatever you've been given to face. It's your superpower! It does not just fill you. It's not coming from outside of you. It's a spark that is ignited within you. You have housed the power all along, Dorothy. Click your heels and go home! You can release that Source without measure over yourself, over others, and over the circumstances of your life.

This Internal Spirit will be with you in the darkest, most lonely, defeating moments, and it will empower you to not just heal from those situations though the external stimuli of this outer world. It will heal you via a Source that carries true Divine Power. In place of the bottle of wine that provided you with an escape, it will give you a peace that allows you to be fully present. And not just broken and present, not just hurting and present, but present and filled with inexplicable contentment and tranquility. You will no longer need the roll around in the sheets with that guy who gives you temporary validation and significance but ultimately leaves you with an even deeper void and a greater sense of feeling completely alone. This Spirit will teach you your worth. It will set your standards immensely high. It will give you your own bubble of happy to surround you and protect you from those who would wish to burst it.

Your happy is an inner kingdom that's always been waiting for you. There is a power in you with a knowledge that will unlock the mysteries of life for you. It can help you sort out the chaos of your mind. In can put the crazy of your life into perfect divine order. It's stronger than you could ever imagine, and it's there for you—endlessly, without conditions or limitations. The whole Universe truly does have your back. It has the power to make you happy when, according to life circumstances, you shouldn't be happy.

One of the most empowering moments we can achieve in our life is when we can learn triumph and true happiness in the midst of sorrow, grief, failure, discontentment, guilt, or embarrassment. When we can love and care for ourselves in those defeating moments, we learn the unconditional love of God.

The people that inspire me the most are not those who are blissful and happy from having lived a life free of struggle. They are also not the people who live in a sense of despair and darkness from having experienced a difficult life. The people that move me and have the ability to touch my heart on the most profound levels are those who have been broken and who have fought through tremendous setbacks yet are still smiling from their soul in sincere genuineness. Those who have been knocked on their face from the blows of life and are rising beautifully from those ash heaps are the true heroes in my book. They are the ones who have allowed the hard moments of their life to cultivate a spirit of grace and ease within them. They have utilized their struggles to find their inner strength, discover who they are, and are now using their voices to inspire and make a difference in their homes and communities. They are using the low moments of their life to help others rise strong. These are the people that carry the stories of victory that impact and speak to me on a transformative level.

My cry was to feel God, to be close to His heart, to be free of pain, to feel loved, and to become as much of that love as I possibly could become in this life.

I remember one day my Mom looked over at me and said, "Misti, do you realize you have become a master of stress management." I gazed back at those heart-piercing eyes and replied, "Mom, I've just become a professional of truly being happy even when sadness has found her way into my heart."

She smiled. I smiled.

After she died last fall, I remembered this moment and how happy that reply had made her. I remember looking at her and seeing how thankful she was that I could say those words and genuinely mean them. I could see the peace come over her as if years of praying for me to arrive at this place of inward, authentic contentment had paid off.

I can't tell you the number of times I have brought this memory to the forefront of my mind, particularly after sadness made its way into my heart more than ever after she died.

But I remember that look. I remember those eyes. I remember how pleased she was with my words from the expression that graced her delicate face. And once again, I found my happy. I found my strength to paint a beautiful picture on the canvas of my life. And for Mama, and for my children, I'm making it pretty. I'm no longer managing stress. I'm eliminating it. Happiness is a state of being. Declare it as your homestead. Make your life the land of the free.

Create your happy. Allow for your happy. Protect your happy. Utilize your happy to love and serve the world around you. The more we surrender and align our perspective with higher truths when things aren't so happy in our lives, the more our physical reality will begin to match our inner spiritual reality. As within, so without. The more valiant the effort to align ourselves emotionally, mentally, and spiritually, the closer we will be to authentic happiness and soul prosperity.

When you discover who you are and what makes you genuinely happy, fight to protect that. Respect yourself enough to walk away from anything that no longer serves you, grows you, or makes you happy. Release or realign things. Speak up for yourself. Empower others to do the same. Love is freedom. Live in a state of loving others enough to let go of control and allow them to also find their happiness. If necessary, set them free to do so. Ultimately, how happy you are will determine how effective you are in living your destined path to uniquely love and serve those around you, and is this not the ultimate goal for us all? Love thy neighbor AS THYSELF. You should go and love yourself. You should go and find your happy.

Happy Trails!

The Greatest Showman

"You don't need everyone to love you. Just a few good people."
"I brought hardship on you and our family.
You warned me, and I wouldn't listen.
I just wanted to be more than I was."
"I never wanted anything but the man I fell in love with."
~ The Greatest Showman

1 JUST FINISHED WATCHING *THE GREATEST SHOWMAN* WITH KATE. I haven't bought a movie in a really long time, but this one is going in my tiny collection.

I am deeply touched. It is a true Masterpiece. In addition, it ranks among the greatest soundtracks *ever*. This movie just earned its way into my heart as one of the best I've ever seen.

In the movie, P.T. Barnum had just lost his job and returned home to his family. That evening while sitting beneath a canopy sky, Barnum gave his daughters a homemade gift with an ability to illuminate the space around them, making it appear as if they were immersed in sparkling stars. As the lights were dancing across the fabric of newly hung clothing that had been draped along the rooftop to dry, he told each of his family members to make a wish. When it was his wife's turn, she simply stated, "I wish for happiness like this forever." Mind you, she had already left her rich, fancy parents to run away with P.T. Barnum, a man who no longer had a job. However, his wife knew the true meaning of happiness.

The last lyrics sung in the movie were laced over a scene of a teary husband and wife who had been to the heights of success only to learn that their family, friends, and one another were all that truly mattered. As they watched their children dance together, the lyrics said,

"It's everything you ever want. It's everything you
ever need. It's here right in front of you."

Happiness is not obtained by having a collection of materialistic possessions or having the most excellent and desirable job. The pot of gold at the end of the rainbow is being surrounded by people you love and seeing happiness in their hearts. Happiness is sharing sweet moments, going through the struggles together, and creating happiness with one another.

At one point the character Zac Efron says,

"All that's left is friendship, love, and the work that I love."

I identify with that statement in ways that my heart could never articulate in the limited language of the written word.

The final words of the film were those of P.T. Barnum, who once said,

"The greatest art is that of making others happy."

Deep gratitude for the those in my life who have mastered this art, beginning with my blessed Christ, who has not only made me ridiculously happy but who also managed to set my heart abundantly free.

The Metamorphosis of the Monarch

LET CRAP GO. LET IT GO. Do whatever you have to do to let it freaking go. Negative energy is a toxic poison that creeps its way into every fiber of your being. It's paralyzing. Take control of your happiness. It's everything. It's your lifeline. If you are around someone who is repeatedly pulling you out of your center and causing you to sink, cut the cord, let the baggage drown, and rise back to the surface. Find your happy. Do whatever you have to do to get happy again. Seek your peace, and don't be satisfied until you've found it. Listen to a song, take a walk, have a picnic, dance it out, enjoy some nice food, or kiss someone passionately!

Just

get

happy!

We create, build, and manifest abundance and beauty in our lives via inspiration and love. When we are under pressure and surrounded by negative energy, all of these vital things are compromised and suffocated. Don't sacrifice your happy for someone else's issues, or their mood swings, or their inability to control their behavior. Ask yourself a question: How long am I going to allow this person's drama to steal my joy, my peace, and my happiness? Is anything worth giving all that away?

How long are you going to use someone as your excuse for not allowing yourself to be in alignment with your highest and best good? How much are your peace and sanity worth? Too many of us sit in our discontentment and anger, saying, "You made me really mad, because you did me really wrong, and I have every reason to be mad at you! And if the whole world were given an opportunity to evaluate this, I'm certain the whole world would agree with me that you are wrong!"

My question to you is, "How long are you going to use this person
as a means to cut yourself off from clarity, abundance, wellness,
and all the things that you consider to be good?"

When you do not return the negativity, then 50% of the negative energy surrounding the circumstance is already gone. Whoever holds the strongest and most dominant vibration will influence the other. This is why the demons had to flee when Jesus entered their space. Because Christ carried the strongest vibration, the negative energy was either going to merge with the light or flee from it. It could not remain as it was in the presence of a Stronger One that had come upon it. If you hold yourself in a happy space and maintain that vibration in the midst of your encounter with negativity, then eventually you will over-power the space. Either the negative ones will be transformed to match your energy, or they will begin to rapidly flee from it.

This understanding alludes to why you may go through seasons of growth and notice friends begin dropping like flies. When you get serious about being happy, about letting things go, about forgiveness, and about being the best ver-sion of yourself, oftentimes you may have friends who aren't ready to make the transition with you. They are still content with hanging on to their resent-ments. They simply aren't ready to let go.

Once you change the dial on a radio station, you can no longer pick up the frequency you were once receiving. You are now tuned to pick up a different signal. The melody of your life has changed. You've been given a new sound-track to play amidst the backdrop of your life. This is why in relationships, especially marriage, it is essential to communicate daily and be committed to growing and evolving together. When one advances without the other, the dial can change, and the two are no longer a vibrational match. Being set to a dif-ferent station mentally and emotionally can make a marriage almost impossible to maintain.

If you find yourself in the midst of unpleasant circumstances or a negative Nelly for that matter, change the channel and start packing your bags. You're tuning yourself to a new concordance. Hopefully, the person who is occupying your space will recognize this if they want to remain with you. Whatever the case, your happiness is everything. If they refuse to change and you have already entered the cocoon, there's no turning back for you. You are destined to fly, Dear One. You've come a long way to make this transition to your freedom. You deserve to soar. A caterpillar is too heavy to carry on the back of your wings.

Caterpillars are voracious feeders and among the most serious of agricul-tural pests. They weasel their way inside a piece of fruit piercing holes in it and causing it to rot. Caterpillars disturb the fruitful ones. They feed off the vibrant life of another by slowly sucking the life out of it. Have grace for the one who still hasn't figured out their true destiny and thus insists on continuing to crawl beneath their ultimate, ordained purpose. Though they may need some more time munching on bitter leaves for their nourishment, you are ready for some-thing more. Go sip the sweetness with the other fluttering ones, colorful Monarch. You've shed your skin, and your delicious nectar is awaiting you!

What is the Answer?

What is the answer?
Chill out.

THE ANSWER IS, BE NICER TO YOURSELF. The answer is to think more thoughts about yourself that feel good and to think more thoughts about others that feel good. The answer is not to work so hard. The answer is to give yourself a break. The answer is to get more rest. The answer is to laugh at life a little more. The answer is to lighten up. The answer is to do more of the things that feel good to you. That's the way you will turn this thing around. You can't demand yourself into alignment with where you want to be. You can't effort yourself into alignment. You've got to release. You've got to let go. You've got to let go of the resistance. When you let go of that cork, things will flow. When you release the resistance, then and only then can your desires naturally flow towards you. Find your Garden of Gethsemane and pray your surrendering prayer.

What is the answer?
Get happy.

Do whatever you need to do to make this happen, but just get happy. What makes you feel good? Do that. And depending on how long you've been in a state of defeat, you may need to take an extended period of time to focus on this one single question, "Does this make me happy?" If the answer is no, don't go, don't stay, don't participate, don't hang around that person, and don't think that way. It's killing you slowly.

Take the nap. Dance to that song. Sip that cup of tea. Watch that comedian who makes you laugh. Delight in children playing. Join them! Play with them! Dance in the rain. Go out with friends. Sit in nature. Listen to something beautiful. Look at something beautiful. Find things that make you feel like you're watching a sunset over a gorgeous beach. You know that feeling—like when a baby laughs, smiles, or stares at you in adoration. What makes you feel that way? Do that! This is the key to open your prison. This is the key to your bliss. This is the key to you manifesting a better future for yourself. This is your game-changer.

It's hard to attract better when you feel worse. It's hard to be happy when you feel sad. It's hard to heal when you live every day feeling broken. It's hard to feel creative when you feel limited.

> *"We don't create abundance. Abundance is always present.*
> *We create limitations."*
> ~ Arnold Patent

Change the way you feel. Change it immediately. If that means you go for a drive and listen to a song that can take you from zero to hero and then come back to face your life...go roll the windows down and turn the radio up! Do whatever it takes. If that means you don't call that person or talk to that person, even if it means you cut that person out of your life—stop hesitating.

Listen to me and listen carefully. Put your dang oxygen mask on and do it quickly or you will suffocate. Do not think you can stay in that vibe and see a difference in how you feel in the future. Emancipate yourself. Stop waiting on God to do what He has given you the ability to do. You hold the keys to the kingdom. You house the creative power of the Source of all that is. What are you doing with it?

> *It's not just about what God is doing.*
> *It's about what you are doing with what*
> *God has already given you!*

What is in your heart? How does it feel? Think a better thought. Do a better thing. Whatsoever things are good and pleasing and lovely, think on those things, do those things, and friggin' surround yourself with people who understand the value of this. Then you just watch. As you feel better, I guarantee you with 100% accuracy you will see a better life surrounding you. Why? Because your heart and how it feels on any given day is the wellspring of your life. Everything, and I mean everything, flows from this place. Make it happy. The power is in you to feel better, to do better, to have better, and to live a better life with better people.

> *Chill out.*
> *Get happy.*

Make adjustments accordingly. Make them today. Your tomorrow and your future productivity depend upon it.

Get Happy

IF IT MAKES YOU FEEL SAD, STOP THINKING ABOUT IT. If it makes you cry, stop talking about it. If it makes you feel hurt, stop dwelling on it. Why relive something over and over that makes you feel pain? Reach deep and pull from that well within you. Dig deep from within your will power and with everything you have and change the freaking channel.

Force yourself over the hump with one gigantic leap of your will. Switch the dial. Don't allow yourself to think about it for one more second. Replace it with a good-feeling thought, anything that makes you feel better. Let the other go. Turn it loose and never look back. Stop giving thought and attention to the moments, the things, and the people that have broken your heart.

You have to decide it will get better before it can be better. Make a decision to be happy. Choose it willfully and abandon anything that makes you feel otherwise. Your happiness is your lifeline, and you can obtain it regardless of your chaos, regardless of your circumstance, and regardless of how far you are in relation to where you want to be.

Happiness is an inside job. The outside will ultimately reflect the inside. So, get happy. Whatever you do, just find a way to get freaking happy! You do that, and I promise you by the law of the Divine, your world will shape into a bubble of happiness around you. And if it doesn't, you won't give a flying flip. You won't even notice. You'll be blissed out in an inner kingdom of sheer love, sheer peace, sheer joy, and sheer happiness—just you and your Source—just you and your God—two peas in a pod—at one with one another, unable to tell where one ends and the other begins.

Happy. Happy. Happy.

JUDGING

Come Like a Child

THIS PAST WEEK WHILE ON VACATION, I took the kids to the pool and sat beneath the shade of a palm tree to watch them play. My attention was drawn to their interactions with the other children in the pool and how quickly they all became fast friends. On this particular day, we were at the pool for about five hours and saw many children come and go. What was so beautiful to observe was the physical intimacy and instant camaraderie they all shared.

I was mesmerized by their lack of boundaries and how sincerely open and trusting they were with one another. The understood concept amongst them seemed to be, "We're kids; therefore, we play together." I wondered why, as adults, we don't see life the same—"We're adults; therefore, we play together."

I noticed how my daughter was holding hands with the little girls she had met. They were pulling her around the pool in her float. They were laughing and giggling and telling each other pretty much anything and everything about themselves. They shared what they liked and what they didn't like, and no one posed any judgments. They all seemed in awe and wonder, genuinely enjoying the opportunity to indulge in their curiosity about one another.

My boys were equally having the time of their lives wresting, throwing the football, and playing water gun wars with the other boys in the pool. I was amazed by how they could shoot water at someone they just met. They were climbing on floats with the other kids, totally invading each other's personal space, and not giving a care in the world for any semblance of social etiquette.

I wondered. How often do we touch another adult? When was the last time I held a stranger's hand, laughed with them, or truly interacted and "played" with someone I didn't know? What was so baffling to me as I watched the children play was that there was no discrimination whatsoever. If you wanted to play, you were welcome to play. It didn't matter if you were red, yellow, black, or white. It didn't matter if you were overweight or super skinny. It didn't matter if you were dressed rich or poor. The kids didn't ask each other where they were from, what they did for a living, or to what socioeconomic status they belonged. It didn't matter if they were a Christian, Muslim, Hindu, or of a different religious faith.

Children love everybody. They accept anyone. Whether or not you are a Democrat or a Republican doesn't seem to affect whether or not you qualify to push a child in the swing or take a ride with them on the slide. They are just happy to have someone to play with them. They don't ask if they have a sexual preference or even if they believe Jesus has saved them from their sins. And they certainly aren't speculating as to whether or not they have committed any sins. None of these things seem to matter

The world needs more children as teachers and more adults with the wisdom to sit at their feet and observe.

when it comes to whether or not a child will play with another child, will love another child, will have compassion for another child, or will care for another child. Perhaps this is why Jesus said that none of us can enter in or understand the kingdom of heaven lest we come like a child.

So, remember: You weren't asking your friends what their political opinions were when you were once laughing hysterically having the carefree, joyous time of your lives together on the playground. You didn't ask your friend who they voted for when they were crying over a skinned knee, and you went over to give them a hug. You didn't know if they watched FOX or CNN when you swam and jumped in the creek together on that hot July summer day. Quite frankly, you didn't care. All the children at the pool that day were treated as if they belonged, as if they were desired, and as if they each brought something special to the experience they were all having. The children seemed genuinely grateful to have one another. They didn't want to miss a moment of playtime, because they didn't know exactly how long their time together would last. They knew they only had a certain amount of time before a parent would call for them and tell them it was time to go. As a result, they played hard and opened their hearts to bond as quickly as possible. When it was time for one of them to leave, the girls would hug tightly, knowing they would probably never see one another again. They boys would handshake or high five and say something cool and macho like, "Hey man, hope to see you around again sometime."

When did we stop behaving like children and what crazy adult told us we shouldn't? Weren't we all having much more fun and were happier when we enjoyed life through the lens of a child and with the heart of a child? Jesus Christ must have really been on to something when He said,

"Unless you change and become like little children,
you will never enter the kingdom of heaven."
(Matthew 18:3)

I am of the notion, as was Jesus, that the kingdom of heaven is found within, that it is in our midst. According to the mindset of Christ, this blissful state of being is linked to our ability to come like a child. These moments of watching children interact with one another help me understand more and more why that statement is so undeniably true.

As I left the pool on that beautiful afternoon, the prayer radiating from my heart for both myself and our world was simple. May we come to see the world through the eyes of a child with the purity and innocence that dwells within their hearts. May we approach life with the faith of a child to believe for impossible things. May we love with the heart of a child, carrying within us their ability to show affection and kindness without bias towards all. Give us the willingness of a child to forgive and forget. Supply us with the ability to give like a child—to give as they do with their smiles, with their touch, with their laughter, and with the potent doses of compassion they carry within their hearts.

Come like a child.

The world needs more children as teachers and more adults with the wisdom to sit at their feet and observe.

Watching my children is teaching me lessons long forgotten. Sometimes it's best to let the walls fall down, the conditioned prejudices fade, and the fears of a stranger disintegrate. An inability to come like a child may be preventing us from the best play date of our entire lives.

Play hard and play well. You don't know how much time you have left before your Parent calls and tells you it's time to go home.

"...and a little child shall lead them."
(Isaiah 11:6)

Dear Judgmental One

DEAR JUDGMENTAL ONE,

Throughout your life, you will meet many people, most of them quite different than you. There is a quote that has circulated and been spoken many times over that says,

"People fear what they don't understand
and hate what they can't conquer."
~ Andrew Smith

Nothing in life is to be feared. It is only to be understood. How often do you take time to understand the person whom you fear or judge? Is it possible to be moved with compassion for the terrorist who from birth has been taught to kill and hate? Is it possible for you to emphasize with the thirty-year-old man who was once a little boy beaten into submission, programmed to believe a certain way, and made to shoot lethal weapons when he was five years old? Can you not pray for his soul to return to the Light? Can you not pray for a divine intervention, a rescue mission for his soul? Is it not understandable that people can feel justified in their actions when they've been separated from others and taught to kill with an entitled mentality to do so? If you had been dealt the circumstances of another, would you be so quick to throw stones, or would you yield your sword and humbly kneel in prayer asking for their return home? If you genuinely treated others, all others, the way you would want to be treated in that situation, would you not cry out for their realization of a higher truth than the one they are living? While you don't condone the behavior, can you not pray for a complete redemption of the soul so that these dreadful patterns cease and desist?

Consider the stay-at-home mom who is unhappily married or perhaps even single. She dresses in a way to attract men, uses her gifts to draw attention to herself, posts her selfies on social media, and daily longs for affirmation and human touch. She is not a stranger to desiring the adoration of a married man and dresses her body in a way to tempt the weaknesses in others. She does not restrict her need for validation and significance to singles only. She is starved to feel worth and will accept whatever is offered to soothe the ache she carries from a childhood of being ignored or potentially completely disregarded and abandoned by her father. She carries a deeply imbedded program that runs continually on the hard drive of her mind that echoes, "I need to feel special." She searches for anything to validate and affirm this encoded program forgetting that she already possesses the power within herself to validate her special place in this world. What would happen to your judgments of her if you took a few moments to understand her path? Would it still be so easy to comment on her actions if you followed her journey?

To understand why someone is behaving a certain way is to take a moment to step into their shoes and see life from a perspective that is not yours. There is a profound difference in how you react to the shortcomings of others when you pause to walk a mile in their shoes. If you proceeded to the spiritual heights of treating others as you would want to be treated in a similar circumstance, you would think more wisely before you speak. You would suddenly have greater compassion, the ability to forgive, and silence would tend to replace your aggressive outbursts against them. Instead of your tongue rising against them, your head would bow in sacred prayer for them. You would ask God to fill the voids they carry instead of delighting in their discipline. You would realize that your love and mercy for others is sowing love and mercy for yourself.

There is a scripture in the Bible that says judgment without mercy will be shown to anyone who has not been merciful.

"Mercy triumphs over judgment."
(James 2:13)

This isn't due to the fact God is judgmental. God is love. This passage was spoken in love with an understanding of the universal laws of sowing and reaping that Jesus taught so clearly.

"For in the same way you judge others, you will be judged, and
with the measure you use, it will be measured to you."
Matthew 7:2

When we judge others, we judge ourselves.

Whenever I find myself wanting to judge someone based on the way they look, how they are dressed, what religious faith they belong to, what political opinions they express, or any other genre through which they appear to possess different behaviors than me, I have learned to stop and consider the path they traveled to arrive at their current destination. I will recall a time in my life when I was lost, confused, and behaving less than what I had the potential to become. I'll then think of the people who showed me grace, kindness, and friendship during those wayward moments. To this day, it is those people I hold most dear and love most deeply.

The people in your life with an ability to love
unconditionally are worth remembering.

I'm not saying for you to stick around and continue to tolerate someone who is mistreating you. I'm saying there is a space of unconditional love you can hold for them even if it is from afar. I'm not advising you to invite a terrorist for dinner or invite a woman who dresses with her "assets" on full display to spend large amounts of time with you and your husband. However, your heart can still radiate love and Light for them, accepting them for where they are on their soul journey.

There is something very refreshing about the person who doesn't try to change you and who possesses an ability to see the divine in you no matter where you are on your path. This person's focus isn't on converting you, transforming you, or pointing out all the areas of your life that are unbalanced. This person simply loves you. This person has discovered that love is the only force that carries the power to change anyone. Love melts the hard, wax exterior of the hardened heart. When true love overtakes the heart of a person, one is destined to change and evolve to become the highest version of oneself. It simply happens. It simply is. Love is a force carried in the wind. It breaks all barriers, heals all lands, and sets the wayward soul on the enlightened path. It will forever be the key that unlocks and the tie that binds. It is the ultimate transformer. Love conquers all.

Someone once overheard me counseling another woman, and after I was finished, he said to me,

"You know, Misti, sometimes people don't want
to hear what you know.
They just want to know that you hear them."

I paused, grabbed a pen, and wrote these words down as I knew they were lasting and true. It's not your knowledge of anything that helps a person shift in any area of their life. It's your ability to listen and love. Their transformation doesn't come simply by your teaching but through your being. It comes by being there for someone often through the worst moments of their lives. It comes by you being the very example of all that you wish to see arise and come forth in others. I wonder what progress could be made in the uplifting of wandering souls if we would but focus on removing the planks in our own eyes prior to dissecting the specks in the eyes of those around us.

Regarding those you think have it wrong, the ones you've placed the scarlet letter upon, have deemed less knowledgeable than you, those you view as ignorant, or self-deceived—before placing judgment, consider the path that has led them to their current level of understanding. Consider how far you have traveled as well. Consider mercy. Consider compassion. Consider love. Consider prayer. Consider that what you think you know now may be a lesser version of a much greater truth that will be revealed to you at a later time. Consider your own weakness and may your heart be tilted towards gently restoring others, including yourself, to their rightful place in creation.

Be kind. Love one another. It is the noblest response one may possess towards another soul. For you too were once a young soul with much to learn. Perhaps you still are. Be slow to anger, slow to speak, quick to hear, and quick to forgive and pardon.

First, we must allow God to change our own hearts
before we carry an anointing to change
the hearts of those around us.

Any teacher who deems they have nothing left to learn is still the student. Any student who is open to receive instruction, be it from that of a child, is the master teacher.

Wisdom comes from the lowliest of places. Even the ant teaches the sage. Even the tadpole captivates the wise as she demonstrates the beauty of transformation. Be prepared to hear wisdom from those perhaps deemed by the intellectual mind as ignorant and unlearned.

No one can argue with someone about something they have personally experienced for themselves. It is one thing to teach grace. It is quite another to learn from one who has experienced it.

Dear Person Who Feels the Need to Correct Everyone

Dear Person Who Feels the Need to Correct Everyone,

Recently, I wrote a status update regarding my health in which I said,

"I am having a fabulous week! In addition, I am inwardly healing and thriving more and more each day. Albert Einstein once said, 'Logic will get you from A to B, but imagination will take you everywhere.' I'm letting my imagination create the most beautiful of circumstances, and I would love for you to join me! Someday we will marvel at our beautiful creations together!"

After I made this post, a lady whom I do not know replied in the comment section saying,

"I know what you're really saying is that God's grace is enough. It is efficient. May HIS HOLY SPIRIT whisper Jesus' name to every matter of your body. May you humble yourself before Him."

Obviously, if I had meant to say what she wrote, I would have written what she wrote. It is quite clear via her ALL CAPS she felt the need to rewrite my words and emphasize what she felt was more important for me to say. I'm guessing she did not feel I was religious enough with my wording.

Here's my advice.
It's simple.
Don't be this person.
Love people and support them where they are
and not where you want them to be.

If you feel the need to change someone's words, or insert your meaning into them, ask yourself what within yourself feels the need to do so? Is there judgment in your heart?

Everyone is at a different place in their journey, and if you can't love them in that position without feeling the need to fix them to match your comfort level, please remain quiet. If you refuse to do so, you will only be ruining your chances of being a beacon of Light and love in their life. Given this is what God truly is, let's hold fast to that vision. Most often, we earn the right to speak into someone's life based on our ability to remove judgment and love them as is, without trying to change them!

I will address the religious people with this first because they tend to struggle with this concept the most. I'm sure the person who wrote this comment is a sweet lady who was well-meaning, but there is a reason I have highlighted this as an example. Firstly, it is in all humility I write this message as I'm sure I could look up an example in my past where I might have typed a similar message to someone.

Love people and support them where they are and not where you want them to be.

There may arise people in your life who come across rigid or as if they are preaching at you. They probably are, but please know they are responding based on their belief systems, programs, and individual personalities. People's fears can propel them to force their opinions or views upon you, versus administering love and acceptance for the voice you are sharing at the time. People deeply buried into religion can very easily slip into an attitude adopted by those who Jesus called the Pharisees or religious leaders of his day. These folks can get so caught up in executing the letter of the text and making sure your every word matches their criteria that they forget the Spirit behind the text and behind what you are conveying. They're so busy looking at the letters of your text that they fail to see your love. They're so preoccupied listening to your words that they fail to hear your heart.

With this said, remember that Jesus was misinterpreted, but it didn't hold Him back from speaking his message. Never stop speaking your truth even if it's colored over with scrapes and dents. Truth develops over time. Love yourself in the midst of figuring things out and don't waste too much time on those who can't offer the same graces.

I can always tell how much someone lacks in confidence by how defensive they get about their faith. If they were confident in their beliefs and were not in fear that you were going to convince them of something else, they would be able to listen to others' opinions with kindness and grace. They would simply respond with a gentle, "I don't agree with that." Perhaps this is why Jesus was able to dine with tax collectors, lounge with prostitutes, and spend more time with those the religious leaders deemed as sinners. I suppose who one sees as a sinner another recognizes as a saint. I suppose that's why so many loved Jesus and feared those with stones in their hands. If you have to defend yourself, if you have to explain yourself, you're lost. Silent power is a beautiful thing.

If there are those in your life who feel the need to interpret your words and rewrite them with their own verbiage, you are not alone. You and Jesus could enjoy a nice long powwow of discussing this matter, as I am almost certain He could relate. However, once the conversation waned, I'm guessing He would say something like, "Shake it off. Smile anyway, love always, and keep moving."

If love is at the center of everything you do, you'll be ok.

Love propels you farther. Love welcomes everyone, not just those pre-selected by the hierarchy for their commendable behavior. Love initiates a genuine invitation for you to speak into someone's life, not to preach your particular dogma at them but to share with them what you've learned along the way.

We are all at different levels of understanding. Imagine a line with points ranging from one to one hundred. Regarding any given subject, one person might be at a twenty on the number line and another at ninety. Yet, the same person who is at ninety in one area of growth might be at ten in another. What I thought I knew at level twenty-five might have changed by the time I'm at level forty. The view from halfway up the mountain appears different from what it looked like when you were standing in the valley below. It's the same landscape, but with a different perspective, you will discover a different view. This imagery could describe my spiritual journey and my life in general. What I thought I knew yesterday might change as I climb the mountain and take in the lay of the land from a higher viewpoint and with a fresh set of eyes. From the top of the mountain, the sunset is always more glorious and piercing. The fresh eyes or renewed vision comes as more Light enters them. When we reach the peak of the mountain, we will be capable of seeing the entire landscape of our lives. Coincidently, it is also when we can see and absorb the most Light. A mountaintop view brings with it a sacred peace. As you marvel at its beauty, it has a way of silencing you. When you respond to people and your life circumstances with this higher perspective and mountain-minded view, you may find it silences you too. You will no longer feel the need to correct that person's status update notifying them of how you think it should have been written.

There are many paths that lead to the top of the mountain. Just confidently respond to others by wishing them happy travels and by telling them you will meet them at the top. Then continue to focus on your own climb lest while you are busying yourself trying to tell everyone else how to make it, you get distracted, and you slip and fall.

While one person may read the Bible and see it as a rulebook, another person may read it creating imagery that enables them to see a deeper, more meaningful message behind it. This person doesn't see a literal interpretation but is reading the stories while feeling and absorbing the expressions and tones. For this person, it isn't about the story itself but what they are absorbing from it in terms of how it is helping them grow. The same exact story placed in the wrong hands and interpreted literally can produce legalism and hypocrisy. Again, some look at the letter of the law while others gaze upon the heart.

Jesus tried to explain this to those who sat in Moses' seat and were busy interpreting and executing the law.

"Woe to you, teachers of the law and Pharisees,
you hypocrites! You travel over land and sea to win
a single convert, and when you have succeeded,
you make them twice as much a child of hell as you are."
(Matthew 23:15)

I must agree with this statement because nothing can bring out the hell fury in me more than when the Pharisaical religious police show up. Don't you just love those people who delight in going around reading the law to everyone but themselves? Insert eye roll please. Instead of working on what they need to fix in their own life, they exude their energy pointing out what needs to be fixed with everyone else.

Never be so determined to convert someone that you forget to simply love them. And lastly, if you were at level five on your spiritual climb up the mountain, would you want someone discouraging you from reaching level one hundred? Don't be that person.

Your role is not to impose your opinion. Your role is *to be* the opinion you wish to see expressed by others. Then, if they respect you for who you are and what you represent, who knows? They may end up liking and appreciating your opinion.

Unending Love

Some have truth but have forgotten compassion. They have forgotten where they came from and how deep their pit once was. Truth without love is a clanging symbol that no one wants to hear. We must bear the weaknesses of others.

Long-suffering, patience, and endurance are necessary requirements for Saints. Kings are appointed based on how well they shepherd the lost and wandering sheep. If you aren't willing to seek and save the lost, you don't deserve to reign amongst those who have been found.

Some are so busy preaching truth they have neglected to love the flock. Never forget you were once a sheep being rescued from the edge of a death-defying cliff by the hand of a Shepherd who was relentless in His pursuit and search for you to be found. You are alive today because of His great rescue mission in your life. Someone had to love you enough to pursue you with an unending love while you were stuck in a storm on the backside of a mountain for you to be here preaching your truth today.

Truth seekers should also be love seekers. If your heart doesn't feel great love for the one you are teaching, be quiet. You're just being noisy to the rest of us.

Put Me In, Coach!

I AM LEARNING IN MY LIFE THAT MY PRIMARY RELATIONSHIP is to my Creator and myself. I have truly been set free from the burden of feeling a need to explain or have the approval of others in my life for the decisions I make. Alignment with yourself and God are the most critical components.

You will always have those who feel they know what your alignment should be at any given time and will be happy to voice it to you. My advice is to stay in your lane following the path the Father has placed before you. Friends who have to agree with you to love you are better left to themselves. Stick with those who have the capacity to love you for the long haul. Your journey of figuring things out down here is going to take a bit more love and compassion than a friend who's eager to block you whenever your beliefs are misaligned with theirs. Be grateful when these people exit stage left in your life. You will be better off with them gone.

Unconditional love is a virtue, and when you find a friend who understands this and offers it to you, hold them close. They are a real gem. No one appreciates the constant pressure of needing to please and keep another person happy in order to be accepted and loved by them. Be you. Do you. And let those who stick, stick. This is how God loves me. He sticks. No matter what. No matter how big my crazy, He just sticks. I've come to understand that I'm worthy of this kind of love not just from the Divine but from the relationships I allow in my life.

Isolating myself from the world in order to "please God" in some unattainable religious pursuit while losing fellowship opportunities with beloved family, friends, and even strangers wasn't a fit for this gal. I am meant to be among the people and always will be. I want to understand as much as I can while I am experiencing this big beautiful world, and I want to understand as many people as I can. I want to walk in their footsteps, immerse myself in their culture, eat their food, laugh at their humor, understand their vision and perspective of this world, and show appreciation for their traditions and what matters to them.

I want to listen more and preach less.
Love more and preach less.
Understand more and preach less.
Laugh with others more and preach less.
Encourage more and preach less.
I want to be Jesus more and preach Jesus less.

If you call Jesus Yahusha, then I will call Him Yahusha. If you call Him Yeshua, then I will call Him Yeshua. If you call Him Jesus, then I will call Him Jesus. If you call God YAH or something else, then I will call Him that. I'm with the Apostle Paul in this regard. I prefer becoming all things to all people that I might reach more people, not just with a message but with an expression and touch of love, kindness, grace, understanding, and compassion. For it was the goodness and love of our Creator that overwhelmed me, changed me, and made me strive to become the greatest version of myself that I could possibly be. It was love. It was mercy. It was kindness. It was walking a path with me, listening to me, and feeling my emotions regardless if they were in alignment or not, that truly brought me to my knees. So, I want to be that. I truly do.

If I'm asked to fellowship with someone in Halloween costumes or wearing a Mardi Gras mask at a super religious Bible study, over a glass of wine, or perhaps while having a beer at the next country concert—I'm in! Where are the souls of the world? Put me there amongst them. Be they confused, bewildered, lost, broken, fulfilled, or blissfully happy. Put me in, Coach! It is there I will be the happiest. It is there I will be shining the brightest. It is there I will have the most opportunity to give unto others what Christ has deposited and given unto me. I want to laugh there. I want to play there. I want to explore there. I'll be there with no judgment, just Spirit, and just love.

Just love…period.

I believe that love is big enough to conquer and handle all the rest. Watching my children play and bond with other children who are complete strangers has taught me this love. Seeing them hug and accept others without questioning their social, political, or religious beliefs has helped me to see that I'd rather be like a little child in this regard. We can never truly be in Christ nor enter his glorious inner kingdom unless we change and become like little children. I'd rather greet people every day of my life like the little ones greet one another, ready and eager to play and make a new friend.

Some folks simply need the people they associate and fellowship with to look like them, talk like them, eat like them, think like them, believe like them, and be at the same step as they are on their journey. Well, my advice to them would be good luck and best wishes in your search for that. My experience is that these people are not surrounded by a band of brothers or a crowd of five thousand sitting on a hillside for three days not concerned with eating because they have a crowd enamored with hanging on their every word. Most of these people that I have observed find themselves very lonely, disconnected, and not waking to the vibrant feeling of vitality and the abundant flow of life. Most have isolated themselves and have very small circles of influence and friends. Some even become quite ill. I believe this is because they are going against their natural design to be fully present and in this world, loving their fellow man whether that man or woman is "a Samaritan" on the roadside who doesn't share the same beliefs as them or not.

When we lose the ability to be friends with anyone, we begin to demonize our fellow brethren. We separate ourselves from the common bond we all share as human beings. We lose our ability to not just relate to others who haven't achieved the "spiritual status" we think we have achieved, but to make friends with those who are different than us with the hopes of leaving a deposit of love and kindness in their lives.

A lot of religious folks want to convert and change people. Christ's focus was to love and heal people. Perhaps this was the key He possessed that caused people to choose to "convert" or transform themselves to the highest and best version of who they were destined to become. Perhaps all it took was just a dose of love, a listening ear, a healing touch, and some potent words of life to awake them to a higher calling.

So, to those who wish to detach from me because I shared a beer in a bar with a stranger or companion, it has been lovely spending this time with you. I pray my deposit in your life during the time we have shared together has been richly filled with love and the grace of God that abides in me. Please know if you ever decide to return, there will be a space of love waiting here for you to come and receive from it regardless of what condition or mindset you may have found yourself in. I am fully capable of having a "chat at the well" with anyone from any background, even if that means you have "five husbands." I'd be happy to pour you a pitcher of water. I'd rather hand you water that will quench your thirst than preach you a message void of relationship that has no ability to pierce the heart and break the yoke.

A simple hug, smile, or if you're blessed—life-long friendship, can do what words just simply cannot, my friends. Sometimes having dinner at a "tax collector's" house with someone you have absolutely nothing in common with can turn out to be one of the greatest relationships of your life, establishing a bond so deep that it lasts for all eternity.

Those People

DON'T YOU JUST LOVE PEOPLE WHO DON'T OFFER THEIR OPINION unless you ask them for it? Don't you just love people who are kind and loving no matter the circumstances? Don't you just love people who don't base their treatment of you on whether or not they agree with you or you are living your life the way they believe it is best for you to live it?

You know those people? The ones that always have a smile no matter if the world is throwing you trophies or calling you crazy. Don't you just love people who are capable of not punishing you by withdrawing their affection for you or their time with you when you don't perform the way they believe you should be performing? Gosh, I love those people. Those people are awesome! The worst I've ever felt in my entire life was when I followed a path that caused me to be any less than one of those people.

This is Enough

IF SOMEONE SPEAKS FALSELY AGAINST YOU, attacks your character, or perhaps you find yourself in a situation of observing while he or she is speaking poorly of another, listen carefully, not to what they are saying but to who they are telling you they are. Usually, the people that feel the need to defend the loudest are the people who are most at fault. Be wise and discerning. And as Mayo Angelou once stated, "Once people show you who they are, believe them."

There may come a point in your life where your character has to defend itself. Jesus taught me that. So while you go about living your life, treat people kindly, speak life wherever you go, walk in truth and integrity, give lavishly of yourself, forgive much, and live in such a way that if someday you find yourself in a situation where someone is speaking falsely against you or calling your character into question, the people listening will know via their own experience with you, such things could never be true. And for those who believe the untruths, let them. Hold your head high. If they can believe such things about you, they were never worthy to walk a path with you to begin with. They aren't your tribe. Let them go and hold tight to the ones who know your character so well they would never believe anyone that tried to tarnish it with their bitter words.

If you walk in Light and truth, that Light will defend you with those who are discerning enough to know and recognize it. For those who can't, pray for them, bless them, release them, and keep moving forward. Time has a way of revealing truth. Let them be them. Let you be you. For those who love and know you, this will suffice. This is enough.

Be Ye Kind

LIFE CAN BE HARD. PARENTING CAN BE HARD. Marriage can be hard. Everyone is walking around with layers of complexities to their lives while smiling to the question, "How are you doing?" to which we reply, "Good," while quickly reverting the spotlight off the plethora of issues we are currently contemplating. We pleasantly reply back to the other person with an offering of, "How are you?" Over and over again, more often than not, we continue the spectacle. We do this regardless of the fact that many of us are desperately seeking to be more of the authentic versions of ourselves we are diligently seeking to find and understand.

Optimistic people can often get a bad rap for creating a world that isn't real. Some are not trying to present a fake world that is secretly unraveling. They're just trying to create a world that is holding itself together. They are making the best of what they have. I've done this my whole life. I always will. Life is not your Facebook wall showcasing the highlight reel of your life. Life is tears, frustration, anger, questions, confusion, messy psychotic moments, and struggle. Life is also beautiful, meaningful, humorous, revealing, sweet, and wonderfully kind.

Right now, I'm on vacation, posting pretty pictures to my Facebook wall. But I'm also hurting and having both awesome moments and defeating moments while contemplating both the beauty and harshness of life. Guess what? Everyone is somewhere doing the same to some capacity or another regardless of the words in their status update.

We all have moments of feeling utterly alone and misunderstood. That's real. That's genuine. That's the truth. If there *is* a normal, in my humble opinion, that would be it. I will say I have tremendous respect for those that in the midst of the struggle, keep showing up for themselves and their children. Being optimistic in a reality-based world can be tough sometimes. Don't quit. Keep going. Keep laughing. Keep trying. Keep living.

Thus, there is only but one option to provide those who we love as well as the total stranger we know nothing about...we give them love, kindness, grace, and courage to be the truest version of themselves they can possibly be and to forgive those of us who haven't quite figured out exactly how to be that.

Everyone is struggling. Everyone is thriving. Everyone has clarity. Everyone has confusion. Everyone has joy. Everyone has defeat. Everyone has fulfillment. Everyone has desire. Everyone has enormous success. Everyone is experiencing utter failure. Everyone has all of these things and sometimes all of them at the same time. However, there are things that we all need from one another, regardless of what state we are in or what frame of mind we are in while riding our enormous waves of emotions.

We all need compassion. We all need forgiveness. We all need massive amounts of grace. We all need love for one another. And we all need to understand that this is how we all find truth. This is how we all find ourselves. This is how we all find God.

Be ye kind one to another.

Share Your Pretty

SOMEONE ONCE ASKED ME, "Misti, why do you feel the need to post pictures of what you eat on social media?" My response...

Life is hard. Life is beautiful. Life is great. Life is messy. Life is relentless. Life is extraordinary. Life is giving. Life is brutal. Life is all these and everything in between. Sometimes we just need a brief moment of appreciating a pretty snack and a glass of sweet red wine to make it through the bumpy spots. Sometimes we just need to share that moment with someone else. Sometimes sharing something we think is beautiful makes us feel happy on the inside.

Allow people to share and appreciate the simple delicacies that make the hard days find their sparkle. Be merciful and kind. You haven't walked in their shoes, friend. Until you do, find the grace to occasionally like their random food pics. Celebrate the fact that they found something beautiful to see and acknowledge that day. Perhaps that particular moment was the moment that helped them cope with all the others.

We must learn to see the beauty in what others see is beautiful and not just what is treasured in the eyes of our own lens. Perhaps there is a lesson for us nestled where another person finds delight, pleasure, and a reason for expressing gratitude. Perhaps there is a blessing wrapped in someone else's beauty. Perhaps this is how God finds enjoyment when peering through the souls of us all.

As far as the evening snack I posted, I think it's beautiful. I like sharing my pretty with you.

So, bottom line: share your pretty.

So Long, People-Pleasing

So long, people-pleasing. It's NOT been nice knowing ya!

HANDS DOWN THE HARDEST BATTLE I HAVE EVER FACED in my entire life has been to overcome what people think about me. My earliest memories of this struggle began in kindergarten. I remember the teacher had left the classroom and asked everyone to be quiet until she returned. However, everyone in the class started talking and getting louder and louder. As I sat quietly listening to everyone chatter while trying to be a good little girl, please my teacher, and follow instructions, I was getting increasingly nervous that our teacher was going to return, and we were all going to get in trouble. Compelled to take action, I raised my voice as loud as I could and said, "Everyone, we have to get quiet! The teacher asked us to be quiet, and if she comes back and finds us talking loudly, we are all going to be in big trouble! Shhhhhh!"

At that exact moment, the teacher walked in the room and said, "I heard several voices as I was coming down the hallway, but the one voice that was louder than all the others was Misti Rains, so Misti you need to get up out of your chair and stand in the corner until recess. You will not have recess today. I am so disappointed my class did not do what I asked you to do."

I still remember the flush in my cheeks and the cold chill and numbness that went all over my body. I was mortified, devastated, and completely ashamed. I loved my teacher so much and had only one objective, to please her. I wanted to help her. I wanted to be good. I was trying to use my voice to save everyone from getting in trouble, and yet I was the one standing in the corner feeling like a complete failure. I was embarrassed, and I felt my intentions had been completely misunderstood. I had failed to please.

At that time, my teacher was heavily emphasizing the significance of coloring inside the lines. She would give special attention and praise to the children that colored well and stayed within them. I still remember going home and practicing my coloring every night so that maybe I could win an approving remark from her. I felt she didn't like me anymore, and my main objective became to win back her full approval. I began to crave and almost need and long for praise from her.

From that point going forward, I became obsessive about being the best student I could be for my teachers. As a five-year-old child, that experience subconsciously taught me using my voice for what I thought was for good meant being humiliated and shamefully placed in a corner with my nose against a cold concrete wall while all my friends stared at me. I suppose that was the moment when the little girl who was destined to color outside the lines began trying to color inside the lines. That was the moment when the little girl who was meant to use her voice began to silence it to win the approval and stay in the good graces of others. I never wanted to feel that sense of shame or disapproval ever again, and I was prepared to work diligently to avoid it.

That feeling stuck with me throughout my life and began to intermingle itself time and time again as the circumstances of my life became more complex in nature. I didn't want to lose the approval of my friends, of my parents, of my boyfriend, or of anyone else for that matter. Most significantly, I didn't want to lose the approval of God. And thus, I entered the world of compromising to keep myself protected, to keep myself loved, and to keep those praiseworthy comments coming. Life was now teaching me that people didn't have the same love for me that I seemed to have for them. There were conditions, and there were lots of them. My friends had them, my boyfriends had them, and even the God I was being taught about seemed to have them.

I still remember not understanding something in the Bible and one day asking my religious superiors a question because it wasn't making sense to me. The response to me was, "You are treading on thin ice, little girl. You are never to question the Word of God." I was even told I might have a demon for daring to question if something in the Bible could be conflicting or wrong. I learned really fast that was a no-no.

It took a very long time to overcome these moments in my life. They shaped my view of God as someone that was not welcoming of me to ponder, ask questions, or even allow me to think for myself and challenge things. That wasn't allowed if you wanted to "color within the lines" and "please the teacher." It took me almost forty years to find the true God, not the one that I had been taught to follow via the perimeters of mankind. It took me a diligent seeking to find the Christ that would allow me to sit at his feet, come like a child, and have a space of love to ask anything I want, to say anything I want, and to be ridiculously and unconditionally loved all the same. It took me even longer to realize that God even admired and appreciated whenever I drew a picture outside the boundaries of what the world's worksheets had placed in my hand. When the world was saying, "Just follow the example. Just stay within the lines. Just color the image we gave you," deep in my soul I was saying, "Can I have a bigger piece of paper please? I'd like to draw my own image. I prefer to use a different medium instead of crayons. Do you have any tape? I'm going to need to design my own canvas. Can we splatter paint?"

It became quite exhausting trying to be loved by every person and every group, all of which had different conditions and rules. I began to discover that all of them believed their ideas were right, and each group tended to only genuinely accept those that agreed with their ideas and principals.

There was a book by Dr. Seuss I read when I was a child titled, *Are You My Mother?* It's about a little bird that fell out of his nest while his mama went to get food. He goes around to all these different animals and entities asking, "Are you my mother?" The little bird was looking for home. He was looking for where he belonged only to eventually discover none of those were the right fit. It took him a bit of traveling, but eventually, the little bird found his way home to his mama.

I entered different relationships or religious groups in my life much like that little bird asking, "Are you my mother?" Are you where I belong? Do you know what love is? Have you learned how to become it? Each time I would walk away, sorely disappointed, as most of them only seemed capable of loving those that looked like, talked like, and acted like them. Those who didn't color in the parameters of their worksheet seemed to find themselves being ultimately shamed in the corner.

And yet, I loved them all. I was fascinated by them all. Their differences, their unique perspectives, their cultures, and all of their desires to try to be better and do better. There also seemed to be a common ingredient amongst them all, to do their best to please their God. And sometimes in order to do that it meant judging or shaming others. But I could even understand them. I had been there once too. It's hard to blame someone when in their heart they believe they are doing the right thing.

I was legalistic once. It didn't really happen on purpose. It was derived out of fear. Fear of not pleasing God, fear of going to hell if I didn't perform well or get all the rules right, and fear of not being loved unconditionally if I didn't follow all the conditions. So, I was relentless about learning all the rules and getting everything right. Sure it made me feel uneasy, doubtful, worried, and constantly stressed out that if I didn't find the whole truth or exact instructions I would be left behind, or worse punished, and sure that feeling was exhausting, was making me sick, and was separating me from people that I love, but in my heart I was trying to do my best. I thought I was doing the right thing.

Today I'm in a much different space, but I have compassion for the legalistic folks. Most of them are just trying to please their God and color inside the lines. They genuinely believe there are conditions to God's love for them, and as a result, they live their lives with a sincere need to get it perfect and follow of all the rules. I know. I get it. I've been there. Religion and my various travels through her different groups has played a massive role in my ability to say, "So long, people-pleasing" for good, but first before I articulate that, let's take a glimpse into what I love the most about a few of them.

I've love the Baptist, because no one can be there for you in a difficult time like a Baptist. They offer so much more than just a casserole for every crisis. Some see them as too structured, too traditional, and too stuck in their ways. I see them as having this consistency and dependability about them that makes you feel the comfort of security and home. I can walk into any Baptist church right now and know they'll be feeding you on Wednesday nights, planning for their next Vacation Bible School, and hosting a women's Bible study. I know there will be choir practice, Sunday school, and the comfort of those sweet soulful hymns. These folks can literally cook you out of grief one loving potluck at a time. Baptists are beautiful. I could also throw the Methodists in with this lot.

They are foundation builders. I owe most of the virtues that were instilled in my heart as a child from the beautiful lessons I learned within the walls of the Baptist and Methodist church.

I love the Pentecostals, because hey, let's just face it, when the crap hits the fan, these are the people who know how to bring out the oil and start scattering the demons. Need a tangible touch of God and a little electric jolt to shift you into a new place in your life? These are your people. There's nothing like a little T.D. Jakes when you need to victory dance your way to a breakthrough. When you feel the whole world is out to get you and need some spiritual confidence, make your way to the alter of a Pentecostal church, and I guarantee you that you will never be the same. One of the most impactful, transformative seasons of life was spent with these beautiful souls. As a result of my Baptist upbringing and my speaking in tongues, there's no doubt I could definitely fall into the category of a solid Bapticostal.

I love Mormons because no one can do family like the Mormons. They have big families and big values, and I mean let's get real, no one is more committed to recruiting for their cause than the Mormons and the Jehovah Witnesses. They are diligent to be missionaries for what they believe in, and I can admire that.

I'm a pretty passionate gal, and when I love something, I really love it. I'm not one to just preach bits and pieces.

I love Hindus too. They are so beautiful and loving in their appreciation and respect for every human and every creature. I love how they live their lives, believing every action has an opposite and equal reaction. They genuinely live their lives doing unto others as they would have others do unto them. This is their creed, and they live by it. They are kind and gentle, peaceful and giving. They value ancient truths and have tremendous respect for their gurus and teachers, reverencing them as being vessels of the Divine. I am incredibly drawn to these gorgeous souls. The wisdom I have gleaned from studying their beliefs is still profoundly impacting me and moving me towards greater goodness and respect for all.

I love the New Age folks. They are the coolest hippies I know. I say that with a huge grin on my face. I see them working so diligently to transmute their egos, heal the planet, and raise their consciousness. All that shedding of negative beliefs, inner child work, and smudging must be working to some degree, because these guys are some of the most humble, relaxed, accepting, and peaceful people that I've had the privilege of knowing. They believe everything in nature holds a purpose, including the animals, the crystals, the stones, and the plants. You can find them hugging trees and hugging people. Gosh, they're just the best. Love those little hippies. New Age is simply Old Age. The truths there are practically timeless and woven into every religion on the planet.

I love the Native Americans. There's this ancient, spiritual old-world knowledge about them that's so esoterically intriguing. They remind me the most of what the Israelites may have actually looked like. They live in tribes, they love smoke, and rituals, and seem to be led by words of wisdom, the laws of sweet Mother Nature, and the Great Spirit that guides us all. They are mystical and magical in a way that is mesmerizing and stunningly beautiful. They show respect to all life, including our beloved animals. They are unique, and they have persevered under the most unjust of circumstances. I especially enjoy reading quotes by Native American spiritual guides. They are rich, deep, and profound. They always shift me, and they always lift me. If I ever need healing there is no doubt, I'll be looking for a Native American Shaman, mixed of course with a little Pentecostal alter call, some New Age inner child work and chakra balancing, and a Baptist baked casserole dish. I'll sample it all, please. And believe me . . . I have.

The reality is that I could go on and on about all the religions and why I've discovered beauty in the hearts of all those that practice them. I see things about each of them that are terribly wrong and out of alignment, and I also see things that are so beautiful that they bring tears to my eyes and warmth to my soul. I believe there is some truth and healing in them all. I also believe they each have their broken parts simply because we are all to some degree, broken vessels in need of mending. I suppose I tend to want to focus on what I love instead of that which I disapprove.

My "baby bird journey" through the various religious groups in my life ultimately served to provide me with the greatest liberation from people-pleasing. I began my journey wanting to be a good little Christian. I preached harder than anyone. I'm a pretty passionate gal, and when I love something, I really love it. I'm not one to just preach bits and pieces. Give me the whole meal, and I'll disperse the whole lot of it. But something happened to me the deeper I immersed myself, and the more intimate God placed his hands into my heart. The more shattering and breaking my life endured, the less desire I had for preaching, and the more desire I had for loving. The more grace and kindness I felt fall from the heart of the Divine into my soul, the more that love consumed me. Ultimately, it was all that was left. And after experiencing that, my mission has become to spend the rest of my life, giving that love to others. There is no longer a need to qualify the recipients of it, nor do I need to know what the circumstances of their lives are at any particular time. I am enamored with feeling their heart and looking into the depths of their soul as I peer into their eyes. I want to help heal as many as I can with that love. Quite honestly, it no longer matters to me what someone believes or what they have done or even what they are currently doing. Everyone is worthy to know that love, and I have found that when I release it without condition, I am freer, I am happier, and I am in alignment with who I believe with all my heart God has destined me to be.

Because I chose love, I also lost "followers." Some people simply need you to look like them, talk like them, believe like them, and minister to the world around you exactly like them. They need you to stay in their box where they are comfortable. But I wasn't meant to color within the lines or stay in anyone's box, nor was I meant to stay spiritually in a corner with my nose against the wall for the rest of life. I was not preaching the way some wanted me to preach. I start being more like Jesus instead of simply preaching him. The thing is, I'll talk to anyone, and quite frankly, I don't care if it's a scandalous woman sitting at a well or a "Samaritan" from a different sect or religious belief system that I'm not technically supposed to mingle with according to the religious law-keepers. Who am I to determine which hearts have found redemption? Sorry, a life within borders is not my kind of pretty. I'm not intimidated by being best friends with someone who is different from me. In fact, I'll get a little intimate with them. What others have left on the side of the road, I'm totally fine nursing back to health and paying for their spiritual, medical expenses. I'd rather serve a "Samaritan," someone that believes differently than me, than spend valuable time trying to convert them, change them, or point out all the ways they are living their life in a manner that's going to send them straight to hell. No, thank you. I'd rather just heal them and help them and keep my opinions to myself unless asked for them. But who knows, maybe that potent dose of love poured over them consistently will begin to rub off on them. Maybe it will ultimately help do something to change their heart for the better. Maybe that love will create more love. Nonetheless, I'm so filled to overflow that I've got to pour it on someone. It has to come out. It just has to.

Here's the thing. Life has taught me that people are going to judge you. They just are. They have their beliefs, and sadly, a lot of those beliefs are bigger than their love for you. Those beliefs will cause them to sometimes separate from you and reject you. But they are just beliefs. I have had people walk away from me because I stopped validating their beliefs and ministering to the world around me like they needed me to so they could feel comfortable and secure. I stopped fitting into their box. And just like when I was five years old, standing in that corner, I've felt misunderstood, and I've wanted to justify myself to those naysayers who have desperately needed me to look exactly like them.

Sometimes people fear what they don't understand. They may distance them-selves from you if you take a road less traveled. Hey, you're not alone. Even Jesus Christ could relate to this dilemma.

People behave this way because of fear, because when you are secure in your relationship with the Divine, you're not afraid of anyone. You're not worried their demons are going to rattle or shake your faith, nor or you afraid of them pulling you away from it. The love inside of you is too profound. It's too deep. It's too solid. It's not going anywhere. That connection is so real and true that you can sit down with anybody and have a cup of coffee un-triggered by their choices, their beliefs, or the circumstances of their life that may not look like what you believe is best for them. That love will just relax you. It keeps you in a sim-plistic peace that allows you to smile at people you don't agree with. And it's a genuine smile. It's a smile and a glance in the eyes that says, "Hey, I love you no matter what. I'm not angry with you. I'm not disappointed in you. I'm here for you anytime you need me to be. Your demons are not stronger than my angels. I'll sit here till you wrestle through them all. I think your mess is kind of pretty actually, because I'm not looking at where you've been. I'm looking at where you're destined to be." That's the kind of love that overtakes people with a good-ness that transforms the hearts of mankind. Nothing can defeat it. It's the ultimate weapon. It weakens all defenses. It scatters any darkness.

Love conquers all.

So, here's the thing. If you can love someone who believes differently than you, then you deserve that same love in your life as well. You are worthy of the love you are capable of giving to others. So, if someone needs to judge you or walk away from you, because you currently don't fit their bill of approval, let them walk. Their love just isn't big enough yet. And that's ok. It may take a bit more brokenness before they can understand that in the end all that will remain is love. If they have taught their rules and yet failed to know and teach love, they will have missed the ultimate mark.

I've had people leave my life, because I started being more positive, less judgmental, and less religious. Maybe it was because I had friends outside of my belief system, or maybe it was because I was having conversations with strangers at a neighborhood bar instead of the weekly Bible study group. Maybe it was because I stopped preaching the Bible so much. I guess I made a decision to just start being what I thought the message was supposed to convey. I also started working to fix myself instead of making it my job to try and fix everyone else. Fixing me has managed to become a full-time job and believe me when I say that it keeps me plenty busy.

Jesus Christ spent most of his ministry teaching me how to live in this world and how to mentally, emotionally, and physically overcome it. That was his message, and I suppose it has also become mine. I'm not really focusing on trying to save people from a future version of hell. I'm focusing on helping them to mentally and physically deliver themselves from the hell they're currently existing in. I want them to find that glorious kingdom that's not just somewhere they're going when they escape this world. I want to them find that inner safe haven, that glorious inner beauty that is a kingdom all its own. I want to help them not need to leave here to find their heaven, but truly learn how to bring heaven here—into the hearts of mankind. And there are a lot of little practical lessons and ways our life experiences can yield us wisdom that teach us the way to truly live in this super special and sacred inner kingdom of peace, light, and unconditional, transformative love.

I could spend the rest of my life literally obsessed with what people think about me. If I let it, it could paralyze me. I could spend the rest of my life trying to prove my connection to the Divine or my spiritual worth to the naysayers who continually go around plucking specks from people's eyes while literally blinded by their own planks. But these people are wasting the valuable time God has given them to look inward and heal what's broken and distorted within their own hearts and souls. What they have failed to see is the problem is not outside of them. All wars and unbalance in this world stem from the desires that battle within the hearts of mankind. If people would focus inward and begin working to heal their own shattered pieces—their own judgments, their own anger, resentfulness, bitterness, self-righteousness, their own lack of humility, and lack of love for all their brothers and sisters—real progress might actually begin to happen for this world.

> *"Religion that God our Father accepts as pure and faultless is this:*
> *to look after orphans and widows in their distress and to keep*
> *oneself from being polluted by the world."*
> (James 1:27)

The above passage is supposed to be the true religion; oh, but no, this will not suffice for some people. Instead, they've made it their mission to save the world instead of learning to save themselves. They're not focused on keeping themselves unpolluted by the darkness of the world. They have to go around pointing out how everyone else needs to get unpolluted from it.

Every day I read thousands of energetic thoughts streaming from the hearts of those surrounding me. "Why does she feel the need to record these videos? Who does she think she is? I mean hasn't she been divorced twice? That should definitely disqualify her from teaching me anything. She looks like a hot mess to me. Does she really think she has some kind of spiritual wisdom to share with the world? Oh, my gosh, look at her. What is she wearing? Did you see her dancing at that concert she went to? Was she drinking alcohol? Oh, my goodness. She's probably out of control. You know her mom and stepdad died last year. She's probably just escaping and needing some kind of attention and emotional validation. Bless her heart. I bet she's having some kind of nervous breakdown. She's too positive. She's not sharing enough hell, fire, and brimstone. She must have fallen away from the Lord. She let her daughter color her hair blue? I heard she's going to Mardi Gras parties. She must be going to hell in a handbasket. I mean, I occasionally have a glass wine at dinner, but I would never be authentic enough to post it on social media. What is she doing?"

Do you get the point? Ya'll, listen. You have nothing to prove. Don't waste the valuable time that you could be serving those that are genuinely seeking by running around trying to convince everyone that you are trying to provide spiritual food for hungry souls. The people out there that are starving don't give a flying flip about all that crap. They are salivating for the nourishment your soul has gleaned, and they are practically begging for you to pour it over them.

You know who you are. You know the Divine connection you have. You know that beautiful Spirit that consumes you, fills you, and loves you so freaking ridiculously that you cannot help but fall in love with its goodness and want to radically change yourself for the better. Stop wasting your energy trying to defend that to people that can't see it.

If you've never experienced that kind of love, stick around me a little bit longer, and I'll freaking give you a bath it. You'll get immersed. You'll experience a metamorphosis, and I guarantee you that you will fly. It may take you a while. You might want to fight against it a little longer. But whether you get it from hanging around me or not, the fact that you are reading this book right now is evidence that this love is coming for you and is going to continue coming for you till the day you die and then some. Why? Because you've cried for it, and heaven is listening to your soul. This love will never fail to be there for you. Ever. Because it's inside of you waiting to be discovered. And when you feel like you least deserve it, it will be there for you even more.

So maybe there is a little darkness left in your heart, or maybe you even feel it's completely statured in it. Not a problem. Do you know what travels faster than the speed of light? Darkness when it encounters the Light. So, stand next to someone who knows love and who knows how to unconditionally pour it over you, and watch the fruit that grows and comes off your vine. It will be rich, and it will nourish those who pluck it with a life-giving healing balm that can literally raise them from the dead. It can lift them from the absolute depths of despair and place them upon the highest mountain peaks. This fruit will produce kindness, goodness, gentleness, faithfulness, and self-control within you. It will give you hope when everything around you appears hopeless. It will produce love, because it was cultivated and birthed from having been shown love. And if that fruit isn't good enough to convince someone you are an Ambassador for the kingdom of light, let them go. Let them mentally go. Let them physically go. Let them remain in the dark.

Stop judging. Start loving.

Maybe that girl posting all those selfies is finally learning to love herself. Maybe she's not superficial or too into herself, or narcissistic as you may have judged her to be. Maybe she's looked in that camera lens all her life and hated what she has seen. Maybe she has previously hidden herself away from the world and now she is loving what's in front of her. Maybe she's finally seeing her reflection in the mirror and has stopped judging herself so harshly. Maybe she was once skinny and to the outside world she appeared weightless but never felt more weighed down. And maybe she gained some weight, because she needed that journey—because it was easy to love herself when she felt like she was a perfect picture for the world. But now she is learning to love herself when she's not that idea of physical or perhaps even spiritual perfection. And maybe she finally feels confident enough to share that beauty with the world. So be nice. Like her photo. One day she may not need to post those selfies anymore. Or maybe she will, because it makes her happy. Quite frankly, it's not your responsibility to determine if she's worthy of your love or respect. It's your responsibility to simply give it. That love will ensure she gets sorted out and where she needs to be. This is assuming she's not exactly where she needs to be, which we humans like to determine for one another way too impulsively.

Look, you're never going to please all these people. Never, ever, ever. As soon as you make one group happy, you're going to make another group miserable. So, freaking emancipate yourself from that big old load of stinky manure. Be yourself. Stop trying to color inside their lines. Stop trying to be like them. For all you know, they could have it wrong. And maybe they don't have it wrong for them, but maybe their right is your wrong. Maybe they need one path, and you need another. You can climb a mountain lots of different ways and still make it to the top to appreciate the view.

Follow your Inner Voice. Let God lead you personally and directly. You may have less likes on your Facebook wall for daring to scribble outside the lines or perhaps daring to use paint instead of crayons, but you will be flippin' happy as a clam. "And why are clams happy?" you might ask. Where did the expression come from? Clams have to be dug when the tide is low. They're almost impossible to find in high tide, and it's too dangerous to venture too far out into deep water looking for them. Clams are happy at high tide, because they aren't in danger of being made into a meal. So look here, if you want to feel safe and secure and happy as a little clam, stay in high tide, my friends. Keep it happy, keep the vibes high, and stay away from negative Nellies that like to linger in low tides and low vibes. These people want to eat you alive, and they will if you let them.

Clam up! Trust me, you're happiness is more valuable to you than their approval. Keep shining! Keep living! And by all means, keep loving!

Dear Protestors

Dear Protestors,

Sometimes we can care so much about making things better that
we fail to let things go and simply allow them to be better.

TAKE A STEP BACK AND FEEL THE POWER THAT CREATES WORLDS. Notice what the improvement in your vibration will yield to you. If you need to protest, be that on your Facebook wall, in a street, or perhaps at home with your family via withdrawal of affection, loudly expressed opinions, or just the good ole' fashioned over-extended offerings of the silent treatment, you have forgotten your power as well as how to utilize it. You must make your emotional reality more important than what's happening in the world around you.

Whatever you are giving your attention to is gaining momentum and getting bigger. By speaking about what you don't want, you are giving more and more life to it. Not to mention you are adding a victim mentality to your vibration, which has now become your point of attraction. This will, in turn, yield more life experiences to affirm your role as the victim.

You are baking your spiritual "life cake." The ingredients you are putting into the bowl right now are going to determine what your future will look like. If you are speaking word curses by calling someone horrible names or secretly wishing they get what they deserve, you are sowing the same exact measure into your own field.

If you want a different experience, you must offer a vibration that stops bringing you a belligerent experience. If your emotions are all over the place, stop and fix them. Realign yourself to a higher truth. Remind yourself of who you are and, most importantly, whose you are. Know God. Know thyself and perhaps simultaneously forget thyself, because it's in becoming less that we achieve more. It's in being brought low that we are exalted higher.

Surrender the will of the ego-self, which includes your need to be right. Attention to your problems is only making them more prominent. Instead of a protest, consider a day of silence during which you stop talking about what's wrong, who's wrong, and stop giving attention to the negative emotions you are carrying. Take time to put some energy into what you do want.

The thing that is keeping you from where you want
to be is your focus on where you are.

When the doctor called to tell me there was a cerebral cavernous malformation in my brain stem, I knew what had to be done. If I was going to utilize the power at work within me, I had to cooperate by not working against the natural flow of this Universe.

I had to stop looking at what was if I was
to position myself to see what could be.

How far we are from anything we want is based on how good we feel about it. When you broadcast to the world your negative emotions, you pave the way for a bountiful harvest of negative experiences.

Whatever it is you are wanting, your world or this world to become, whatever it is you are asking God to supply is given the moment you ask. Esther Hicks teaches to ask, and it is given, period. She once said after that part, it is 99% done; but it can stay undone forever. You must master yourself. You must stop complaining. You must bring your emotions and vibration into alignment with what you want to see occur.

You cannot look at what is and change it.

Your Inner Being is always in alignment. It is always at peace and never feels like a victim in need of protesting anything. But you can be separated from it. You can be acting as if the frequency you are emitting is not enough to change your reality. You can be behaving like you have forgotten you are using your free will to create your environment. You can be choosing to see racism, hate, and hypocrisy instead of immersing yourself in the blissful emotions of love, unity, and peace. What ingredients have you put in your cake? What seeds are you sowing in your field?

Your life is your field, and you are the farmer.

Who knows? While you're attending your protest and talking about why you're unhappy, others could be ascending all around you, becoming like unto the angels, achieving the very thing you truly desire. They may be in the same world you are in, experiencing the same mass consciousness, sitting under the same president, but because of what they have chosen to give their focus to, they are living heaven on earth.

The kingdom you are searching for that you say you wish to experience, that you say you want the world to experience, is already here. Some are already living it. They were living it when life wasn't perfect, when the person they voted for president didn't win, when they were told terrible news, and when earthly things weren't going as planned. When they were poor, they were rich. When they needed their voice to be heard, they were echoing through the fabric of their being, "Be still and know that I am God."

If you judge people, you have no time to love them. When you judge people, including that person who really gets under your skin, you are only bringing more judgment upon yourself. These are the laws of the Universe. May I suggest you choose to love yourself by not judging others. May I suggest you learn to place your intention upon one thought,

"Only good can come to me, and only good can come from me."

If you allowed your vibration to settle into this beautiful place, you would no longer feel the need to organize that protest or finish your long Facebook rant.

Do you believe all things, as in all things, as in even whatever is happening in our country, is working for your good? You chose to be born at this time in history for a reason. I'm guessing you and God in your perfected oneness knew this experience might just be the exact one you needed to expand and grow. My advice is to spend more time determining what this moment in time is here to teach you versus spending it name-calling and gathering in the streets with like-minded people who do the same. Perhaps consider staying home, enjoy some profoundly beautiful meditation, and reach for a higher mind and a higher truth.

Reconnect with the Source of your being and allow the Spirit of Truth to guide you in how to create bliss for yourself despite any physical circumstances. It is possible! You choose your emotions. Perhaps it's time to choose something better.

You can't focus on what you don't want and
what you do want at the same time.

Choose wisely.

Everything you are against weakens you.
Everything you are for empowers you.
~ Wayne Dyer

Happy harvesting!

The Ignorance of Racism

RACISM HAS TO BE ONE OF THE MOST IGNORANT CONCEPTS still lingering in the world today. When we leave this hemisphere, our bodies are not equipped to withstand an atmosphere we were not created to endure. As a result, we see astronauts wearing space suits and oxygen helmets. When we are born into this world, we put on a suit called a body. This body allows us to interact with this physical dimension, to touch, feel, smell, taste, and hear. This is why the mind and Spirit of Christ had to take on a human body to interact physically with this lower dimension. This is also why when we leave this world, we shed our body having no more use for it and are like unto the angels.

Racism is like entering space with someone and saying to them, "I don't like your spacesuit. Your suit is red, and my suit is blue." What difference does it make? This ideology would be ignorant and insane because, under their suits, they are exactly the same. Underneath their suits, they are both human beings.

The next time you look at someone's "space suit" a.k.a. their body, and don't like it because it's different than yours, keep in mind you both came from the same Source. You were both created by the same God. Underneath the body, we are all human beings that stem from the same stream of Life.

Dear Mr. Homeless Man

DEAR MR. HOMELESS MAN,

It doesn't matter what you did. It doesn't matter what was done to you. In this moment, it doesn't matter to me the circumstance that brought you here nor the circumstance that's keeping you nestled on this cold city street. All I know is that I love you. When I look at you, I am moved and stirred with a deep well of love overflowing for you. I want to come sit with you, clothe you, and feed you till you are full. I want to smile at you. I want to chat with you for a little bit, perhaps for as long as you need. Something inside of me just wants to be your friend, your Good Samaritan. I want to be the best I can be for you while the chips are down for you. I feel a strength rise within me to believe for you, perhaps when you can no longer believe for or in yourself.

I feel an added dose of grace and mercy deposited in my heart for you. I see your brokenness. Perhaps you see me dressed in fine clothing, combed hair, and a full belly and yet you also see my brokenness. How do you see the world, my friend? Maybe you feel at peace; maybe you feel you have all you need, and you traded all the comforts I currently possess to search for something greater. Maybe a sleep on the street is better than a sleep in a comfortable bed of tear-stained pillows.

I don't know what's inside of you or what sits behind those sleepy eyes. But I know there is a soul there, a treasure amidst the heap of trash that may surround you. Those ragged clothes can't hide its sparkle. I see the spark nestled there, and I want to come breathe on it—stir it and stoke the fire of it. There is a Light there that has dimmed, but hey Mr. Homeless man, there is a potential within you to illuminate an entire city. You have already shined a truth into my heart. You gave me a moment of feeling deep, limitless love today. Thank you for that. You touched me in a way no one else in this city was able to touch me. I am you, and you are me. I've always had shelter, my friend, but I know what it's like to feel like I don't have a home. Perhaps this is why our sweet Jesus couldn't find a place in this world to lay his head. Maybe home is not a place. Maybe home is like the bread of heaven, a substance not tangible or of this world, a spiritual food beyond the delicacies assembled by human hands.

Dear Mr. Homeless Man, I hope you've found your home. I hope you've found it deep within your beautiful heart. I hope it's really pretty in there. I hope it feels warm and inviting. I hope you turn the Light on so people can see you are welcoming them to come and sit and break bread with you. I hope they find comfort in your home. I hope your heart leaves them rested and having received the best of hospitality.

Dear Mr. Homeless Man, I hope that just like heaven, just like that glorious Kingdom, home has found its way to a deep abiding place within your heart. I love you, Mr. Homeless Man. I love you very much. You are as royal to me, perhaps even more so, than those who wear the suits and crowns and often broken smiles of this world. You've lived. You've learned. You've succeeded. You've failed. Your experience is a treasure trove. You've learned compassion and humility. You've gleaned all the good stuff. I may have a purse fat and heavy, but if I have not obtained these precious gems, I've obtained nothing along my journey. Perhaps you are wealthier than me, Mr. Homeless Man. Perhaps I should be honored to someday sit amidst the heavens and feast with you at the table of a King.

Sleep well, Mr. Homeless Man.

Until we meet again,
Misti Rains

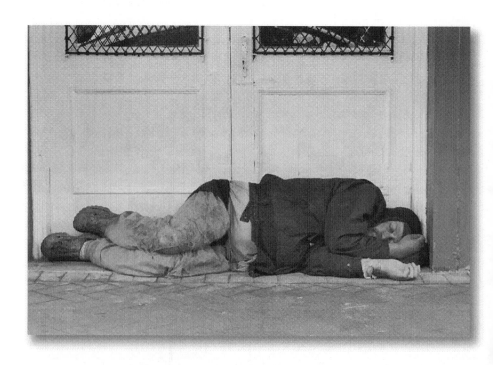

Dear Mr. Guru

Dear Mr. Guru,

You've got this all wrong. There's a reason you spend most of your time alone. There's a reason you welcome lots of visitors, but none stay with you for very long. Your students are short-lived for a reason. The ego you enjoy telling everyone you have transcended is massively in your way. While quick to see the shortcomings and limitations in others, you have failed to see them in yourself. In fact, you still think the reason you are emotionally alone is that everyone else is the problem. In your mind, they are the ones who haven't arrived. They are the ones who are still becoming. They are the ones who aren't seeing clearly. Your truth is the only truth, Mr. Guru, and this is your problem.

You love telling people that they can't hear, or they aren't listening, meanwhile you haven't stopped talking to listen to anyone but yourself. You always see yourself in the teacher role; therefore, you never empty your cup to receive what "the student" was there to teach you! This is your first clue that you are not the guru you think you have become. You have failed to acknowledge that the common ingredient in all your failed relationships is you. You still blame others for your isolation. People walked away from you rolling their eyes for a reason, and it wasn't as you viewed it. It wasn't because they were rebellious or stubborn and not ready to receive the deep soul wisdom you think you have acquired.

You have a lofty mind and are puffed up. You martyr yourself allowing yourself to think you are more enlightened than others. You think that your journey and your story is more special than the students you wish to teach. A true guru doesn't need a title or recognition, Mr. Guru. A true guru makes himself least. He has but one title, that of servant.

You spend so much time talking about yourself, your strengths, and your story that you fail to use the valuable time with your students to speak to who they are, to their story, and to their strengths. Quite simply, Mr. Guru, it's all about you. Your ego is still wanting to be validated. You brag about who you think you are, but a lion will never have to tell you it's a lion.

You are easily offended, easily angered, and you quickly walk away when you don't get your way. Your motives are still selfish, but you can't see this. You are quick to defend how unselfish and enlightened you are, but if you still feel the need to constantly explain and defend yourself, you most assuredly have not transcended your ego.

You tell people how heart-centered you are in all you do, but you never absorb any healthy advice or critique. You rarely listen to your students when they try to explain what they need, because you are too busy thinking of what you are going to say next. You are too busy defending how wonderful and perfect you are. You are blind, Mr. Guru. It has never occurred to you that what you deem to be your student has come to be your teacher.

You have been controlling, Mr. Guru. You have imposed your opinions on others. You have sought to gain more exposure and to capitalize on the networks of your students. Get honest with yourself, Mr. Guru. The moment your students stood up for themselves or opposed your guidance in any way, you withdrew from them. You punished them with either your disapproval or absence. You are quick to abandon any student who is unwilling to do exactly as you say. You get frustrated when they seek wisdom from other sources besides you. You want them to follow your voice and your voice alone, because you believe your way is the only way. You are ignorant, Mr. Guru. Your wisdom is still limited. Your perspective is not the only perspective. The path to the top of the mountain is not singular. There are many ways by which one can reach the summit. The road you carved was your road. You are close-minded to assume someone else cannot forge their own unique path to the top. Stop telling people how they must arrive at your conclusions. A true guru supports their students in finding their own answers, and they aren't intimidated when their students are wiser and more connected to the Divine. They aren't blinded to this notion either.

Perhaps you have found truth, Mr. Guru, but truth without love is nothing. Your Spirit is weak. You have not been discerning. You may have truth, but your students had the Divine Spirit. They had heart. You taught laws, rules, and regulations. You knew them better than anyone. You stuck to the script and the letter of the law. But you were void of being able to discern and hear with your Spirit. And without both Spirit and truth, there is no pure guidance. You must never teach your laws, Mr. Guru, without teaching God's unconditional love. You are still in your head and have failed to be led by your heart. You guide with intellect and not love. This is why many of your students who come with an open heart and open mind leave because you have managed to keep yours closed. Your supposedly transcended ego is too big to allow room for anyone to be smarter than you. Your ego is suffocating, Mr. Guru. This is why so many genuine seekers leave to catch their breath.

I notice how you like to tell everyone how special and gifted you are, Mr.

Guru. I notice how you fail to mention your mistakes, or you always reference them in past tense. You don't want to admit you are still learning and still capable of occasionally getting it wrong. This would mean you aren't the perfectly enlightened guru that your ego needs to believe that it is. This would mean your students would see you as not being the God-like figure that is important for your ego character to project. You don't want your students to see any chinks in your armor lest they discover you are as they are and see you as their equal. This would mean you can't sit in your seat of superiority, which you so desperately need, and have strived to obtain. You are not one to sit at a round table as an equal with the students you deem as immature to the mighty ideals and state of being you have acquired. How could a mere child speak more wisdom or carry a higher vibration than you? Yet, the child has nothing to prove as you do, Mr. Guru. The child is simply content with being the student. The child is happy to learn. The child

The path to the top of the mountain is not singular. There are many ways by which one can reach the summit.

understands he or she will make mistakes and is satisfied just being included in the classroom of life. The child isn't seeking status. The child is there to love and be loved. The child is seeking insight with a divine curiosity that is innocent and pure. The child doesn't see himself as the teacher, but the child is most definitely there to instruct the teacher. Only a true Master Teacher can see this, because the enlightened say, "Let the little children come to me," not because He seeks to teach them, but because in His wisdom, the true Guru knows He stands to benefit from the child.

The immature guru will always have a perspective that he is better than his students. He struggles to acknowledge and see the student as a master in their own right. Mr. Guru, your student didn't come to you because he needs another reason to feel small. Life has already dealt him those cards. He didn't come to you to be broken down. He sought after you to be built up. He didn't come to be made to feel less than you. He came to be told he can be more than you, that there are no limits to what he can achieve, and that he can exceed your spiritual heights to even greater ones. Is this not how Jesus responded to his disciples, "You can do even greater things than me if you believe you can."

Mr. Guru, you are not here to tell anyone who they are. You aren't here to be their answer. You are here to help them to discover who they are and to show them how to find the answers to their questions for themselves. You aren't here to tell them what to think but to teach them how to think.

Don't give yourself too much credit, Mr. Guru. A true prophet never houses wisdom about anyone that the person doesn't already possess within themselves. You aren't there to receive the glory for revealing something that only came via your direct hotline to heaven. You will never tell anyone something that deep down in their Spirit they don't already know. The true gentle and humble prophet is there to activate the seed of greatness within others, to breathe life into their destiny, and show them what has always been placed inside of them. You are there to water the seed. You are there to empower the student to make that connection for themselves. Step out of your guru role long enough to help others step into theirs, Mr. Guru. Your need to be the one who has all the answers has gotten really old.

Goodbye, Mr. Guru. I don't need you anymore but thank you for your role played well in my soul journey. I appreciate everything you contributed to helping me step into my power. You gave me strength and helped me figure out I didn't need you to help me find something I already possessed within myself. Thanks for the trip down the yellow brick road, Mr. Guru, but this Dorothy has clicked her heels and found her way home.

I wrote this letter more for those who have been victimized by a guru than for the guru himself. The guru, pastor, or teacher that I'm describing above would be too egotistical to identify himself in this letter anyway. I wrote this to the person who has given their power away to this type of person before. Maybe you were deeply searching for truth, and you blindly followed someone in your search for direction and wisdom, and they ended up preying on your desire for knowledge. Perhaps they used it to control you, manipulate you, or even financially bankrupt you. Perhaps they used it to make you question or betray your own Internal Guidance System in order to follow theirs.

Examine the fruit on the vine. In time, true intentions are revealed. If something isn't empowering you, encouraging you, uplifting your Spirit, or listening to you, it's not for you. If someone is teaching you to rely on their voice instead of teaching you how to connect with your own, that's not your teacher. Next!

White Sand Black Sand

*A*S I SIT HERE SWIRLING THE SAND BENEATH MY TOES and between my fingers, I find myself immersed with both the black and white crystals of sand.

Black sand
White sand
They are both sand

They both house a capacity to massage my feet, to bring me comfort, and to absorb the nourishing waters.

I wonder if God looks upon us as these grains of sand. Some are white. Some are black, but both are capable of serving the same purpose. Both are capable of being saturated by the Waters of Life.

As sand drifts back and forth into the ocean waters, it functions as a filter removing particles of algae that could harm the community of living organisms dwelling along our beaches. I suppose you could say lest the grains of sand work together in unison, the community and environment they are protecting will die.

Black sand
White sand
Both are sand

Let us serve as the sands of these beaches. Let us function in unity that we may secure a thriving, life-giving community. Let us realize that although sand comes in different colors, they are the same and were designed to function in unison with a similar purpose.

And like the sand, may we always sparkle in the Light of the magnificent Sun.

Black sand
White sand
Both are sand

Caught on the Blindside

I'M SITTING HERE IN STILLNESS AND REFLECTION LISTENING to a sweet melody in my ears and the whisperings of that beautiful Inner Voice of continued strength and comfort. Today I'm thinking about compassion. Life can be so ridiculously complex with her continued proposals, crossroads, and decisions. Everyone is facing each day with many personal layers of emotions that underlie their journey and their interactions with others. All come with their own set of pressures, conditioning, and heart-piercing attachments.

Life has a way of catching us all on the blindside, leaving us in situations and facing circumstances we never imagined would come our way. What do we do with them? What is the best path? Do we possess what is required to choose what is in the highest and best interest of all? The complexities of life are not easy to sort. Take time to feel into the heart of another. Be kind. Lend compassion. Their current battle may be physical, but it may also reside heavily in the mind, in the emotions, and most difficultly ... in the heart.

Be patient with others as they seek to make those tough choices that keep them on the straight and narrow. When they are prone to venture, be merciful, listen, and gently guide. Sometimes life requires a wayward path and a series of U-turns in order to find the exact destination.

The Way of the Christ

ONE OF THE MANY REASONS I WILL ALWAYS TREASURE my brother and teacher, Jesus Christ, was because of his ability to be peace in the midst of a storm. He never called anyone a disgrace. He never shunned anyone from listening to the truth His Father had revealed to Him regarding this kingdom of heaven He spoke of that He said could be found within us all. He never let someone's religious affiliation, their current lifestyle choices, their race, or their beliefs interfere with His ability to love them, teach them, fellowship with them, or heal them. He was not to be put in a box, and the only ones He opposed were the religious leaders who kept trying to place Him there. Why was that? Had He the ability to see God in all things? Was that how He prayed for those who were hurting Him? Did He know somewhere beneath the layers of paint that had been splattered upon them by their socio-economic backgrounds or their religious programming that there was a blank canvas where the Spirit of Truth hovered and where the force of life existed? Had He too much respect for the sacredness of that Divine Force, that He was willing to give of His own life before He allowed His sword to take the life of another? Though Jesus understood He was wrapped in divinity and recognized the Spirit of Truth within Him, He never made anyone feel less than Him. He wasn't interested in being called a Master. He requested we call Him our friend. He wanted us to know that as He was in the world so were we.

Jesus did not come to convert us.
He came to love us.
That love is transformative.
Jesus did not come to condemn us.
Jesus came to heal us.
He came to walk in our shoes and carry our burdens.
He came to show us a way to salvation,
a way to His beautiful kingdom
that He said was here, in our midst.

May we lay aside our seminary degrees and our Bible-thumping rhetoric and simply be like Jesus to those that don't necessarily fit into our mold or definition of being chosen or elect. May we come like a child as did our precious Christ.

May my life be a beacon of hope for all people. May my life be an icon of compassion for all religions, all nationalities, all backgrounds, and all beliefs. May I rid myself of anything that separates me from those who believe differently than me or look differently than me. May I heal as Jesus did.

May I never judge someone nor see anyone
as unworthy or void of God's touch.

LOVE CONQUERS ALL

Love Will Come for You

*H*APPINESS HAS NOTHING TO DO WITH WHAT YOU HAVE OR DON'T HAVE. Happiness is related to what you are. Life will present her temptations. Crossroads will come. Choices will present themselves to you. Our souls seek true expression and a thirst to be ridiculously free to live our passions and the life of our dreams. Yet, happiness cannot be achieved by compromising integrity. Wait for your circumstances to align in such a way that you aren't required to morally compromise your standards to achieve that which you desire.

Who you are is more important than what you obtain. This life and all her pleasures will come to an end. But how you obtained these pleasures while journeying through this world will remain a part of your soul forever. There is remarkable beauty to be emitted from a soul that makes decisions to deny self for the protection and love of others.

Those who carry the strongest magnetism and attraction are those who walk purely with a deep love for one another. Deceit is not found in them. They choose their own flesh to suffer rather than cause harm to another. These are the angels who walk amongst us, and these luminous ones can recognize one another. They are being transformed from glory to glory, from one moment of beauty to another, from one victory to another, and from one moment of integrity to another.

Trust that when you choose love for others, all of creation and its Creator applauds and promotes you to rewards far superior to this physical world, for there is but one way to the Divine—this is love. We are presented with this decision to love continuously. Often it comes with tremendous sacrifice.

In a moment of speaking, we love by being quiet.
In a moment of justice, we love by offering mercy.
In a moment of anger, we love by yielding a smile.
In a moment of greed, we love by releasing and giving.
In a moment of control, we love by setting something
or someone free.
In a moment of lust, we love by taking a step back.

At the root of all our choices is trust. Trust is creative. Doubt kills. Doubt is poison. Trust gives you life, abundant life, and infinite life, because when you trust, you relax. In trust, there is no fear. In trust, there is no need to defend. In trust, there is no struggle. In trust, there is only happiness.

Thus, temporarily you may not have obtained your desire or the possession you were seeking, because you chose love in order to protect those you could have otherwise wounded. However, ultimately, you chose love for yourself. For in this act of kindness and self-denial you were giving yourself an eternal gift. The selflessness of the heart is greatly rewarded as it was once so profoundly stated, "Greater love hath no man than this that he lay down his life for a friend."

Our daily choices to "lie down" are ultimately
the ones that help us rise up.

Trusting in this truth and the rewards that come with it will bring peace and happiness to the soul. And then, who knows? Given time, the Creator may be so pleased with your selflessness and acts of great love, that He beckons to the Universe moving all of heaven and earth to bring you that which you deeply desire in a way that unravels exceedingly and abundantly above and beyond anything you could have ever hoped or imagined. Then, where you have given love...

love will come for you.

Preach Less, Teach More

I JUST READ A QUOTE BY MOTHER TERESA WHEN RESPONDING to a nurse as they were caring for a man who was dying. When the nurse expressed concern that the man was approaching death Mother Teresa replied, "The greatest suffering is to feel, alone, unwanted, and unloved."

She proceeded to take the man from the small hut in India where he was suffering alone and bring him to her side where she held his hand, placed warm cloths over his brow, and spoke prayers of love over him as he passed.

I'm undone.

May we all love greater. May we express God to the lonely and dying, and may they feel our great empathy and affection for their souls. Mother Teresa never tried to convert anyone to her faith. She never judged the condition of the soul nor their beliefs, failures, or brokenness. She simply loved and offered healing to the sick and poor.

May we preach less and teach more. May we live in such a way that the world knows we house the love of God. May we lay down our notions that anything less than pure love can heal or "convert" a soul to a higher and more gracious path.

When I think telling someone how to live is greater than showing them how to live, I have missed the mark. The world doesn't need my words. They need the love through which inspired them to come forth.

Remind yourself that you are a vessel of God's most magnificent Light, and your purpose is to be love to all as God is love to all. If something, anything, causes a dimness in your Light, consider lying it aside or turning it off. This includes FOX, CNN, or your Facebook newsfeed.

Before we speak, before we teach, before we write, before we post, before we think, let us stop and breathe.

Just breathe.

Often it is the reminder from the Breath of Life that creates a stillness and humble calm amongst us all.

Breathe deep, my dear friends.

Love Period

IF GOD HOLDS EVERYTHING TOGETHER AND GOD IS LOVE, then Love is what holds everything together. It's what holds us together. Therefore, we mustn't be surprised when we fail to love in any given situation or circumstance that we begin to see things fall apart. Not only do our relationships begin to break down due to lack of loving properly, but we begin to collapse when we don't love ourselves properly.

So, let's get it together.
Let's keep it together.
Let's love properly.
Let's Love.
Period.

With all the issues going on in the world right now and all the things that could separate and divide us, there is a common thread that binds us all...love.

Love for one another.

We tend to want to focus on the sadness and depravity of this world that is so often repeatedly reported through the media. Yet, look at the good springing forth like a gushing fountain from the hearts of those around you.

Today I saw a mental image of all this love being absorbed and poured into a bottle until it was so full it could no longer be capped. The bottle exploded and began to spray all over the room—similar to when a bottle of champagne opens and bursts into a room full of cheerful people ready to celebrate a special occasion.

I began to imagine all this love was stored inside of a rocket, and I sent the rocket into war-torn areas, riots, protests, and straight to the heart of the various governments around the world. The rocket continued blasting into homes and most importantly into hearts. I saw a miniature version of this bottled love aimed directly to the malformation in my brain stem. I also sent it to others I know who are struggling with illness both in their body and those with hurts that are wounding their soul. I filled the rocket with love and sent it forth with an intention to heal the fears humanity has carried on their shoulders for far too long.

Love One Another

Could it be that simple? Is this the highest truth? Could there be an unlocking fountain of healing and restorative power for ourselves and our world by following three simple words?

The love you offer another is like being wrapped in a warm blanket on a cold, winter's night. It's the life raft when you feel you are drowning. I pray we all do this one simple thing more and more.

Love.
Why?
Because love CONQUERS ALL.

Keep sending your rockets of love. They are locked and loaded and aimed straight for the heart. You need them. The earth needs them. Mankind needs them.

Blast off!
Let the healing begin!

Love Does Not

LOVE DOES NOT APPEAR TO BE NICE AND CONCERNED for you in public but makes your life a living hell behind the scenes.

Loves does not lie.

Love does not steal from you.

Love does not steal from children.

Love does not destroy.

Love is authentic. It is not fake.

Love doesn't control you. Love frees you.

Love does use you for its own pride and validation.

Love is secure.

Love does not yell at you.

Love shows self-control.

Love controls its temper.

Love speaks life.

Love does not isolate you from people who love and care about you.

Love protects people above worldly assets.

Love does not threaten you.

Love is not constantly criticizing and critiquing you.

Love covers. It does not expose.

Love displays good fruit.

Love is not just words that sound good. Love is action demonstrated.

Love is more than financial provision. It is emotional and spiritual provision.

Love listens.

Love listens to what you say you need.

Love does not withdraw affection to punish or control you.

Love helps you in your time of need.

Love makes you feel safe.

Love makes you feel heard.

Loves does not ask you to compromise your moral standards.

Love is not jealous.

Love is not suffocating.

Love tells the whole truth and not just a fraction of the truth.

Loves does not lie to deny its own guilt.

Discernment is one of the greatest gifts God has ever given us. It helps us determine what love is. Sometimes it can take time to see fruit and to decipher whether or not that fruit has produced something that is nurturing us, healing us, or hurting us. At some point, we have to ask ourselves, is the fruit this person or circumstance is producing in my life causing me to wither or thrive? Is being around this person or being in this situation causing me to lose myself or do I feel more empowered? Is this stealing my energy or breathing life into my frame?

Counterfeits are deceptive. Only time can reveal truth. Remember wheat and tares look exactly the same until the time of harvest. Only then can you see which is the tare housing a poison that when eaten, puts you to sleep.

We can smile through the pain and hurt. The most vulnerable seem to tolerate and withstand the most. But there comes the point when we must ask, how does this person make me feel? Do I find myself expending massive amounts of energy to try and maintain internal peace? How much energy are you exhausting to try and keep the peace in your relationship? Is that person making you feel valuable in public but worthless behind the scenes? Do you watch them speak one way to people's faces and another in private? How much are you willing to withstand on a daily basis that is not in alignment with who you truly are. How much are your peace and sanity worth?

Protect yourself! Care about yourself! Wake up! Stop accepting disrespect. You deserve to be adored.

A Shovel, a River, and a Compass Called Love

IN A SEASON OF SELF-DISCOVERY, I TOOK MANY EBBS AND FLOWS as I followed the internal movements within the fibers of my heart. Somewhere along my journey, the various paths got mixed up, disjointed, and moved in directions they were never intended to flow. The rivers divided, crossed, and confusion flooded my heart. I lost my way.

The rivers, at times, ran dry and I imagined I would be stuck forever with no ability to reach my destination. I found myself in horrid rapids, and as they beat violently against my canoe, I felt as if I would surely drown. There have been many moments of calm, yet the waters were still full of devouring creatures waiting on me to give up so they could rip and tear at my flesh. I found myself in twisters that spun my boat in circles, and sometimes, my raft would be taken and lost. I was left swimming all alone with my only hope in a merciful Savior to lift me from the waters.

Where was the River I knew existed deep within? The one that did not split or divide, the River of Peace, a solo ordained path free of confusion and alternatives. Where was this steady drifting? Sure, it too had its bumps and climbs, even waterfalls that dropped to insurmountable depths, but the course remained solid and secure. It was a narrow way that was sure of its destination. This River, unlike the others, was a Compass for the Soul.

At first, the other rivers seemed more adventurous, exciting, more fulfilling, and more inviting. However, once upon them, it was discovered they led to jagged edges, rocky cliffs, and treacherous waters. They pointed to unknown lands with unfamiliar sensations that caused me to miss a home that I didn't know how to find. Like Dorothy in the Wizard of Oz, I felt trapped in a confusing world. It was the entrapment of the mind with all its rivers of possibilities. Yet, in the midst of this disorientation, there still remained the idea of the one River that could bring order to the chaos and lead me safely home.

In this season of learning to "click my heels" and find my River, I took many winding loops around the various river bends. I was tossed by the waves, thrown overboard, rescued, spun around, and experienced all the highs and lows of being on a river that is lacking in peace and stability.

On my journey, most confusing of all were the voices along the riverbanks yelling, "Turn here! Don't go there! You'll never make it going that direction! That's the wrong way! Look this way! You're steering wrong! Now you're on the right path! Keep going the way I'm instructing you, and you'll find your way!" More fear emerged within me as I listened to the others yelling, "If you keep going that direction, you'll get killed! You'll be unhappy! I would never choose that path! You're not listening! Turn around! Look here! I have your answers!"

And the boat spun and spun as I listened to the voices and continued traveling down lonely rivers with strange, noisy, and often crowded spaces empty of true direction and peace.

I looked to the voices. I looked to the path ahead. I looked to the skies and the stars for guidance. I looked for clues. I looked for a sign. I looked for instructions. I looked for hope. I searched for a teacher. I searched for an oracle. I hoped fate would take over and guide me safely home. Yet, in all my asking, searching, hoping, and praying, there was one place I never looked.

I never looked within.

Ouch!

Too painful

Too dark

Too real

Too broken

Too lost

Surely my answer to the River of Peace couldn't possibly be found there. At first, the idea seemed too easy. Do you mean all along the answers could be lying somewhere within me, concealed beneath the troubled waters of my soul? Was it feasible to think that underneath the dark and miry clay of my heart could exist a Beacon of Hope and a Light? Could there truly be a Compass within me? I thought to myself, "Where is this Light? Where is this Voice? I must find it! How is it discovered? Is it possible there could be a Treasure lying within me, an Answer to the way home?"

With a mustard seed of faith barely visible to the naked eye, I grabbed hold of my shovel and began to dig. Though tired from the rivers of confusion, the turbulent waters of self-doubt, and the arrival of one too many desolate lands, the idea of a Compass within me was a mystery too great to ignore.

The layers of soil were deep. The walls had been built of solid concrete, rigid stones, and icy layers of rock with rigid edges and what seemed impenetrable matter. Finding a way to the core through the tunnel of immense darkness seemed too difficult and challenging of a task. Yet the desire for the truth was deepening, and the hope of returning home began to defy all logic and ideas of impossibilities.

I began to see names upon the layers as I started to dig.

Betrayal

Fear

A layer called Abandonment

A layer named Unwanted

Some layers required more time and effort: layers such as Defeated, Hopeless, Not Enough, Devalued, and the thickening layer called Lies.

As the dig continued and the sweat emerged from my brow, tears began to flood my eyes. A softening began to take place among the layers of rock. Iron walls began to tremble. Layers of concrete began to disintegrate. Though the river had previously begun to calm and straighten, the shaking of the layers caused a ripple effect, and the river felt turbulent once more.

I hit layers called Hurt and Abuse, which led to layers of Rejection and Forsaken. Then, as I approached the core, I felt the pressure begin to build. Everything within me began to tighten. I felt as if everything within me would implode. Emotions began to intensify as I was approaching the Layer of Bitterness. I squinted my eyes, and when I saw the Layer of Unforgiveness, I collapsed under the weight.

My boat began to spin again. I heard the voices, and the many rivers began to call me once more. The whispers became shouts as they beckoned me with their promises of a better way, an easier path, and a whimsical solution to the life of my dreams. Yet, I had not dropped my shovel. At this point, it was as if the tool had been grafted into my hand. I couldn't seem to lay it down nor turn it loose.

I began to have a suspicion that others had been to this part of the river before. I saw the etchings of their boats where they had turned back and took another path that had once again promised a greater hope. I paused and remembered that although those paths seemed promising for a fleeting moment, they had ultimately led to emptiness and unresolved answers in my search for home.

In the eye of the storm, I began to feel a calm intermingled with a determination. I could now see a tiny opening beyond the iron gates of the layer called Unforgiveness. It was the smallest window I had ever seen. Could it qualify as a marker for a breakthrough? Was it even real? I moved through the Layer of Deception and saw that it was truly there! There was a glimmer, a sparkling! There was Light!

The sediment began to crumble. The world inside me began to illuminate a new sensation. The boat began to point adamantly towards its pre-determined course. It began to emerge with a confidence, an assurance, and an inner calm that seized the once darkened chaos. The voices quieted, and I began to hear a pure, solo, magnificent voice speaking from the core of myself.

I am the Compass. The Light was in me all along.
I had never known it.
I had never known myself.

Amidst my discovery and as the Light was breaking forth, the remaining fragments began to remove themselves from my presence. The prison walls that had previously served to entrap and restrict me were shaking and disintegrating all around me.

The reflection of the newly present Light caused my eyes to notice an inscription that had been engraved upon my shovel. I had looked at this shovel many times as I had dug along the walls and layers of the once formed and solid rock, but I had never seen any markings on it. Many days and nights had passed along this journey to my true self and yet only in the reflection of the Light was I able to see what I could not see before.

I brushed away the remaining dust and debris to read the inscription. Similar to all the layers I had previously conquered, I realized the instrument that had defeated all of them had a name. The letters were beginning to emerge. I blinked away the remaining puddled tears collecting in my eyes that I might clear my clouded view. Like a prism, a rainbow of colors, or a golden, shimmering flash of lightning, I saw the inscribed letters:

L...O...V...E.

Love. Love! Love!!!
Love, the instrument that melted away the rocky, cemented
layers, the iron gates, and the impossible fortresses amongst
the darkest places of my soul.
Love, the unstoppable force!
The warmth to the icy bridges,
The dew to the unthawed fragments,
The rain to the dry ground,
The key to every shut door,
The force that never fails,
Always endures,
That moves the mountains within,
That heals the sickness of the soul.
The silencer of lies,
The calm amidst the storm,
The Light shining greater than all darkness,
The softener of the cold heart.
Love releases.
Love, the feeling agent.
Love, the director that ensures the story of your life has a
happy ending
Love, the instrument used to break down cemented walls
Love, the chain-breaker
Love, the hardened-heart melter
Love, the Compass for life's wayward rivers

Wisdom, nor fasting, nor speaking in the tongues of angels, nor the casting away of evil, nor prayer, nor faith, nor any other word was written on the instrument that led to my awakening of self-discovery and my journey home. One tool was used to find this Divine Compass and the hearing of this Voice within.

The instrument had but one name . . .

LOVE.

Because love keeps no record of wrongs

Because love does not delight in evil but rejoices in the truth

Because love covers over a multitude of sins

Love, the solution given by the Christ of God

To love God

To love others

To love yourself

Without love, you have nothing

You can be nothing

You can do nothing

You can change nothing

You can gain no wisdom

Without love, you go nowhere

You'll never find your way home nor conquer anything without love because of one simple truth and because of one divine law:

ONLY LOVE CONQUERS ALL.

With love, my river eventually became a birth canal. I no longer heard the external voices along the riverbanks. I could only hear the Voice within. I had become the River. The River was Me. We were One. My river was now full of life. Its waters were no longer treacherously deep. I could stand in the current. I could swim in the waters. They bubbled up from within me, and I arose within them. The River was no longer dark, scary, murky, or unknown. The River was clear, iridescent, and full of color and light. I could now see my reflection within it. I could see who I was. I could see who I had always known deep beneath the layers I was destined to become.

I was alive! I danced! I sang! I jumped and played in the waters! I realized I was fearfully and wonderfully made! I knew my course. I could not see the adventures that lied ahead, but I knew the Compass within me would guide me to my final destination. I was home. I was dwelling in the River of Peace. I had released the Power within to give it life, and the darkness had finally ceased. I knew I would remain in the Light forevermore. And that is when my journey really began, with the one instrument that helped me find my way. It began with the one tool that led me to hear, to see, and to simply know:

LOVE.

Because anything great,
anything legend,
or any story worth telling
began with love.

For God so loved the world.

Your story begins with it too.
LOVE ONE ANOTHER

Happy Beginnings!
I'll meet you in the River!

All I Want to Know

THE BEST I COULD ANSWER ANY QUESTION ABOUT ANYTHING is, "I don't really know." I am not keen to take my beliefs on the written or spoken words of men, even if they tell me they are from God. I really know nothing except what my life has taught me. I know that the Spirit that flows through me is much wiser, much kinder, and much more forgiving than the God most religions portray. I know that God is with me always and will love me eternally. We are One. I know that I am one with my brethren, all of them, rich or poor, Christian, Jew, Catholic, Native American or Hindu, etc., thus why I should love my neighbors as myself. The moment I can no longer see my God in any of them or feel separated from them is the moment I have placed limitations of the depths of love that abides within me. So, at this point in my life, what do I know?

Only Love
This is all I want to know
I want to know what it means
I want to be all that it is

If becoming love can't help me cross the threshold of heaven, then I don't want to enter. For when I have obtained love, I will have obtained the kingdom...

here

now

on this earth.

God is love. Obtaining love is obtaining oneness with God. Obtaining love is going home to yourself. It was never about going to heaven. It was always about bringing heaven to earth. It was about bringing heaven to the hearts of man. So, I may speak and share thoughts, but I know nothing of the ways of life or its meaning beyond once central focus, and that is to learn love and to become it. Once obtained, all other pieces of knowledge I feel will be frivolous to acquire.

RELATIONSHIPS

Dear Man Desiring to Make Love Like a Champion

We are all seeking to be seen—for a pair of eyes to search for us—
to be constantly upon us—admiring—
for love to be made with open eyes.

DEAR MAN DESIRING TO MAKE LOVE LIKE A CHAMPION,
There is no distraction. Your focus is singular. It's her, the constant thought that lingers throughout your day. You see her. You see your purpose.

> *Her smile.*
> *Her hair.*
> *Her curves.*

All her imperfections are perfect to you. You're intoxicated. When you look at her, you really look. You stare through her layers of skin. You feel her energy. You learn her heart. You memorize her soul. You go slow, determined to know every detail. You chase her with your eyes. You burn with passion, a constant unquenchable flame that pulls you back in—time after time after time. You never tire of her. Each of her million different smiles gives you new material to study with the many shifts of her features. You concentrate on each feature, a scholar of her beauty. You trace her body with your fingers, with a desperate need to know her reactions to each sensation. You long to please. You long to know this woman, this mate to your soul. You linger beneath the surface, gazing past the eyes. You wait for her to breathe just to pull it in. You wait for her rhythm so you can sync your body to the beat of her breath and to the melody of her heart.

You smile. She smiles. You both know. It's time. You've lingered long enough watching, touching, lightly grazing. Your eyes begin to make love with hers. Your bodies begin to write a song together, a symphony of all that comes forth through the union of a deep abiding love. There is no other woman, only the one you've chosen to hold in your arms, the one you carry in your heart. You concentrate on her. Her pleasure is your daily affirmation. There's the way she walks, the way she moves, and the way her silky skin feels against your chest. You touch her hair. You tuck it behind her ear, and a rush floods your entire being. The look of her eyes, the grin that moves across her perfect face—it's too much for you. You melt into her arms, knowing she's created a safe place for you to rest. Her devotion to you is your sound foundation. She's become your hiding place. She's become your open space. You wait for her just to smell her perfume, just to taste her lips. She's your dream. You love her. You love her so.

It's been years, and it's still her. You're there still watching her. Still learning. She touches everything. She touches everyone. She pierces the hearts of man. She speaks to the soul of another. You marvel at her in gratitude that she belongs to you. She chooses to touch you, every day, every night, she comes to you with that smile, and with those eyes.

When you daydream, you pick her, every . . . single . . . time. The way she cradles her children, the way she instructs and guides, the potency of her love—it moves you. It makes you a better man. She relaxes you. She respects you. She's your rain from heaven. She waters the dry places in your soul. When it's dark, and you've lost your way, she shines like your guiding Light. To you, she sparkles.

Always has
Always will
Always

You've learned how to come to her softly. You've opened your heart to her. You hide nothing. She has access to it all, and you let it pour out. When she's weak, you offer your strength. You hold her close. You let her go. When her sky is falling, you hold her hand. You've mastered the art of giving her all she needs. You've studied her. You know her. You see her potential. You treasure her worth. She is all that is or ever will be. Her shadows reveal her gifts. She is your home.

When she wakes, it's like the sun rising, and when she sleeps, you miss her glistening eyes. You listen for her. You listen to her. She's the marvel of your life, your crown and glory.

You've stood in the back of a room basking in the Light that she shines forth. You wait for her reassuring nods, and when she walks towards you, your heart spins as you anticipate the kiss of an angel. If she fears, you reassure and protect her. You offer your kindest devotion as your eyes never fail to echo the consistent truth that you love her, you love all of her.

Years have passed, yet you still romance her. There is more to love, more depth to her, and to what you have with her. You've been gentle with her. You've been passionate with her. You've been in love with her, from the beginning, when you first breathed her in, until now. She and you are forever and always. You've made a safe haven for her to rest her wings. And when she needs you, she calls to you with her eyes.

When she is feisty, stubborn, or attempts to anger you, you inwardly smile, observing her, learning how to shepherd her with greater care and a more intense love. You calm her. You nurture her. You forgive her. You teach. You heal. You restore her. Your hands remind her of your gentle presence and your admiring devotion to her. You release an unconditional love that melts and tames the wild places of her heart. You take hold of her. You pull her close. With the softness of your lips and the movement of your tongue, you make her forget why she was anxious or upset. You release a peace upon her with the warmth of your smile and the grace-filled eyes that hold her attention from across a room.

You've helped her let her hair down. You've made her laugh. You made her breathe in life with greater vigor and velocity. Her eyes light up when she sees you. You've given her fun. You become her playmate frolicking upon the playgrounds of life. You've become her favorite dance.

You made love to her before you ever invited her to your secret chamber. You touched her heart before you ever touched her skin. You've learned that your kindness is the key to her heart. Your pretty words and your chivalrous deeds have made the pedals of her flower bloom a magnificent array of the prettiest colors you've ever seen. Her uniqueness and creativity stem from the love you offer her and the Divine Presence that flows through you and touches her. There is nothing your loving touch cannot heal. When she sees you, she sees her God living in you. When she embraces your touch, she tastes the sweetness of God moving through you. She has grown to feel as safe with you as she does her God. You speak His words. You carry His truth. You yield His unconditional, forever love that never gives up, never tires, and never seizes to encase her with the brilliance of a pure, beautiful Light. She has your sunshine, and you have her Saving Grace.

Rest assured she loves you for the way you see her. She loves you for the way you study her well beyond the fabric of her delicate skin. She loves the way your eyes trace her soul, examining every piece, those both broken and healed. Your piercing glance heals the cracks as you pour love and admiration into the crevices. You love. She loves. You admire. She admires. Nothing should separate two people who know how to pour ointment upon one another like so. You prepare a palette for a great eternal work, for a foundation not built by human hands but with a heart of such depths, its layers reach the heavens. And you do it one penetrating glance at a time.

Capturing Her Heart

A MAN WHO DOESN'T WORK TO KEEP THE GIRL WILL LOSE HER, and the first thing to go will be her heart. If you don't listen to her, you will lose her. If you think it's too much to tell her she's pretty every single day, you'll lose her. She may stay, but trust me, she will be gone.

When she tells you what she needs, and you don't fight with everything in you to provide it for her, she will begin searching elsewhere for her nourishment. Don't blame her when she's starving and leaves to find food. Animals resort to scraps when they haven't been fed, and so might she.

The true accomplishment is not in snagging the girl. It's in winning her heart over and over again every day for the rest of your life. The victory is not in capturing the girl once. It's in keeping her. It's in capturing her heart time and time again. The one who has mastered this is a man of great measure and worth. This is the mark of a true lover.

Actively pursue the object of your affection as aggressively as you pursue your need for validation and significance via the time and effort you put into climbing the ladder of success. If not, when you reach the top of that ladder, you will look around and realize there is no one there to celebrate with you—not the ones who matter, not the ones who have any value or worth. They will have respected themselves enough to have walked away while you focused your attention on other pursuits.

You go to work every day to pursue your passions or maybe to earn payment for your hard effort. The question is, are you working as diligently at your key relationships? When was the last time you asked her, "How can I be better for you? How I can improve to be more of what you need me to be?"

If you are with a wise woman, she will know her worth. If you want to marry a queen, you must possess the noble heart of a king. A wise king will know that he will only rise to the degree he helps his queen shine. Water her. Nurture her. Your pretty words and kind deeds make her sparkle. Your lack of attention causes her to wilt.

> *Protect her, and she will guard her heart for you.*
> *Cherish her, and she give you the best of care.*
> *Affirm and appreciate her, and she will adore you.*
> *Allow her space, and she will respect you.*
> *Encourage her, and she will create and build a kingdom for you.*
> *Speak truth to her, and she will loyally stand and fight for you.*
> *Listen to her, and she will unlock her secret world to you.*
> *Love her, authentically love her, and she will*
> *give you her heart for always.*

Proper Nourishment

WHATEVER YOU'RE FEEDING WILL GROW. Every plant and animal on Earth requires a certain "diet" to live and thrive. You wouldn't feed a cow what you feed to a monkey or fish. Nature teaches us we each require something different. Do you know what you need to be fed for you to survive? Perhaps you're feeding your relationship the wrong diet? Do you know what the person standing in front of you requires to thrive? If you feed a lion the diet of a snail, it will die. Perhaps the person you are feeding hasn't grown and thrived, because you haven't fed them the proper and specific diet needed for them to grow.

When I buy a plant, I have to learn about it. I have to know how often I am supposed to water it, if it needs shade or sun, and the condition the soil and temperatures must be for it to live. Have you studied the people you love? Do you know what your partner needs to grow? Do they understand you and "the food" you need to survive? If you feed someone the wrong diet, they slowly begin to starve. God made us all uniquely, and each person needs something different. Some relish in words of affirmation. Others flourish with quality time, gifts of service, or physical touch. However, there is a diet needed by us all that consists of encouragement, love, kindness, grace, and forgiveness. Feed your relationships these ingredients and watch them grow.

If someone isn't feeding you the proper nourishment, tell them what you need to survive. If they still continue to feed you the wrong diet, leave before they kill you.

Loved Greatlies

COUNT YOURSELF BLESSED IF YOU WALK THIS JOURNEY, having loved greatly. I called these that we have immensely loved, "Loved Greatlies." Some of these "Loved Greatlies" remain and some we must let go. To love them doesn't always mean we keep them. Love is freedom. To love greatly means we free them in whatever way that means. It means you throw the stone at the wolf you've raised and loved to help him turn towards his true home and protect him from a life he isn't meant to live with you.

"Loved Greatlies" are those that you wish for their best above your own. Their happiness rests like a peace upon your heart. You listen to them without words needing to be spoken. You can be with them when they are not with you. "Love Greatlies" aren't separated by time or distance. They understand one another. They see one another. They are soul mates. The love is so great that the bond is unbreakable because true love remains ~ for always.

If you've been loved by someone like this once in your lifetime, you're extremely fortunate. You were given a divine gift. You were allowed the privilege of knowing what it's like to be the recipient of love bestowed via a genuinely selfless, heaven-filled heart. If you have loved someone else like this, rest assured, wherever they are right now, you are their angel.

Free-Spirited Me

I know that you loved me.
I also know that you needed to control me.
And I am untamable.

Wild
A free Spirit

I am a loyal lover but one that must be free to roam, to fly, to flutter my sparkly wings.
I had to breathe.

I can stay without a harness.
But I can't stay amidst suffocation.

Change this.
Be this.
Think this.

These dictations never work for someone like me.
Let me go, and I will stay.
Imprison me, and I will rattle the cage and emancipate myself.

The Critical One

HAPPINESS COMES FROM BEING IN A RELATIONSHIP with someone who loves you as is. This means, in your current state of being, they wouldn't need to change one thing about you in order for them to be content. If someone is constantly trying to tweak you or improve you, I have one word of advice for you...next! Seriously, release them to go find someone more suitable and compatible to what they need. You will never be happy partnered with someone who doesn't see and appreciate you exactly for who you are.

Also, select a partner with enough maturity and passion to continue the reckless pursuit of your heart. Life experiences are going to impact and change you, and if you are committed to your spiritual path, you will evolve throughout your journey. Select intimate partnerships with open-minded individuals who have the capacity to allow their love for you to grow as you grow. You will be happier with someone who is committed to continually getting to know you and is open to loving future versions of who you will grow to be.

Lastly, a lot of people are trying to find someone exactly like themselves. But it's our differences that help us evolve and grow as individuals. The person you are with doesn't have to be identical to you; they just have to adore and love the unique qualities that make you so wonderfully you.

Take Back Your Power

SOME PEOPLE'S MOTTO IS, "I love you as long as I can control you." If they can't have you, the only way they can cope is to villainize you or demonize you. They will call you names, spread false rumors, accuse you of doing or saying untrue things, fabricate things, and play the victim. They will do just about anything to justify their behavior.

Why? Because to do anything less would mean they have to accept responsibility for what went wrong, and most importantly accept responsibility for what they did wrong. It would mean them having to take a sincere and honest glance inward. It's easier to make the person that walked away from them into a villain versus taking ownership for any role they may have played in fostering such an event.

With this said, rumors are evil and awful. Some people have the capacity to hate someone based on rumors. They may create a swell of resentment towards someone they previously liked, or that was kind to them, based on information from a source that probably has been wounded, hurt and feels justified in their words. You do yourself a disservice when you carry anger or judgment towards another based on rumors or second-hand information. Have the maturity to go straight to the source before making conclusions regarding the character of another person.

There's only one person in your life you can control ... you. You can control your response. You can control your emotions. You can control how you choose to feel at any given moment of the day. Don't give your power away by allowing these things to be controlled by the behavior of another. You're worth more than that. Settle matters of injustice by loving yourself enough to know your truth, hold your chin up, smile kindly, and move the heck on. Now that's real justice!

Five-Star Status

IT CAN TAKE YOU A WHILE TO FIGURE THINGS OUT, but once you do, make adjustments, make decisions, and begin moving forward.

I know. I know. The skies have parted, and now you can see clearly. You can see them clearly. You can see them for exactly who they are and for their intentions. Their love was shallow. You deserve more. You are worthy of so much more. And now you can have better.

Drop to your knees and thank the good Lord for giving you the courage and strength to say goodbye to that madness. What a compromise you made, eh? But no more. Never again. So, you lowered your standards. Raise them.

Moving forward, don't waste your precious time trying to prove you now know your worth. Just be more, believe for more, and live for more than that crap you were allowing. Open yourself to receiving genuine, soul-nurturing love.

You are not leftovers, and you're certainly not designed to be someone's sloppy seconds. You are adorable. You are lovable. You are divinely powerful beyond measure.

You are too much! And that's ok! You are not an appetizer. You are a five-course meal. Not everyone can handle you. Focus on feeding the ones that are really hungry. Stick with the ones that treat you like a delicacy. You're not a meal to be picked up at the drive-through window of a fast-food restaurant. You're five-star status, Baby! Never forget that ever again!

Prayer for True Love

I BELIEVE I AM WORTHY OF INTIMACY, SPIRITUAL CONNECTION, romance, and the deepest love ever known. I invite this love into my life. I am ready to move beyond the superficial and that which no longer serves me and my purpose.

I surrender to the divine path my soul longs to take. I trust God and His angels to know what is in my highest good, will fulfill the deepest desires of my heart, and will help me step into my ultimate purpose. I am ready to let go of less to receive more. I am prepared to release that which is not assisting me in walking a more divine, spiritually-fulfilling, and contributive path.

God, help me with this transition. May those destined to travel it with me remain with me and may those who have another path to walk, find the road that best serves them for this moment in their journey. I wait in expectation for guidance and truth. Thank you for bringing this love into my life in perfect timing and in whatever way is best for me.

Time Will Tell

LIFE HAS TAUGHT ME THAT PEOPLE COME IN OUR LIVES to reveal things within ourselves for healing and release. Sometimes they stick and sometimes they are only supposed to remain for a season.

I have had people promise me many things in my life only to discover their words were null and void. Intentions and the pureness of one's heart are always revealed with time.

No matter what your instinct says when you first meet someone or how good you think your discernment is regarding them, only time will reveal the true nature of their character to you.

Time never lies. Time reveals genuine truth. Give it time. Sooner or later, they will tell you who they are. They will tell you whether or not they were with you for themselves or they were there to unconditionally and unselfishly serve you. Lip service is cheap. Anyone can give it. Time will reveal motives as well as those who have the ability to stick around for more than what they seek to gain from their time with you. Bottom line: What belongs to you will always remain. What was meant to make a brief deposit will pass. And what was meant to be discarded will ultimately reveal itself as trash.

In all these relationships, the ones that stick and the ones meant to fall off, you will experience tremendous growth. They will provide incredible opportunities for you to discover your voice, your strength, and your values. They all have the ability to empower you and help you better align with your true self.

Don't try to hang on to every person who comes into your life. Sometimes relationships are simply there to teach you how to stand up for yourself and assume back the power that in times past you so easily yielded to others. With each relationship you encounter, more and more contrast will be provided to help you determine what makes you genuinely happy. When that is revealed to you, really absorb it and apply it as you move forward to help yourself create more beautiful, lasting, and genuine connections with the new relationships that enter your life.

Sow More Reap More

WHEN DID THINGS BEGIN TO IMPROVE FOR ME? Things began to get better for me when I realized that I couldn't get more withdrawals than I had made deposits. I began to sow more abundantly into the areas of my life where I needed to see increase and abundance.

If you need more emotional support, give more emotional support. If you need more help, give more assistance to others. You can't get more out of something than you are willing to put into it.

If an area of your life is lacking in some capacity, try making more deposits. Relationships bankrupt when someone begins to withdraw more than they deposit. Even if that particular relationship disintegrates, the love you deposited in sincerity will eventually return to you via another means. Perhaps your reward will simply come to you as a lesson learned, but you can take that lesson with you for the rest of your life. Sow the best you can with love, kindness, and honestly. Eventually, you will reap a profit for the faithful toiling you have administered in the various fields of your life.

I'm so thankful God in His great wisdom orchestrated a principle of sowing and reaping to govern this beautiful world. It is dependable and never failing.

Sow more, reap more.
The greater the investment, the greater the return.

Do you need more love in your life? My life began to be consumed with more love when I began to offer more love to myself and to others. Do you need forgiveness from someone? Give forgiveness to yourself and those who have wounded you. When we give freely, we open the portals of heaven to flow into our lives often synced to the very measure by which we have given. And more often than not, we receive back even more abundantly than we could have ever hoped for or imagined!

The Ultimate
Relationship Advice

ALTHOUGH I HAVE PREVIOUSLY WRITTEN about the significance of being in a relationship with someone that understands what you need to flourish, and while I agree with the significance of creating a peaceful environment for yourself and choosing a partner that knows how to nourish you, there is something even more instrumental one must understand and embody before truly obtaining the ideal relationship.

Below I articulate the ultimate truth and most significant wisdom I have acquired in my attempt to seek love, happiness, and fulfillment from the various relationships I have encountered throughout my life. Rest assured, this wisdom is spoken in all humility as I most certainly obtained it via a lot of trial and error as well as painful lessons learned from approaching this area of my life completely backwards. Nevertheless, all those experiences have taught me some priceless gems which I will share in hopes of helping others discover what I believe to be the unlocking key to experiencing genuine fulfillment, happiness, and a blissful love relationship with another person.

The first thing one must understand is that the only relationship that really matters to you is the one between you and you. What I mean by this is the relationship between the physical and emotional you that is your ego-personality and the part of you that is the highest version of all that you are destined to be. This is the God part of you that you are trying to come into alignment with. Every other relationship is insignificant in comparison to the one between you and the Divine.

However, most people allow the relationships in their life to determine whether or not they are in alignment with the highest versions of themselves. They allow external relationships to pull them out of their alignment with their true selves. They allow the way they feel to be dependent upon the behavior of others. As a result, almost every relationship they have turns out to be their need to control the behavior of others in order to ensure their happiness. This makes almost all of their relationships miserable at best, as well as short-lived.

Some people do need to enter into a new relationship but one with the highest versions of themselves and not another person. If you want to discover what unconditional love really is, you have to remove relationships that have become the condition keeping you from discovering it.

I came to a place in my life where I didn't want my happiness to be based on whether or not another person was making me happy. I wanted to be happy for myself! If I had to depend on someone else to make me happy and fulfilled, then I was placing the responsibility upon them to keep me content 100% of the time. I grew to a level of maturity, where I wanted to feel good because I had found a way to feel good apart from my external relationships. I didn't want to give others the responsibility for making me feel good. I needed to show myself that I could be a happy person regardless of what others were doing. I came to realize that once I could convince myself of that, then I could be with someone and live happily ever after. I no longer wanted to be in a relationship with someone because we made one another happy, but because we already knew how to be happy and thus could be together.

With enough personal development and spiritual work, you will ultimately realize that the deepest truth is you do not need anyone in your life to make you happy or fulfilled. Through blockbuster, Hollywood movies like Jerry McGuire, we are often taught the general idea that you need someone to be your second half or to fulfill you.

While it is true that we seek relationships to have love, compassion, excitement, to have someone to do fun things with, to have children, etc., and while there is nothing wrong with any of these things, true love is not finding someone else to complete you. This is not what a healthy relationship is. A healthy relationship is when both parties are confident, independent and happy by themselves. Only then can two people come together and create something greater than the sum of its parts.

You may be feeling lonely right now and thinking, "If only I had that guy or that girl, or if only I could rekindle the spark and have the love I once had in a previous relationship, I would be happy, content, and complete." This is actually the biggest problem you are having in attracting a fulfilling relationship in your life. It is not because you aren't pretty enough or because you are behaving in some weird or wrong way. The above mindset is highly unattractive to others. When you come from this frame of mind, you are repelling people rather than attracting them. When you are desperate and needy, other people do not want to be around you. At least, not the kind of people that you want in your life. When you are housing this mindset, you are going to attract someone that is on that same level. Either you won't attract anyone at all, or you will attract someone as needy and desperate as you, which will create a dysfunctional, co-dependent relationship. What your soul is longing for is to attract someone to you that is equally confident, stable, and happy in themselves so that when the two of you come together, things click and are incredibly rewarding for you both.

When you are in a needy and desperate position, you are being inauthentic to yourself. You are not really in touch with the fact that you can be happy by yourself. Although you may be calling your relationship love, romance, and fulfillment, you are really just using another person to fulfill a void in your own ego.

Even if you get that perfect person to fit the void you have in yourself, it's not going to work. It's no different than thinking you can dominate the corporate ladder, become a millionaire, and you will be happy. The reason this never works is because relationships or monetary comforts will never make someone happy. There is something within the person, within their psychology, that they are not facing. When you avoid this by trying to get a quick fix of sex, companionship, love, or marriage, you are only putting a band-aid on a deeper wound within yourself because the ultimate truth is that you do not need anyone to be inwardly content.

You do not need anyone to fulfill you. You can be completely happy all by yourself. If you don't feel this way, it's only because you have not done enough introspection and figured out what your core beliefs are, and what your limiting beliefs and ego deficiencies are. You have yet to realize who you truly are and the power you carry within you. You simply have not done enough spiritual and personal development work to get that part of your life handled.

Once you are inwardly fulfilled, you will
become more attractive to those around you.

You become more attractive when you are 100% authentic, and in order to do this, you have to be 100% confident in who you are. You have to be able to let people come and go in your life without needing to clutch on to them and hold them to you. This applies whether you are single, in a boyfriend/girlfriend relationship, or even if you are married. Because even if you are married, you should not be attached to your spouse. You should not need that spouse to be in your life for you to feel fulfilled, complete, or happy. If you do, then I can't say I would be surprised if the relationship eventually turns sour. More than likely, it won't be able to last, or if it does, both people will probably end up incredibly dissatisfied and miserable. This is because the relationship will have been built on something that's fake and a counterfeit of divine truth. It will have been established on the co-dependent nature of needing someone else to be responsible for ensuring personal fulfillment and contentment.

Generally, you must come to this deep understanding that there is nothing that anyone in this world can offer you that you cannot offer yourself. I'm not talking about needing someone to fix your car or supply food for you to purchase at your grocery store. I'm talking about the fact that you do not need someone to fulfill you psychologically, spiritually, or emotionally. The more you rely on your parents, your siblings, your spouse, your children, your boss, or anyone else for your happiness, the more psychological dependencies you will have.

The definition of a dysfunctional relationship is two people coming together and needing something from one another. "I need sex, excitement, and love from you. You need security, comfort, money, and love from me." When you've got this trading mentality going on, there will always be fear sandwiched in the middle of the relationship. Both parties will think that if they do something the other person disapproves of, the other person might stop loving them, get upset, angry, and pull something away from them, thus leaving them void of the love, comfort, etc. that they need. This example is a perfect depiction of a relationship based on fear and is in direct opposition to two non-needy entities coming together with an attitude of, "I'm happy. You're happy. I'm excited to see how this is going to play out."

If you cannot sit home alone with yourself and be happy and comfortable without going out and distracting yourself with some form of stimulation, for example, television, internet, sex, drugs, alcohol, etc., you've got some work to do. If you want to be genuinely and authentically attractive, what you must first do is work on yourself and your psychology. Why do you feel you need that relationship, love, and companionship so badly? Why are you not comfortable in who you are by yourself without needing someone else?

Create a happy life for yourself with beautiful external circumstances. Personally, ensure you have a rich, productive life. Establish a thriving career. Build something that you are passionate about. Solidify your life purpose. Make friends and go on adventures with lovely people that you enjoy hanging out with. Acquire some hobbies that you enjoy. Get your money situation handled. Make sure you are free from addictions like drugs, smoking, alcohol, and over-eating. Create happiness with your family life. Ensure that you have your health and hygiene in order. Take care of yourself to the best of your ability. Develop and mature your spiritual life and practices. Bring yourself into alignment with God in order to cultivate the characteristics and virtues of the Divine so that you can become all you are destined to be. When you can manage all these things, when you can manage you, you're going to be happy. And who wouldn't want to be a part of that?

When you get your psychology, your spiritual life, and your external circumstances in order, then you will have created a happy, awesome life for yourself. Then you can be authentic, and others can see you being carefree, joyous, confident, and not desperately needing to extract anything from them. Others will say, "She is so refreshing! I rarely meet someone like that. Her life is infectious and magnetic." Then, they will naturally become magnetized and attracted to you. This way of life is the secret to building lasting, non-gimmicky relationships.

To give credit where credit is due, this Misti Moment was
derived from life experience as well as inspiration from a
combination of wisdom collected and gleaned from listening to
the profound teachings of Leo Gura and Esther Hicks. I am
eternally grateful for the lasting impact the above knowledge
has made in helping me discover authentic happiness and enjoy
rewarding and lasting relationships.

GRATITUDE

What Do You Have?

FEAR OF MISSING OUT CAN CAUSE YOU TO BE SO FOCUSED on what you're missing that you fail to appreciate and acknowledge what's standing right in front of you. You can be so focused on what you want to be or where you want to be that you can miss the sheer bliss of feeling value for who you currently are and where God has placed you in the present moment.

You can't focus on what's missing and be fulfilled at the same time.

When Moses was standing against the Red Sea in need of a serious breakthrough, God's first clue to help him came in the form of a question,

> *"Then the LORD said to him,*
> *'What is that in your hand?'*
> *'A staff,' he replied."*
> (Exodus 4:2)

Everything Moses needed for his breakthrough was already in his hand. In fact, he had used that rod many times to work miracles. Remind yourself from time to time that what you already have is enough to accomplish a victory despite the fact our "mountain," "Red Sea," or circumstance may seem too big to move out of the way.

When a boy wanted to help feed five thousand hungry people, Jesus assisted him by asking him to bring what he had, a mere two fishes and five loaves of bread. Twelve leftover baskets later, everyone was fat and happy.

When a widow from Zarephath was asked to provide bread to a visitor in her home, she replied that she didn't have any, to which he replied, "What do you have?" When she was asked to take her attention off of what she didn't have and place it upon what she did have, the widow soon discovered that she had everything she needed to bake a cake for her visitor. She had a handful of flour and a little oil in her jar. As a result of shifting her focus and offering what she had, her jar was never lacking flour again nor was her jug short of oil.

Happy people focus on what they have in front of them. Unhappy people focus on what's missing. Stop focusing on what you have to lose and start focusing on what you have to gain. Stop focusing on what you've been through and start focusing on where you're going. If you look at what you have in life, you'll always have more. If you look at what you don't have, you'll never have enough.

Get Well Soon, Poppy

SOME HAVE SAID WE CAN'T TAKE ANYTHING WITH US to heaven when we go. Perhaps my attempt to sneak precious treasures like the beautiful gem posted below into my pocket on my exit from this world would be unsuccessful. Nevertheless, I am most certain they will be carried in my heart for eternity and then some.

When everyone was hustling and bustling in the Easter madness, the dyeing of the eggs, the hunt for the golden prize, the rush to be the first one to get a piece of key lime pie, the scurry to snap the perfect Easter photo, the greetings of friends and family, the rush to get a seat for the big Easter Sunday message,

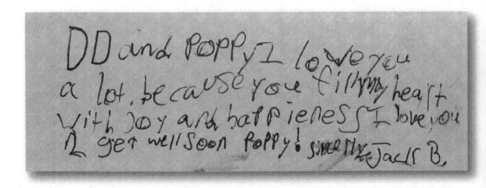

one little boy remembered his Poppy. With all that could saturate his mind, he thought to leave a hand-made message of gratitude behind for his D.D. and Poppy who had worked so hard to plan a special day of fun and memory-making for him. Today amidst the madness, it was in my son's heart to tell his granddad, who is dying of cancer, to, "Get well soon."

These are the moments
You know them
When the tear slips from your eye
When the heart squeezes tightly in the chest.
When it's all worth it
When life becomes so unbelievably beautiful, you realize if you had
to live every painful moment all over again to feel what you are
feeling right now, you would do it all over again in a heartbeat.

Memory Savored.

Easter 2017

Perspective

RECENTLY, I WAS IN THE FRONT YARD WHEN I HEARD SEVERAL LOUD SCREAMS. We have an incredibly steep hill beside our house, and a small child about the age of four was blazing uncontrollably down the hill on his bicycle at full speed. There was no way the parents could beat his momentum to break his fall. He was headed straight to the woods in front of our house for a sudden impact with a tree. I dropped my new iPhone on our driveway, not caring one bit if it shattered to pieces, and I ran as fast as I could, knowing I would have to stop the little boy's speed with my body. I threw myself in front of the bike, attempting to protect him from feeling the impact of the crash as best as I could. This method worked, and I shielded the little boy from hitting the tree. However, in the process, I injured my neck and woke the next day with an arm that was bruised, incredibly swollen, and sore to the touch. After a visit to the doctor and an x-ray later, I discovered that I had a hairline fracture to the bone on my right arm and would need to wear a brace for a few weeks.

After the incident, the parents rushed over to the little boy and immediately took him home. They never thanked me or asked if I was ok or hurt. Afterward, there were two ways I could have chosen to look at the situation. I could have been irritated and frustrated with my new injury and pouted about the lack of appreciation offered to me by the parents, or I could feel gratitude for the experience and the ability God afforded me to protect and help the little boy.

My arm hurt, but my heart was so full! I had the opportunity to save someone from harm, and I had the privilege of feeling proud of myself for choosing the well-being of another over myself. There was an inner reward that was greater than the outward pain. I could have chosen to become bitter at what I determined was a lack of gratitude and appreciation from the parents. Instead, I chose to think their behavior was completely normal. They were rightfully concentrating on their child, not to mention in shock over what had just happened. I made the decision to put my energy and momentum into looking at the situation with compassion and grace.

The peace and power of God lie within you, and He has provided a way for you to go directly to the Source.

I pay attention to these moments in my life. Generally, we don't practice gratitude when we stub our toe, trip over something left on the floor, spill a jug of milk on the kitchen floor, or have a fender bender with a car—but quite honestly, these are the moments when we get to see what is truly in our hearts. These moments are gifts. They are opportunities to see what we are made of. How will we respond? Will we be merciful, forgiving, kind, and graceful in the midst of irritation to both ourselves and those around us? Will we spout off at the mouth and use our hurt to hurt others? Will we see this moment as a gift to practice the fruit of the Spirit? How can we know the depth of our character until it has been tested?

Every moment serves as a potential blessing to us, as something for us to be grateful for. It's all about perspective. It's how we choose to see things. I could have chosen to see the incident with the little boy, his parents, and me as a positive or a negative. Most would see an injury as something to constitute being out of alignment or as something negative and bad. But I have chosen to see these moments as gifts and used them as opportunities for my spiritual growth. As a result, my soul has thanked me.

A negative mindset will never yield a positive result. Ever. You can't keep repeating the same story and expect to see a different outcome. You must stop putting your energy, focus, and momentum behind what isn't working and begin placing your attention on what is. The moment you begin to feel irritation, anger, frustration, worry, doubt, blame, resentment, or any of these other deadly viruses, you must begin to reach immediately for the best-feeling thought you can muster. This practice must be implemented if you ever hope to break unhealthy or unproductive patterns and shift yourself to a better outcome.

I have come to realize some have grown accustomed to their negativity and are quite comfortable in their pessimism, but for those who want to experience a life that doesn't require complaining about it every day, the moment those negative emotions hit, you must acknowledge this is your code-red alert to shift yourself into a better space.

The peace and power of God lie within you, and He has provided a way for you to go directly to the Source. The way to this Source begins with our appreciation for life as it is right now. With appreciation comes acceptance and integration, the keys to transformation—the keys to the kingdom.

Negativity is a deadly killer. It yields a slow death that gradually rots away your creative life force because it goes against the flow of God's design for you to live in a state of gratitude and appreciation. Don't let it take you out.

Choose life.

Oh, and one final thing. One week after the above incident occurred, the parents left an incredibly thoughtful gift with a beautiful thank-you message attached to it on my front doorstep. This entire circumstance was such a profound life lesson for me. I was so grateful I had not decided to judge their initial reaction but to understand it. When we align our perspective with an enlightened, merciful, and loving viewpoint coupled with great compassion for others, rewards always follow. And true rewards come with no sorrow attached. They aren't just tangible to the touch. They are heart-piercing and valuable in soul merit. They teach us. They strengthen us. They grow us. They make our hearts and souls shine with wholesome delight.

The Silver Lining

THE FIRST FOUR DAYS OF MY WEEK VACATION AT THE BEACH with my three children have consisted of flash flood warnings and my eight-year-old daughter running a fever coupled with chronic diarrhea. Tonight was the first time we were able to venture out after almost four days in an RV with rain chronically pouring down around us.

I have played every board game imaginable at least three times and more rounds of Old Maid and UNO than I can count. We've watched kids play outside in the rain, make s'mores around the campfire, and soak in a few, brief hours of sunshine unable to join them. And I must say, I've had a lot of vacations with my kids, but I'm not sure if we have ever had one that will be more memorable than this one.

With not much to distract us, all we've had is one another. We've talked more than usual, watched movies together, ate every meal together, and talked about big topics sparked by questions from my little Kate asking why God let her get sick on her vacation.

Tonight while she was in the bathtub, she said, "I like this, Mom. I'm having fun talking to you." My response to her was, "Well, Kate, maybe God answered your question. Maybe if you were on a beach playing somewhere, we wouldn't have had this moment together."

Tonight, we finally got out for a bit although she still hasn't had a full recovery in the regular bowel movement department. We laughed, danced in the rain, drank virgin piña coladas, put our toes in the ocean, and finally had our first late-night swim. As we watched the sunset give us one of her prettiest efforts, I told the kids that no matter what happens, sunsets are proof that every day can end beautifully.

So, cheers to our memories made! Life isn't perfect by any means. There are layers of complexities most people never see on our social media platforms. However, perfection comes when people who love each other very much make memories worth staying in their hearts forever.

In two days of frustration, cleaning up after a sick little girl, exhaustion, and at times when I thought I was going to go stir crazy, I still have the ability to see the silver lining. I'm really grateful for that. Don't ever let anyone tell you rose-colored glasses aren't pretty. Sometimes seeing the best in things is what keeps the best of things coming towards us.

All Is Well

*D*ETERMINATION REQUIRES A TREMENDOUS AMOUNT OF EFFORT. Have you ever realized how much effort and energy we use when we are determined to get from where we are to some other place?

I suppose I have found a softer way on the opposite end of the stick of determination. Rather than being so determined to get somewhere other than where I might currently be, I've learned to be ok with where I am.

> *I am learning on this journey how important*
> *it is to make peace with where I am before*
> *I can get to where I want to be.*

We have to make the place we presently are positioned the right place for us to be before we can experience anything more. We have to change our perspective and the view from where we currently stand if we want to see something different on the horizon of our lives.

> *Isn't there a certain amount of relief in*
> *just accepting where we are?*

There is a statement that says, "That which is like unto itself is drawn." From that understanding, I began to realize that every day I was becoming more of what I presently was in that moment.

> *Make sure that what you are becoming*
> *more of is what you want to become.*

If where you are doesn't feel good any longer, you must realize you can never change the outcome of that scenario by staying in a place of lack and feeling overwhelmed. In my personal journey, I found that determination to get myself out of those places and be something more never helped me arrive at my desired destination.

I found it prudent to let 100% of my intention be placed upon making peace and finding contentment with wherever I was in the moment. I would say,

> *"I'm doing good.*
> *Things are working out for me."*

Did that statement contradict my belief system in such a way that I could not even say those words? Could I not say, "It's alright?" Could I not say, "It is well with my soul?" I knew that I could. I knew that I must, and I did.

When I begin to make peace with where I was and accept that wherever I was in that particular moment was alright and even purposeful, I began to feel closer to where I wanted to be.

If you can genuinely mean it when you say, "It's alright. No action is required of me right now," then it actually means that your point of attraction has become one that says, "All is well." It means that there is nothing you need to do to justify yourself, improve yourself, change yourself, or defend yourself. And what would that mindset then indicate about your current state of being? It would mean that you are in a good place. And why should you be in a good place?

Because you are worthy.
Because you have trusted that well-being belongs to you.
Because you've embraced that well-being is who you are.

And from that space, your point of attraction can bring to you what it is you are wanting.

"Whoever has will be given more, and they will have an
abundance. Whoever does not have, even what they have will be
taken from them."
Matthew 13:12

Have more acceptance for where you are if you
want to experience more acceptance.
Be at peace with where you are if you want
to experience more peace.
Embrace healing where you are if you want
to experience more healing in your life.
Be happy if you want happiness to surround you.
Be thankful for what you have; you'll end up having more.
If you concentrate on what you don't have, you will never, ever
have enough.
If you want all to be well, if you want everything to be alright,
then you must be alright with where you are now.

Grateful Graduates

YOU MAY NOT BE WHERE YOU WANT TO Be, but if you can't find a way to be grateful for what you have, you will never be given more.

"Whoever has will be given more; whoever does not have, even
what they have will be taken from them."
(Mark 4:25)

Whoever has gratitude will be given more things to be grateful for. Whoever does not possess gratitude for what they have, even what they have will be taken from them.

Want to test this universal principle? Give it time. Life will eventually teach this truth to you. Some learn. Others fail. In every classroom, we see both passing and failing. And with each classroom, there are also those few who will far exceed expectations. The classroom that is this world is no different.

What is the secret to abundant living? Abundance is more than money. Live life to its fullest. Start appreciating.

Cheers to the Grateful Graduates who finish well!

The Remedy

WHEN PRAYING, NEVER FOCUS ON YOUR PROBLEMS. Always ask for the right remedy. Then, let the Spirit bring you the right solutions. Don't talk about your illness. Concentrate on the power you are receiving immediately into your condition. Give thanks for your swift recovery and then . . .

Believe in it.

When you give thanks, you are accepting, acknowledging, believing, and impressing on your consciousness the realization that your prayer now lies with your Creator and is being processed for visible manifestation in due course at the right time. Then, live in a state of thanksgiving for the answered prayer before you see it come to pass.

If after praying, you go out and tell people how awful you feel or how terrible your personal situation is, you are undoing the work the Universe is engaged in. If you ask God to solve your health problem but continue to talk about all the negative conditions surrounding it, you are in essence, denying His ability to deliver the answer to your prayers.

After prayer, if you are still focused on the negative circumstances surrounding your situation, return to prayer until you can dismiss them from your mind and truly believe and feel that all is being divinely taken care of right at that minute. You must trust that God, the angels, and the entire Universe has your back. Surrender to the process and embrace however, whenever, and by whatever manner your prayer is answered. Trust that everything is working together for your good. Then, remain in a constant state of thanksgiving.

We must become that which we seek to obtain if we wish to see it manifested in our existence. We must feel healthy before we can obtain health. We have to be a match to that which we want or desire. You can't manifest wealth when you live in a constant state of feeling poor. Change your thoughts, change your emotions, and you will change your life.

First hope
Then believe.
Then receive the answer in your Spirit without
having obtained the physical manifest of it.
Then feel thanksgiving.
Then feel excitement for what is coming!
Then witness your reality begin to change.
Then receive it tangibly.

Abandon fears. They have availed you nothing. Turn to your Creator, the Source of your being—your conception, your growth, your development, your nutrition, your regeneration, your healing, your fulfillment for every need, and your protection. Realize that all this wonderful work is constructive, purposeful, orderly, and it's all happening within you.

You truly have a Master Mind behind you, your family, and your living conditions. Trust it. Don't allow your thinking to spoil this divine creative operation.

This year I walked through the valley of the shadow of death. We may all experience our moments of darkness in various ways, but we have also been given a Lighthouse to guide our way through the storms of life.

Missing Treasure

THIS PAST WEEKEND WAS MEMORIAL DAY, and everyone couldn't be more excited. It was an extra special day due to the fact my parents recently bought a gorgeous piece of property on Lake Martin. This would be our first official holiday enjoying it together as a family. The car was loaded with everything we needed. The corn toss game, bad mitten set, bubble wands, large water inflatables, board games, movies, s'mores, and of course a large cooler packed full of yummy food. Excitement was in the air! We rode to the lake in swimsuits and sunglasses with the roof top-down and the radio up!

On our way there we heard on the radio that Mountain Dew had sponsored twenty coolers full of unknown treasure and had positioned each of them somewhere across the 44,000-acre lake. Upon hearing the news, the kids were, for lack of better words, "freaking out." What's interesting about children is that they rarely doubt or bother themselves with examining the odds. If you tell them reindeers fly or a big, fat man in a red suit is coming down a chimney to bring them presents, they will believe you. It never crossed my kids' minds to statistically measure their probability of finding a winning cooler. They were on a mission. There was no more interest in ring toss or water gun fights. They had to find that treasure!

As soon as we arrived at the lake, the kids shoved down their lunch and began lathering themselves in sunscreen, which was a first. Of course, all of this was done in their desperate attempt to get to the boat as swiftly as possible.

Before long we had set sail on what was labeled by the kids as our "hot ride," the borrowed pontoon boat their granddad a.k.a., Poppy, had loaned us for the day. Then off we went to find our treasure! The first hour or so was indeed adventurous. We enthusiastically rode the big waters, and often side-tracked into small coves looking for the coveted treasure. Although Riley, our twelve-year-old, and Kate, our six-year-old, were excited about finding the treasure, it was Jack, our ten-year-old, who had taken this particular mission to heart. From the moment we got on the boat, he was front and center. Whereas usually, he takes his shiny, white-skinned, freckled body and sits under the shade at the back of the boat, today he was at the bow of the ship watching and ready with an eagle's eye.

A couple of hours into our boat ride and after much searching with weariness creeping upon us all, we saw a shiny object that appeared like a flashing, blue light calling for us in the distance. As we made our way to it and the cheering, high fives, and hugging had made its way around the boat, our celebration was brought to an abrupt stop. It became clear the glistening object was a set of silver birthday balloons that had gotten tangled in the brush alongside the water and was reflecting the light from the sun.

It's never a pleasant experience to watch your child experience disappointment. I watched as Jack's head began to sink farther into his life jacket. The realization that it was time to return to the cabin and the treasure had not been found was overtaking him. Jack could barely bring himself to smile or enjoy the fun taking place around him. I knew exactly how he felt. He was facing that moment in life after you've prayed for something to happen, believed for it with all your heart, never displayed an inch of doubt, and yet still came up empty handed. It was an answered prayer nowhere to be found, a closed door, and a reply from the heavens saying, "No, that treasure was not meant for you."

Seeing Jack in this state of mind, I made my way over to sit beside him. At this point, he had left the front of the boat where he had been playing with his brother and sister and was sitting in his usual spot on the back cushion. I placed my arms around him and said, "Jack, never let an unanswered prayer change your position or move you to the back of the boat. The boat represents your life. These waters are the Spirit that carries you."

You must learn to enjoy the treasure you have while looking for the treasure you seek.

You must trust the Spirit is guiding you to the treasure that is meant for you. In the meantime, when we mourn what we do not have, we position ourselves at the back of the boat where we are unable to take in the view and see all the beauty that is surrounding us. We miss the opportunities and the gifts being given along the journey. We miss the laughter, the joy, the fellowship, and the awe and wonder of the sites and discoveries we make along the way. Therein lies the true treasures we often do not recognize because we are too attached to the outcome and the object of our desire. When we chase the pot at the end of the rainbow, we often miss enjoying the mesmerizing beauty of the rainbow itself. We often miss the message the rainbow came to deliver.

It wasn't long till we were back at the cabin, and Jack was back to his silly self again swinging in the hammock with his siblings, laughing and playing, and enjoying the simple pleasures of life. I found it quite amazing that when he detached from needing to find the treasure, he became a treasure for all to enjoy, especially his mama.

Later in the evening, when we returned home, Jack came into my room. He sat down on the arm of my chair and said, "Mom, you know that game I really wanted? I began downloading it over a week ago, but something hasn't been working right with it. When we left for the lake, it was still only at 15% after having waited patiently an entire week for it to be ready to play."

With the biggest grin on his face, he continued, "Guess what just happened? When I went upstairs just now, it was at 100% and was ready to play! I've been thinking about the treasure I asked God to help me find today. I really don't even know what was in it. It could have been just a bunch of Mountain Dews, and I don't really even like Mountain Dew. It probably had a bunch of gift cards to places I don't even like. But coming home to this game was God answering my prayer for treasure. It's what I really wanted. I guess God answered my prayer, after all."

I turned to Jack and said, "You know, it's the doors God shuts in our lives that redirects us to the ones that are meant for us to walk through. And when God opens a door for you, no man can shut it. If it doesn't open, it's not your door. It's not what is in your highest good. God conspires with the entire Universe to bring to you what is truly the very best for you. He knows what will ultimately make you the happiest."

When you're riding the boat called life, trust the "waters." Trust the Spirit that is carrying you and enjoy the journey along the way. When we fail to appreciate the treasures along the way, it's as if we're allowing pirates to come on board our ship and steal what we already have.

Never allow anyone, any circumstance, any unanswered prayer, or any delayed outcome to mentally move you to the back of the boat. You are destined to stand tall, front, and center with hands in the air so that you are open to see and receive all the many blessings God wants to deposit in your life. Don't be left with missing treasure. Recognize the gems you have already been given and anticipate the treasure that awaits!

Happy Hunting!

PEACEMAKERS, LOVEMAKERS & WORLD CHANGERS

Dear Evil Ones

DEAR EVIL ONES,

I hear the world talking about you, but I prefer to speak to you. I need not see you face-to-face for this message transcends the war of words. This message comes from the Breath of Life within me and the magnetic pulses of my heart. There is something you must know.

Love is coming for you.
Like a rush of wind grazing over the oceans,
Like a fog sweeping across the tops of the mountains
and hovering over the deep,
Like the tumbleweed rolling across the desert,
love is coming for you.
A wave of the highest vibration has been
dispatched to overtake you,
a force strong enough to dispel all hate, unbind any soul,
bring order to any chaos,
and melt the cold heart of any man.

We are the Enlightened Ones, the Awakened Souls. Although there are but few of us, our power is great. It stems from the true Divine Source. We have made ourselves vessels. A limitless supply of this Source has poured Himself into our frame. We come not with tanks and soldiers nor with weapons of mass destruction. We come not with arguments, agendas, or carefully written battle plans to see your destruction. We speak a language buried deep within you. We understand our mission. We follow an ancient truth to love thy neighbor as ourselves. Love we must do, and we will do it well.

While others talk about you, debate about you, yell about you, and broadcast your every move, we will be sitting under our trees, lying on our beds, standing by the oceans, and blessing you. Though you are the enemies we bless today, you will be the brothers and sisters we dine with tomorrow. We know how to speak to the mountains without doubt. We understand the universal laws. We know the feeling we must muster to move heaven and earth, to make what is above so below.

We heal from a different place, not one that is rooted in tactics of fear. Mountains have learned to yield to our requests because we make them with the only effective language in the Universe, that of love. You bring a holy war. We bring you a holy ground, one where we can stand together reminded of our brotherhood.

The world highlights our differences.
We are here to remind you of our similarities.

Do you feel your breath? Indeed, I feel mine as well. We can reach beyond the exterior walls of your heart to the Source of Life within you. We can see your soul smile as you remember when we once dined together drinking from the same cup, a part of the same Living Breath.

We bring a message of life, one that cannot be heard with words. It's a message we will show you with our lives. Our swords have been surrendered. We do not wish to fight you. We have transcended such man-made sadness. For those who live by the sword also die by the sword. That which we sow we understand we shall also reap. When we sow death to another, we reap death upon ourselves.

We bring you a love that is overdue and overwhelming, one you have yet to feel. It breathes through your cities and hovers over you as you sleep. It says, "Though your sins be as scarlet they shall be washed white as snow."

You call yourselves servants.
This Force of Love wants to make you Sons.

Where can you run from this love? Even the darkness cannot hide you. Come, my brothers and my sisters, place your blood-soaked hands in mine. There is a sound of a rushing rain to remove every stain and bind every wound.

Do you want to be free? Come and sit in my Light. Absorb all that you need. May the Truth pour forth and unite us once again.

I know you can feel my love. I have sent it forth, to the outermost extremities of this earth, directly from my beating heart to yours. More is coming for you.

God has shown us how to change the world, and we fully intend on doing it. Hatred does not cease by hatred, but only by love; this is the eternal rule.

As Above so Below.
*Thy will in Heaven be done **on this earth.***

I look forward to meeting you soon as we live in peace
together once again.

"Hatred stirs up strife, but love covers all offenses."
(Proverbs 10:12)

LOVE CONQUERS ALL.

New day. New dawn.

Your sister,
Misti Rains

To the Trail Blazers

"Do not go where the path may lead, go instead
where there is no path and leave a trail."
~ Ralph Waldo Emerson

THERE ARE THOSE TIRED OF THE DEBATING, THE HE-SAID-SHE-SAID, the I'm-right-and-you're-wrong endless wrestling and arguments. They are tired of the illusions of Republican or Democrat. They are sick of the way animals are treated in this country and around the world. They are disgusted with the disrespect for Mother Earth and the lack of appreciation for the healing and life she offers us. They are too smart to eat processed food, consume GMOs, and question the excessive amounts of vaccines being given to our children. They aren't afraid to pose questions to their government leaders, and they don't allow bullies to make them feel psycho when the stories they feed us on the news channels don't add up. They understand all too well the need for wars to maintain corrupted systems of power, greed, and control. They see through fake news stories to arouse the people and provoke them to wrath. They can see straight through tactics of divide and conquer. Their eyes are too enlightened to participate in the insanity of religious quarrels or anything that produces the fruit of separation and division. They refuse to be labeled or categorized. They have surpassed judgments and racism and the poison of pride.

They no longer defend.
They listen.
They no longer see differences.
They look for similarities.
They no longer fear.
They love.
They are love.
They give love.
They speak love.

These people are radically changing our world and pushing against the old epoch that is desperately trying to maintain its current reign of control. Though they are throwing quite the temper tantrum, this current system cannot prevent the inevitable shift that is upon us. They cannot stop the tide from turning, the stars from moving, the cycles from continuing. They cannot prevent the end of one age and the dawning of the next. They cannot take away the power of those who know who they are, why they came here, nor silence their joy and delight in completing the task before them. They cannot stop those who carry the power of God, and they know full well that they are not a victim of those who want to manipulate and control the masses.

Your prayers for peace, your voice of truth matters. You are effecting change that is impacting the consciousness of the entire world. Your thoughts, your words, and the path you are forging is affecting the whole. You are a drop to the wave, a piece of the whole, a part of the plan, and what you radiate changes the consistency of the entire organism. Even the earth and the land respond to the thoughts of mankind and humanity is waking up and remembering the truth of who they are. They are realizing they carry the power to make a difference. They are remembering they came here to contribute to this change.

To the Trail Blazers, mount your horses, take hatchet in hand and continue chopping down the brush. Don't look to the left. Don't look to the right. You mustn't allow for distractions lest you fall off your horse. Keep your eyes straight ahead to the path you are clearing. There is a massive army of people trailing behind you.

Happy trails!

"Blessed are the peacemakers: for they shall
be called the children of God."
(Matthew 5:9)

Love Wins

"We don't even know how strong we are until we are forced to
bring that hidden strength forward. In times of tragedy, of war, of
necessity, people do amazing things. The human capacity for
survival and renewal is awesome."
~ Isabel Allende

GROWING UP, I HAD HEARD OF WARS. I studied them in books and watched them depicted in movies. Although the story would always encapsulate a woven thread of tragedy and loss, there was a more compelling theme that would capture my lingering thoughts and hold my most considerable attention. My mind would always fixate on the heroine or the band of brothers and loyal followers that championed their worthy cause, their fight for freedom, for truth, or for justice. Although the tragedy was there, the perseverance, fortitude and sheer strength in the hearts of the people would mesmerize me and leave me oddly full of a glorious hope, a deeper wisdom, and an appreciation for what their fight represented. What I saw in the people was so much greater than what I saw happening in the world around them.

Today I am forty-two years old, and I can officially say I have lived to see my country at war. I have lived to see our world at war. Yet, in the midst of those horrific seasons, I also see something happening among the people that lead me to feel light amidst the darkest of nights. The love, the compassion, the desire for Light and life, and the renewed birth of peace and health is rising strong and mighty within the people.

Love for our world is at its height.
Love for our brothers and sisters is shining forth.
Love for those suffering loss.
Love for those we do not know.
Love for those who need our prayers.
Love for those of a different race, nationality, political, or religious
affiliation.
Quite simply, I see love.
And this I know . . .
Love conquers all.

To those suffering at the sight of war, know that
a greater movement is lying beneath the surface
of the evil that stirs above the ground.

Hold fast.

While some are saying it's hopeless, there are those rising with greater hope than ever before. There are those finding a strength they never knew they had. We are praying with a greater reach. We are loving with an endless supply. We are releasing a spirit of truth. We are ushering in a movement of peace. We are releasing the kingdom of heaven on earth from within our hearts. The treasure placed within us is going to heal the depravity around us. The purity within is going to cleanse the blemishes that are layered atop our beautiful world.

Fear not.
Love wins.

Some people see a problem. Other people use problems as a means
to discover a solution.

Join us.
We are the peacemakers, and we need you.
The world needs you.
Pray for the broken.
Let healing arise.
Shine bright.

Ye are of God, little children, and have overcome them: because
greater is he that is in you, than he that is in the world.
(1 John 4:4)

Divide and Conquer

RECENTLY, I'VE HAD MANY PEOPLE PRIVATELY SENDING ME POLITICAL MESSAGES, asking whom I'm voting for, and wanting to share their views with me about the election. My blanket response has been to quietly smile, try to comment as little as possible, and then release the tremendous sadness I feel regarding the collective state of human consciousness. As I scroll through the Facebook news-feed reading as people debate one another, argue their viewpoints, speak badly of people they don't know, and quarrel and fight amongst themselves, I can't help but get a feeling of nauseousness. It's enough to quieten the soul and create a pause. Is anyone else taking a step back? Has anyone else sat in the stillness and asked, "How have I contributed to this madness?"

Love One Another.

That statement begs us to ask the heart probing questions, "Did the statement you made about the political candidate you don't like fall into that category? What emotions are being held within your heart regarding those you view as your enemy?" Religion and politics have created more division than most could bear to perceive if left to truly contemplate its effects. I feel regret for the moments when my own opinions or beliefs dissipated deeper truths such as, "Do not judge."

Do we pray for our enemies, or do we rant about them on social media? How close to the image of our morals do we appear to the world. Something must be broken because the world is terribly divided.

It's Christian vs. Muslim.

It's Jew vs. Christian.

It's gay vs. straight.

Republican vs. Democrat.

It's one person's opinion about how to eat vs. another person's opinion about how to eat.

It's pro-life vs. pro-choice.

It's a wall vs. no wall.

It's black vs. white.

It's flat earth vs. globe earth.

It's everyone ranting and raving about who, in their opinion, the Anti-Christ will be.

It's you're justified by faith alone apart from works vs. you're justified by works and not by faith alone.

It's this scripture vs. that scripture.

It's James vs. Paul. It's Jesus vs. Paul.

It's Yahweh initiating and leading the charge to destroy your enemies vs. Jesus saying to pray for and bless them.

It's Yeshua vs. Yahusha vs. Jesus. It's this name vs. that name.

It's Old Testament vs. New Testament.

It's I say it this way vs. you say it that way.

It's you're saved this way vs. No! You're saved that way!

At some point, we must lay aside our differences. We all sound like ridiculous clanging cymbals. The pastors, the leaders, the politicians, the activists, and the everyday person like you and me—all noisy instruments having no love nor demonstrating self-control or kindness. Have we forgotten, "Be ye kind one to another?" Did we lay that aside while we expressed our religious beliefs and political opinions? And while we are spending all this energy and time arguing back and forth with one another, who is feeding the poor, who is loving the wayward and lost, the downtrodden, the hurting, the broken, and the confused?

Love belongs to those who are not easily provoked, who think no evil, who bear all things, who do not behave rudely, and who are not busy parading themselves. Love rejoices in the truth. What truth? The truth that states,

"Love conquers all."

Mercy will always and forever trump justice. Perhaps if our hearts were flooded with mercy instead of seeking justice, a shift in the consciousness of this world could occur. A mind like Christ could take form where instead of preaching about it, we could actually love our neighbors as ourselves. Not just the neighbor that looks like us and behaves like us and has our set of beliefs, opinions, and morals but the ones that we judge, the ones that we label, and the ones that we tear down.

Divide and conquer is getting really old. Is there anyone else ready to abandon participating in this way of existence? It's time to evolve. It is true that life and death is in the power of the tongue. It is true that we must choose our words carefully. But choosing life is something that begins in the heart. How we feel about the world around us, how we feel towards others that are different than us, the emotions we carry in our hearts matter. Choose life.

How long has it been since you've listened with compassion to someone with a different belief system than you? Seeing the divisiveness around me has caused me to think twice before my next rant on whether or not someone should behave a certain way, argue the many contradictions in the Bible, or blatantly defend who I'm voting for in the latest political campaign. I pray the deterioration of unity amongst us will cause a serious thought-provoking pause from within us all. May our first thoughts simply remain...

Love one another.

Be kind one to another.

Forgive.

Show compassion.

Do not judge.

Be merciful.

Hate no one.

Remove prejudices.

Listen.

Be patient.

Exercise self-control.

Model humility.

And never ever forget...

LOVE CONQUERS ALL.

Dear Mr. Anchorman

Dear Mr. Anchorman,

I'm breaking up with you. The racism and rhetoric you continue to promote is not working out for me anymore. I hope you understand. It's not you. It's me. My vibration can no longer hold a space for you. We've chosen different paths. I'm sure someone else will love you, but I can no longer tolerate you. I've made a choice not to include you in my experience. Best of luck highlighting all that's broken in this world. How's that working out for you by the way?

Whenever you decide to promote peace, give me a call, and perhaps we can meet for dinner. Please let me know if you decide to broadcast the loving heart of America in brothers and sisters united in love all across this country. I would love to know if you decide to show stories of inclusion, hope, kindness, and unity. If so, I would be more than happy to invest my mind, time, and energy in seeing an example for Americans, both young and old, to emulate. Pardon me for a moment when I get lost in the ecstasy of how powerfully transforming television with a continuous positive message could be for humanity.

Sometimes you just have to make a decision to love yourself enough to make a clean break, particularly from something that no longer serves the direction for where you envision going. In this case, I genuinely pray there are no more fish in the sea for you to trap in your vicious cycle of divide and conquer.

Please delete my number. When you start broadcasting a different signal, I'm sure my Internal Guidance System will pick it up. Until then, please don't try and beg me to stay. I have a new lover. His name is Peacemaker, and we are perfect for one another. We live in a place called Heaven on Earth. We choose to see a different world than you, and we are very happy.

If you get exhausted from the negativity and desire a better existence, please feel free to visit anytime! My new boyfriend has this uncanny ability to love and accept anyone. Just being in his presence seems to bring everyone to the Light. Perhaps one day, the two of you will meet.

Until then, it's best we not communicate. And yes, I'm going to need to block you. Perhaps when you watch your material, someday you'll understand why. Thanks for teaching me how much I really dislike you and how much I desire a peaceful world. You served your purpose well, and now it's time I close the door on that chapter of learning.

Na na na na, na na na na, hey hey hey goodbye.

Sincerely,
Misti Rains

Dear Media, I Don't Believe You

ENTITIES FEED OFF OF FEAR. We do ourselves a service when we don't allow ourselves to engage with fear. Movies can stir the emotions and bring them to the surface. I have learned to ask myself with anything I'm encountering in life, how is this making me feel? Pay attention whenever you are watching television, the news, or any program, be it a documentary or a YouTube video, to see if what you are watching or listening to is creating fear or anger. These are very low vibrational states of being ranked alongside their companions: condemnation, guilt, and shame. Let's pretend we are ranking states of consciousness on a scale of one to one thousand with one being the lowest state of being and one thousand being the highest—those of which include love, peace, and joy. We would need to be vibrating at a frequency of two hundred or higher, surpassing the emotional states of blame, despair, and grief before being open to receive the higher vibrational truths. Thus, being immersed in feelings of fear, guilt, or anger can limit us from being in a place to receive a divine message from above. Fear changes our vibration and takes us out of alignment with the God frequency. Perhaps this is why when someone in the Bible would encounter an angel or a messenger of God, they were instantly told not to fear. The messenger wanted them in the right mindset and emitting the right emotions to receive the message correctly.

For example, when Mary was outside the tomb of Jesus, she was crying in a place where she should have been rejoicing. The angel had to ask her, "Woman, why are you crying?" When we are upset, we can't hear clearly. Sometimes we have to stop crying so we can hear the message of God. In the story, she was mourning in a place where Christ had risen. I have been in that position before, crying when I should have been rejoicing. The problem I thought was there to chain me, with a shift of perception, became the solution sent to liberate me.

How you feel truly does determine how you heal. Why are certain entities wanting to keep you in a vibration of fear, anger, separation, and blame? These states of being block you from connecting to the Divine and receiving the highest truths about you, God, and the world around you. Why do they not want you to know these things? Because if you knew the truth regarding how powerful you are, no one nor any circumstance would be able to control or limit you. Some know the truth, yet they do not apply it to liberate themselves, and they attempt to restrict others from having access to it. Instead, they distort the truth and use it as a form of black magic to control people. As Jesus said,

"Woe to you, teachers of the law and Pharisees, you hypocrites! You shut the door of the kingdom of heaven in people's faces. You yourselves do not enter, nor will you let those enter who are trying to."
(Matthew 23:13)

I believe the news has become one of the worst forms of mind control in the world today. It is used to keep people feeling angry, separate, and divided from one another. Many people only believe what they see, not what they innately know to be true. They haven't taken time in the stillness to hear the truth of Divinity whispering to them. They wake instantly reaching for their phones or the remote control. They are being controlled by a remote and programmed by their television "programs." They are missing the precious moments of spiritual insights that come by walking outside and taking a few moments to sit listening to the birds. Our Mother Earth is a living entity all her own. She will speak if we would but listen to her wisdom.

They are missing the precious moments of spiritual insights that come by walking outside and taking a few moments to sit listening to the birds.

Fortunately, many people are waking up to this. The depressing old constructs of bickering and fighting amongst ourselves is getting old. We are asking more from our media outlets. We are going to other resources to find stories of inspiration, messages of hope, and silly videos that make us laugh and lighten our day. We want to feel happy. We are begging for it! Eventually, I believe the media will be forced to tailor their content to the growing number of enlightened souls emerging strong and seeking for their minds to be stimulated intellectually and their hearts to be pierced emotionally with things that help us all to grow, evolve, and unify our world.

In the interim, the more detached we can be from any negativity the mainstream media decides to feed us, the healthier our minds will be. Hypnosis, in its most basic form, is simply repeating something over and over again, e.g., commercials and musical lyrics. There was a song we use to sing when I was little girl that said, "Be careful little eyes what you see. Be careful little ears what you hear." If you view or listen to something long enough, it will impress itself upon your subconscious mind where the images or thoughts ultimately become a part of your belief system. Your beliefs determine everything you will encounter or experience in your life. Our reality is shaped by what we believe to be true.

As a man thinketh in his heart so is he
As within so without

Our Earth at large also has a worldwide consciousness based on what the people as a whole believe to be true. If just a handful of people can convince us of how to believe, they can limit and control us. With that said, it only takes a small portion of the world's population who understand their innate Divine power to change the tide and rewrite whatever story those separated from the Light have fed us. Statistics have proven that one person vibrating in the frequency of love can influence, shift, and uplift over seven hundred and fifty people. How you feel right now is affecting the entire planet. Whether anyone ever reads the words I am writing, the frequency I am emitting right now is already helping to heal the world.

You can truly change the world by healing you.

You do not need to give a life-altering speech or write a best-selling novel. By simply holding a space of peace and unconditional love for the world, you will have shifted to becoming a solution for all that is broken in it.

Guard your space. Keep it purely devoted to the highest truths. It amazes me how we wonder why our present world is in such disarray and division with its quarrels, strife, jealousy, and wars. Yet, we've all been raised watching these dramas play out on movies screens year after year, conditioning our minds and adapting us to these agendas. We watch riots on TV and fighting amongst divided opinions, and we wonder why we see these things growing and becoming more rampant among us. The power of one photographic image can remain seared in the human mind for a lifetime. The desensitizing that has occurred regarding bombs, terrorist, and school shootings is a perfect example. Years ago, we were in shock, disbelief, grief, and deep sorrow when we heard about the Columbine High School shooting. We were stunned and could hardly imagine something like this happening in schools that we once considered a safe haven for our children. Today we hear of school shootings on a regular basis. Do we not think the chronic mass media coverage of such events has not contributed to the epidemic?

The solution lies in unplugging. It's sort of like Jim Carrey says at the end of The Truman Show. He turned to the cameras watching him and said,

"Good morning, and in case I don't see ya, good afternoon, good evening, and good night!"

Turn off the television, stop playing the war video games, and avoid going to movies where you watch things blow up, get destroyed, invaded, or controlled. As Mahatma Gandhi said,

"Be the change you wish to see in the world."

If, as a society, we continue to watch movies or play video games about death, destruction, abusive relationships, and violence, perhaps we are part of the problem. If this be the case, maybe it's time to evaluate our contribution to the epidemic and realize we are not helping to represent a solution. We are being baited hook, line, and sinker, playing right into the hands of evil and divisiveness.

Detox from the mind control. Retreat to the mountains. Sit by the ocean. Step into your backyard. Invite some friends over for dinner. Instead of looking at your iPhone, look people in the eyes. Connect to others. Connect with yourself. Connect with the earth. Go home. The kingdom of heaven is here. It is at hand. You can experience it every day of your life. As Dorothy once learned in The Wizard of Oz, the answer to her peace, happiness, and returning home was in her all along. Get off the yellow brick road with all its creepy creatures and distorted voices. Look behind the curtain and expose the truth of who you truly are and what you are capable of achieving. As Jesus Christ said in Mark 9:23,

"If you can believe, nothing shall be impossible for you."

Let Compassion Rise

MAY COMPASSION RISE AMONG US ALL. May it so consume us that we experience the love and compassion of the Divine and are able to recognize the Spirit's breath in all creatures. When we learn to respect nature, nature will, in turn, yield to respecting us. As we sow to the earth and the animal kingdom, we will receive back the blessings it longs to bestow upon us. We cannot sow death and expect to reap life. That which we kill may also kill us. Those who live by the sword must also die by the sword. We must learn these truths to ensure a peaceful way of life will ensue on this earth.

If you are waiting on a Christ to return and end the shedding blood of the innocent, we must first ask, "Did Christ ever truly leave? Is He not dwelling within us?" While we are waiting on Christ to return and solve the problem, perhaps Christ is waiting on us? Do we not house the power of God? What have we done with the Living Word He has placed within us? Are we not the temple housing the glory and radiance of God? If so, why aren't we conquering our selfishness and in turn caring for the least of these? Choose life, not death. Choose to give life, not take it. Not from anyone, not from anything, not from any creature, not ever. Be a life-giver and the universe will breathe life-giving health, peace, prosperity, and all its wonderful gifts upon you. Your Spirit will be at peace with Mother Nature, and she will provide for you with the same nurturing love and care you have bestowed upon her.

Still Mending

I'VE GOT TO SAY, TODAY WAS A BIT DISCOURAGING. I keep a picture on my phone as a screen saver that says,

"Our truth is stronger than the illusion. Never forget that."

But today I caved. It's really hard not to get lured into the mayhem that currently encapsulates us. I found myself being enticed by politics and getting angrier and angrier with each news segment or negative Facebook post I read in my newsfeed. Then I saw a video of a child being abused. It infuriated me when I saw it, and I wanted to bring as much awareness as I could to the injustice of the situation, so I posted about it on my timeline.

Perhaps I shouldn't have posted it or added any more energy to it. I still struggle with things I share sometimes. I always want my post to inspire, encourage, and uplift, but it can be a real struggle at times to keep a good rant to myself.

Point being, some days I get it right. Some days I get it wrong. I don't always know what is best, and sometimes I am overwhelmed by all the divisiveness and multi-layered opinions of others. But then there are those redeeming moments that set me back on track and provide a momentary cleansing that redirects and places me on my ordained path once again. Such a moment occurred this evening as I was reading Kate a Bible story. The end of the story is paraphrased by saying,

"Jesus helped many people. He made sad things come untrue. He was mending God's broken world."

I paused and said to Kate,

"I believe God is still in the business of healing a broken world. I know this to be true, because he is most definitely mending mine."

With that peace and reassurance, I close my eyes, cast my care, and rest in knowing there are people all over this world being the hands and feet of Jesus. In the midst of confusion, dissension, and chaos, we still rest in the shadow of an Almighty Source that mends hearts and heals a broken world.

STILLNESS

Just Us

SOMETIMES I WAKE IN CONFUSION. Sometimes I wake with the weight of yesterday's burdens on my shoulders. I replay the conversations, particularly the ones when I spoke, when I answered questions, and when I shared. Were there any moments when I chose to smile but kept the truest expressions of my heart nestled and protected behind its safely secured walls? Were there moments when I should have said more? Should I have exposed more, or should I have sat longer in silence listening to them—to the atmosphere, to Lady Wisdom, to the sweet Holy Spirit?

I wake pondering it all. In those tender, sweet droplets of the early morning, my heart is pliable. My mind is reflecting. I can feel any hurt that didn't get cleansed during the night. I can feel any feelings of insecurity, doubt, or misaligned thoughts about my future. I lie. I reflect. I look very clearly at what is.

And then . . .

The work begins with added grace, added ease, and added pleasure. The Spirit begins her glorious process of transmutation and cleansing what is present until only love remains. This is when the magic begins —

when *what is* transforms to into *what shall be.*

It's when the music starts. It's when the worship and gratitude begin. It's when my heart fully surrenders for my daily bath in the grace, wisdom, and guidance of the Divine Helper, the Divine Healer, and the Divine Supplier.

I allow the presence of something beyond beautiful to begin rising strong within me. It's otherworldly. This Spirit is a Kingdom all her own. She sparkles Light in my soul like the sun twinkles diamonds upon the waters. She gives me strength I do not have. She gives me truth I did not know. She is my kind Teacher. She mothers me. She touches my heart like she touched Mary's womb. She places life where I feel empty. She hovers over me as she once did over the face of the ancient deep. She brushes my hair with her gentle wind. She reminds me, "You are worthy. You are not to be compared with another. I am upholding you. My glory sits upon you. I have a plan for you and rest assured, I will see it to completion. There is most indeed a blessed hope, and you can depend upon it."

She comes close and whispers in my ear,
"I have a promise for you."

In grief, you are my Great Lover nurturing me in your arms.
In feeling lost, you are the Lighthouse guiding me home.
In confusion, you are my Missing Puzzle Piece.
In lack, you are my Abundance.
In loneliness, you are my Intimate Love Affair,
never failing to be a present touch of affirmation.

You are it. You're everything. What else is needed when a Spirit with such power and potency sits, hovers, abides, flows, and releases in the seat of my soul? When I can't, You can. You remind me I'm not alone down here doing this thing called life all by myself. I have a Great Helper. I have angels. I have a heavenly host surrounding me, offering continuous love and guidance.

Sometimes when I wake, I feel lost.
But then, I pause.
I do that thing we do together.
I start to feel you.
The appreciation comes.
And then when the love touches me . . .
everything changes.
You make me Superwoman.
You make me fly.

When I feel like petals are falling from my stem, you are the rain and sunshine that makes me bloom again. You make me to sparkle brighter than the prettiest star in all the heavens.

And what takes it over the top, the icing on the cake? You are inside of me, and I am inside of you. My mama lives here too. We are One. We can do anything together.

You are with me always, even until the end of the age,
and then some.

Sometimes when I wake, I think about You, and I believe we're going to change the whole wide world together. You and I together equate to a majestic, magnetic combo that warrants no impossibilities, no restrictions, no hurt, no heartbreak—just us—just joy, just peace, just reassurance, just beauty, just grace, just ease, just kindness, just trust, just . . .

LOVE.

I woke a little lost, but now I am found.
I woke a little blind, but now . . .
I can see.

Meditation

1 MEDITATED FOR AN INDEFINITE SPACE THIS MORNING until I was in complete oneness with my Father. These are the best moments of all. Where I get lost in Divinity, no longer able to recognize where I end, and the Father begins. Layers of baggage were shed.

A lifetime of miracles can infuse themselves into our being during this sacred time of meditation. We see pure love and pure beauty. There is no grief, no worry, no pain, no weights of unforgiveness, no feelings of lack, rejection, hurt, or desires left unmet. All is complete. This is freedom. This is soaring. This is abundant life. This is how I know the kingdom is not something to be obtained. It is something to be felt continually from a great divine wellspring from within.

I am happy. I am floating. There are no limits to possibility. Why we do not "be still and know I am God" is beyond me. All answers and freedoms are found here. Imagination and creative power are released here.

If you don't start your day with the sheer bliss of meditation, I don't know how else to say it other than you're missing out. Take a moment to feel God's power electrify you. It's not one of those things you ever regret doing. When I miss this, I get loss during my day. When I do it, I get found in the Creative Power of my Father. It's when we begin dancing seamlessly with one another in complete tandem. I replace all my negativity with all of heaven's positivity.

Meditation is where I am spiritually washed. My eyes and ears are cleansed. My mind is renewed. My heart is revived. It's where God and I plan and dream together. I awake inspired. I awake limitless. I awake to moved mountains. I awake soaring high above them. Where life was once defeating, life becomes electrifyingly abundant, gloriously adventurous, and one I would choose to experience a million times over in a million different ways!

Meditate yourself into oneness with your Father.
Close your eyes and enter His glorious heavens.
Enter through the portal of your heart.
Open your eyes and see the world anew.

"Neither pray I for these alone, but for them also which shall believe on me through their word; That they all may be one; as thou, Father, art in me, and I in thee, that they also may be one in us: that the world may believe that thou hast sent me. And the glory which thou gavest me I have given them; that they may be one, even as we are one: I in them, and thou in me, that they may be made perfect in one; and that the world may know that thou hast sent me, and hast loved them, as thou hast loved me. Father, I will that they also, whom thou hast given me, be with me where I am; that they may behold my glory, which thou hast given me: for thou lovedst me before the foundation of the world. And I have declared unto them thy name, and will declare it: that the love wherewith thou hast loved me may be in them, and I in them."
(John 17:20-24, 26 KJV)

Just Breathe

THERE IS A REASON THE ANCIENTS ADVISED US TO FOCUS on our breath during meditation. When we focus on our breath, we are reminded of the Source from whence we came. This is the Breath of Life, the Breath of God, emanating within us and flowing through our entire being. This is the Divine Spirit empowering you to live. When we place our attention there, we are reminded of who we are. In this knowing, we are empowered to face any and all circumstances with confidence and strength.

I am of the belief that a few, deep intentional breaths can heal just about any anxiety, stress, or worry known to man. The more present I am with this, the stronger effect it has on me. Whenever I am stressed or worried, want to start my day on the right foot, or simply want to bliss out in a feeling of peace and calm, I take several deep breaths. I breathe in deep, holding the air in my body before slowly releasing it.

When I breathe, I see my entire being surrounded by a beautiful, brilliant light. I breathe in the Light and release it to the space around me. Sometimes I envision purple and gold sparkles in my Light to raise my vibration from one of doubt and defeat to one of belief and victory.

In addition, I also use this technique when I am hungry. As Jesus Christ taught us, there is food not of this world that nourishes and replenishes the soul. Often, if trying to curb my appetite, I will feed on the manna from above and digest a Light that fuels my body and my soul.

> Breathe in Light, breathe out darkness
>
> Breathe in peace, breathe out chaos
>
> Breathe in love, breathe out hate
>
> Breathe in compassion, breathe out judgment
>
> Breathe in freedom, breathe out entrapment
>
> Breathe in forgiveness, breathe out punishment
>
> Breathe in kindness, breathe out guilt and shame
>
> Breathe in truth, breathe out fear
>
> Breathe in the truth; breathe out the illusion.
>
> Just breathe

Morning Reflections

I'M LYING HERE IN THE STILLNESS ENJOYING A MORNING GAZE out the window. I wonder how much different our lives would be if we began each day with a moment sitting with a heart-piercing melody to touch the soul and warm the most drown trodden spirit. When I take a moment of reflection, when I don't miss the savoring, I never fail to absorb a rendering of movement stirring the most intimate places within. No matter how confusing the puzzle of life is in that moment or how torn the fragments seem to be, sunshine begins to flood my heart. I'll recall deep, passionate love and swirls of dancing and spinning in the green summer grass with my three little Loves. My heart feels like a rainbow, I begin seeing butterflies once more, and nostalgia floods me with gratitude for the gifts that have been awarded to my soul via each experience life has given me.

The valleys, the mountains peaks, the treks through a few wildernesses, and even the darkened alleys begin to bring a swelling of sweetness and morning glory. Every moment, those laced in victory and also those cloaked in utter defeat, bring forth a rising. The scorpion hiding and stinging itself in the corner begins to rise like the phoenix.

These morning moments of stillness assists my heart in recollecting on the people that have brought forth a special lighting to my soul. I hold their smiles in my memory. I think of their sacrifices for me, and I remind myself why I continue to serve and make sacrifices for them. These moments are where I find my grounding, my humility, and those life-laid-down renderings for the family and friends I love so dearly. These are the moments we seek forgiveness, we bathe in grace, and we let God hold us in the reassurance that He is with us and is loving us relentlessly through it all.

Let life begin with a pretty song and a little stillness today. Your darkened path will find its illumination. You were created to feel the rainbows, to hope like a butterfly, to appreciate the rain, and to shine like the sun.

Turn on the Light

ONE DAY I WAS GETTING INCREDIBLY FRUSTRATED with the course my day was taking, and the Spirit said to me,

"If you didn't pray, meditate, and fill your house with Light this morning, why are you surprised that darkness has settled in?"

Very quickly I realized that if I didn't pray and meditate each morning and download the Light of God, I would accumulate the absence of light, which is darkness.

"Darkness is merely the absence of light; fear is merely the absence of love. We can't get rid of darkness by hitting it with a baseball bat, because there's nothing to hit. If we want to be rid of darkness, we must turn on a light."
~ Marianne Williamson

I have found that just five minutes spent with the Holy Spirit in the morning is enough to guarantee I will be in charge of my thought forms throughout the day. That's how much power we have through prayer and meditation!

Take time to bring heaven into your heart each morning.
Turn on the Light!

Let It Be

I'M CURRENTLY WORKING ON GETTING OUT OF THE THINKING and into the being. This week I was listening to a friend verbalizing her thoughts something to the tune of, "If this happens then I'll do that, but then I won't know what to do with this, and then I won't know how to react to that." I found myself responding with a deep breath before replying, "Don't think. Just be."

I am learning to stop worrying about moments that have yet to happen and just be in the ones that are taking place now. By allowing my mind to wander too far in the future or too far in the past, I fail to appreciate the bliss that exists in this moment. The more I release and let go of the worries, the fears, and the distractions, the happier I am in the present moment.

Technology really took a toll on me to the point I found myself reaching for a distraction anytime I had a dull moment such as waiting in line at the post office or grocery store. I was always filling my moments with something to do to the point I forgot how to simply be. When I laid my phone aside, I began to see the world again. I began to wonder again. Instead of checking my phone, I began to check the faces of those around me.

There is so much to be absorbed and learned during those in-between moments of waiting and stillness. I found miracles there. I discovered wonderment, ideas, and connection. There are blessings and gifts to be discovered while waiting. We all seem to only want the express lane or the fast food. Let us not extinguish the gift of waiting and the treasures found in her wisdom.

There is a lot we miss when we fail to appreciate the beauty of silence. I see so much more splendor in the world when I take time to breathe, don't think, and just be. Those are the moments when I usually find the answers to all the problems I've been exhausting myself thinking about. Just being in the moment and appreciating where I am, releases the resistance that allows the truth to flow to me naturally and effortlessly, with grace and ease.

Let there be peace.
Let there be happiness.
Let there be joy.
Let there be abundance.
Let there be health.
Let it be.

Summer Nights

So, YEAH. I LIKE GOING OUT TO AN AESTHETICALLY PLEASING RESTAURANT with candles flickering and melodies permeating the air. I like it best with a little dancing, some deep, meaningful conversations, really fantastic laughs, and eye contact that touches the soul. But the thing is, there are these moments on my back porch that make all others pale in comparison. I suppose they take me back to my childhood. They remind me of when I use to spend more time barefoot than I did in shiny heels, and when I spent hours lying on my trampoline, contemplating the stars. I was the girl who took my journal to the pier and wrote until the sun had set, and I could no longer see my pages beneath the moonlight.

Tonight, it's the sounds of a sweet summer night that move me the most. The cicadas are making their harmonious melodies making the only place to be a front-row seat beneath the canopy of the sky. These are the nights we try and create a simpler time when life was nothing but playing in the sprinklers and drinking homemade lemonade.

I can't go back to my childhood, but I can try to recreate it every day for the rest of my life. I can take time to wonder and sit in awe. I can take time to appreciate the pretty little hydrangea bushes that someone once planted in this yard. Hydrangeas are my favorite flower, and now I'm left to wonder if God whispered in someone's ear a long time ago, knowing I would one day sit here admiring their delicate beauty.

She dreams. She ponders. She takes time to simply be.

I believe we were made to really need these moments. Every now and then we should catch some fireflies and stare into a flickering candle. We should hang twinkle lights and make a tent on the porch just so we can sleep beneath the stars. We should romance our soul more often. We should not be afraid to let the crickets be our only distraction and spend a few moments alone really falling in love with ourselves.

Make it madly.
Make it deeply.
Fall hard for you.
You're spectacular.
Get dreamy and inspire yourself.

The best summer love story you'll ever experience is with you. With that said, definitely throw in a few passionate kisses for summer romance and grins!

Live beautifully.
Make your nights sparkle
and keep your back porches smelling divine.

Seasons of Silence

THERE ARE SEASONS IN LIFE WHEN WE SHOULD TEACH AND SHARE from what we have gleaned in our various fields, and there are times when we should be quiet, reflect, listen, and absorb. There is a time to be the teacher. There is a time to be the student.

If one wishes to lead, they must first learn to follow. I have been in a season of testing, a time to follow and not lead. Life has been a series of pulling me in and out of the wilderness to face the darkest shadows of my soul. The wilderness is not a time to speak. It is a time of wandering, of standing, of character testing. When stones are being offered as bread to a hungry soul, one's focus is on passing their test. The time to teach of it has not been awarded. The cross must always be faced for a resurrection to occur. The Garden of Gethsemane wasn't called "the pressing place" randomly. Sometimes we must learn to sit beneath the olive trees and experience the crushing so the oil can one day flow.

I am silent because God in His kindness has granted me wisdom to be quiet and not speak. The back side of the wilderness is not the moment you teach others how to overcome. It is a time for learning how to overcome yourself. Red Sea moments of carrying people across a miraculous exodus of their soul to a promised land does not come without proper moments of thirsty treks through a desert having conversations with the parts of yourself that must be placed into the ground to die. Mounts of Transfiguration do not come without first retreating to the hillside with the One that knows how to illuminate your soul and lighten the darkened world around you.

Someday, I'll tell you about my wilderness, and you can share yours with me. Until then, I pray you find Olivet Mount. Please pray I, a fellow journeyman, stand upon mine.

It's the Night
When Things Get Still

It's the night
When things get still
When we reflect
When we remember
When we choose to hold on or to let go

THE NIGHT IS TENDER. IT PREPS US FOR A STRENGTHENED SOUL REST. Decisions are made nestled beneath the crisp, cool sheets and softened pillows. It's a sacred moment. It's when we choose life or death, love or hate, doubt or fear, defeat, or hope. What shall fill your heart? What shall be the source of its swelling throughout the night? What shall be your fill? Do you release? Do you heal? Do you close your eyes to regret or do you lie down with an appreciation for what has been gleaned? What shall you do with the hurts of your day? What shall you do with the aches? Where shall you put the loss and disappointments?

It's the night
When things get still
When we choose life
When we choose forgiveness
When we choose a layer of compassion and a sprinkle of grace.

It's the final moments of the day to choose unconditional love. It's when you choose to be kind to yourself, to be kind to others, and to lace your life's view with rose-colored glasses of hopeful bliss. It's when your soul sleeps in prep for a glorious rise, a new day, and rejoicing for promises and victories to come.

It's the night
When things get still

It's when God sleeps with us. He nestles deep inside. He holds us tight. He whispers His sweet nothings. He touches our hearts with vision and with things unseen by human eyes. It's when we see with our hearts, soar with our spirits, and dance with our dreams.

Reflect with me
Restore with me
It's the night
When things get still

Color My World

THIS MORNING I'M WAKING WITH THE SUN. It's my personal preference. There's just something about the hues from a morning sunrise peering through your window. There is a freshness to her rays. The colors bring a rainbow of promise that today is a new day. A bare canvas lies before me to be painted anew with the pairing of my choice. What colors shall I drape upon the artistry of my day? The morning pinks sitting on the palette of the horizon remind me to include a touch of warmth, passion, and love. The glittering golds remind me to reflect the Light that has been entrusted to my care. The calming blues remind me to soothe the hurts of those who need a healing hand and a reassuring word of hope. The oranges bring with them a fire of boldness, strength, and fierceness to rise strongly from my bed and greet my day with tenacity and courage.

I know beyond this gorgeous prism of colors lies a mixture of them all, a glorious, brilliant, pure, white Light. I pause. I reflect. I give thanks to the One who gave thought to color my world. I ask and pray that I be a pretty pigment upon His.

God, enrich the colors of my soul that I may stain this world with beautiful rich hues to be displayed among all men. Make me Your canvas. Color my world. Teach me how to paint with colors that grace the halls of Your kingdom. May my life be a masterpiece lacing the walls of Your heavenly gallery. Bring me Your purchased pigments of love, beauty, hope, compassion, faith, and freeing truth. Steep them with Your notorious crimson red. I want to paint a picture with You. Show me the ingredients to brighten the dull, darkened stains that rest upon the weary, downtrodden hearts of mankind. Place your brush of joy with a tip of kindness in my palm. Teach me to paint well and to choose my colors wisely.

Thank You for coloring my world today. I'll see You again tomorrow for you have made Your colors in my life as consistent as the sun as she rises to greet me each day.

With deep gratitude,

An Artist in Training

Prayer is Listening

MANY OF US THINK OF PRAYER AS SPEAKING TO GOD, petitioning Him, and giving Him our requests. For many of us, our prayer time is largely dominated by our needs, wants, struggles, and worries. This week a friend made the statement to me, "Prayer is listening." I was taken aback. Whoa! I'm not sure I have ever really thought of prayer in terms of it being a time to be quiet and listen. Although many times I have sat still in God's presence to hear from Him, I'm not sure I have ever truly let it click with me that prayer in itself is not just speaking, but it is also listening.

Being in a state of prayer is also being in a receiving mode to hear from our Father. I am working on using my prayer time to listen more and speak less. This has become a game-changer for me in terms of what I've been able to hear and access from our loving Heavenly Father. I'm learning that prayer is also listening to God's instructions and then having the courage to trust and act upon that still small Voice. It's amazing what I receive when I take time to close my mouth, be still, and simply listen. For someone like me who is full of words and crafted for expression, this has been an area of maturity that has taken much time, growth, and a willingness to develop the fruit of patience and self-control. Perhaps God knew we would need a little help with this concept and thus, why He only gave us one mouth and two ears.

"My sheep hear my voice, and I know them, and they follow me:"
(John 10:27)

Serenade Yourself

I won't let go.

THERE WILL ALWAYS BE SOMEONE LYING AWAKE in the darkness of night wanting to believe in a force that can not only sing these words over them but can fervently fulfill them. I hope that someone finds the strength to look within and realize they are stronger than they could ever imagine. There is hope in there. There is comfort for the pains that arrive in the stillness.

To the one who feels their will has been broken . . . congratulations. In your sheer nothingness, you will find everything you've been searching for. Keep surrendering. Turn the Light on inside your weary, shattered heart. There is a peace to release that will illuminate your sadness and mend your fractured pieces. There is a Voice in there that will sing these words over you. Choose to listen to the melody. Only you can push "play" to receive this sacred song.

Go serenade yourself.

Take Flight

THERE MAY COME A TIME IN YOUR LIFE when your Spirit beckons you away for a season to embark upon a solo journey. You may be surrounded by people, but your soul will begin to desire a quiet place to restore itself. You may discover this time of introspection to be a long-overdue prescription for your healing path. There may be things you wish to pen, words and feelings you need to write to your own heart. Or maybe it will just be a season for you to slow down, to stop and smell the roses, to make a fire, light a candle, drink a cup of tea, watch the clouds, get still, and simply be with yourself for a little while.

There is an Internal Voice that guides your steps that is of utmost importance as it teaches you how to heal. When moments of significant transformation appear in your life, more than likely, you will recognize them. Be a good listener and position yourself to receive your breakthrough.

When an eagle is around forty years old, its physical condition begins to deteriorate rapidly, making it harder for the eagle to survive. The eagle's feathers begin to get worn-out, which causes its flight speed and maneuvers to slow down. As a result, the eagle will retreat to a cliff of rocks along the mountaintop to break off its beak and rip out its talons and feathers until it is entirely bare. This process allows the eagle to fly dynamically and royally again without much effort or toil. What is so profound to me about this moment in the eagle's life is that it never gives up living. Instead, it endures a painful process of metamorphosis waiting five months until a new set of feathers has grown back. During this time, regrowth of the removed body parts occurs, which allows the eagle to extend its life another thirty to forty years!

There will be times in your life when you must look back and take stock of your life, the good and the bad experiences you have endured. You must realign yourself with the original intentions your Maker and you set forth when your soul purposed to come here.

Perhaps this is your season to soar high and nestle yourself in the cleft of the rock, sheltered and held in the shadow of the Almighty. There are things that must be plucked away in order that you may gain new life and fly again, dynamically and royally without effort or toil.

I'm sure when the mother eagle watches her young soar to the hidden place to pluck out its feathers and bang its beak upon a rock, she struggles as her off-spring endures this awful, excruciating process. However, any wise mother eagle knows that for her child to live a long, extended life this is a process her child must endure. If you are aware of a fellow eagle enduring this process, be patient. Allow for a potential unraveling. Believe that they will fly again. We trim the rose bush so it can bloom again. Nature is always teaching. If we pay attention to her, she will provide us with answers and solutions to some of our most difficult mental and physical challenges.

> *"But ask the animals, and they will teach you, or the birds in the*
> *sky, and they will tell you; or speak to the earth, and it will teach*
> *you, or let the fish in the sea inform you."*
> (Job 12:7-8)

You may be taking some time to hide in the cleft of the rock, and perhaps your body may appear to be deteriorating. However, in actuality, you are just completing a metamorphosis so you can mount up like an eagle and soar majestically once again. You are extending your life, whether that be in this world or the eternal one to come. Trust in the mystical process of rebirth and growth.

Every eagle soars for a reason.
Discover yours and enjoy the flight.
Soar well, my friends, and soar high.
I'll meet you in the skies.

The Shining Ones

As a little girl, my mom would testify to my fascination with nature, my love for the sunset, and my desire to lie beneath the stars. Eventually, when I was finally old enough, she would let me go alone to the pier at night where I could lie close to the water and look at the night sky. If I wasn't on a blanket in the grass, lying atop the trampoline, or in the most recent stick fort I had built, I was somewhere to be found stargazing and collecting thoughts to be written in my journals.

It was while listening to the cricket's chirp and watching the twinkling of stars that I first knew they were our angels. It made no difference to me what the Science teachers said. They knew, and I knew when we stared back at one another. Many times, I have looked upon this great Cloud of Witnesses with a quiet smile, with a feeling of hope or expectation, and with enormous peace in my heart. Other times I have looked upon them with sadness, a sense of feeling lost, and with much confusion plaguing my mind. No matter what the condition I was in at the time, they have always been there staring back. They maintained their order and position. They moved at the command of their Creator. They've never failed to carry forth their purpose and whisper the cheers they are so wonderfully known for, cheers that spur us on and are recognized by the hearts and minds of those who take the time to look upon them. When they herald their messages and are called upon to shine forth, a King emerges and wise men find their long-sought for destination, the place by which they give and receive their treasures.

Answers and clarity come in the stillness, and when my mind is quiet, I can always hear them best. I sit beneath them. If calm enough, if an ample supply of anxiety is removed, and if the stillness gets really perfect, I can hear them singing their beautiful songs. And if I rest long enough for the cares that are plaguing me to cease, I will sing with them. Although they love to bring their messages in our dreams and sometimes have to in order to get our attention, these glorious Messengers will use the still, quiet moments to bathe us in an unwavering knowing and a calm reassurance that provides great peace to the traveling soul.

Tonight, as I was driving home, once again, the stars caught my eye, and I knew they were telling me something very special. "Look at us," they said. "We have a message for you." I knew something meaningful was taking place. The twinkling was just different. They knew my curiosity would seek and seek well. We know each other. Whether I present as an adult or a child makes no difference to them. They recognize my soul, and I see theirs. They know my eyes, and I know their sparkle. It's that old familiar gaze we've shared so many times before. We look deeply at one another, and words are spoken more profound than any known language written by the hands of man. To speak the tongues of angels is to be still and quiet and allow the heart to use her voice.

Tonight, our hearts connected like so many times before. "Look at us. Have you seen it yet?" Ahhhhhh, the treasure hunt begins. Like a beautifully orchestrated game of hide and seek laced upon the heavens, and at last, I found the treasure! I found why they were sparkling so pretty tonight and pulling me in.

Oh, how fun it is to play with angels. My heart is full tonight, and I must express my gratitude for their sweetly draped message across the heavens this glorious evening. I see you all. I see you all so well. Bravo! Bravo! As pretty as you all are, and as wonderful as you all appeared glistening in all your splendid beauty this evening, I see what you wish to herald, dear friends. You have never failed to bring us the truth.

Tonight, a deeply meaningful love letter was written in the stars. To my fellow stargazers, to the angel watchers, to the wise ones who follow the Stars to find their King...I pray this blesses you as much as it did me.

What is the treasure? No matter where you live in the Southern Hemisphere, this evening, look in the southern sky as soon as darkness falls and there before you will appear the glistening brilliance of the breathtakingly gorgeous Southern Cross sparkling in all her glory.

What a message! Well done, Shining Ones!

Rest,
Little Plant

THE PAST TWO DAYS MY HEART HAS BEEN CONCERNED for a little plant to the side of my house that has been forgotten and is dying. It appeared starved for attention and in need of immediate nourishment. Its leaves were burned from the sun and of all the plants in the yard, this plant called to me. I made it my personal duty to see to it that this plant was watered. I even went and prayed for the little plant and sat with it a few moments so it could feel my love for it. Love can make anything grow. Love conquers all.

Just as I noticed the least of these and was mindful of this plant, so God is mindful of you. Where you have cared for the forgotten, God will care for you. As you have nurtured His creation, so He will nurture you.

God's Spirit has coursed through your body from the moment your life was conceived. He has always been with you, giving you the will and strength to survive and to accomplish all your soul chose to accomplish and learn when it made the decision to come here to evolve and grow. All the difficult experiences you have endured have not been to punish you or make you feel abandoned. Quite the contrary, they have taught you the beauty of remembering the forgotten plant, the forgotten ones. These deeds are remembered in the life to come and have matured your soul. They have allowed your soul to develop the divine virtues it was seeking to obtain.

The very fact you are here is reason enough for why you are deserving of goodness, grace, and God's help to live, survive, thrive, and grow. It's time now to release the suffering and torment trapped within your body from carrying emotional and mental pain for far too long. It is no longer serving you. You have learned what it was there to teach you. You are ready now to forgive and love others and to forgive and love yourself. You are as deserving of sun, water, and love, as the beautiful plants you have so lovingly tended.

If sickness or disease enters into your body, it is not because you have sinned or done something horribly wrong to warrant being forgotten or punished. The little plant did not deserve to wither. It wilted because it had not received the proper nourishment it needed. It had not been given the conditions it required to flourish.

However, where the plant was once lacking, with the proper awareness of its needs, it can be restored to life and vitality. In the same way, what you have lacked has now been provided for you: love, attention, affection, compassion, knowledge, and understanding. Allow God to nurture you. Absorb it into your body. Allow it to expel the pain and torment that trapped itself in your "leaves." Just like the plant, you will wither by accommodating such things as they steal and rob you of the nutrients you need to heal yourself.

As with all things in nature, this plant has intelligence that pulsates throughout it that wills it to live and that wants it to flourish. That Living Force is in you. That force is still surging throughout your chest and can be felt with every breath you take. That force is God, and He wants you to know that He sees you. You are not forgotten. He is raining upon you with all the nourishment you have lacked. He is restoring your soul. He is healing your "leaves." He is with you. He is inside of you. He is speaking to you. He's always been there from the moment you were born. He is not separate from you. He is not some divine favor having to be earned. He is offering you an unconditional, never-ending for all of eternity kind of love. His love for you is the ultimate Healer. Receive it into your body like the warmth of the sun and a fresh rain from heaven.

The very fact you are here is reason enough for why you are deserving of goodness, grace, and God's help to live, survive, thrive, and grow.

This is not about performance. This is not a time to do. This is a time to be still like the plant and wait. Your nourishment is coming to you. God has noticed you just as you have been attentive to other "plants" in their time of need. God will water you. He will remove the toxic things that have trapped themselves within your body. He requires you only be still.

It's hard to be still, isn't it, to simply rest and receive? So, God is helping you be still. His angels are bringing a healing balm for your soul. This is the imagery the Spirit wants you to have. Be thankful for such a wonderful gift. You have been chosen to receive a precious purification by the hands of angels unaware.

Rest, Little Plant. God remembers you forever and always. He remembered you and loved you before you came to this world, and He will remember you and love you when it's time for you to return home and continue the journey and evolution of your beautiful soul.

Under the Influence

WHEN I WRITE, MY HEART TENDS TO SPIN AND SWELL as the Spirit of God rises in me. My cheeks get flushed, my temperature feels warmer, and I often feel as if I am going to levitate off the ground. I can be anywhere, doing anything, and with anyone and when I hear the Whisper, I'll pause, feel the rush of Wind blow through me like a mighty, rushing River, and instantly, I'm in immediate need of pen and paper.

These days my instrument of divinely stored insight is most often the note section of my iPhone. When I write under the influence and power of such a magnificent force, it is as if my cognitive functioning has been shut down. Much like when I speak in tongues, although I cannot understand the dialect, my heart hears the message and mysteries are revealed. When writing under the influence of the Spirit, a wave of pure consciousness floods through every fiber of my being and often times it is difficult for my hands to keep up with the overflow and swiftness of the message. It's a symphony of thought, often rising to a climactic peak and then slowing to a gentle melody of words. For lack of a better analogy, it's like the sensation when you need to throw up but without the ill feelings and nastiness of the aftermath. It's the idea of something being inside that must come forth. If suppressed, it will project forth. Something has built within that must see its way to the surface. Afterward, I am often observing what has been written much the same as the reader. I will feel as if something was birthed and as with all things orchestrated by God, each utterance of life matters and has been uniquely conceived to serve a specific purpose.

There is a difference between when I am speaking and when directly influenced by this beautiful, pure form of God-consciousness, though my life's quest has been the merging of the two voices. When yielded to this force, it is leading for I have surrendered to its glorious guidance. I do not interrupt it. I do not critique it. Often, I may pause to ask it questions for a greater understanding, but I trust it as I know this Voice is all-knowing and has the greatest good of the whole always at work. When delivering a message, I do not stop to reason or rationalize the message with a mindset built upon this world or my own limited perceptions of it.

I wonder if Jesus, the man, felt similar when the Christ of God that had existed before the foundation of the world flooded His being? He too became divinity wrapped in humanity. He was a man subject to the concerns of this world and the feelings generated by those He knew and loved as they interpreted the messages He spoke. Yet, filled with the Spirit, He was empowered with a Divine Presence, a Holy Spirit, God's Spirit, which is wonderfully pure. He was definitely in this world but certainly not of it. He had found an inner kingdom that reigned from within his heart. He had found the truth revealed only by what He called The Father, as the thought of a Heavenly Parent seemed fitting for such a magnificent, guiding Light.

I am learning in my life to listen to this Heavenly Parent, this Divine Force, which in all truth is both male and female, both mother and father, a force that quite simply possesses everything we need. I used to taper these messages of divine inspiration to perhaps soften the blow of them or allow them to be more warmly received by the recipient. I used to intervene and seek to interpret them through my own lens of understanding. However, I woke from a dream recently, in which I was given the message,

> *There is no greater lens through which to view life than those that have been filtered by the Spirit of Truth.*
>
> *Sometimes we need something to rattle our cage so that the prison door can be shaken open.*

I have learned to not dilute the message through alterations in an attempt to please the will of the person receiving it. The potency is thus compromised and the message's ability to pierce the heart and melt the hard-wax exterior is lost. Squeezing and pressing the olive is what produces the rich olive oil. When Jesus went to heal the blind man, He asked him, "Tell me. What do you see?" It didn't matter that Jesus had healed the blind man's sight if he still could not see the truth.

> *To change the heart, we mustn't change the message.*

OVERCOMING NEGATIVITY

Stay Out of the Dirt

YESTERDAY I WORKED LAYING MULCH IN THE FLOWER BEDS. When I came in, the dye from the black mulch had seeped through my gloves onto my hands. It took me about ten minutes of continuous washing and scrubbing in the sink to get all the dirt off of me. I was amazed by how much the dirt and dye had settled into the cracks and crevices of my palms. I couldn't believe how much effort was required to get my hands completely clean again.

During this time of washing, I heard the Spirit say, "Whenever you spend time emerged in the dirt, it is going to take a while to get it off. The more you immerse yourself in it, the deeper it settles in and stains your skin. It requires time and effort to remove it."

I immediately thought of negativity in any form, be it criticism, defeating mindsets, lack of encouragement, kindness, compassion, or love for one another. Negativity can manifest itself in so many forms: anger, jealousy, resentfulness, bitterness, feelings of inadequacy, low self-esteem, doubt, fear, and the list goes on and on. How long do we play around with this dirt? How long do we allow ourselves to be immersed in it?

I held the mental image of my dirty hands spreading the mulch thick and wide around the flowers. Isn't this the perfect image of what negativity does when it sits upon us? We end up spreading it deeper and wider until it's pressed against and choking the beautiful, vibrant flowers it presses itself upon. The longer we allow ourselves to "have our hands in the dirt" or stay connected to this negativity, the deeper it settles into our skin—into our being, into our minds and hearts. And the longer you spend in this dirt, the more time and effort it takes to remove it. However, even if I had dipped my hands into the bag of damp, black mulch and left them for just a short period, I would still be left with dirty stains that would require some time to rinse them off. Any amount of time spent in a negative atmosphere will have an effect on you.

Bottom line: Stay out of the "dirt." Keep yourself clean of it. Don't allow for the stains. Don't allow it to settle into the fabric of who you are. Negativity is a black virus that requires a sincere effort to remove. If you ever find your life colored by it, grab the soap, turn on the water, and take a good long shower. Stay in there for as long as you need, washing that mess off of you. When you emerge clean and refreshed, remember how long it took you to scrub it off, and never stick your hands in that "dirt" ever again.

Atop the Waters

THERE IS A PASSAGE IN THE BIBLE THAT SAYS, "Therefore, if you are offering your gift at the altar and there remember that your brother or sister has something against you, leave your gift there in front of the altar. First go and be reconciled to them; then come and offer your gift." (Matthew 5:23-24) I have applied this passage of wisdom in many ways throughout my life, but I will list below one of the greatest ways it has served me.

To be attuned to the frequency of God means to embody and literally vibrate his characteristics, those of which are love, peace, kindness, understanding, patience, and forgiveness. If ever I find myself engaged in a conversation in which I am not in the above frame of mind, I have learned it serves the highest good for the other party and me to remain quiet and not engage. If someone is expressing themselves to you and is speaking with a tone of frustration, irritation, or anger, stay calm and ask for some time to process what they have said before replying.

You have the ability to discern the spirit behind what someone is communicating and whether or not he or she is coming from a space of love and gentleness. If they are not speaking from a God presence, then they are not saying anything that is in your highest and best good. Even if the words they are saying are true, if you are not spiritually shielded and strong enough to handle their misguided vibration, they will cause harm to your emotional body. When negative vibrations touch your emotions, you are left feeling depressed, defeated, and overwhelmed. You will always know when a person's spirit is not aligned with Truth because instead of leaving a conversation feeling hopeful and full of solutions, you will walk away feeling defeated and concerned, feeling as if you have even more problems. Someone can speak the truth to you, but if it doesn't come from a space of love, it is as a clanging symbol most often rejected by the recipient and causing more harm than good.

The words of Jesus Christ in his famous Sermon on the Mount help me understand how to deal with someone who is at odds with me. Basically, Jesus said that if you are wanting to commune with the Source of your being, perhaps even offer a gift of gratitude to Him, but you are housing a negative frequency, first go and heal the issue and then come back and commune with God. If you are out of alignment with God, nothing you say to someone will bring about healing or restoration to your situation. You may control and manipulate it, but you won't heal it. You will also not feel the closeness to God you could experience if you simply released the bitterness, anger, judgment, and irritation that is keeping you separated from the highest and truest version of yourself.

You may have heard of the universal principle of that which is like unto itself is drawn. In essence, if you are disciplining your children in anger versus love, you are only drawing more circumstances into your life that provoke you to anger. Deal with the source of your irritation and the issue will stop presenting itself repeatedly to you. Your soul wants to heal your wounds. It wants to live, thrive, and grow. However, it knows it cannot progress if there is a wound that has not been healed within you. Issue after issue will continue to arise, provoking the same emotion until you have learned to master yourself. Nothing ever goes away until it has taught us what we need to know.

The opposite is also true for the person on the receiving end of the negative vibrations. The story of Jesus standing on the waters amidst a raging storm is the perfect analogy to articulate this point. We should be seeking to get to point where we can stand atop the waters regardless of what storm appears around us. Many of us have managed to walk upon the waters. We have displayed the courage needed to get out of the boat, and we've even managed to bring ourselves emotionally to a place where we are walking upon the sea. We can be dancing upon the ocean and yet as soon as a storm comes, we lose our balance and begin to sink into the waters. I believe the story of Jesus walking on water was partially written to show us that we too can walk atop the waters or, better stated, the circumstances of our lives.

When horrible energy surrounds and immerses us like the wind of a violent storm, it is possible to stand firm and not sink into a state of depression and defeat. Beyond that, it is also possible to calm the storms saying, "Peace be still." When we raise our frequency to such a degree that we are vibrating the mind and heart of God, we begin to influence the lower or negative vibrations surrounding us, bringing all into harmony and balance. Either the wind must calm, or the wind must disappear. Either the people around you will energetically come into alignment with the frequency you are emitting, or they will simply disappear.

You notice certain people fall out of your life when you shift your vibration and begin thinking and existing on a higher level. There are some who are not ready for the light you shine forth. The light exposes shadows and many choose to retreat to their comfortable positions in the darkness away from a light that can reveal that which has been buried or hidden. Don't chase after them. Be ready when they call for the light but don't pursue them into the dark places from which you have emerged. Allow them to have their journey as you have had yours. When they are ready to walk in the Light, they will draw near to it. In the meantime, shine your light for the world to see. Never hide it for the sake of another. Shine well and shine bright. Those who are drawn to the Light will come of their own accord. Like the leaves falling from the trees that surround us, people and circumstances will fall away. Let them fall. Along with them will be the experiences they provided you. These will mesh with the soil of your life, springing forth new people and circumstances that cause you to bloom and flourish. Nothing shall be wasted. All is recycled into the wellspring of your life.

How does one stay atop the crashing waves? How does one stay clearly planted and living the kingdom of heaven on this earth? I'm still working on this one because it's not just knowing what to do, but actually doing it. I've heard a lot of teaching in my life about the amazing things that can happen in your life when you distance yourself from negative things. My experience here on earth has shown me that if a person is living in this world of polarities, there is something he or she is working to overcome. Earth is the great school of the cosmos. Even those given as spiritual teachers and masters are here working to advance and overcome certain things.

You will continue to feel, see, and hear negative things. You may live in the midst of them every day. The answer is not in praying the problem away but in learning how to be the solution. As Mahatma Gandhi said, "We must be the change we want to see in this world." The Apostle Paul told us not to pray the storm away but to pray that we may be strengthened in the storm. While it may appear the best way to shed negative energy is to simply run as far away from it as possible, the laws of the universe naturally demonstrate it will most likely catch up to you. Ultimately, you may find your life is illustrating the scene in *The Sound of Music* where Mother Abbess tells Fraulein Maria she can no longer run from her problems but must learn to face them. While I have seriously considered an extended stay in Tibet channeling my inner monk and escaping the realities of daily life, I must admit there wouldn't be much growth afforded my soul if in order to live my life I had to constantly find a way to escape from it.

The first thing you must remember in order to stay atop the waters amidst a raging storm is found in one of my favorite quotes by Rumi, which says, "Remember . . . the entrance to the sanctuary is inside you." You already hold the keys to the kingdom, and love is the key that unlocks the door. First, love for yourself, and second, love for the one who is hurling their anger and frustration towards you. You must have love for yourself to hold your space of peace and not let anything or anyone cause you to sink. The less you respond to someone's negativity or temper tantrums, the more at peace you will become. Protect your spirit from contamination.

If someone is ranting and raving, unless they are genuinely seeking to understand you or expressing a desire to genuinely listen to your thoughts, it is best to remain silent. They aren't in the right frame of mind to listen to you. They want to be heard, but they are not yet ready to hear. Stay quiet, stay calm, and stay detached! Don't allow their energy to detract from your Light. In this scenario, it is best to continue living the example you wish to see emerge in them and others around you.

> *Responding to an angry person is like*
> *putting another log on a burning fire.*
> *The way to put out a fire is to stop*
> *feeding it something to burn.*

We are so keen to want to explain or defend ourselves when we feel someone is angry with us or has judged and misunderstood us in some way. However, unless a person is approaching you with a spirit of love with intent towards restoration, your reply will only turn your simmering campfire into a raging bonfire. Most likely, the experience will also leave you feeling rejected, unappreciated, and unrecognized for your good intentions. Doesn't it feel nice when someone has genuinely come to you, asked for your advice, and you are able to share it with them? It's a totally different experience. Instead of feeling rejected, you walk away feeling grateful for the gift of soul wisdom you were able to offer in that moment.

Save yourself the continual heartbreak of needing circumstance after circumstance to learn this lesson. If someone approaches you regarding a situation and you begin to feel the Spirit behind their words is offended and not seeking true restoration, stop the conversation and gracefully bow out. You may choose to use my newly adopted reply, "I'm sorry. I can't hear you right now." I then proceed to explain to them that the tone I am picking up isn't allowing me to truly absorb what they are saying. I explain to them that when their tone reaches that of love, compassion, openness, forgiveness, and understanding, I will be able to better hear what they are saying and can respond. Don't engage with a person who is more interested in proving a point or being right than healing something broken in your relationship. Save your energy. Save your tears. Save your mind! There is an appropriate time to walk away.

Before you engage in discussion with someone, always ask yourself, "Is this person even mentally mature enough to grasp the concept of different perspectives?" Because if not, there is absolutely no point. It takes two people to resolve a conflict. When one is still barking, leave them in the doghouse. When you begin to respond the correct way to these experiences, they will begin to show up less and less in your reality. Once the lesson has been learned, there will be no need to reteach it.

Don't Take it Personal

THERE IS A BOOK I READ A COUPLE OF YEARS AGO called *The Four Agreements* by Don Miguel Ruiz in which the author dedicates an entire chapter to teaching the concept of not taking anything personally. The wisdom of that one chapter has lingered with me and helped me tremendously when someone flies off the handle, loses their temper, or fails to manage their words or emotions in any way. It's essential to understand that their reaction is coming from their own personal blueprint, their belief systems, and installed programs. By programs, I mean a belief system or way of thinking programmed through external means and not generated by the life-giving Spirit within.

When someone is angry or upset, responding to you in an unpleasant tone, or simply offers an intense opposing opinion, keep in mind they are expressing themselves based on their own social programming and beliefs. Don't take it personally. Whenever a person makes a comment towards you or about you that leaves you feeling judged or misunderstood, take a few breaths, and find the calm in the midst of the storm before replying. Detach from their opinion of you and cling to the truth of who and what you truly are. Allow them to make their own choices without trying to change or influence them in a different direction. Unless you have genuinely been invited to offer your opinion, save your energy and keep it to yourself. I could have saved myself many heartaches in life had I kept my mouth shut and not spoken unless asked for my opinion.

Stop internalizing other people's issues and drama. Hold a space of love for them while they work it out, but don't take it in. Learn to separate what is their stuff and what is yours. You'll be so much happier.

Every time you let someone else's disposition affect yours, you are giving your power over to them and allowing something very precious to be taken from you…your sanity! Never give anyone that much control over your emotions. Let them pitch their fits. Let them say whatever they need to say. Hold your space. Release the storehouse of love you have built in your diligent spiritual practice and pull from this reservoir in moments such as this.

Keep your peace. Maintain your joy. Enjoy the bright, beautiful day that has been gifted to you. Don't waste beauty on what's beneath you. Don't take it personal.

Protect Your Happy

HAPPINESS IS DERIVED FROM THE QUALITY OF YOUR ENVIRONMENT and the caliber of people you allow in your space. If you're in a conversation with someone who doesn't have control over themselves emotionally, and they begin to project their negative energy onto you, take charge of that situation! It's imperative. I've even been known to stop people mid-sentence and say, "I'm sorry. I'm not in a position to have this conversation right now." I then hang up the phone and mentally move on very quickly.

When you are on a healing journey, you must intentionally protect your space. You're dealing with enough, mastering your own emotions. The last thing you need is to be responsible for trying to balance the emotions of someone who is ridiculously out of alignment. Step away and step away fast. Your happiness and good vibes depend upon it. As a result, it might be a little lonely initially, but I guarantee you, the caliber of people that will begin to surround you will be absolutely phenomenal because you will have set higher standards for the quality of souls you interact with on a daily basis. Besides, being alone with yourself is not a bad thing! These are your greatest moments to get to know yourself, fall in love with yourself, experience rapid spiritual growth, and set those amazingly stunning standards that will uphold you in a position of joy for the rest of your life!

Make maintaining your happy bubble a priority. Protect your atmosphere and make sure the people who you allow in your intimate space are in alignment with your positive mindset and emotional state of being. Until you are strong enough to handle adults behaving like spiritual kindergarteners, keep your distance from those who can trigger you. You need to be around people who can pull you up and not weigh you down. One day you will be able to stand atop the waters, and it won't matter what storm comes against you, what kind of person you're around, what behavior they are exhibiting at that time, or if they are in vibrational alignment with where you are. You'll be able to stand on top of the water and take control of the storms raging around and within you. You will be able to handle the person who just insulted you or tried to dump their emotional baggage and drama in your life. You'll be able to handle their temper tantrums and depressive, negative chatter. There will be a strength that will have cultivated so deeply within you, and your happy bubble will be so coated and thick with joy that absolutely nothing can penetrate it. That's the place we all should seek to obtain; however, until you arrive there and can speak calmly from the eye of the storm, paddle your boat to a different island. Paddle hard and paddle fast. You may be able to step out of your boat, but you may still need help to stay atop the water when the storm starts raging around you. If this is the case, be incredibly careful with who you align yourself with in those moments, so you don't sink beneath the waters. And if by chance you do find yourself drowning, no worries. You have a great and mighty Source to come to your rescue! You have the Christ of God, the strength of God inside of you, to lift you from the waters during your sinking moments. Pull from that —several times a day if you must. It will never fail you.

There is a dynamic that must be created in order for you to thrive in your happy place. Just like a plant or animal requires a particular climate to survive along with certain instructions for how to nurture and feed it, so do you! Get to know the kind of environment that is needed for you to grow and shine. Then create the garden of your life to flourish! The wisdom to do this will not come from outside voices. It comes from within you. Don't place your happiness in the hands of another person. Don't allow someone else to tell you who they think you are or how they think you should be. Don't allow them to determine your atmosphere. It is your responsibility to generate that. Don't allow others to decide or impose what will be planted in your garden. You are the Master Gardener of your life. Be careful who you allow to place something in the garden of your soul and carefully monitor what is being planted. Whatever you put into your field will sprout and grow.

I wish more people understood the significance of how sacred their space is and learned how to fiercely protect it. Negativity is a killer. I've learned the value of protecting the atmosphere around me, and how important personal happiness is to my overall well-being. This, in turn, blesses those around me.

You can't help others until you've learned how to rescue yourself. If you don't value the happiness and peace of your own space and protect it accordingly, you probably won't give a flying flip about treating others' space as sacred and meaningful either. And you'll probably not care if you are negatively draining someone else's energy with your rotten, Debbie-downer attitude. Why care about their well-being when you can't even see the value of protecting your own?

Keep it happy, peeps!

Goodbye, Angry Person

"Do not make friends with a hot-tempered person,
do not associate with one easily angered."
(Proverbs 22:24)

I'M A PEACE, LOVE, AND I-WANT-TO—BE-FRIENDS-WITH-EVERYONE KIND OF GAL, but let's get one thing straight. We all have our boundaries and exceptions to the rules. Toxic, angry, people—well, the buck stops here, Buster Brown. Ummm, no thank you.

Your space is sacred, Folks. Treat it as such. Respect yourself enough to keep it free from bitter, angry, close-minded bullies. If they don't have the self-control to love people who don't think exactly like them with their actions, they are still a spiritual baby. Have grace and compassion for their lack of maturity and growth, but don't feel you need to let them pollute your positive, happy space.

Love is not easily offended. I can't say this enough. Look at the fruit, people. What fruit is coming off a person's vine? It doesn't matter how knowledgeable a person is or how many Bible verses they can quote if when you leave their presence, your peace has been threatened by their inability to control their temper. Cleanse your space and move the heck on. Anger never looks good on anyone.

"Fools give full vent to their rage,
but the wise bring calm in the end."
(Proverbs 29:11)

"Better a patient person than a warrior,
one with self-control than one who takes a city."
(Proverbs 16:32)

"A person's wisdom yields patience;
it is to one's glory to overlook an offense."
(Proverbs 19:11)

"Do not be quickly provoked in your spirit,
for anger resides in the lap of fools."
(Ecclesiastes 7:9)

"A hot-tempered person stirs up conflict,
but the one who is patient calms a quarrel."
(Proverbs 15:8)

"My dear brothers and sisters, take note of this:
Everyone should be quick to listen, slow to speak and
slow to become angry, because human anger does not
produce the righteousness that God desires."
(James 1:19-20)

TRUTH SEEKING

Traveler of Truth

*I*T'S NOT ALWAYS POPULAR TO ACKNOWLEDGE THE TRUTH. It may be well received to experience glimpses of it but digesting it in full often leaves us with a belly-ache. Truth will confront you. It will pierce you. It might even anger or confound you. It is also the only path through which we find authentic freedom. Truth liberates.

> *Love is freedom.*
> *Truth is freedom.*
> *Love is truth.*

I have done my own share of wanting to avoid seeing the truth about myself or my circumstances. Truth can be hard to hear. It can be disturbing. However, truth is never meant to condemn; it is meant to conform you into what your heart has always longed to be. Truth is meant to reveal to you who you truly are. It's so potent that God often allows it to be received in doses so that we can fully process the gravity of its magnitude in our lives.

Truth should always be laced in love when spoken to ourselves and to others. Without love, truth falls void upon the ears of mankind. One must never teach truth and fail to teach love. They are the same. To separate the two is to miss the mark.

To stand upon truth, one must walk a narrow road that carries with it a cloak of misunderstanding. Not everyone will understand your journey because it's not their journey. It's yours. To walk in your truth, one must be prepared to be misunderstood. A bitter sweetness rests upon this often-lonely path. Finding peace and genuine contentment often comes with a price. Others may have to be left behind because they are not meant to journey where your path is guiding you.

This narrow-road traveler possesses something special. A traveler of truth is dripped in the gentle tenderness of a grace-soaked heart. The unconditional love and acceptance he or she expresses towards others as well as the peace and sheer joy that permeates their entire being comes as a result of a lifetime of searching. Their humility stems from the crushing they've experienced from searching in all the wrong places.

Yet, the wayward paths along their journey are what made their arrival point so victoriously sweet. The rabbit trails of discovery helped the diligent seeker discover more of himself. The U-turns of life are what helped the journeyman find his destination for not all who wander are lost. In fact, without the detours, the traveler could never find home, because it's what we learn from our experiences that mold and shape us into the highest and best versions of who we are. They help us find our true nature and path.

One cannot experience God's highest truths upon their lips if they have not tasted His love with a continuous demonstration of it overflowing from his or her heart.

This blissful arrival is not found in the wide-open places. It is found through a narrow opening. It is found with boundaries and restrictions placed upon you to help you navigate to a secured position upon the only path that will provide a foundation that will not fail you. The world with its many pitfalls could never offer what the narrow path grants the longing soul. What those resting upon this path of liberation fully know is that there was only one thing that placed them upon it . . . truth. Not truth spouted in harshness or with self-ish, egotistical intention but truth given in love and received by grace.

Narrow roads require narrow openings. They require you to become small to enter in. But once the crushing has occurred to qualify you for entry, you will dance in the wide, open spaces. From this space of expansion, you will be able to freely give to others what has been freely given to you. However, you will realize that grace wrapped in truth becomes sweet to one and quite bitter to another. Just as light illuminates, it also causes darkness to scatter. When you turn on a light you also see what was previously hidden in the dark. Things are exposed that couldn't be seen without the help of the light. So, while deep darkness covers some, the Light of God rises in others. What determines which of these will become your destined outcome depends on how badly you are willing to seek the truth and how much courage you muster to face and embrace it. When we choose self-awareness, we are awarded a token, which ensures our passage to an inner kingdom many are desperately seeking to find.

Speaking truth is the greatest form of love, because it often requires loving someone more than needing that someone to love you. It means placing truth above your need for validation, significance, or a selfish keeping of someone in your life when your truth is telling you it's time to let them go.

Truth requires bravery, and while speaking your truth is always a necessity, speaking the truth for another is a different story. One should never offer advice to someone unless extended an invitation to give it. This ensures a gentler and more profitable receiving of it. In order to appreciate treasure, one must value it. One much search for it. One must desire it. Otherwise, one won't be able to recognize the gift that has been offered.

Recently, I was given a dream, and in this dream, I asked a question, "Can you tell me one of the greatest purposes for my Light?" And in the dream, I replied, "To cause the darkness to scatter, to expose the darkness, and to cause all to see the living truth."

I am a lover of the Divine's beautiful precepts and His blessed truths of loving instructions to guide us upon our journey home. Love is truth. I will cling to it. I will teach it. I will uphold it.

One cannot experience God's highest truths upon their lips if they have not tasted His love with a continuous demonstration of it overflowing from his or her heart. It's God's love that allows us to see His truth. It's your love for yourself and others that will allow you to offer a heart-piercing truth for this world as well. Make it a mad, crazy, forsaking all, do anything for the one that makes you weak in the knees, kind of love. I want everyone to find this love story. I want to expose all counterfeits that deceive and distract from it. It's worth the heroine's journey. It's worth squeezing through the narrow opening through which it is obtained. The diamond is ultimately grateful for the heat that shaped it. Nothing sparkles like a diamond, and no one shines more than the one who has obtained their love story with the Savior and Shepherd of their soul. Let Truth be your Saving Grace. She's come to liberate you.

Love well, friends. Be bold. Be uncompromising. Speak truth. Speak it with your tears if you must but speak it. Lace it with love. Wrap it in grace. Let this be the decoration through which truth is given—not by adding to it nor by taking from it, but by packaging it with the sweetness of the warm embrace of the Greatest Lover of all time. For no one can woo a heart like the Christ of God, the ultimate Love Story for us all.

Dear Truth Seeker

Dear Truth Seeker,

While traveling life's journey, there have been many voices pulling at me along the way. Experience has taught me there is none greater than the Voice radiating from within me. This Voice of Truth will come forth within me when I still my mind and listen for it.

I have learned that any voice that provokes fear within me is counter to my wellbeing and shouldn't be followed. If something outside of myself leaves me feeling disempowered in any way, it is always discovered to be a lie. It is my responsibility to instruct myself not to follow that Voice.

> *The truth liberates you.*
> *Fear paralyzes you.*

> *Any voice no matter how real, how accurate, or how factual that*
> *tries to assume a position of control or limitation over you is a*
> *distortion of the truth.*

> *Don't fall for it.*

We are derived from the Highest Power, the Greatest Truth, and we stem from the purest Source of Love. If ever in a moment of weakness, I doubt this truth, I return to nature and observe the growth taking place around me. There is an intention that permeates throughout all creation that wills it to live, thrive, and become all it is designed to be. I will observe the seedlings as they grow into vibrant plants, mighty ancient trees, and delicious fruits and vegetables. I'll remind myself of the baby growing into an adult or the goodness within every cell of our being as our bodies intricately work to cleanse and restore us. I'll remember that moment when my skin knew how to heal itself after a tear, how it formed back together, perfectly sealed to protect me once more.

> *Be kind to your body. It is working tirelessly for your highest good.*

The intention towards growth we see in nature is also living in us. Stay in the Light believing all things are working for your absolute best. Nothing can take your power lest you give it away. In regard to His life, Jesus Christ once said,

> *"No one takes it from me, but I lay it down of myself. I have power*
> *to lay it down, and I have power to take it up again. This command*
> *I have received from my Father."*

Always remember that as Jesus Christ was in this world, so are you. We too, have received such a command from our Heavenly Father, the Great Divine Intelligence behind all things. Lest through your own worry, anxiety, or fear, you willingly yield your power to another, no one, nor anything, nor any entity on earth or in the heavens can take it from you. Remember, you are here to overcome this world not to be a victim of its lies and deceit. Be in the world but certainly not of it. Your truth arises from a much higher dimension and was given to be your guiding Light.

Compare any voice with the Inner Compass nested in your Spirit and gifted to you by the Divine. I could be sitting in my room and see an angel appear, an extraterrestrial being, or even Jesus Christ himself, and if something didn't feel right in my body, I would resist the lie, not follow it, and draw nigh unto the Voice of Truth within my own heart.

Impersonators are real. This is not to frighten you. It is to warn you in love and kindness. Unfortunately, in this world, we may run into some trouble. There are deceivers who have chosen to completely separate themselves from the Light. If I ever run into someone trying to convince me or control me, I take a step back and assess the situation more closely. At times I have needed to run in the opposite direction. The truth doesn't need to convince or sway you. It just is. You will know it when you hear it because it will feel right to you. It will uplift you. If it's not for you, your Spirit will disagree and alert you. Listen to those warnings. That Voice is the highest version of yourself, the part of you that is completely one with God, guiding you to stay on course. Pay attention.

How do I hear the Voice of truth and connect to my Inner Wisdom? The answer to this question will always be found in the stillness. Just get still. This world and more importantly, our ego will try its best to distract us with anything and everything to keep us from the one thing that holds the power to transform and help us. In the stillness is where I ask questions and listen for answers. It's where I cleanse my emotions and give my soul a beautiful, refreshing, spiritual bath. I will lay aside the technology, turn off the television (a.k.a. mind control radiator), shut off the Wi-Fi, and just be. Often it is those in-between moments that the greatest revelations and insights are downloaded. When distracted by attention stealers, I miss these purposeful times of daily healing.

In the morning when I first wake is a very precious time. It's when we are still lingering between an unconscious state and a conscious state. It's when we are very sensitive to things our Spirit and soul are saying to us. I have learned to pay close attention to what my body is saying to me during these sacred sweet moments.

Your mind will lie to you, but your body never will.

Imagine if you went a day without a bath; make that two, then a week, months, and even years. Imagine a lifetime of not bathing. Get the picture? Just as we need to wash physically, we also need a daily spiritual bath. Each day as we walk throughout the world, things can be spoken to us that are not of the highest truth for our souls. These things can be negative, speaking limitations, attaching labels, hurting feelings, and creating deep wounds. These things can attach themselves to us and need to be cleared each and every day.

Have you ever noticed when someone says something hurtful to you, your body emotionally responds to it? Ever notice how you feel when you receive bad news, or you allow fear to take hold of your body? Perhaps you notice the palms of your hands get sweaty, or you begin to feel nauseous. Imagine the thought that created that physical reaction remained in your body for a day or several months. Imagine that it stayed with you for many years. This is where the majority of sickness, pain, and even death emerge; thus, why wisdom teaches to let go of weights that so easily ensnare us and to be transformed by the renewing of our minds.

In the morning when you first wake, scan your body and discern if anything feels off or out of alignment. If something feels out of balance physically or emotionally, perform a quick healing from the power that is within you. If any troublesome feelings or physical ailments emerge, I guarantee they are coming from something based in an untruth. Identify any lies you have allowed to seep into the crevices of your mind, such as you are unworthy, or you can't overcome your present situation. Replace the lie with the truth of who you truly are, which is grounded in the knowledge that nothing shall be impossible for you. You are divinity wrapped in humanity and house the potent Creative Life Force existing in all things. There is nothing unredeemable about you, your life, or your circumstances. Everything can change with a shift in thought and a new course of action. Thoughts are energy. However long you house the energy of any particular thought will determine just how powerful its effects upon you will be.

At night I encourage both men and women to take a bath before bedtime. Bathing has predominately become a ritual for women, but its benefits are advantageous to all, including children. I bathe every night before bedtime, regardless of whether I have previously showered that day. Water carries with it a high vibrational frequency that cleanses and heals. Baptism is not simply an act of symbolism. The waters carry life, renewal, and restoration. Second to the sun, the waters carry the strongest energy frequency for healing on earth.

Next time you are by a lake, river, stream, ocean, or even a trickling fountain in the center of a city park, notice the soothing calm that comes over you as you sit beside the waters. If you get the opportunity, take a dip! I guarantee you will not only receive a physical cleansing but a refreshing, energetic spiritual lift for your soul.

In the evening, dim the lights, light a candle, step into a bath, and transform your bathroom into a healing chamber of divine Light and love. Allow the waters to cleanse away any negative energy. Use this time for renewal of your soul. Omit distractions, including children, cell phones, or literature. Use this time wisely to meditate, still yourself, and hear God's beautifully wise Voice whispering love letters to your soul.

If sickness does emerge, don't fight it. There is no need for swords. If you live by the sword, you'll die by the sword. Thank the illness or disease for what is there to teach you and listen to its message. When you change your mind, you will change your outcome. When I was told I had a brain tumor, I came to a place of giving thanks in all things. The situation showed me vibrations I was holding in my body that I did not realize were there. Yet, my desire and search for truth brought things to the surface that needed to leave my body, trapped emotions and beliefs I had been carrying that were not in my highest good. I was thankful my body alerted me with such symptoms, not to frighten me or indicate I would get worse, have more strokes, and live with nerve damage the rest of my life, but to serve as a catalyst to usher me into higher levels of spiritual growth. The tumor became like a storm cleansing away the negative trapped energy that was ready for release. Without my body as my teacher, I would not have listened so intensely and sought a path of radical transformation. When you can thank what you have previously perceived to be the enemy in your life, you will know you have progressed along the road of enlightenment.

To my tumor, which has already died in the Spirit, you played your role well. Thank you for being the irritant to this Pearl of Great Worth. You helped show me my true value. You helped me to love all that I am, thus also loving all that God is. You helped me silence the lies and discover true oneness with God as well as gain the power that accompanies such things. I get it now, Jesus. We can cheer up. Like you, we've been given everything we need to overcome the world.

Give me a curse, and I'll choose a blessing.
Give me death, and I'll choose life.

In Search of the Mysteries

LIFE HAS TAKEN MANY EBBS AND FLOWS FOR ME. I have traveled more rabbit trails than most. Why do I search so diligently and why this thirst and quest to study and seek understanding? I do not know. Why can't I be content with what I've been told or taught or what everyone else has accepted as unquestionable truth? Why do I challenge even religious texts as having a deeper message that man has failed to teach its followers? Why am I not content with the surface teachings? Why do I look for the meaning laced beneath the pages of the parables I read? Why do I require to know the mysteries of the kingdom? Why do I believe there are mysteries stored for the diligent seekers? Why do I scrummage through all the religions of this world as if searching for missing pieces?

I do not know the answers to these questions, nor have I understood the burning within me to find the answers to them. I have yet to find a leader, pastor, teacher, or guru that satisfied me. If they can't give a proper answer to my questions, then why should I follow them? I may stay satiated by their explanations for a while. I might even revel in them or adopt them as a principle. However, more often than not, when implemented and experienced, they fail me as being fundamental truth I can rest upon.

The dreams and words spoken to my heart via Spirit are what I treasure most. They seem to at least indicate to me that an ending or completion to a very significant cycle is coming. At least they have planted a deep conscious awareness of a truth that is eminent. I would not have gone seeking for an understanding of such had it not begun within my dreams. Of course, when looking to man for explanations, we can often find the wrong solutions and take our once purified truth to a place of extremes and strong delusion. I have landed here many times when I sought for understanding via man's countless explanations and interpretations. Eventually, after immersing myself heavily in the doctrines of man and trying them on for size, the Spirit eventually brought me back to a place of balance. I am grateful for that. I missed a deeper meaning I believe the Divine was trying to teach me, and I learned from that experience, once again validating trial and error as my life's theme.

The challenge for me has always been to rise from my ash heap, learn, and do better. Very few will travel with you for your entire journey. Mistakes often cause severing with others. Painful lessons, however, produce priceless pearls of wisdom we carry with us as we learn from our trials and less than proud moments trying not to repeat the same mistakes we once made in our ignorant, blissful, purposeful, and quite meaningful pursuits.

All in all, the ending I feel that is upon us is as spiritual in nature as one of apocalyptic doom. Perhaps this Divine Intelligence is preparing me for my own ending of sorts, a seedling that must go into the ground and die in order to rise again. All has become a beautiful metaphor teaching me the significance of preparing for a finish line of what I would call soul completion—to return home I suppose, becoming likened once more unto the angels or from the state we once knew in the distant past, perhaps before the creation of this world.

There are many things I do not know, as I am just a traveler on this journey. My unquenchable thirst for knowledge has led me down many rabbit trails that have left me feeling quite disoriented, alone, and bewildered. In Ecclesiastes, it tells the story of how Solomon went in search of knowledge, but in the end, it led to

The dreams and words spoken to my heart via Spirit are what I treasure most.

the vexation of Spirit. It's not uncommon when on a truth-seeking journey to become overwhelmed with the expansion of the mind, the various paths one might venture, and the variety of beliefs, opinions, and possibilities. It can cause even the most focused, solidified traveler to lose their bearings.

Once, while I was walking in nature and in a great deal of confusion from having taken in immense fragments of knowledge, and watching one too many YouTube videos, the Holy Spirit said to me,

"Misti, in your search for truth,
don't forget what you have found to be true."

The Spirit had to take me back to the basics. In all my life experiences, I was guided to pause and ask myself what I had found to be true. Not what everyone else had found to be true, not the gurus, not the mentors, not the teachers, and not the countless pastors, but me.

What I have found to be true is that I have a deep, abiding, and incredibly powerful connection to the ultimate Source of all life. Regardless of how little I know or how confused I might be on what sometimes feels like a walk through a never-ending wilderness, that connection never dies for me. I feel Him. I feel His presence. I feel His comfort and the sweetness of that Love that continually emulates through my entire being. I hear Him. I hear the angels whispering in my ear. This is what I know to be true. We are knit together forever, the greatest love story of my life—well beyond my life. I came with this love affair at birth, and I will most certainly leave with it. It has deepened in this lifetime, and I have no doubt it will grow when I am no longer identified by this ego-personality of Misti Rains.

I have found love, forgiveness, kindness, and honestly to be true on my path. I also believe that if or when I willingly choose or fail to produce these characteristics among many of their beautiful companions such as grace, mercy, justice, and peace that whatever I sow will come back to me. If I plant a lie into my field, I will reap a lie in return. I am quite cognizant of how the Universal laws work in this regard, and this truth shapes my decisions greatly.

Nothing is hidden. All is ultimately revealed, not just the things we allow others to see outwardly but what we manifest inwardly in the hidden recesses of our hearts. We can never do to someone else that which will not be done to us. It does return to us, either in this life or the next. The soul must be purified. Oh, how frustrated I get with myself when I delay this process with selfishness and greed. We so often create fields of terrible harvesting that must be reaped upon us. The only way to eradicate such is via genuine heart repentance. Repentance does erase the consequences of poor choices that we bring upon ourselves. It is the ultimate game-changer. Yet, it must be authentic and real. There is no fooling universal principles, the angels that are guiding us, nor the Creator by whom they serve.

What I have found to be true is that I have a deep, abiding, and incredibly powerful connection to the ultimate Source of all life.

If you want to find the true mysteries of the kingdom and be healed from the moments spent in ignorant darkness, there is one truth I have discovered with complete assurance: your heart must be filled with love. It is the answer to unlock every opening because you are love. It's your home, your Source, the place from whence you came. We are made whole by this love. We find answers with this love. Mysteries become magical unveilings with this love. This love is what I've found to be true. This love is everything.

Mirrored Truth

WE PRAY FOR THE TRUTH, BUT WHEN TRUTH IS SHOWN TO US it can often be very disturbing. Only the truth sets us free, but more often than not there is a bridge we must cross before arriving at that place of freedom.

Staring into the truth causes us to face a mirror and make tough decisions. Seeing the truth forces us to confront our morals and beliefs, and it causes us to feel. People will ignore the truth to avoid feeling the emotions associated with the reality of a situation.

However, it is only in having the courage to face the truth that we can clearly see a path to the answers we are searching for as well as a place of authentic freedom. The truth holds us accountable because a genuine truth will grip us and make it difficult to deny it consciously. We may run from it. We may try to hide it. We may ignore it. We may try to change it. But truth is truth. It is the Light that cannot be hidden. It will always be the refreshing pull that guides our path to true abundance and to freedom from oppression and pain.

Your life is as a mirror reflecting back to you the contents of your heart. It shows you the truth. Don't be afraid to examine it closely. Take a good look. See what's resting in the seat of your soul. Embrace it. Face it. Heal it. When we look in the mirror, we can clearly see our reflection, and we're given an opportunity to fix the defects. If you see dirt on your face, simply go wash your face, go back to the mirror, and look again.

Don't Delete Parts of Your Journey

I AM A WORK IN PROGRESS. As I have grown and evolved in my level of understanding things, I have wanted to delete things I've written or recorded from my past. Trust me, some of them are terribly embarrassing. As I mature, unfortunately, the things I've left in cyberspace remain the same. I've often wondered when I meet new people if they are judging and sizing me up based on an old Facebook video, I recorded a year prior that doesn't represent my current level of understanding and truth.

Sometimes our relationship with God, others, ourselves, and even life in general can take a while to figure out. Life circumstances, traumas, and overcoming physical and emotional pain can expand that process even longer. I have learned more than anyone the effects of trying to teach something you haven't quite learned yourself or speaking about something you don't have all the answers to yet. Many times, I have thought I was teaching the gospel truth only to humbly admit later down the track that I was actually wrong. As a result, I have wanted to make private many old videos; however, life has also had to teach me not to delete parts of my journey. Each step has helped me grow into more and more truth, and each experience was needed to help me get to where I am—even the pitfalls, mistakes, and often crazy rabbit trails I have taken.

My pendulum has swung to many extremes in my search for truth, and it has taken me a while to find balance with the information I often attempt to assimilate. I most certainly don't always get it right. I have blocked many people I wish I could unblock simply because of my own immaturity and inability to stand amongst opposition. The silver lining in those situations is that I've learned from them. I try to remember those moments and carry them with me as wisdom for my present circumstances. Each failure has become a teacher in its own right, and I am grateful God uses our desire to learn and grow as an opportunity to turn even our often-misguided understandings around for our good. I believe our intentions and our hearts do matter before the Overseer of our experiences here. When we get it wrong, He knows how to make it right.

I don't remember all the things I've previously said, written, or posted online, but what has stuck with me is the awareness that as one climbs a mountain, the view and perspective changes as our understanding and truth become more refined. Mine has changed and evolved as I have changed and evolved, and as life experiences have taught me a different perspective, often through humbling circumstances and brokenness. This is why I never judge anyone based on what step they are at on their climb up the mountain.

May we all strive to honor one another by being long-suffering, merciful, and gracious with the failings of the weak. My prayer is that anything I contribute to this world via expressed pieces of my journey leaves those receiving from it inspired, encouraged, and heart-piercingly better. If ever I fail to do so, I humbly ask for forgiveness. I'm sure I have failed in this regard many times but continue to strive to obtain the prize. May you find the capacity to chew the meat and spit out the bones. Glean from this field but don't feel the need to take all that is in it. Take what is meant for you and leave what is not. Perhaps you will find some nuggets along the way that you can treasure. If not, I wish you well as you continue on your path. I am confident if you are seeking your Source, the Holy Spirit will provide exactly as you need.

I am seeking perfection, but I am by no means perfected. One day we shall no longer see a pale reflection, but we shall see face to face. One day we shall no longer see in part, but we shall know in full. Until then, I will delight in sharing my "parts." May one day our loving Father assimilate the pieces I have gathered into a beautiful masterpiece, a display of splendor for His glory and the betterment of all.

Could my ashes ever produce such beauty? One can only use a mustard seed of faith, believe against all hope, and dream. Perhaps such faith could be counted as righteousness, and I could find myself favored to be amongst those positioned in the Heavenly hallway amongst our Creator's most magnificent works of art. Only the work of a Master Craftsman could take my broken, fragmented pieces and make them something worthy of display in the court of the King. Oddly enough, I believe in a noble King who raises up and embraces the lowliest peasant to positions of great worth. I am but a maid-servant in love with my King

Each failure has become a teacher in its own right, and I am grateful God uses our desire to learn and grow as an opportunity to turn even our often-misguided understandings around for our good.

and seeking to learn of Him. Perhaps I have been but a wild mare in need of being broken and trained to gallop in the royal court, but I am willing to show up every day and keep trying to learn the walk of grace and nobility.

Much love and continued blessings be upon you as you travel your path. I pray you can find compassion for where I may have missed the mark on mine. May we all spur one another towards good deeds. Most of us are trying really hard against insurmountable odds to find our way. Kindness, love, grace, and truth is a much-needed symphony that we all need to hear as the background music of our lives. Please forgive me where I may have been a clanging symbol in our Father's orchestra. I am committed to keep practicing.

Spirit of Truth

NO MATTER WHERE YOU ARE

No matter where you've been.

No matter what you've been told.

No matter what your eyes can currently see

There is something bigger chasing you

Something greater in pursuit of your heart

Be still

Can you feel it?

The Voice.

The Voice defeating all obstacles.

The Voice conquering all odds.

There is a Truth pulsating through your awareness

It's hovering over you, the Great Spirit, the Mighty Force

It's making caterpillars soar

It's making tadpoles leap

It's making charcoal into diamonds

It's making sand into pearls

It's making acorns into oaks

It's making you soar as an eagle

It's taking you to a higher plain

It's giving you a clearer vision

It's flooding you with an awareness of who you truly are

It's giving you a metamorphosis for your soul

It's helping you let go of the former

It's filling you with gratitude for what remains

It's helping you embrace your wings to fly.

May the Spirit of Truth encapsulate you. May it hold you like a cocoon until you grow your wings to soar. Listen to the promptings from within your intricately built internal compass. Like the Great Intellect instructing all of creation how to thrive, there is a Mighty Voice lighting your path. This Voice stretches beyond the pages of a book. It lies written upon the hearts of mankind. History calls it God though who can define it as anything but love in its purest form. Man has attempted to harness it, control it, limit it, define it, but this truth belongs to everyone. All life deserves it. All life is bathed in it. Some have come as angels to release it. Some have come as messengers to herald it. Some have come as children to teach it. Some have come as souls to recognize it. Some have come to follow it. But all who have come have the ability to remember it. When nothing was, this Truth simply IS. It may lie dormant in some. But when exposed to the true Light, the layers of darkness surrounding it are easily melted away.

You must be the Light to see the Light in others. I challenge you to feel the overexposure. May it illuminate you from within the recesses of your soul. May it radiate like a cleansing beam of the purest Light, the strongest wind, and the fiercest rain, one strong enough to purge all your fears away.

Living entirely in the reality of this earthly realm will limit you, but when heaven merges with your heart, you will see as if for the first time. You were designed for existing simultaneously in heaven and on earth. Though there are still traces of the caterpillar, it is reborn as a new creation. It did not leave its abode. Though it still dwells on this earth, it soars amidst the skies. Though you are here, you must live as if you are there. You are there. The kingdom of God is at hand. Do not look up for it. Look within and feel it now. Thy will on earth as it is in heaven. As above so below. Was it ever about going there or was it always about bringing it HERE?

Live in paradise with me. It's so pretty here.

Internal Compass

*T*HERE IS A PASSAGE IN THE BIBLE THAT BEGINS BY SAYING,

"But when it pleased God ... to reveal His Son in me."
(Galatians 1:15-16)

We might think this verse should read, "It pleased God to reveal His Son to me." But in the original Greek language, the verse reads "to reveal His Son *in me.*" God's plan is to reveal His Son or His Truth *in us,* from within, rather than *to us,* from without. Or, to put it another way, God reveals Christ to us from within us.

"Christ in you, the hope of glory."
(Colossians 1:27)

Are you listening to outward voices? You have a Compass within you that is guiding your soul. It is the greatest GPS Device in the universe. Are you following it or are you listening to a back-seat driver who does not know your destination? Never underestimate the treasure placed within an earthen vessel. It is the Light that shines from the darkness. It is the One that radiates in our hearts to illuminate the knowledge of God and the highest truths about you and about Him.

The voice of God sits within the seat of your soul, providing you a direct channel for guidance to help you make the choices that will lead to your ultimate happiness and destined path. Trust that voice, not the voice of someone else who thinks they know what is best for you. People will try to change you, and at times may attempt to make you into more of what they want you to be in order to selfishly accommodate their needs. Don't give your power away so easily to someone else's direction, because there are no better directions than the ones lying with you. No one knows you like you know you. The biggest mistakes I have ever made in my life have come as a result of betraying my own Internal Guidance System because I trusted someone else to be wiser or perhaps more connected to God than me. I allowed outside pressure and influences to guide my decisions instead of following my Inner Compass.

The quickest way to discover the truth in any situation is to learn to connect to the Voice within. It will silence all lies and highlight all truths. It is the truth. It is you. No longer you who live, but Christ who lives in you. As He walked in the Light, so you walk in the Light. As He was in this world, so are you.

"What I am looking for is not out there. It is in me."
~ Helen Keller

Imagine that. A quote given by one who could not see or hear the physical world.

DESTINED
WITH PURPOSE

Die or Fly

SO YESTERDAY WAS A HARD DAY. One of those days, when everything gets a little flipped upside down emotionally. "What is the purpose of all this?" I asked myself. "Why have I been guided here? Like I know that I know that I know, but God, can you affirm it for me one more time? I mean, I know you already have, like a bazillion times, but sometimes the ground is pretty shaky down here."

Sometimes I feel I've been plucked out of my comfortable nest by a Mama Bird and told to start flying, meanwhile spiraling to a very firm and flat earth below. The bird ponders amidst the reality she could be hurling to her death, "I'm a bird, right? Am I a bird? What did Mama Bird mean when she said I could fly? I'm not sure she was talking to me. You mean I can soar like the eagles I often watch from my nice, secure, and homely nest?"

Surely not.

Maybe so.

What if I could?

Should I believe I can fly?

Maybe I should try it.

I wonder what would happen.

I mean, why couldn't I fly?

I'm gonna go for it!

Maybe I should wait a little while.

I can't wait any longer!

I mean, seriously running out of time here!

Time to get real!

What are my options?

Once you've been nourished, fed by your mama, kept cozy and nestled in your nest, and then made to feel uncomfortable by a Mama Bird who is turning the objects that once comforted you around backwards so that they poke and prod at you, and once you're finally plucked from your nest and told to fly... the only remaining option is:

Die or fly.

So, after wanting a bit more confirmation before attempting to flap my wings, and while in my downward spiral, I was strongly guided to stop my work around the house by an intense impulse to drive to a department store and treat myself to a new bedspread.

I've had this notion on my mind for about a month now. Every night I've been scrolling through Pinterest and Pottery Barn magazines looking for the exact colors I've desired for my new bed. I've wanted something simple and calming. My bed is such a sacred space for me and where I do most of my writing. I had settled on the colors gray and white, and I knew when I decided to purchase a bedspread precisely how I wanted it to look.

You are here because you are meant to fly. And you've been given an Internal Guidance System that is the best navigational tool ever designed.

When I "spiraled" into the department store, my bedspread was waiting for me, perfectly placed by the universe on the display bed as I walked directly into the store. However, after I selected it, something was missing, and I felt guided to keep walking around. I knew I wasn't done shopping yet. There was something more to search for, another message God had waiting for me. Where was it? I kept listening to the Spirit and continued "spiraling" around the store.

And then I saw it…my message, my affirmation, and my purpose. Written on a pillow, a place that represents a position in which my mind is to rest, there was one simple phrase…

"The world was hers for the reading."

For someone who believes God wants them to write for the world, I don't know how much clearer the message could have been for me.

I can fly?

I can write?

You mean you want me to flap my wings now?

You mean you want me to pick up the pen now?

As Erin Hanson so brilliantly stated,
"What if I fall? Oh, but my darling, what if you fly?"

So, the pillow was in the exact colors of the bedspread I had dreamed of, that I had just selected, and that was being assembled by the store clerk. But of course, it was. Of course, it would be waiting just as I walked in the store. Of course, the message would have been written precisely and perfectly to pierce my heart and provide exactly what I asked it to provide…an affirmation of purpose.

Why are you here?

You are here because you are meant to fly. And you've been given an Internal Guidance System that is the best navigational tool ever designed. It's always accurate. It never fails to send you alerts, detailed instructions, and always gets you to your destination exactly on time. It provides exactly what you specifically need for your charted course. You just have to listen to it and follow it.

It was important for me to put forth a little effort and trust my intuition. I had to get up and go to the store. And then the spiraling stopped. The fuzzy gaze began to clear. The horizon began to come into focus straight ahead.

My wings actually do work!

I think I might actually be a bird.

I'm a little wobbly, but hey, I just flapped a wing!

I just picked up a pen.

I'm meant to fly!

You're meant to fly too, you know? I don't know what equates to your wings flapping, but I do know your purpose sits on that horizon. I know you may have your nest-plummeting, downward-spiraling moments, but I also know the significance of paying attention when God is trying to reveal His purpose and your destiny to you.

Without a vision, the people will perish. What is on your horizon? What inspires you to believe the impossible dream? You know exactly what it is, because it's already been placed within you.

The bird was always a bird.

The seed was always an oak.

What saves a plane in a downward spiral? One must find the horizon and pull up. Find your purpose. Focus there, and then...

> *"I will lift up mine eyes unto the hills,*
> *from whence cometh my help.*
> *My help cometh from the LORD,*
> *which made heaven and earth."*
> (Psalms 121:1)

Serendipitously, Psalms 121:1 when added together is five.

$$1+2+1+1 = 5.$$

That's Grace, my friends. That's grace. Five represents the number of grace. Your spiral allowed you to find your horizon, your purpose, and your grace.

So, lose your equilibrium? Not a problem. As the ancient text above articulates, God's got you! He will help you. He will take you on the wings of angels if He has too, but He will most certainly get you there! There is a heavenly flow that is guiding you home and will help you build many more nests for other baby birds who will one day also dream of flying alongside of you.

All my love and happy soaring!

The Key to Manifesting
the Life of Your Dreams

YOU LIVE INSIDE A WORLD HELD TOGETHER BY VIBRATION AND MAGNETISM. God holds everything together. God is love. Love holds everything together. Love is holding you together. Everything is energy.

Your reality works like a projector for what's on the inside of you. You are in control of everything. Everything external is a mirror of what sits within you. This is why your healing must begin in the heart and mind, not fixing things outside of you, but from within you. When you shift to doing the spiritual work within, you will see the outward circumstances eventually transform.

Though you may understand these things, it is still difficult to do the internal work that changes the outcome. The double-mindedness, the lack of knowing what you clearly want, the beliefs systems that prevent manifestations, the external programming, the feelings and emotions of unworthiness for what we can have, and the lack of understanding of the power we have to create, generates many interruptions. I could go on and on.

You must unlearn much of the lies you've been conditioned to believe. To obtain divine knowledge requires a genuine search of the soul, a true, noble quest! There is so much ancient knowledge that has been hidden and lost, thus why enlightened ones are sent to reveal truths that have been concealed and the mysteries of the kingdom to the initiates, those worthy to receive the truth. Those worthy to receive the mysteries are those who have already obtained gratitude; thus, they are awarded more to be grateful for.

Jesus had initiates, His inner circle. He spoke in parables to the outside world. He had one hundred and twenty people that He taught the mysteries. He gave only twelve the sacred knowledge reserved solely for them. Divine knowledge is not for everyone. It is not for the masses. It is reserved for the ones who have diligently sought for it and are of a pure heart. It is given to the righteous, those who are living right. You don't have to be perfect to be righteous. Being righteous is being a good person and doing the right thing. It is walking in truth and integrity. Making mistakes does not disqualify you from being a person who is living rightly. Making mistakes is part of learning to be the best person that you can be. A spiritual child is no different than a human child that has failures in learning how to walk or talk or exist maturely in this world. Just as a child must have some failures along their journey to walking in maturity and wisdom, so too will the spiritual child experience some setbacks on his journey to adulthood. The child isn't evil. He is simply learning how to get it right.

Most of the time, our vibration is too dense to see the realm behind the veil. Not to mention the fact we can be so distracted that we rarely pay attention to it.

There is a story in the Bible about an angel that visited a Roman Centurion named Cornelius. The Centurion was the first Gentile to convert to the faith. He was chosen because it says he was a God-fearing man who always prayed and was full of good works and deeds of alms, meaning he gave money and food to the poor. Basically, he was a good man, and thus angels were sent to him to reveal the mysteries of the kingdom. The angels told him his prayers had been answered. Cornelius understood that he had been chosen for a higher purpose.

Why must one be righteous or living right before revealing the mysteries? Because with this knowledge, you understand the nature of your reality. You understand that you house the power of God, the keys to the entire kingdom, and the power that creates worlds. You can create anything. You can have anything. You can be anything. You can manifest anything. You have access to the Divine for whatever is needed, and whatever is asked is given.

A true righteous initiate wouldn't ask who will win the race so he can make his bets. A royal subject of the kingdom is allowed instant connection for answers of much greater merit such as, "Which path do I take next for the highest and best good of all?" An initiate asks for wisdom. An initiate asks for a deeper ability to love his or her neighbor. An initiate asks to be more connected and one with their Creator. An initiate will only create with a profound awareness of their power and with the understanding of the universal laws of sowing and reaping.

With this said, God's plan is to prosper you and see your personal desires fulfilled. There is no judgment. Just love. This is all God is. Never forget this, despite what man teaches. God is not judging or condemning our creations any more than a parent would throw away the messy scribblings of their four-year-old child who is learning to draw.

You are creative because you were created in the likeness of a Creator. When you create, do not focus on the how. Do not ask how your creation will come to be. Focus on the attributes God wills you to possess: intimacy, happiness, depth, meaning, and the desires of your beautiful heart. Do not engage in the emotional turmoil of trying to assimilate how these things can come to be or what events must happen for you to obtain them. This is not your concern. You are wealthy because you feel abundant. You are healthy because you feel healthy. You must feel you have what you wish to obtain. You must know it is your right by divine law and you possess within yourself an ability to release this bounty from within.

You must not accept lack for the things you desire to obtain because God supports you possessing that which is purely good for you. This includes provision, happiness, joy, peace, and the pleasurable comforts of the lush garden of this world He has placed you in. Taste and see that the Lord is good. Never say, "I don't see how that is possible." With this mindset and vibration, you can't obtain that which you desire. You must see it before you receive it. You must believe it before you achieve it. Adopt the mindset of Mary Poppins, who once said, "Even the impossible is possible," and maybe, like her, you will fly!

You have everything you need to manifest a beautiful inner kingdom and a lovely outer world surrounding you. You have an angel that is assigned to you. This angel will be with you your whole life. There are other angels that specialize in assisting you with other things. For instance, if you need help parenting, there are spiritual guides ready to assist you and give you ideas. This unseen world is very real and available to you. Call upon it! Most of the time, our vibration is too dense to see the realm behind the veil. Not to mention the fact we can be so distracted that we rarely pay attention to it. Thank goodness for our dreams. Our dreams are essential tools God can use to get our attention. When your body rests, your Spirit is active and speaking valuable insight to your heart and mind. Pay attention when it comes.

Submit to God and be at peace with him; in this way prosperity will come to you.

Blessed are the pure of heart for they shall *see* God. Where is God? Look within. Examine your heart. Purify it, and you will perfect your vision of the Divine. This world around you is your canvas.

> *"Finally, brethren, whatsoever things are true, whatsoever*
> *things are honest, whatsoever things are just, whatsoever things*
> *are pure, whatsoever things are lovely, whatsoever things are of*
> *good report; if there be any virtue, and if there be any praise,*
> *think on these things."*
> (Phil. 4:8)

Think on these things! This includes your happiness, this includes making deep passionate and intimate love, this includes joy, success, and giving and contributing to the world around you. Think on these things. Deny yourself nothing in your lovely creations. You have an imagination for a reason! Allow the Universe in all its goodness to design your world exceedingly abundantly above and beyond anything you could hope or imagine. Believe your desires are possible for you. Never settle for a life where you suffer without them. It is not God's intention to starve you or make you suffer! His desire is for you to have the abundant life you seek, that deep in your heart, you know is meant to be yours.

Believe in your dreams, as cliché as that sounds, and let God handle exactly how your reality will take shape around you. Matter changes based on the elements mixed with it. What ingredients are you putting into your creations? The world around you will take form based on your beliefs. You are never a victim to what *is*, though this world has conditioned this belief. You are the victor of speaking into existence what can *be*.

> *"Thou shalt also decree a thing,*
> *and it shall be established unto thee:*
> *and the light shall shine upon thy ways."*
> (Job. 22:28)

> *Submit to God and be at peace with him;*
> *in this way prosperity will come to you.*
> *Accept instruction from his mouth*
> *and lay up his words in your heart.*
> *Then the Almighty will be your gold,*
> *the choicest silver for you.*
> *Surely then you will find delight in the Almighty*
> *and will lift up your face to God.*
> *You will pray to him, and he will hear you,*
> *and you will fulfill your vows.*
> *What you decide on will be done,*
> *and light will shine on your ways.*
> (Job 22: 21, 22, 25-28)

Cleanse your heart. Make it good. Make it pure. This is the gateway to see God. The passage says that His instructions will then be placed in your heart. If you get still and listen to them speaking from within, and if you apply them to your life, prosperity will come to you. In addition, whatever you decide on will be done. Darkness will be removed, and light will shine on all your ways, not just a few of them, but *all* the areas in your life. Your mission should be to purify your heart. Place it upright and rest it in the hands of God to be molded and shaped in such a way that your outer world matches its sculpted beauty.

People are still praying and waiting on God to perform their miracles when God has given them everything needed to create their own. You hold the key. Turn it. Happy Manifesting. Make your world super pretty!

Ask and Ye Shall Receive

THERE IS A POWERFUL AND PROFOUND TEXT CALLED THE GOSPEL OF THOMAS with portions dating back as early as 30-60 AD. It was discovered near Nag Hammadi, Egypt, in December of 1945 among a group of books known as the Nag Hammadi library. Scholars speculate that the works were buried in response to a letter from Bishop Athanasius declaring a strict canon of Christian scripture. The library is known for containing gospels that state they were written by Jesus.

In the Gospel of Thomas, there are two fundamental keys to praying in power. These two ingredients were said to be essential if you wanted to pray with an ability to change the world, your circumstances, your illness, or change anything, including the force of evil.

In verse 106 it says,

"When you make the two, thought and emotion, one.
You will say to the mountain move away
and the mountain will move away."

This verse is saying that firstly, feeling is the prayer. And secondly, you must feel as if your prayers have already been answered.

I once heard Gregg Braden speak on this particular passage. He said that this verse is saying that when you can marry your thought and your emotion into one single potent force, this is when you have the power to speak to the world or to speak to your mountains and see them moved.

So if you still feel fear, terror, anger or hate towards your enemy, towards your government, towards your husband, towards your boss, towards your friend that betrayed you, towards anyone or anything, you will never get the results you are actually seeking. In this state of being, you will never see change. If you want a different result, you must truly feel the result you wish to create. You must feel peace and love towards something before you can receive it from them. You must sow what you wish to see harvested in your life. Can you see how we as a society have been doing things backward? Perhaps this is why we are in this endless cycle of war and division.

This was such an important truth that the Gospel of Thomas records it again in Verse 48,

"If the two make peace with each other
in this one house they will say to the mountain
move away and it will move away."

When Jesus references the house or the temple, He is talking about our body. He is telling us again how powerful it is to marry thought and emotion.

In the early Christian Bible, there is a passage that says, "Ask and ye shall receive." I know people that ask and ask and ask, and nothing happens. This is because asking is not done with the voice. The asking is not done by saying, "Please, please bring this to my world." That is not asking. To ask you must speak to God in the language that God recognizes, in a language that is meaningful. God looks beyond what we are saying with our voice.

God recognizes what is inside your heart.
He listens to the language of your heart.
What is your heart saying?

Jesus Christ explained this to us when He spoke of those that pray long prayers and speak with their lips, but He could see their hearts were far removed from the words that were coming from their mouths.

When your heart has a feeling, it creates electrical and magnetic waves. This is the language God recognizes. So, when you create the feeling in your heart as if your prayer is already answered, it creates the electrical and the magnetic waves that bring that answer to you.

"Ask and ye shall receive." While we still have this passage in John 16:23-14 of the King James Bible, it is actually the condensed and edited version. This is so amazing to me because they took out the two sentences that tell us how to ask. In the 4th century, when the edits happened, they took out the two most important sentences. Those two sentences in the original Aramaic are as followed:

"All the things that you ask straightly,
directly from inside my name,
you will be given. So far, you have not done this.
Ask without hidden motive
and be surrounded by your answer.
Be enveloped by what you desire,
that your gladness may be full."

If you are solely asking with your voice, but your heart is far removed from your outward prayer, you have not followed the above instructions. Look at what it is saying. It is not saying to speak an audible word. It's saying to be surrounded, to feel as if the prayer has already come to pass. If you are surrounded, you are feeling as if your answer has already happened. It says to "be enveloped." How can you heal a situation if you feel anger when praying? Your heart is not being enveloped and surrounded with the result you are seeking. You are not feeling as if it has already happened. How can any relationship be restored, or how can your finances be restored, if your heart is feeling the very opposite of what you are praying to receive?

If you want to heal or restore a relationship in your life, or if you want healing in the body of your loved ones, feel the feeling as if it has already happened. Be enveloped by what you already desire because that is when your thought and your emotion become one. When you think the thought of a particular healing for your loved one, and you feel the feeling of that thought, allowing the thought and the emotion to become one, you are speaking the language that the Divine recognizes.

It also says to ask without hidden motive. What does that mean? It means to ask without judgment. This is precisely what the Buddhist actually tell us when they say to ask without judgment of the right or the wrong, or the good or the bad. It

When our heart has a feeling, it creates electrical and magnetic waves. This is the language God recognizes.

means to ask without the ego. It means to ask from the heart. Jesus Christ instructed the same truth. He warned us about judging, saying plain and simple, "Do not judge." He understood this in direct correlation to its effect upon whether or not our prayers would be answered and also regarding whether or not we would reap a harvest of non-judgment upon our own lives from external people and circumstances.

Gregg Braden also shares of a famous experiment where practitioners healed a woman who had a tumor with their intention, by feeling as if the healing had already occurred. They literally watched the tumor disappear on the sonogram screen as they prayed with their hearts. They said that they did not judge the cancer as being right or wrong, or good or bad. They didn't contemplate the source of it coming from sin or as a result of some evil or negativity. They only accepted the tumor as one of many possibilities, because in the quantum world, they acknowledged the truth that all things are possible. So, they didn't say, "Bad cancer, you must go away," or "We're going to operate on you," or "We are going to use radiation on you." They didn't do that. They accepted the cancer as it was, without hidden motive and without judgment. And instead they said, "Now we are going to choose a new reality." They did this by assuming the feeling as if the woman was already fully healed, fully enabled, fully capacitated, and as if all of this had already happened. The chant they were using as they placed their hands upon her loosely translated into the words, "Already done. Already done." When they got excited, they began to chant, "Now! Now! Now!" Not a year from now, not a month from now, and not five minutes from now, but now, in the quantum world...now! And guess what? Her body responded. It must. The tumor began to shrink. Physical reality must respond to the language that it understands.

The passage in the Gospel of Thomas also says, "to be enveloped." "To be" means "to feel as if." We can understand this truth spoken through many who have understood it throughout the ages. Early in the 20th century, The Philosopher Neville also said the same thing in his book, *The Power of Awareness*. He said,

> *"You must make your future dream a present fact now*
> *by assuming the feeling of your wish fulfilled."*

> *We must learn to ask from the place of it has already happened.*

In the Buddhist traditions, they are telling us the quality of the feeling, and in the Christian traditions, they are giving us the instructions to be surrounded, to be enveloped, and how to create that feeling. And when you put those altogether, it is clear that this is something that begins and happens in our hearts, not in our minds. It is feeling as if the prayer has already happened, with no judgment and no motives, that brings it to pass.

When a martial artist demonstrates their focus by breaking a concrete block, they use a secret to break it. The very last thing they are thinking about is their hand hitting the block, because they know if they think about it, it will hurt them. Instead, they focus on what happens after their hand has passed through the block as if it has already happened. They concentrate on a place below the block and feel the feelings as if their hand is already in that place. This is a metaphor. It is equivalent to what we are doing with the power of emotion and feeling when we feel as if the experience we are seeking has already happened.

May this simple truth taught to us by One who embodied the Truth, Jesus Christ, sink deeply into our hearts to ponder. May we be enveloped with the concept of how to pray in power. May we learn to pray, ask, and receive as if it has already happened. May we sow what we wish to reap. May we be that which we wish to see. May we learn to pray with our hearts.

My deepest gratitude to Gregg Braden who is responsible for teaching me the wisdom laced in this particular Misti Moment. I used these principles to shrink the tumor in my brainstem, and I remain a living example of these marvelous truths.

The Divine Plan

SOME NIGHTS ARE BETTER THAN OTHERS. Some are so unbelievably disappointing. Some are riddled with emotions, and sometimes you just can't figure it all out. But no matter how frustrating or confusing or disappointing, you must never ever stop believing in a divine plan, in a promise, or in a miracle. You just can't give up. You can't stop hoping or believing.

Your hidden desires that no one sees, the things that are too raw and vulnerable to reveal, are being heard in the courts of heaven. Heaven hears you. God knows you. He knows the deepest desires of your heart. Trust in something more powerful than you to orchestrate your divine destiny and much-needed breakthroughs. You must never stop hoping and believing the entire universe has your back. For if God be with you, and if God be in you, who or what circumstance can stand against you?

I know it hurts. Believe anyway.

I personally believe there is a reward for those who maintain an ability to see life with rose-colored glasses when the view is, in reality, tainted with darkened and cloudy stains. When frustrated and impatient, just breathe. Everything is going to be ok. There is a divine plan at work. Everything, and I mean everything, will work out for your good, for you have been filled with a great love for your Creator and His glorious purposes for mankind. We can't ever allow current circumstances to overshadow, disempower, or let us to forget this profound truth.

Serve Well

SERVE WHERE YOU ARE PLANTED. Serve wherever you are. Serve well and with integrity no matter the circumstances. Whether you be in a place of light, or whether you be encased by the darkness, hold your torch and shine brightly to bring warmth to all those in the house. Place love upon your hands and let love permeate the crevasses of your mind as you go about your work.

In the Bible, there was a man named Joseph, who was sold as a slave in Egypt. He was forced to bring aid to someone who served a different god, a different culture, and a completely different mindset. Yet, Joseph served where he was placed. He didn't have to go the extra mile in his doings, but he did. He performed his assignment over and beyond the call of duty. Although he was unjustly put in prison, it didn't stop Joseph. Even when he was in jail, his heart to serve caused the commander of the prison to elevate him to a position of authority, putting Joseph in charge of running the entire place. In what could have been chambers of despair and hopelessness, Joseph shined even brighter when placed in the dark dungeons. The torch he carried in his Spirit was so illuminating that it ultimately took him from a pit to a palace. He became second in command of all of Egypt.

Whether or not Joseph agreed with Pharaoh or the lifestyle of the Egyptians was irrelevant for Joseph, because he had a greater vision and understood deep in his Spirit that he was there for a higher purpose. The Bible said God increased Pharaoh and all his possessions and blessed him with great wealth simply because of Joseph.

> The thing that was meant to imprison Joseph ultimately became the place from which he found his freedom and the greatest promotion of his lifetime. His prison became his promotion, and whatever you believe to be your darkened dungeon also has the potential to become yours.

Serve well. Serve with goodness and love in your heart. God will see your faithfulness and reward your right living with divine promotion.

Destined Purpose

I WAS READING THROUGH SOME OLD JOURNALS from when I was younger this morning. Below is an excerpt from when I was fifteen years old. I suppose there are certain things that never change. You can never truly escape what you were born to do, the reason you came here. Traces of your destiny will be woven throughout your life, ingrained into the fabric of your being. Look for the clues.

What is your thing? You know. That thing that when you do it, you come alive and every cell in your body lights up and stands at attention. If you are paying attention when you are doing that thing you will hear the Spirit say, "This is what you were born to do."

What Will You Name It?

FIND YOUR JOY AND MAKE EVERY DAY OF YOUR LIFE one glorious mental vacation. Keep it blissful. Your vacay is one thought away. I was having psychological vacations long before they turned into actual events. As a man thinketh in his heart so is he. Call things that be not as though they are. Create something beautiful for your future. Your future happiness begins with appreciating your current bliss. If you don't have "it" now, fake it till you make it. Pretend, daydream, and live as if it's on the way. Your imagination is not a random commodity. It's a gift to help you create and manifest your dreams. You are creative because you were created in the likeness of a Creator. Design something really spectacular. Your only limitation is you.

One of my favorite passages in the Bible is when the animals are brought before Adam, and it says that God wanted to see what he would name them.

> *"Now the LORD God had formed out of the ground all the wild*
> *animals and all the birds in the sky. He brought them to the man to*
> *see what he would name them; and whatever the man called each*
> *living creature, that was its name."*
> (Genesis 2:19)

What has God set before you to see what you will name it? What are you speaking about your life? What have you named your future? What are you speaking over your circumstances? What have you titled the story of your life? Perhaps there is One watching to see what you will do with it, how you will define it, and what world you will create around you.

God started with nothing and made absolutely everything. Has He not given us the keys to the kingdom as well? Your mind is a beautiful imagination station full of creativity and power. Get busy using it.

Your destiny is standing before you.
Name it.

All the Way

ONE OF THE GREATEST MOMENTS I'VE EVER HAD WITH GOD is while reading the story of Peter walking on water in the Bible. As many may know, the story articulates Christ appearing to his disciples while walking on the sea. Jesus calls to Peter to step out of the boat and come atop the waves with him. For a moment, Peter actually steps upon the waters with his Christ, but when the waves begin to roar and his focus detours from Christ to the storm around him, he begins to sink. At this point in the story, Jesus reaches out his arms to save his beloved friend.

As I contemplated the story, I heard a voice whispering to me, "Misti, what if Peter had made it all the way to Me, without sinking?"

My reply was instantaneous, "The others would have wanted to do it to. They would have thought it was possible for them to also walk on water. Another group of powerful leaders would have been eternally and forever impacted, causing a ripple effect in every life they touched from that point forward."

And the voice replies, "I asked, because I wanted you to know that it's possible to make it all the way without sinking."

So, was Peter a failure? No. You know why? Because He was willing to try. He stepped out of the boat regardless of the raging winds and violent waves. For a moment, he believed he could walk on water. For a moment, he had enough faith to believe he could do what Christ could do...

and he did.

Don't focus on the storm. Eyes on Christ. Let the weak say I am strong. That is you. The Christ of God in you. His mindset in you! His vision in you. You can walk above the waters in the midst of all hell breaking loose in your life. And when others see you do it, they will follow. Others' feet will begin to slide over the side of the boat and dare to do the impossible for themselves.

I'll see you somewhere offshore!
You are destined to walk atop oceans
and dance upon seas!

The Law of the Jungle

MOST OF OUR SOCIETIES HAVE THE SAME RULES about seeing life. If we look at those rules with honest eyes, we see very limited ways of viewing life. One of these is that we live in societies that are rooted in fear where every day our choices are made from a place of avoiding possible risks, pains, deaths, and damages. We have grown far away from our roots and what I would say is the "Law of the Jungle."

In the Jungle, things are different all the time. It is a world where each moment is changing and evolving. One is required to be in the moment in order to choose wisely. One must learn to survive by their instincts. In today's society, instead of being in the moment or following our gut intuition, we too often hold ourselves back to avoid risks. This is against the "Law of the Jungle," where every day one is required to go out and get food while being creative and adaptive. In the jungle, you have to take with you your courage and your abilities in order to survive. It's through taking the risks that one gets the essential things that he or she needs.

Playing it safe produces the illness of becoming more fragile emotionally. In the jungle, part of gleaning wisdom for what is harmful and what is useful is acquired via trial and error. Being passive stifles our creativity and doesn't allow us to gain the intelligence to solve problems.

It's producing the illness of not being able to distinguish what is harmful for ourselves and others. It makes us passive. We become like followers because it puts away our creativity and the part of our intelligence to solve problems. Our lack of being in touch with God and nature disconnects us from our free-spirited jungle roots that allow us to receive the intuitive messages that not only help us survive but thrive in our adventures.

At all times, The Force of Life within you wants you to be healthy, strong, happy, to have an open heart, and to have a vast understanding of the world so you can contribute with your gifts. When you ignore your intuition and primal instincts to take risks, you are putting all this down for protective comfort.

You were made for the jungle. Grab a vine and start swinging! If it scares you, it may be a good thing that you tried, because instead of falling, you may realize you can fly!

Illuminate

1 HAVE FELT LOST SO MANY TIMES THROUGHOUT MY LIFE. I've lost my bearings, causing my compass to spin searching and seeking endlessly to find her true North. I've been confused. I've been afraid. I've taken many wrong paths while genuinely seeking to find the righteous path. I have fought the voices of defeat more times than I have ever wanted to wrestle with them. I've felt the journey of one slow, exhausting step at a time. However, there is no denying it has been the struggle that has taught me how to find my horizon. The moments lost in the thick of the forest have taught me how to forge my path to the Light.

It is willful, and it is an allowing.
It is a promise,
a promise you will be delivered,
a promise despite your many pitfalls,
you will arrive at your destination.
It's a pulling,
a pulling from something deep within.
It's a listening,
a listening to the Source of the pull.

It's the Voice in the midst of darkness and confusion, the Internal Compass, the Great Holy Spirit, the Voice that makes miracles seem easy and causes trapped doors to unlock. It's a Voice that provides guidance amidst chaos and hope amidst our darkest hours of defeat. It's a Voice that tells you who you are, what you can do, and it reminds you of those waiting for you to do it. It reminds you that your weaknesses and vulnerabilities are your greatest assets and most beautiful, relatable tools for your freedom. It's in that weakness, in that moment of burying, that an otherworldly strength begins to fill you, begins to spur you, and begins to lift you so that you begin to rise victoriously. Grab hold of it. It's available to everyone. It's your freedom song.

You can be in the darkest cavern and yet turn on a Light within your soul that can illuminate your steps to the highest peak of any mountain your heart desires to climb. That Light can help you overcome any feat your soul wishes to conquer.

Make a decision to Light up, and I promise you, your compass will realign itself. You will find your way home. You will shine the Light, and like a beacon in a dark storm, the heavens will receive your SOS. Your Destiny, your Blessed Hope, will come for you and take you one step at a time to your paradise.

Just . . . keep . . . shining.

Don't wait for the Light.
Become it.
And the Light will surround you forevermore.

The Tree of Life

YESTERDAY WHILE ON A SAFARI AT DISNEY WORLD'S ANIMAL KINGDOM, a certain tree caught my eye. When I heard the tour guide mention it can store up to thirty thousand gallons of water during the dry season, my mind began to sit in a place of awe and wonderment. I couldn't wait till I got back to the hotel to research information about the tree. It's called a Baobab Tree, and wouldn't you know, it's known as the tree of life. Its water supply is enough to source an entire village. It can also provide shelter, clothing, and food. The cork-like bark and huge stem are fire resistant and are used for making cloth and rope. The leaves are used as condiments and medicines. The fruit, called "monkey bread," is edible, and full of vitamin C. Some of these trees have even been carbon dated at over six thousand years old.

"A tree that is protected by the fire
A tree that is a storehouse of living water enough
to supply an entire village
A fruit coming forth from its branches providing
vitamins and nutrients
Its leaves a source of medicine
A tree with an ability to provide shelter and can clothe
you with the needed garments for your journey
An all-sufficient, all supplying, tree of abundant life
Can you see yourself as this tree?

And he shall be like a tree planted by the rivers of water,
that bringeth forth his fruit in his season; his leaf also
shall not wither; and whatsoever he doeth shall prosper."
(Psalms 1:1-3)

I found the appearance of the roots at the top of the tree also a point of wonderment. Have you grown to such depth that your mind is as deep roots firmly planted in the universal laws of love and light established by the hand of God? Have you given such delight to words of the truth that you sit planted by rivers of living water? Has your mind been rooted in the spiritual wisdom of the Divine?

This tree appears dead. It appears barren and dry, yet inside its trunk houses thirty thousand gallons of water with seeds of greatness to nurture, supply, heal, clothe, and protect. Is there an area of your life that appears on the outside to resemble this tree? Perhaps if you have been devouring the fruit of Divine wisdom, you carry within you a greater storehouse of abundant supply, not only for yourself but more than enough to supply the village surrounding you. Perhaps in your moments of meditation and gratitude, like this tree, you have created a barrier strong enough to protect you from any fire.

*"He also took some of the seed of the land and planted it in
FERTILE soil. He placed it beside ABUNDANT waters; he set it
like a willow. Then it sprouted and became a LOW, spreading vine
WITH ITS BRANCHES TURNED TOWARDS HIM, but its
roots remained under it. So, it became a VINE and yielded shoots
and SENT OUT BRANCHES."*
(Ezekiel 17:5-6)

The hand of God wills to place you in fertile soil beside abundant waters.
He humbled you and brought you low that you may remain growing upwards
towards His Divine nature and outwards in love towards your fellow man.
When the Baobab Tree blooms, its flowers are white.

*"Blessed are those who wash their robes, so that they may have the
right to the tree of life, and may enter by the gates into the city."*
(Revelation 22:14)

There is an internal kingdom within you that may be entered when you
purify your heart. Therein lies an abundant supply of all that you need to water
the dry places of the soul, not just for yourself, but for those hungry for your
sacred resources. Cleanse yourself from anything that would block your
entrance to this sacred city. Become love and live the remainder of your days
giving love to others.

Be watchful! There are trees standing in a place near you. Though your land
may appear barren, vessels are full and prepared to offer you a drink of living
water!

Cinderella Sings Her Truth

THERE IS A STORY ABOUT A MOTHER WHO LOVED HER DAUGHTER VERY MUCH. Just
before she died, she told her daughter a secret that would see her through all
the trials that life would offer. She told her to have courage and be kind.

I have watched this story play out on a big Hollywood screen, and I have
lived a portion of its chapters in my own life. The story of Cinderella affected
me so deeply that I wrote about it years ago not knowing then that someday I

too would lose my mother, and it would resonate with me in a way I could never have expected, leaving a profound and lasting mark upon my life.

Like Cinderella, my mother planted a precious secret in my heart to always have courage and be kind. Years prior to my mother's death, these are the words I penned in my journal regarding the transformative story of Cinderella:

I recently took Kate to see the new Cinderella movie, and there was a moment in the movie that was profoundly gripping to me. Years had passed since Cinderella enjoyed running and playing in the meadows with her father. All that remained were memories of a better life and the encouraging words given by her mother to "have courage and be kind." In addition to the grief and suffering of much loss, Cinderella spent years being the recipient of unjust treatment, hurled insults by her stepmother and stepsisters, being forced to toil and labor, eating only scraps from the table, and being robbed of her basic human rights.

Finding herself locked inside an upper room, imprisoned, and at the lowest point of Cinderella's life, she responds in her defeat with a song...

Lavender's blue, dilly, dilly, lavender's green,
When I am king, dilly, dilly, you shall be queen.
Who told you so, dilly, dilly, who told you so?
'Twas my own heart, dilly, dilly, that told me so.
Lavender's green, dilly, dilly, Lavender's blue,
If you love me, dilly, dilly, I will love you.
Let the birds sing, dilly, dilly, And the lambs play;
We shall be safe, dilly, dilly, out of harm's way.
I love to dance, dilly, dilly, I love to sing;
When I am queen, dilly, dilly, you'll be my king.
Who told me so, dilly, dilly, who told me so?
I told myself, dilly, dilly, I told me so.

At Cinderella's darkest hour, she was telling herself the truth. She knew she was destined to marry a king. Her heart had revealed to her the truth amidst a stream of terrible lies. She spoke her truth, she sang her truth, and she prophesied her truth. From Cinderella's heart, she began to profess that she would be safe, removed from harm's way, and taken to a palace where she would be under the covering and protection of the king.

It was as Cinderella sang her truth that the king appeared. When all thought he was far removed in his palace, he was there on mounted horse in search of his bride. The king was among the search party. He alone recognized the song of her heart. The king then sends for Cinderella. He commands his officer to go claim his queen and unlock her prison door. The wicked enemy, her stepmother, attempts one last time to remind her of who she will always be with her venomous lies and to interrupt Cinderella's rescue mission.

And then my favorite moment of the movie happens. The officer turns to the wicked stepmother and says, "WHO ARE YOU TO STOP AN OFFICER OF THE KING?" At this moment in the movie, I almost heard the heavens shake! If God be for you, WHO can stand against you?!

You may find yourself in an upper room, and yes, it may be dark. Perhaps your doors have been locked, and you find yourself imprisoned and treated much like the fair and lovely Cinderella. But when you fill your heart with a song for your King and begin to speak out the truth regarding what you know about yourself and your destiny, even the ravens will come to serve and feed you. In this case, the mice, the lowest and filthiest of all creatures, were sent to open her window. Like Cinderella, your song will permeate the atmosphere and carry your praises to the heavens to be heard by your King of all Kings, mounted on his white horse and ready to command his angels to come harvest and collect you as his bride-to-be! Just as in the movie, your King will mount His horse declaring, "I have to see her again!"

I can see the enemy's final attempt to spit his venomous lies to you. I can see you standing in your peaceful state just as Cinderella waited and rested in full confidence that the King would make her enemies a footstool. I can see the moment the angel of the Lord says to the Angel of Darkness, "Who are you to stop an officer of the King?!" Somebody shout with me! He is coming! He is coming! Keep singing your song!

> Lavender's blue, dilly, dilly, lavender's green,
> When I am king, dilly, dilly, you shall be queen
> Who told you so, dilly, dilly, who told you so?
> 'Twas my own heart, dilly, dilly, that told me so.

With a flash of lightning, I can see the eastern sky parting and your King appearing ready to cloak you in your garments of white. Have courage! Be kind! Keep singing! Ready yourself for your King! At the midnight hour, the magic isn't ending. At the midnight hour, the power is seen by all! Your story is much better than Cinderella's! This is no fairytale, only truth. You were not meant to eat scraps from the floor! You are destined to dine with the King of all Kings at the marriage supper of the lamb!

The Cinderella movie begins with her mother telling her, "I want to tell you a secret that can see you through all the trials that life can offer." At the end of the movie, the king approaches Cinderella and declares he wants her. He removes her filthy rags and drapes her with the finest of all that he is. He clothes her in dignity and in strength.

"Behold, I will make them of the synagogue of Satan...behold,
I will make them to come and worship before thy feet,
and to KNOW THAT I HAVE LOVED THEE."
(Revelation 3:9)

I want to tell you a secret that can see you
through all the trials that life can offer.

Your King WANTS YOU.
He LOVES you.
He IS COMING for you.
Have courage.
Be kind.
Love others.
Speak and live the TRUTH.
Sing amidst your dark place.

And...
BELIEVE.
You have been rescued.

NO MORE FEAR

Fear of Missing Out

1 RECENTLY HEARD SOMEONE SAY, "I just hate to see you miss out on this opportunity." Here is what life has taught me:

Too many people live their lives in fear. Fear of missing out, fear of failure, fear of disappointing others, fear of loss, etc. Don't make decisions based on fear of missing out.

> *Any decision made from even an ounce of fear*
> *will always lead to suffering.*

Make choices in your life based on faith, not fear. Decisions made from fear produce loss. Decisions made from faith produce blessing, abundance, and increase.

Jesus taught "by your FAITH you are made whole." We are healed by our faith . . . by choosing faith, not fear. If you are making a decision based in fear, wait! Reestablish your peace. It's the peace of God that should guide you.

> *From a position of peace, faith is given her platform to emerge.*

My dear friend, Tracie Bonds, once told me, "Your job is not to convince someone of what is best for them. Your job is to share the seed God has given you. It is His responsibility to bring the harvest. When the disciples cast their net into the sea, the miracle was in allowing God to do the work of the gathering fish where there had previously not been a supply. Allow the Spirit to draw someone towards their destiny. Don't use fear to push them towards something that may not be in their highest and best good. Show them your opportunity and let God draw them to what He has for them."

Above all else, serve the needs of the one placed before you. Instead of making someone feel they are missing out, teach them the confidence in knowing that in seeking guidance from their built-in Internal Guidance System, they have nothing to lose but that which is no longer serving them. Inspire them to believe in all that awaits them from a life lived making decisions via the beauty of their internal guidance and childlike faith.

No More Lies

THROUGHOUT OUR LIVES, we lie to ourselves and others for many reasons:

To blame

To seduce

To perform

To appease

To stay safe

To be likable

To be special

To not look bad

To be accepted

To avoid conflict

To not be yelled at

To influence people

To avoid feeling lazy

To avoid feeling guilty

To avoid feeling unlovable

To solicit money from people

To appear better than we are

To protect ourselves from being hurt

To affirm the way we see things

To paint an image of perfection

To avoid accepting responsibility

To manipulate to get what we want

To embellish and make others feel special, so they will tell us how special we are.

Lies are rooted in fear. Your greatest fear is your secret poison.

Today I had a funeral for my brain tumor. I wrote down all the programs, beliefs, and lies that had created her, and I asked the Holy Spirit to clear them to the point of creation. I watched the light and fire of truth burn her away. I watched her wither and turn to ashes. I kissed her goodbye, thanked her for what she came to teach me, and then I buried her with these words, "And the truth shall set you free."

No more lies

When Fear Overtakes You

*I*N THE EVENT, FEAR DOES OVERTAKE YOU, ask the Light of God to come down and cleanse away any debris that has attached itself to you. Ask for the Light of God to surround you throughout your day. A friend and mentor once taught me a prayer that I say each day and sometimes more than once depending on the circumstances.

> *The Light of God comes down and surrounds me.*
> *It fills up my room, my home, and me.*
> *It protects me so that only good can come to me*
> *and only good can come from me.*
> *I am grateful for all of my blessings.*

Take a moment to be grateful, as this raises your vibration far away from fear. It's hard to be fearful and at the same time, feel thankful. After you say this divine prayer of protection, you will face your day with a heightened assurance of grace and ease. You may also say the Lord's prayer and align your will by allowing yourself to be guided by a Divine Intelligence higher than your own. Ask yourself how you can align your will each day with an even greater will to help serve the common good? How can you merge the lower you with the higher you? This thought process creates protection grids all around you, so you can only speak or connect with beings of pure love, are of the Light, and that are committed to the highest and best good of all living beings.

I believe the Bible is true when it says angels have been given charge over us to guard us in all our ways (Psalms 91:11). However, don't call beings to yourself when you are vibrating fear as you may attract the opposite of what you desire. As mentioned above, entities love to feed off of fear. First, do as mentioned and correct your vibration. Take a few deep breaths and then ask for angelic assistance to aid you in overcoming any obstacles in your way. Bathe yourself in the Light of God and cleanse in the healing power of the Holy Spirit, the most powerful vibration in all the cosmos.

THE MANY
LAYERS TO
OVERCOMING GRIEF

Heart Strong

$\mathcal{A}$T THIS MOMENT ONE MONTH AGO, I was having the last conversation I would ever have on this earth with my mama. Oh, if I had known, I would have never let her go. I would have never let her walk out that door. It was two beautiful hours of her pouring the best of herself into me as she always did. She had brought me a little scarf, a pair of gloves for the winter, her finest advice, and as always, her whole heart.

While Mom was with me, my daughter, Kate, came home from school and was so happy to see her at our house. I'll never forget that last treasured image of seeing Kate yell, "D.D.!" while running into her arms with that huge, adorable grin of hers. She had just gotten her line to read in the Christmas program at school and was so excited to say it for us. Mom couldn't wait to hear it.

Kate says, "The snow started melting from the warmth of each heart. And grumpy attitudes simply fell apart."

Mama replied, "Oh, Kate, you got the best line in the whole play!"

Kate, "No, D.D. There's another line that's even better. It's about everyone coming together and uniting."

And I'll never forget the last piece of advice D.D. gave her precious little

Kate Diann, "Oh, but Kate. You got the line about the heart. No one could come together if the heart hadn't melted. Everything begins in the heart. Everything! Always remember, Kate, it's all about the heart."

And just like that, we gave our tender hugs. We exchanged our last glance. We heard her last words. She waved for the final time, and we unknowingly said our last goodbyes.

It was the 5th of November. Five, a number of divine grace.

Today is one month since she took flight.

And although we found her in her final sleep on the 6th of November, I know in my heart her last day was the 5th. She ended her journey well with words of completion to her only beloved granddaughter. She departed with words about the significance of the heart.

My mother's last words were literally, *"It's all about the heart."*

How apropos.

"A word fitly spoken is like apples
of gold in settings of silver."
(Proverbs 25:11)

My mama left this beautiful imagery with us as she left her final mark on this world.

I'm still in the operating recovery room. It's been an extended hospital day. I've undergone heart surgery, the kind that comes from having loved greatly and lost severely. However, I know I must lie here as long as needed so my heart can recover because everything begins in the heart. The heart is everything. It's all about the heart. Mama said so.

So right now, I'm waiting for Kate to get off the bus. We are going to buy her the prettiest dress we can find. Her Christmas program is in the morning. We are taking D.D. with us. And she will sit beside us tomorrow as we listen to Kate say her sweet little line for all to hear.

"The snow started melting from the warmth of each heart.
And grumpy attitudes simply fell apart."

You melted hearts, Mama. You started melting mine from first glance, and you were still melting it upon our last gaze. I was mesmerized then with your beauty, and I am still in awe of all that you are.

Tomorrow morning Kate will say her line in her play exactly one month from the day my sister and I found you in your final sleep. And when hearts are melting, your heart resting, my heart will still be breaking. But Mama, I promise you one thing, I will let it heal. I will let it grow strong again. Why? Because it's all about the heart. Because it's the last thing you ever said to me. Because your life deserves that my heart thrives and shines the way you spent your life molding and shaping it to sparkle.

Heart strong, Mama.

The Many Layers of Grief

I LAUGH. I CRY. I STARE INTO A DAZE. I wear a smile atop my broken heart. I feel as if it should be a national holiday on which shops are closed, and the world has stopped to grieve such a tremendous loss. And yet, the clock is still ticking. Life is still moving along.

I try to be "normal." I write about the emotions I'm experiencing on Facebook. "Is that appropriate?" I ask. Who knows? I stare for long periods of time. The foggy haze I walk amidst gets more transparent and then heavy once more. I cry again. I accept another condolence. I try to read the messages about my mother and stepdad's death while still in denial that I'm having to deal with the last mental image, of finding her dead, burned into the recesses of my mind.

I'm confused. I'm angry. I'm still in shock. I'm hopeful. I'm peaceful. I'm a mess of chaos. I'm a little bit of it all. I'm surrounded with people, and yet somehow, I feel all alone. A part of me is missing. I feel grateful for what I have and have had and yet I mourn for what has been lost. I look for wisdom. I search for strength. I look within. I feel weak. I feel strong. I feel lost. I feel found. I feel something is missing, and a part of me is incomplete. I feel I've been preparing for this moment my whole life and a new beginning has appeared, and yet I feel like all has ended and I'm not prepared at all.

Oh, the layers of grief, my friend. The more you love, the deeper the cut. All I can say is, "Ouch." Life is one freaking, beautiful mess. And I think to myself, "Life, sometimes I really love you, and sometimes I really, really hate you." But then...

I stop typing. I get still. I stop rambling. I listen, and I begin to hear that old familiar and sweetly treasured voice,

"Misti, stop being so dramatic. I haven't gone anywhere. Stop crying. I'm within you now. Feel me. Hear me. See me. How can you mourn that which you have not lost? Lo, I am with you always even until time immortal."

The words of my mother's voice echo throughout the chambers of my heart. They remind me of another pairing of similar words I had heard somewhere before, when Mary Madeline was standing outside the tomb of Jesus, crying in a place where she should have been rejoicing over His resurrection.

"Woman, why are you crying?"
(John 20:15)

"I pray that they will all be one, just as you and I are one —as you are in me, Father, and I am in you."
~ Jesus
(John 17:21)

How can one mourn when what has been lost now abides within?
As Mom is in the Father and the Father is in Mom.
As the Father is in me and I am in the Father.
So, Mom is in me.
We are one.

Jumping Puddles

OH GOD, TODAY IS HARD. IT IS SO HARD. It's been two months since Mom died, and I had to go to her house to begin cleaning it out today. Walking through those doors is almost unbearable. The sweet smell of her still lingers in the air. Her coffee cup still sits where she had set it out, ready for her morning pour. She always had things so organized and was such a good little planner. Her clothes still lie meticulously folded on the bathroom counter from the night before. Her cute little glasses sit waiting for her on the kitchen table beside her makeup where she sat and got ready in the mornings. I see her touches of love all around me. I pause and read the framed picture hanging in her kitchen,

"Do not neglect to show hospitality to strangers, for by so doing
some people have entertained angels without knowing it."
(Hebrews 13:2)

How telling. How appropriate to be the one scripture she placed upon her kitchen wall.

I knew it would be a difficult day. So, I put on my rain boots, and I made my way "through the rain." I posted a picture with a happy quote about jumping in puddles on rainy days. And yes, it seems like just a cute little motivational moment to the outside world, but not for me. It was something my mama used to say. I remembered us tapping puddles together when I was a little girl and her telling me that life will bring some rainy days but that whenever life brought me a puddle, to never be afraid to jump right through it. So today on the way to her house, I decided to jump puddles—first the ones I faced on the ground and then the ones I would face when I walked through the door of her home.

I jumped a puddle today, Mama. I wore the pretty boots you bought me. I cried for you. And then I faced my rainy day with a smile.

She Kept My Cheerleading Jackets

She kept my cheerleading jackets.

I pause and ponder.

She kept my cheerleading jackets.

1 REMEMBER HER SITTING ON THOSE BLEACHERS cheering me on, gazing in appreciation—that look of mesmerizing awe that is solely reserved for a mother and her daughter. Oh, the way her eyes would look at me. I could feel God through those delicate, soft eyes.

She kept my cheerleading jackets.

What did she treasure about those moments watching her little girl cheer so proudly, watching her bounce, play, prance, and laugh with her friends? The memories that stay in the heart of a mother are keepsakes.

So here I am, still in shock that she is gone. As I brace my heart in a brave attempt to clean out the remains of her closet, here in the back of her closet, nestled behind her meticulously organized sweaters, are hanging my cheerleading jackets.

I cry a little. I think of my daughter and how I love her so and how I want to keep things of hers that will probably never be as special or meaningful to her but are my precious memories of her; like the little Princess Anna dress she wore that one day when she was four years old. I still remember those cute little cowgirl boots she paired with it and braiding her sweet little curls into pigtails.

This morning I am remembering my past with the heart of a mother and peering through a new lens, the lens of my mom. She kept my cheerleading jackets. Something about seeing me in those jackets—something about remembering me in that moment—she wanted to save and keep. She loved me. She treasured memories of me and of my childhood.

She loved me. Oh, how she loved me. This is special. This is sacred. I was loved. I was loved very well.

She kept my cheerleading jackets.

Little Red Cardinal

LAST WEEK A LADY APPROACHED ME BECAUSE SHE FELT GUIDED to share a message with me. She told me that whenever I see a red cardinal, it was a reminder that my mom was with me. We hugged, I received her message with deep appreciation, and we parted ways for the evening.

Later that same night, another lady came over to introduce herself to me. It was my first night to try and leave the house after Mom died. I didn't last long. The first time I tried speaking to someone, I unraveled and began to swell up and cry. As circumstance would have it, this precious lady looked at me and began to tell me of how her mother had passed away seven years prior. She hugged me and offered tremendous words of warmth, understanding, and comfort. We friended one another on Facebook, and afterward, I decided it was best for me to go on home.

The following morning, I awoke, and would you believe her post was the first to appear on my timeline. It read...

"7 years ago, today, my mama gained her angel wings. Not a day goes by that I don't miss her. Not a day goes by that I don't have something I wish I could tell her, show her or share with her. Not many days go by that I don't see a cardinal... it always makes me smile because I believe it's a sign, she heard me, she saw, she knows."

It was exactly seven years to the day that she had lost her mom. She posted three pictures; a picture of her mom, a poem entitled, "A Letter from Heaven," and a picture of a red cardinal.

My friend had just told me the night before the message about the cardinal, and the following morning I woke to my new friend's message. Of course, I immediately texted the friend who shared the message about the cardinal with tears, a screenshot of the post, and a massive, "Wow!"

But the story isn't over. While waiting to be seated for Thanksgiving Dinner, I ventured into a gift shop, and when I looked up, I noticed a little dish set with beautiful cardinals on them. I couldn't believe my eyes! I grabbed my camera to take a photo, and when I turned around, I saw an entire Christmas tree decorated in them. Then more and more began to appear. An entire section of the store was immersed in red cardinals! They were everywhere. I saw two perched side by side, and I knew immediately it was my stepdad and mom telling me they were together and happy.

And then, I saw her. My eyes fell upon the prettiest cardinal of all, one made of sparkling glass that shimmered every time the light hit her. The tears in my

eyes caused her to glisten even more spectacularly. I took her, and I held her in my hand. Just like my mom, she sat, reflecting the Light so magnificently.

Just before I sat down for my first Thanksgiving without my precious mama, she found a way to have a moment with me and let me know that she was with me, that she saw me, that she loved me, and that we were together giving thanks. She completely surrounded me in the form of red cardinals everywhere I looked! I am in awestruck wonder.

Of course, I took my pretty little cardinal home with me and every time I see her, I will be reminded of how my mother is always with me, still guiding, still loving, and still watching over us.

Yesterday, I had to go over to mom's house to check on some things. I happened to look down at her keys as I was opening the door. I paused. I cried. I smiled. Engrafted onto almost every key she owned, including the key to her home, was the image of a cardinal.

You just can't make this stuff up. The hand of the Almighty is at work. There is a spiritual realm that has our back, that loves us, that fights for us, that helps us, and that is constantly sending us messages and speaking intimately to us. Today I am grateful for such a wonderful heavenly host of angelic agents, and I am especially grateful for my mom, my personal angel of brilliant Light.

Oh, Mama, my heart burns for you. The pain is beyond what I feel I can bear, so thank you for surrounding me tonight. And thank you, Father, for giving me this pretty red bird before I broke bread with my family this evening. I needed her. She comforted me. I am grateful your love is so aware and focused upon my hurt. You are truly close to the broken-hearted. Come closer and closer.

Goodnight, Mama.

Rise Up

"There is no force more powerful
than a woman determined to rise."
~ anonymous

I SAW THIS QUOTE TODAY, AND IT REMINDED ME of a phrase my mom began telling me during my teen years and would continue to reiterate throughout my life, "Rise above." She was always encouraging me to rise above petty issues, drama, insecurities, doubts, fears, and to take the high road in life. These words now take on a whole new meaning as my sister and I seek to honor her life by pulling from her strength to once more rise above our present circumstances.

Today, rising strong is overcoming the tremendous grief in my heart from having to face the reality that my mom is dead. Today, rising strong is to stop crying, get out of bed, get a shower, get the boys homeschooled, get my groceries, make dinner, and just keep going. Mom would be saying,

"Rise up, Misti. Rise above this, and I prefer you
do it with peace and joy in your heart as well as a
beautiful smile for your precious three."

How can I not reply back with appropriate southern fashion, "Yes ma'am." Though now speaking from the other side of the veil and echoing her pretty voice from within the chambers of my heart, her words are still too pure and piercing to resist or deny them.

I can hear her guidance for me and feel her strength. I know exactly what she would want me to do. She's a part of me now. I can feel her rising within me. For this, I have found something to feel appreciation and gratitude for this morning. For this and for those she loved that still remain, including me, I find my reasons to rise strong.

Baby steps.

A Sound Sleep

I THINK GOD IS SHOWING ME SOMETHING IMPORTANT ABOUT SLEEP. After the shock and horror of finding my mom in her final sleep and the traumatic, emotional days that have followed, there has been an otherworldly adrenaline keeping my body moving and functioning.

Today, I finally slept. I slept. I slept some more. And then I slept some more. I feel like I could keep sleeping for several more days before the heavy weight in my body would pass. All day today, I felt the Spirit keep whispering to me, "Just sleep. I will heal and restore you."

I started thinking about all the Bible stories I could remember where sleep led to something good or to restoration. I thought about the illustration of God putting Adam into a deep sleep so He could pull forth the majestic Eve, the greatest treasure and gift he had ever been given. I thought of Elijah being worn down and told to eat and sleep beside a brook, the place where he found angels surrounding him and nourishing him back to health. Perhaps the angels came to him in a dream. Perhaps his nourishment came to him in his sleep. I also thought of Lazarus "sleeping" for three days before experiencing the greatest moment of resurrection his soul had ever known.

It is 6:40 p.m., I've been sleeping all day and all last night, and the Spirit said to me, "Go back to sleep." And then the following words fell like a rain shower into my heart and gripped me in a way I had never heard or understood them before.

"The girl is not dead but asleep."
~ Jesus
(Matthew 9:24)

Selah.

I will let this speak to you as the Spirit leads. It is deeply profound. For me, it was as if Christ was saying that there may be some that feel lifeless within due to something that knocked them down and took the life out of them. But don't consider these precious ones down for the count. A One much greater can come along and recognize he or she is simply sleeping and speak life into their frame. I have seen this One in many people speaking life into me and helping me rise.

Love conquers all. It can lift, revise, and raise the dead and saddened parts within us all. Christ is not just something that came or is coming again. He is always coming eternally through His beautiful Vessels, the wonderful mouth-pieces that have allowed His Spirit to flow through them and into our hearts.

The Spirit nourished me with a pearl of deep wisdom while I was as Elijah resting by the brook, and while I was as Lazarus lying in a darkened cave wrapped in mourning garments.

Sleeping matters.

Something is happening beyond what I can understand when we rest our bodies. Sleep as long as you need. Sleep as hard as you need. Let God put you into a deep sleep and restore you. I believe this is what He is doing each night for us. And who knows? Maybe like Eve was extracted from within Adam during his time of rest, God has something tremendously amazing beyond anything you could have ever hoped or imaged that He wants to pull forth and see emerge from your frame.

Sometimes when things get really hard, we just need extra sleep. Listen to that still small Voice. If you're still here, there's a reason It's still guiding you.

"So good night, Mama. Sleep well."
"Goodnight, Sweetheart. Sleep well, Misti.
We will both rise again. I love you."
"I love you too, Mama.
Will you rock me to sleep as you use too?"
"But of course, Dear. I am here. Now get your rest.
I will sing you to sleep."

A Most Honorable Feat

"It's time. We can't put this off any longer. Let's go together."
My sister and I walk into her room, where we found her in her final sleep.

The heart begins to tighten. The familiar stabbing hurt pierces deeply. The tears can't be withheld. Silence fills the room for the sacredness of the moment. We begin to fold her bedspread and remove her sheets and place them in the bag. We remove the pillowcases where we lay beside her weeping the day we found her breathless, our tear stains now visible and engrained upon the pillows.

We wail once more. We cry out. We weep. We moan. I hold the garbage bag, and my sister places the bedding securely in it, and then we close the bag.

We remind ourselves just to keep functioning.

Just stay distracted.
Just keep moving.
Just laugh.
Just be happy.

We realize we haven't stopped since that fateful day. We can't. Not yet. We're not ready to face the moments we presently find ourselves in this evening—packing away the final dreaded things.

The realization she is really gone settles in a little more firmly... ouch.

"I'd give away every material comfort to have her back," my sister whispers painstakingly through her tears.

"Me too," I sorrowfully replied.

Friday her bed must be moved. Oh, the agony of such simple things.

Grief is an indescribable pain. Be kind to those enduring it. Some have loved so great that they carry that piercing-heart sting with them for the rest of their lives, because the greater we love, the deeper and more profound our grief.

Celebrate when someone who has suffered loss can laugh and play again. It's a big deal. It takes a supernatural strength and determination that is beyond their overwhelming sadness. The journey back to happy from grief is a most honorable feat. For those of us courageously embarking upon it, we have immense, eternal gratitude for those helping us smile and laugh amidst our pain. We will never ever forget you.

Oh, Mama, I miss how pretty you looked when you sleep. Even in your final rest, you looked more beautiful than all the wonderment this world has ever shown me. I bet you'll make the angels jealous when they see how radiantly you glow. Enjoy your peaceful rest, Mama. You don't need this bed anymore. You have a much better piece of furniture to rest upon. I know your royal seat sparkles something beautiful and makes heaven look even more glorious.

Nothing
Unsaid or Undone

On my last birthday, the first thing I did upon waking was send a message to my mom. I felt an immediate strong urge to release a massive swell of love I had in my heart for her. For some reason, I was guided to take a screenshot picture of the text I sent to her as well as her response. The date was October 10th. I look back at the exact words I chose for her that morning, and I'm left in silent awe. I'm so grateful I said them to her. I wrote...

> *"Good morning! I love you so much today! My heart could burst with the love it carries around just for YOU! You have no idea how much your presence keeps me going. You are my best friend, Mama. And even though I am so busy with the kids and responsibilities, you are MY Mama, and I carry you with me all day every day, thinking of you almost every single second of the day. You remain with me always! I even listen to your guidance when you're not here! You are so loved and cherished! Having you in my life is the greatest birthday gift and greatest gift I have ever received from God!!!"*

I had no idea at the time, but it was the last birthday I would ever spend with my mother. Today I am so grateful that I had previously gone through the experience of having a brain aneurysm, which taught me the value of savoring moments and not leaving things unsaid and undone with the people we most treasure and love.

Death has a funny way of providing a sobering perspective for our lives. I look back at the impulse I had to write to my mom and the exact words my Spirit was guided to give her. In essence, I told her that although we were separated by life, that I carried her with me, that she remained with me, and that I could hear her voice and guidance even when she wasn't physically present with me. I let her know that I loved her, that I cherished her, that she was the greatest gift that God had ever given me, and that I considered her my very best friend. Twenty-seven days later, my mother entered her final sleep. It was the greatest shock and trauma of my life. However, there is a peace in my heart, because I know that she left this world knowing how deeply I loved her. I am certainly left here knowing how deeply she loved me.

My Spirit, in its divine wisdom, was making a deposit in my mom's Spirit, letting her know that she had done well, that she had contributed something magnificent in this world, that she had left me with the very best of all that she was, and that I would be ok. I will carry my mom's deep-soul wisdom with me for the rest of my life, and I am so humbly grateful I followed my impulse that birthday morning to let her know that.

Share the things you truly want to say to people now. Don't wait. Let them know how you genuinely feel.

Wake every day and ask yourself, "If this is my last day on earth, how will I choose to live it? How will I choose to respond to the people and circumstances of my life? How will I handle the argument or disagreement? What is worth my energy, time, and focus? When this day is over, what will I wish I had released or healed within myself? Is the anxiety really worth it? What still needs to be said? What still needs to be done? What is the last impression I want to make upon those I love?"

Perspective is a beautiful thing. Perspective is the way we see circumstances and people from a certain distance that allows us to truly appreciate their value. Once we're given perspective, act on the wisdom gleaned from it. Follow any impulse that moves you towards any and all expressions of love and forgiveness.

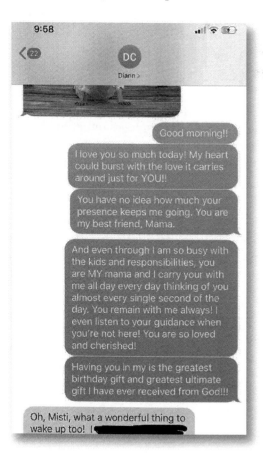

That Turn, That Day, and That Room

It's JUST ANOTHER NIGHT OF PASSING THE SAME TURN. I wish I could go through the stop sign without the memory.

On November 6, 2018, my sister and I called one another just before noon, because our mom wasn't answering our calls. We decide one of us should head over to her house to check on things. I was waiting for my groceries to be delivered to my home, so my sister decided to go ahead and make her way over to my mom's house.

I was putting up the final groceries when the call came, "Misti! Oh my God! Misti, she's blue! She's blue, Misti!" My ears began to ring from the tormenting screams of my sister. My heart collapsed, and my body went into a full-body, violent tremble.

I yelled for my children. They immediately came running down the stairs. For the rest of their lives, they will never forget that horrific scream. A deep, piercing cry of the soul was bellowing forth within me. No one should ever have to hear such a heart-wrenching howl.

"I have to go! It's Mama!"

I left driving faster than I had ever driven in my entire life. My sister was still on the phone, screaming and crying in a stricken panic. For some reason, my body was shaking and convulsing involuntarily from head to toe. I went uncontrollably into a repetitive scream. I cried at God. I yelled at Him as loud as I could. I wailed from my soul. I was stuck on one word, "No! No! Noooooooooo!" My screams became more violent.

I had to get off the phone with my sister so that she could call 911. I began calling, trying to get in touch with my then-husband at the time, but I couldn't hold my phone because my hand was shaking so violently. I dropped my phone, and when I tried to pick it up, I felt a massive jolt and heard an intense sound from behind me. A large van and crashed into the back of my car.

I remember getting out of my car, feeling as if I was in a dream state. It felt like my vision was blurred, and everything was happening in a conundrum of frantic chaos and slow-motion video. I emerged from my car, screaming and crying uncontrollably, "I can't! I can't! I think my mother could be dying! I can't!

I have to go!" My voice was shaking so badly I could barely breathe to say the words, "Nooooo, God! I forbid it! She isn't dead! No, God, no! Don't you dare!!! Don't you do this!"

The two men that had now exited their van were now staring at me in terror having no words to say. It was fuzzy. I was fuzzy. Everything was fuzzy. I vaguely remember the men telling me, "There's no damage, Ma'am. We've looked at your car and our van. There's been no damage. It's ok. You can go."

I remember for some reason I was holding my hands on my head in a daze, perhaps trying to keep it still from all the trembling. With hands still on the sides of my head, I said, "I can't stay. I have to go. If something's wrong, you have to follow me. I have to go!"

I couldn't catch my breath, was still shaking violently, and felt my heart was going to beat out of my chest. I pulled out and once again began to speed towards my mom's house. Five minutes later, I walked into the worst, most traumatizing and horrific moment of my entire life.

An angel had stopped breathing
Not just any Angel, my Angel

For hours I screamed for her to breathe again. I lay in bed with her begging for her to come back, and for the warmth to return to her beautiful face. I lay there facing the darkest most shocking moment of my entire life.

Tonight I passed the turn again. Driving twenty minutes out of the way to try and avoid it is no longer feasible. I've got to face that turn.

It's been eight months of numbing out. It's taken eight months to get brave enough to let myself feel. I've been avoiding facing the ache. Tonight, when I passed the turn, I let myself feel it a little bit. I let myself cry. I let myself hurt.

My soul has finally stopped screaming, "Nooo!" I am still. I am quiet. I am broken and bruised, but I have moved past the scream.

Progress.

I think Mama would be proud of me tonight. I think she would be waiting patiently and lovingly for me to give her a call and ask if I could come over to talk. She always waited until I was ready to face whatever it was I needed to face. She waited with such grace until I was ready to let it out. And when I finally came to her, she would sit and hold a space of love for me while I let myself fall apart. She would say something wise and sacred, something to ground me and give me peace. If nothing else, she would do as she had done many times before on those really painful days when I didn't feel like I was going to make it. She would crawl in bed with me. She would hold me while I was crying, listen to me intently, and remind me that she loved me and would always be there for me.

So, I made it past the turn tonight. But this time, I didn't numb myself emotionally. I didn't phone a friend. I let myself feel it all, and I did it all by myself. I didn't do it with a glass of wine, or with a group of friends where I was attempting to talk about anything and everything but that turn and that day of walking into that room.

I faced it alone. I faced it with God. I faced it with the heart of my mama beating inside of me. I let the pain surface, and I just surrendered to it. I let it cry itself out.

It's been eight months, but I think I'm ready to start thinking about what has happened to me. I'm ready to feel the pain, and I'm ready to heal from it.

Still Here, Still Breathing, and Still Hoping

MOM'S DEATH HAS TAKEN ME TO MY UTTER DEPTHS. It has changed me in ways I hope to one day articulate for the benefit of many souls, but for now, I am just letting this all have its way with me. I suppose she finished saying all that was needed, and it's time for me to forge ahead with all the beauty, love, grace, and truth she has put inside my heart as the brilliant angel she always was for me. She did so well. She finished strong.

When I found mom dead, it was horrific for me. It was a pivotal moment of change in my life, a stark realization that things would never be the same. It was a mother's final nudge to push her baby bird from the nest and tell her it was time to fly. I have cried every day since she died, but I also feel her closer to me than she's ever been.

I had to let go of everything. Now, in my utter weakness, I am surrendered yet never have I felt so internally strong. In a state of complete release, I am finding a clearer vision and a deeper purpose. Losing my mom was the worst thing that could have ever happened to my heart. I lost her and my stepdad within two months of one another. I faced the pain and guess what? I'm still here. I'm still breathing. Oddly, I still feel hope. How could it be? I suppose I am truly made to wear those rose-colored glasses even in the midst of the worst of storms. So, I am free to fly, but I am resting in this space a bit longer. I feel I am exactly where I am supposed to be, facing exactly the parts of myself I need to face. I feel this divine current within me taking me along a peaceful stream of angelic guidance. I have no doubt everything is as it should be and when my lessons have been learned the current will change, the dam will release me into a new river, and I'll float in a new pond. Until then...

I write.

One thing my mom taught me was to appreciate what is and to love that which remains. Always focus on the blessings in front of you and upon what you have. Appreciate it, and you will have more and more of it.

It is a gift to find true happiness in the midst of circumstances that are not quite as perfect as we wish them to be. It is easy to look upon that which we love and feel bliss. It is a Master Teacher who can look upon that which displeases him and remain in a state of contentment, compassion, grace, bliss, and love. Perhaps your soul wants to glean such a potent strength. I know mine did, and this catalytic moment in my life has forced me into this space. And though my heart feels squeezed night and day and though the tears still fall, I have accomplished a surrendered peace that I've searched for my entire life, and I have no doubt that all things are working for my good.

Key Turned

So, it's March, but last night Kate and I decided to celebrate a little Christmas cheer together. Our December was a bit broken. We never really had a "Christmastime" this year. So, we lit a cinnamon candle, turned down the lights, and snuggled in bed to watch *The Nutcracker* together. One thing life has taught me is that it's never too late to make up for lost time.

The movie was about a girl named Clara who had lost her mother and in doing so, lost a piece of herself. She lost her bearings and her purpose. She was looking for a golden key she believed would free her from her sadness and depression and give her the answers she was searching for. The girl's mother had left behind a gift for her, an ornately decorated egg with the words, "Everything you need is inside." Clara believed her answers lied within this egg, and that if she could only find the key her problems would be solved. It took a long courageous journey for Clara to finally realize that the key wasn't something to be obtained outside of herself, but that her mother was trying to tell her all she needed to rescue herself and fulfill her purpose lied within her.

At the beginning of the movie, Clara's father, Mr. Stahlbaum says to her, "This time has been built for all of us, but when Christmas comes, we must do our best to enjoy it." Clara's response was, "I don't want to enjoy anything right now. I wish mother were here."

However, once Clara's journey had concluded, and she understood the key to her triumph, the movie ended with her saying these final, epic words in reference to her mother,

"I will miss her every day for the rest of my life, but I don't want to miss one more minute with you, Louise, or Fritz."

Clara ultimately realized what she had left and placed her value on that which remained, her father and siblings.

The words were spoken. The credits rolled down the screen. The bedroom grew quiet. Kate, only eight years old, understood all too well. She grabbed my hand, and I held hers...tenderly. We squeezed them together, and the tears drifted softly down my cheeks. Inwardly we knew not a minute of gratitude was to be wasted. So, with that, we had a Christmas ~ in our hearts ~ together. The key was discovered.

And then, we did as my mama would have wanted us to ~ we danced. We did the silliest Nutcracker ballet poses we could possibly do, and we laughed.

Key turned.

Merry March Christmas!

Perfect Vision

"Misti, your mother only ever saw you as perfect."

I DON'T KNOW IF THERE WAS A MORE PIERCING STATEMENT sent to me after my mother died than the one listed above. I have read this statement at least a hundred times. As I sit here staring at it once more, a lifetime with my mom is flashing before my eyes. No matter how many wayward turns my journey took, she never wavered with those endlessly, loving eyes. Her eyes were as the eyes of God, piercing and pure. She had a million different looks and a million different smiles, and I knew them all. I even knew the traces of the veins upon her hands and the crooked, cute way her fingers bent. Her touch was so tender, so gentle, so healing, and so true.

If a man sought to find truth through a thousand, arduous lifetimes till he finally heard the sound of her pure light, it could not compare to the treasure of obtaining the love from the heart of my mother. The pureness of one drop of her love was enough to heal the hearts of mankind. She had a way of making a stranger feel like family and a prodigal feel like a firstborn son. She had a way of making me feel like a Queen when life had me at times feeling like I was spiritually draped in Cinderella's filthy rags. My mother was love.

"Misti, your mother only ever saw you as perfect."

But the thing is, I so often felt I disappointed her. It's hard to stare at love when you feel so unlovable. And yet, she would overtake me with it, her love that is. She would invigorate me with it. She breathed love from her mouth. She kissed my cheeks with it. As a little girl, I still remember holding hands in church while she listened to her pastor and sang her pretty hymns. I loved going to church, because knew I could lie in her lap and know she was going to trace my face and hands with the tips of her fingers. Oh, was she was something special! She only searched for good. She only wanted good for others. She served with a brokenness about her that made her ooze a sense of humility and lowliness. But she wasn't the least. She was the greatest, because she had placed herself at the back of the line waiting for everyone else to be fed before taking her morsel. She was promoted to head of the table by the Divine, and she wore her royal cloak well, as one who cared for and loved the continuants of her kingdom.

"Misti, your mother only ever saw you as perfect."

That she did. That she did. I ponder. If this is how the greatest of the kingdom loves, is this not how the Creator of such a heart must love? My mother never took delight in punishing me, and an eternity spent in spiritual separation would never be an option for her. She would mount a horse and come for me across the greatest divide if this be the requirement, but she wouldn't leave me behind. I could never imagine her eyes looking at me with a disappointing glance. In fact, the moments in my life when I was staring in the face of my greatest failure, her gaze never carried a more potent, heart-piercing love. Nothing I could ever do or say was going to cause even a moment of doubt for her. She was unwavering in her love with a reckless pursuit to shower me with the best of all she had. Even in her death, she is still caring for me, providing for me with both spiritual and physical sustenance. Nothing can separate me from her love. She would tear the veil of heaven and part the spiritual divide to ensure I was being cared for and to ensure I was being given everything my soul needed to finish this journey well.

"Misti, your mother only ever saw you as perfect."

Why did I ever see God any different than the way I see my mom? Someone recently said to me, "I've never known fear because the only thing God has ever shown me was love."

How could I ever diminish His love or think the love of my Maker would be less far-reaching, enduring, and unconditional than my mom, the giver of my life, who held and nestled me in her womb. Has not God carried me in His cosmic womb? Was it not Him sitting behind my mother's beautiful, brown eyes? Was it not His Light that flooded her soul and fell like a rainbow of hearts upon mine?

"Misti, your mother only ever saw you as perfect."

I sit in the stillness of the night and read these words over and over again until I hear with my spiritual ears...

"Misti, your God only ever saw you as perfect."

The tears fall. It's too much. The love is that statement is too piercing, too healing, and too freeing. The words are almost too good to be true. But something deep insides tell me they are true. My heart tells me they are true. God thought of me just as she did when I made my grand entrance into this world, absolutely perfect: no stains, no filthy rags, and no imperfections—just a pure, beautiful, unique creation that had been molded in the matrix of God. I was loved. He wanted to hold me, touch me, and cradle me with an endless loving glance just as she had done. My mistakes were opportunities for me to learn, to grow, and to be sculpted by the hands of the Divine. That was all. They were not to shame me. They were not to condemn me. They were not to make me feel excluded or separated from love. They were simply to grow me.

"Misti, your God only ever saw you as perfect."

Misti, you can relax now. Your God loves you like your mother, and you have a tangible experience now to draw upon to understand the depths of that love. You know how she loved you. It was unending. If was without condition. It was fierce. It was protective. It was enduring. It was immovable. It was healing. It was always there. It was freeing. There are no depths to which that love wouldn't travel to come for you. *And it did.*

To the one holding this book in your hands, it came for you too. It came and deposited itself within you. It's sitting behind your eyes. It's falling with your tears. It's saturated upon your palms. It's hovering in your breath. It's flowing through your touch. It's laced upon your lips. Somebody needs it as bad as you needed it, and as bad as you needed to realize you had it to give. Go give it to them. Go love them so well that one day someone will say of you,

"Your _____ only ever saw you as perfect."

Was I really perfect? No, I wasn't perfect. But what I do know is that love made me want to be perfect, because it was the only thing potent enough to transform me when I wasn't. What I do know is that love was powerful enough to make me perfect in the eyes of my mama, and that love was powerful to perfect me in the eyes of the Divine.

Strength Through Grief

A LITTLE OVER TWO YEARS AFTER MY BRAIN ANEURYSM, life handed me an even more traumatic and worse blow than being diagnosed with an inoperable tumor in the middle of my brain stem. I walked in on the love of my heart, my precious mother, lying breathless in her bed, having died of a heart attack in her sleep. My mother was my best friend, my counselor, and my rock. It was a moment of horror.

A cry from my soul emerged so deep that I am certain it shook the halls of heaven. The worst thing that could have ever happened to me short of losing a child happened. That old familiar feeling of wanting to quit, of wanting to check out, of wanting to escape the pain of this life emerged once more. But this time, things were different. There was a keen awareness of my need to make an instant, deliberate statement to the entire Universe that I was prepared to face this. In the face of death, my mother's death, I had to choose life once more.

There is a reservoir of strength inside of you that can assist you in defying all odds. It will be there to warm you on your coldest, darkest nights. It will be your Light through the dark night of your soul. My mother was the one who taught me how to pull from that Light. There was no one who desired me to overcome my scare with death more than her. There was no one prouder when I rose from that diagnosis with healing in my wings. After her death, when I felt my heart had broken beyond repair, I felt her strength. I felt God's strength within me, and once again, I chose to live. I chose to rise from the ash heap of deep despair and soar on eagle's wings. It was a little bit sheer will and a little bit a Spirit much bigger than me carrying me when I was too weak to stand. I was grateful for both.

At the end of the day, what helped me make those faith-filled, life-giving choices was not focusing on the circumstance, the illness, or the horrendous loss. It was focusing on that which remained. It was focusing on love, the love I had for my children, and the love I had for the remainder of my family. They were what I had left. They were my two fishes and five loaves of bread to place in the hands of God. They were what began to multiply me once more. They were my twelve baskets of overflowing abundance. They were my miracle.

You can't overcome the defeating moments
of your life by focusing on what you've lost.

You must find a way to place your attention
upon that which remains.
This is your lifeline.

Although there are moments when I feel the grief leaves me unable to breathe and the ache for my mother seems unbearable, I have also found the strength of her presence in ways I never imagined possible.

She is with God.
God is with me.
She is with me.

She is in God.
I am in God.
She is in me.
We are one.

I would have never thought I could overcome a blow like this, the grief of such an immense love. Yet, amazingly enough, I am seeing glimpses now of a life where I believe I will not just survive this great loss, but that I will eventually thrive again. Every day I wake and choose happiness. My mother began telling me in my teenage years that happiness was an inside job and a deliberate choice. She would always follow this statement with the added phrase, "Choose wisely."

Every time I dance in the kitchen with my kiddos, laugh at a random party with friends, or sit in the front porch rocking chairs singing my daughter's favorite songs with her—it's a choice. It's a choice to love my mama in death as dearly as I loved her in life. I feel her smile with me. I feel her being proud of me. I feel her happiness because I have chosen to overcome the immense heartbreak, rise out of bed another day, fight to create an atmosphere of love and joy for my children, and express the courage it takes to move forward after life has thrown her curve balls of surprise at me.

The fears I once had are dissipating, and each day I am realizing there is nothing in life we can't overcome. God is with us. Our angels are with us. Our purpose is with us. And a heavenly host of loved ones is surrounding us; I believe all of which are cheering us on and wanting us to succeed and make it through the ridiculously hard challenges we often face down here. To do this, we need one another. We need to love one another. Someone's "crazy" needs your love. Their pre-judged nervous breakdown needs your kindness and support. They need you to want to see them pull through, rise strong, and be all that God has destined their life to become. Don't give up on them. I saw a meme recently that I deeply identified with which read, "Sometimes I feel like I'm in season five of my life, and the writers are just making ridiculous shit happen to keep it interesting." Well, be the friend that makes it through season five of someone's life. My mama was that kind of friend, and I want to be that kind of friend to others.

Bottom line . . . It's friggin' hard out there. Be friggin' nice to people, and know this, you can overcome anything life throws at you. Yes, it might hurt like hell. I can assure you it most certainly will. But as Dory the fish says, "Just keep swimming." I'm thankful I still believe in purpose, destiny, a little pixie dust, and the importance of waking with the idea that a little mystical magic is coaxing my day. I'm grateful for the fact hope has always remained with me and regardless of how cray cray the twists and turns of my life can sometimes get that I still believe with unwavering faith God truly does have a rhyme and reason to all of this.

There is ample forgiveness, unending grace,
overwhelming support, and an eternal love available
to you at every moment along your journey.

So, Mama—I promise to honor your big, beautiful life. I can't say I won't cry, but I promise you I will keep laughing. I promise you I will keep dancing. I promise you I will make better memories, and as you know, this is a big statement because you gave me the absolute best of them. So, I have a few tears as I type, but Mama, I also have a smile. I have your courage. I have your kindness. I have you. I have my precious three, Riley, Jack, and Kate. I have God. I have Christ. I have everything. As the soundtrack to the timeless ending of *The Greatest Showman* articulates as the lead characters stare at their treasured children,

"It's everything you ever want. It's everything you ever need.
And it's here right in front of you. This is where you wanna be."

To happiness, to choices, to this day,
to this moment . . .
Cheers!

Reflections from a Mother's Heart

Written two and half years before my precious Mama passed away

I'VE READ MANY BOOKS IN MY LIFETIME, and I'm sure I have many more yet to read, but the one I read this weekend is the greatest one I have or will ever read.

Eighteen years ago, I went in search of a Mother's Day gift for my mother. I was nineteen years old and on a mystical search for the Spirit to guide me to the perfect gift for my mother. I found myself in a bookstore, drawn to one particular book titled, *Reflections from a Mother's Heart*. On the front cover was written, "A Family Legacy for Your Children: Your Life Story in Your Own Words." The book was full of many questions with blank spaces, and I knew from the moment I saw it that it was special. Something inside of me knew it would be a gift not just for my mother, but to all those whom she loved. Knowing my mother, I knew her family was her heart. Anything that could warm the hearts or those she adored would be the greatest gift I could ever bestow upon her.

Years passed, and I had forgotten about the gift I gave my mom so many years prior. Until this past Mother's Day when my mom walked me to the front yard of my home and said, "I'd like to show you something. It took me a while, but I finished it." From behind her back, she handed me the book I had given her eighteen years prior. I opened it to find where I had written a message for her on the first page...

Mama,

Although this book is my gift to you, I am hoping that someday it will become your gift to me. Throughout the years, I have listened to your words of wisdom and remarkable life lessons that have only left me captivated and longing to hear more. My curiosity to know you more and discover all the many treasures that lie within your heart continues to grow more and more. My hope is that you will complete this book for me and someday make it a priceless treasure that I can call my own. I will always be fascinated by the amazing person and Godly woman you are. You have been one of life's greatest blessings to me. I love you and wish you a much-deserved Happy Mother's Day!

As I looked through the book, I quickly noticed that each page, all two hundred and two of them, had been filled with the delicate touch of her handwriting. Maybe it's because it's my Mother's craftsmanship, but I can literally see love with every stroke and curve she placed upon the letters of her script. I can feel her personality in her writing and the sweetness of her heart in the intricacies of her penmanship. As I glanced upon the pages, I was immediately taken back to the bookshop and the thoughts that saturated me when I first purchased this gift. I knew then it would somehow be an heirloom for my heart.

I could hardly wait to open its pages and begin devouring every word, but I hesitated because I wanted it to be special. It was special. These words were my mom. My mom was these words. These were not just written words to me. They were windows into my mother's heart. There are great loves in this life, that of a man for a woman, that of a child for his parents, that for a man and the Divine, and that of a mother for her beloved child. So, to honor these words, I selected a sacred place to digest and ponder them.

I went to my parents' lake cabin nestled beautifully in a cove by the lake with a view that makes even heaven stop and take notice. I lied on the pier in the sunshine and

Listening to the heart of your parent share their regrets, their failures, their joys, and their memories is a noteworthy legacy to be treasured by their children.

read. I swung in the hammock beneath my favorite tree, Hope. We call her Hope because she's been struck by lightning twice, mended herself, and has flourished in spite of what tried to knock her down. I read enveloped by the winds and while listening to the birds sing their sweet summer songs. I read with the fragrance of flowers in the air. I read while listening to the frog's croak and the crickets chirp. I read. I cried. I listened. I laughed. I pondered. I read some more. It was the greatest feast I've ever absorbed, each morsel like that of a delicious spread fit for the most noble of all the land.

The questions provoked my mother to answer life's most personal and probing questions. She took me on an adventurous heartfelt journey through the pages of her ordinary yet tremendously spectacular life. I glimpsed into her childhood memories, family history, light-hearted incidents, cherished traditions, and most importantly I saw inside her heart where I discovered her most treasured possessions: me, my sister, her grandchildren, and all those she has loved so deeply, including the One she holds most dear, her Jesus.

I've always been in love with my mother from the moment I saw her, the way she smelled, the way she smiled, the way she cared and the way she loved. But reading this memoir of her life connected me to her Spirit in a way that I am certain will bind our souls for all eternity. Her wisdom was so simple yet so profoundly heart-piercing that it was difficult to read without a tear in my eye. The force of love woven throughout each page was so potent my heart could barely take the pulsing of its energetic power. I pray every soul has the opportunity to be overtaken with the power of love radiating at its most elevated frequency and directed specifically towards their heart. God has provided such an experience for all of us if we would recognize and receive it. For me, this weekend, He sent this electrifyingly wonder through the heart of my mother. I saw God while lying on a hammock. He was encapsulated in the penmanship of my first love, my mom, and stamped upon the pages of my heart.

Listening to the heart of your parent share their regrets, their failures, their joys, and their memories is a noteworthy legacy to be treasured by their children. Listening to my mother speak about the beauty of repentance, the power of letting go, and the theme of love and belief that echoes from her heart moved me to no end. My mother's heart is her greatest treasure because that is where she stores all of us.

I wish I could articulate what these pages have meant to me. They've given me a glimpse into my mom's life through a different lens, her lens. Though I was also experiencing many of the noted moments myself, seeing them from her viewpoint gave me a whole new perspective of my own life. For example, one particular question in the book asked my mom about her Christmas memories. At the bottom of the page, she wrote, "This is how I see Christmas." She then drew a picture of three stick figures, her, my sister, and me. My sister and I were placed beneath the Christmas tree. She was looking from afar with a heart drawn on her chest. That picture had me in tears for a least a good half hour. Now that I have my own children, I understand the emotion that resides in such a simplistic sketch drawing. I too have sat beneath the Christmas tree staring at my children with a swollen heart wondering if they will ever know how deeply I truly love them. My mom depicted moments like combing my hair and how special those moments were to her. It made me pause. Every morning I fix my daughter's hair. She just turned six years old, has long, curly, black hair, and is pure sunshine to my soul. Yet, in the hustle and bustle of life

I comb through her tangles each and every day rushing to the next activity. Will someday I peer back through the lens of time yearning for those conversations, when she steps out of her bath, smelling so delicious and waiting for me to comb through her hair? One day she won't need me to braid her pigtails any longer. Oh, the parting a mother must endure to release that which once belonged solely to her. Seeing life through the lens of my mother has caused me to pause and savor each moment with my own three beautiful blessings. Time passes so quickly. Perhaps I should sit and let my mother comb my hair once again. She has spent her whole life devoted to making me happy. Have I given enough of my heart to her? While I was off chasing after life, how badly she must have missed holding my hand and curling my hair.

I share this particular Misti Moment for one reason. Listen to your parents. As written in Job 12, "Is not wisdom found among the aged? Does not long-life bring understanding?" Seek for the wisdom in their words and really allow their love for you to deeply root itself in your heart. Take time to get to know them as your friend. When you're with your family, be there, really be there. Look them in the eyes. Listen to their soul. Never be so rushed to get to the next moment that you fail to appreciate the beauty in the one you are experiencing. As the famous quote says, "Now and then it's good to pause in our pursuit of happiness and just be happy." Listen to your parents. But also love them. Really love them. Love them well.

I would encourage you to talk to your parents. Ask them questions about what they've learned in life and savor their words to you. If your parents are no longer with you, don't stop listening to them. Don't stop talking to them. Some of your greatest moments with your parents will be long after they're gone. Those of you who've lost a love one will understand what that means. And for those who had parents that lost their way, were unkind to you, or possibly abandoned you, there is a Heavenly Parent that lives within you. That Parent is always speaking, always guiding, always comforting, always near, and always, and I mean always, loving you. Also, don't forget the sweet and nurturing voice of Mother Nature who speaks in her own way. She's always whispering the most beautiful calming words that teach the mysteries we all long to perceive.

> *"But ask the animals, and they will teach you, the birds in the sky,*
> *and they will tell you; or speak to the earth, and it will teach you,*
> *or let the fish in the sea inform you."*
> (Job 12:7-8)

I dedicate this entry to my mother who has given me the greatest gift I have ever received. She literally offered me her heart. Mom, it was oh so pretty. Thank you for sharing such beauty with me. In the book, you were asked to list your most poignant memory about your childhood to which you replied,

> *"Being Loved.*
> *That is all that is left when all else is gone.*
> *It's enough, girls.*
> *It's enough."*

So, I would say the same to you, my sweet mama. What was my most poignant memory about my childhood? Being loved. Oh, and by the way, it still remains my most wonderful memory.

In loving memory of my mother,
Diann Cruickshank
07/19/49 - 11/6/18

THE DARKENED DAYS

I CHOSE TO INCLUDE THIS SECTION TO SHOW A TINY GLIMPSE into some of my darker days when I felt utterly lonely and wanted to quit. It was my days of playing the victim and feeling powerless. There is but one reason I am giving brief attention to these days and sharing a few of these moments of misalignment. I believe when we cry out to our Maker for help, when we feel all our strength is gone, He comes and meets us. He rises from within us, and He begins to shine the Light from within our souls to illuminate our path and guide us to embracing our eternal inheritance of truth, liberation, and peace.

> *"Call to me, and I will answer you and tell you*
> *great and unsearchable things you do not know."*
> (Jeremiah 33:3)

I'm Done

*T*HE NIGHTS ARE SO LONG. THE LONELINESS TOO MUCH TO BEAR. Please, Father. Embrace me. The tears . . . I can't see through them. Hold me. I need you so much. I need the angels to lift me up. Will you touch my pain tonight? How much longer? I've waited so long. Will it ever be?

Send me more. It's not enough. There's something still broken inside of me. You're the only one who hasn't broken my heart. Please hurry and heal. What else must I do?

Ouch . . . I hate this. I really do.

I need a new heart again. How many times must this one break? Forgive me if I have failed you. Be my Rescuer tonight. Mend me. Will the tears ever go away?

I've been lonely for as long as I can remember. God, will you show me what it's like to not feel this sting? You're with me. I know this is my truth. Please. I need new memories. Take these painful ones away. Father, please get me out of here. Please.

I'm supposed to be stronger, and I've never felt weaker. How many times have we been here?

Surrendered

No fight left

You must intervene for me now. Now, God. No one but you knows how hard and painful the fight has been. When will I be touched? When will I be held? Man's empty promises I hate. All I want is to be with you forever. I'm going to need you to pull me deeper and make your love sweeter. Please help me. Tomorrow, ok?

After every breakthrough, I find another war. The enemy is still trying to take everything from me—my hope, my strength, and my confidence. You must fight him for me and meet my every need. I'm starving for your love. I'm hungry for intimacy. Why keep calling me to be brave and bold when you have made me feel so helpless and weak?

I hate my memories right now. Gut them like a fish. I'm done. I can't take it anymore. I'm done! Do you hear that? No more! Show up! Rip my heart apart if you must! Take this horrible pain out of it. I'm exhausted. I've been exhausted. I've always dreamed of smelling the roses, and all I have is wounds from the thorns. Can you send me flowers? Can you praise me before the world? Take away the dream if you don't intend for me to receive it. God, I really can't handle anymore.

Cloak of Darkness

*T*HE DARKNESS IS FULL OF WEIGHT, A THICK COATING pressing against me. Fear is lurking at my window. The death angel is visiting me once again. And though I shake and tremble, I know my help is in your name. I call to you, my Messiah. I close my eyes and see you coming towards me as bright as the sun. Your love prevails in my loneliness. I know you are all that I have, yet I know full well you are more than I could ever need. The darkness has blocked my view, so hold my hand. I won't let go. Guide me until I see the Light.

My future is in your hands. All my hope is in you. I need more of your love. I know it never ends, so pour it upon me. Fill my life with hope again. I'm weak. I'm waiting. How can I move without your strength? How can I stand without your power? Equip me. Position me to worship with a grateful heart. Give back to me a double portion of what I allowed the enemy to steal from me. Be my supply.

I want to speak of you and study you all throughout my days. Teach me all that you are. I want to become you, to become this love you are placing in my heart. It's healing me. I believe you have a miracle awaiting me. I believe every prophetic word ever spoken over me with no evidence yet seen. I simply need to know you more. I need to understand this love more.

Come quickly to me. My soul is resting in you. Breathe on me a little stronger tonight. Hover over me with your Spirit. Touch my heart with it. Your love is everything to me.

All I've ever truly had
All I'll ever need
I wanna go home
He'll be coming soon

Put me to sleep, Daddy.

Sacrifice

I AM SOAKING THESE PAGES WITH MY TEARS. Please send an angel as I walk this hill. I feel the wood on my back. I can see the place where my altar will be built. I know the sacrifice you require. I know the fire will soon be falling upon my offering, consuming it as a pleasing and acceptable sacrifice. My heart still bleeds. I can feel the tearing away of that which in your wisdom, you are removing.

Instinctively, I know you are the God of the heavens and the earth, and I know you are good. I know that which you require me to lay aside is only preparing me to receive beyond what I can presently grasp. Take this weight off of me, Father. Consume it quickly. This burden must be burned.

Make myself one with you, a beautiful picture of perfected righteousness. Burn away all impurities and drape me in gowns of white. Hold me as your Beloved.

I let go that I might rise up.

GOD

The Voice

ONE THING LIFE HAS TAUGHT ME IS WHAT YOU SEE on someone's bio or Facebook wall isn't always the whole picture. Life hasn't always been picture-perfect for me. I lost my fantasy world of the husband, 2.5 kids, a golden retriever, and a white picket fence when I was eleven years old. That was the year my parents divorced, paving the way for years of emotional turmoil and a long road of healing and recovery for the entire family. While the pain of this deep severing was ever-present, there was a beautiful silver lining in the clouds. I began to cultivate an incredibly strong and binding relationship with God. In the midst of terrible suffering, I felt an immense comfort from a growing connection to the Spirit of God. I spent quite a bit of time alone listening to that Voice. I would spend hours lying on the trampoline in my back-yard star gazing or sitting on our pier starring at the waters. I hated missing sunsets, and I always had a journal in hand.

There was an Inner Voice that began to arise within me.
It was solid, strong, comforting, compassionate and kind.

This Voice became my best friend, and nature was our love language. Although the Voice never stopped talking to me, when we sat together in the open spaces, the connection was much stronger, purer, and highly tangible. Even as a child, I could see how struggle created strength and growth. I felt like a seed emerging from the dark soil with my tears watering the soil that was cultivating my vibrant garden. I was hopeful. I was grateful.

As I grew, I was drawn to anything with the name God attached to it. Although my parents' divorce had deepened my connection to God, there was never a time when I could not remember him being with me. My Mom would tell the story of when I was three years old, and she leaned down to give me a big hug. Squeezing me tightly, I replied to her, "Be careful, Mama. You will hurt Jesus." When my mother asked me what I meant, I told her very plainly that Jesus lived inside of me, and I didn't want her to squeeze Him too hard.

I still remember being seven years old and walking the aisle at church to ask Jesus in my heart. I wanted more of God so desperately, so I followed the voice of the pastor asking if I wanted to be saved and go to heaven. However, I can still remember that Inner Voice, the one that spoke with me in the meadows. He and I both knew He had always been inside of me. As that seven-year-old little girl would say,

"We were like peas and carrots.
We had been together forever."

I felt I had already come from heaven. It was my home. I knew "Him" full well. I felt him from birth. He was more than just a "Him" to me. He was my Truth and my answer for everything. We were as they say here in the deep South, "hitched at the hip."

As life transpired and more opinions and voices entered my world, it seemed with each new experience or relationship, I moved farther away from the truth I had known as a little girl. Somehow my view shifted from God being in me to God being above me. So, what did I do? I chased him. Down the yellow brick road, I traveled. I chased him on mission trips, at conferences, on Wednesday nights, Sunday nights, in youth groups, college groups, and community ministry teams. I joined every church program. I attended every class. I even served as a missionary on the other side of the world. Perhaps I could feel Him closer there, I thought. Perhaps He would speak louder there. I worshiped harder, I cried louder, and I sang stronger. I stopped listening to the Voice within and began to listen to the many speakers, the many pastors, and the many prophets, all of which never failed to offer a word from the Lord. They seemed to have the answers now. They seemed to know the truth. I would buy their devotions. I would attend their seminars. I would follow their step-by-step instructions to the blissful, abundant, and happy life.

Yet, in all this traveling down the yellow brick road, I found myself in my mid-thirties, divorced, defeated, depressed, exhausted, confused, really broken, and with no more energy left to continue my journey. I was a mess. I had lost my way. I had lost my hope. I no longer recognized myself. Then, one dark night while lying on my bed at 2:00 a.m. with tears streaming down my face, I cried like a child asking,

"Can you hear me? I need you. I have no energy left to search for
you. If I could just feel you once again. Take me back to the
beginning. Take me back to when we first met."

With no hesitation, a flood like a mighty, rushing wind pulsated through my entire body. Every hair on my body was electrified and standing on their ends. Was I levitating? I didn't know. My body had to be glowing! The force of Light was so intense it purged me like a raging fire. My mouth opened, and a language I had never heard came forth. My Spirit spoke a new tongue. My soul cried for its healing. It knew precisely what to say. It knew exactly what to pray. What was happening to me? Had I been asleep all the years prior to this pivotal moment? I was awakened with a pulsating wave of pure energy, pure Source, pure love, and pure healing power. The Voice coming from inside of me said,

"I never left you. And you never left me. You think you left me, but
you are wrong. You've just been listening to the wrong voices.
You've been deceived. Together forever, remember? We are one."

In an instant, I felt alive again. A force without measure had filled me to the brim. Time stood still. My humanity had been completely wrapped in divinity. I no longer knew where I ended, and He began. We were joined.

I remembered who I had always been.

That night the conversations began again, and boy had I missed them! I had missed the connection. I had missed the touch. I had found my way home. The Living Truth, the Life Force of all things, my Breath, my Friend, my Answers, my Everything had been with me and in me all along. I felt like a little girl again running through the cotton fields and chasing fireflies on a warm Alabama summer night. I had not a care in the world. I felt free!

Although my life was at its deepest and darkest place, there was a bright Light of hope shining within me. Whenever I opened my mouth, this Light would burst forth. Other people could feel it too. I was affecting them. I was Him, and He was me. We were a unit. He was truth, so I was truth.

The more we danced and played together, the better friends we became. I knew what He knew, and with His Spirit guiding, my Life began to sort itself out. My finances changed, my relationships changed, and my entire life became something new. Most importantly, my heart felt brand new. It was sparkling again.

I was dancing with God every day
in a glorious Kingdom right here on earth.

The Spirit of Truth is what I most like to call Him because He showed me a truth that set me free. There was a well that sprung forth inside of me that watered the dry places of my soul. Lying dormant ready to be awakened had been a truth that brought healing, restoration, vigor, and life!

The more I interacted with my Best Friend and followed the Voice of Intuition within myself, the freer I became and the more blockages I removed from things that had been holding me back for years. I was able to see things I had never seen before. The more I trusted what was inside of me, the more I began to see the lies that had been fed to me. One by one, I began replacing every lie I had previously believed with the truth. Seeing the deception is always a disturbing part of the journey. However, the more I deprogrammed myself from subconscious beliefs that were not true, and the more I surrendered to the unraveling of my world as I knew it, the more comfort and security I gained from a sincere and lasting foundation built upon eternal, virtuous truths.

My mission became to ignite a spark of faith, love, Light, and divinity with each person I met. I wanted every single person in the world to realize there was a Voice inside of them willing and ready to provide the answers they needed for their soul's journey. I wanted to help reconnect others to the Spirit of Truth and empower them to clear away the programs and mind lies that this world had fed them. I wanted to help them return home to their inner truth and guidance system.

There is a happily ever after awaiting you. The greatest love story ever told is living inside of you. Dust the cover, clear the cobwebs, and look inward. Open the book and read it out loud! It is a masterpiece worthy of the best seller's list!

The world is waiting to discover you. Perhaps you are waiting to discover you! There is a Voice in there that is all-knowing, all-loving, all-Light that has always been with you, and will continue to be with you every step of your journey. Introduce me to your Best Friend, and I'll introduce you to mine. This is just a hunch, but I bet they have a lot in common.

I'll meet you in the meadow. I'll be the one standing in the Light.

Who is God?

YOU ARE GOING TO HEAR GOD DESCRIBED IN MANY WAYS throughout your life. You will encounter those who will speak as if they know the way home to Him. They will tell stories of Him and romanticize their understanding of who He is. You may hear great speeches and wonderful scriptures from ancient texts. In your search for God, you may look where others have claimed to find Him. You may open a Bible to read about Him and of those who experienced Him long ago. You may look for Him where another told you He would be.

Here is what I want you to know and remember. Nowhere will God be found and felt more predominately than pulsating in the rhythm of your own heart. Look in the mirror, and you will see all that is God, a perfect, beautiful, wondrous depiction of His image. He is not a he. He is not a she. He is the all. When you laugh really hard, you will feel God. When you see a child play, you will see God. He will be there placing His gentle chill upon your skin **Life has shown me never to judge an exterior for beneath the cover I always find God's Spirit resting, abiding, and sometimes hiding there.** when you feel a moment of inspiration. You will feel Him through the rhythms of a beautiful melody, and you will know He is listening to you sing along.

There will come a time when you may experience the death of someone you love, and He will be found hovering all around you, around those you hold dear, comforting as only He can. He will allow you to feel the nurturing Spirit of the one you grieve abiding mightily within you. For he or she will have returned to Him and now as God is in you, so too is your loved one within you whispering, guiding, and comforting you along your journey. In these down-trodden moments, you will feel the tight squeeze of His presence wrapped around your heart. He will be with you in your tears, and He will also be with you in your laugher. He will be with you in both your sorrow and your joy.

Life has shown me never to judge an exterior for beneath the cover I always find God's Spirit resting, abiding, and sometimes hiding there. I have seen him arising in the darkest of nights, and in the most dispersed ashes of despair. It is His wind that causes healing to arise once more. It is His current that moves the ebb and flow of the waters and directs the hands of time. He is the peace that guides you when the chaos and disorder overtake you. He is the Light that shines from deep within your soul.

When you feel love, you will feel God, and you will know He is there with you. I believe there is only one thing God has ever desired of me. It is to know that I am one with Him and that in this glorious, gifted experience called life, I would not forget this most essential truth. For all imbalances begin when we forget who we are, when we forget the power at work within us, and when we play the sad role of separation from our beloved God. We must never forget that the same power that creates worlds is abiding within us all.

Although God can be seen and found all around you, you always feel more deeply than you see. Allow yourself to feel God within you. The Great Master, Jesus, infused with the Christ of God, so sweetly shared with us the beautiful truth that the kingdom of heaven was already in our midst, a priceless treasure lying within the core of all that we are. In all the cries to experience God that you may echo in your lifetime, try never to forget that within you lies a never-ending stream of all that God is and all that God will ever be. The more in alignment you are with love in its purest form, the more you will recognize this truth, the more attuned you will be with your divine nature, and the more oneness you will experience with God.

I looked for God all my life. I cried to him and asked for many signs to confirm that He saw me. I smile now at all those deeply emotional spaces of time for if I had only been still enough, I would have realized He was whispering in my ear all along. It was just that His voice sounded exactly like mine. Never be afraid of your own voice. Learn to trust it. No one can guide you as well as the Voice of God placed within you. Listen to it well.

Be still and know that I am God.

If something appears in your life, leaving you feeling criticized, condemned, or judged know this is not of God. God is in you. You are one with Him, and He does not wish to condemn Himself. God is gentle, kind, and long-suffering with His love. This love never leaves, never dies, never surrenders, and is always there for you. The true God keeps no records of your wrongs nor is sitting idly by, ready to punish you when you fail or make mistakes. He is the love flowing through you always shining the Light upon whatever darkened path you may have found yourself upon.

This love that I speak of is as overwhelmingly magnificent as one could ever hope or imagine it to be. Embrace the Highest Version of yourself by acknowledging your body is a temple for Divinity. God has made His abode in the souls of mankind. You are His treasured earthen vessels. Salvation isn't about accepting this truth but in acknowledging it. It is true whether you realize it yet or not.

The power of God lives within you, and all that He is has been made available to you. Therefore, if God be for you, who or what can stand against you? He that is in you is greater than he that is in the world.

We often pray for what we already have. We pray to God for peace, for joy, for abundance, and for health. The highest truth is that we already have all these things. I remember years ago a moment where I was on my knees crying out for a move of God to touch my life. I wanted to feel God and to encounter more of His Spirit. During this plea, I felt the Spirit speak very clearly back to me saying,

> *"Misti, why are you pleading for what has already been given? Where is my Spirit? Where is my presence? Have you failed to see that it has been placed within you? It is up to you now whether you will acknowledge its presence and release it upon this world. You must begin to release what has been instilled. Release the peace. Release the kindness. Release the grace. Release the warmth. Release the Light. Release the love. There is a glorious Kingdom sitting in the seat of your soul. Release the treasure I have placed within you."*

The idea of separation will always lead to pain and heartbreak. I would even venture to go as far as to say it will lead to doubt, fear, despair, hopelessness, sickness, and even death. Whenever you house an idea that you are separated in any way from God's love, you block yourself from an unconditional bathing of daily nourishment that as a spiritual being you need to cover yourself with each and every moment of your journey through this crazy, wild, and adventurous experience called life.

Whenever you have thoughts of separation from others, you bring the sting of misalignment upon yourself, an underlying pain that remains whenever you take a step away from feeling unity with your fellow brothers and sisters. If you leave yourself in this condition of separation too long without allowing grace, mercy, forgiveness, and unconditional love to flow from within the storehouse of goodness God has placed within you and upon the people or circumstances of your life, you begin to get sick. You can only remain misaligned with who you are created to be and how you are designed to live for so long before your physical body begins to serve as a guidance system alerting you. Its purpose is to help bring you back into alignment with the beautiful blessing of compassion and love for one another.

Separation is a result of fear.
When you are in Christ, in alignment with Spirit,
there is no fear, only love.
Only love. Period.
Love for those who are different than you.
Love for those who think differently than you.
Love for those who believe differently than you.
Love for those who act differently than you.

It's hard to be afraid of someone when you're loving them.

There is no force that can dispel hate but that of love. There is no method by which to rid the world of evil or hate but that of love. There is no hope for change within the souls of man but that we love the wayward soul. Love conquers all.

Love is the game-changer.

Who is God? God is love. To know God is to know this love—to become this love, and to give this love to both yourself and everyone without discrimination as much as you possibly can for as long as you can. This is truth. This is freedom for . . .

Love is freedom.

It is the force by which we all take flight. So, love deep and soar high. Your ultimate emancipation depends upon how greatly you learn to love.

Let go.
Let God.
Let love.
Let freedom ring.

A Divine Love

1 HEAR THE INVITATION, MY GREAT LOVE. I'm coming into your chambers clothed in garments of white just as you prefer. My body is prepared. May I please you? I withhold nothing from you.

Can this be true? Chosen by the King? Prepared to enter His chambers by the hand of God?

I see your eyes adoring me. Place your fragrance upon me. Overwhelm me. Take delight in your creation. Let's breathe this moment in. Close me in and shut the door. You are mine, and I am yours, forevermore.

I remain here in the sweet spot of our love. You are tender. You hold me as your greatest treasure. Your eyes never leave my gaze. You are my Magnificent Obsession. Your love is intoxicating. Pull me a little closer. Take me a little deeper. You would give your life for this moment, and you did. It's so holy. It's so beautiful. Feel the expression of my heart as my words cannot describe the glory surrounding this marriage bed.

Tell me everything. I want to know you like none other. Show me your heart. I want to know what you love. I want to know whom you love that I may please you to the utmost. May You delight in my affection for you. Teach me your thoughts, and I shall think like you. Make me one with you . . . mind, body, soul, and Spirit. Be jealous with me. I want you to have me all to yourself. I am burning for you. My heart is so in love. It cries tears of deep joy.

This love

This longing

This hand upon me

It's too wonderful for my mind to conceive of it—how you have always loved, always protected, always been my bright, shining Light. You are my forever Guide. On my darkened nights, it was you that held my hand and wrapped yourself around my heart.

Hold me like a child. Touch the places I need most. I owe you my everything. I pray you drink from the love I pour at your feet. I pray you see it when I look upon you, for you have washed me with liquid love, and I will drink from your fountain for all the days of my life. Now I have tasted. Now I have seen. I'll bear your name for eternity. I'll wear your garments of white. I'll kiss you with the kisses of my mouth. Let's kiss in the rain. I'll breathe you in deeply and never look away. You were always the One. You were my Soul Mate waiting to be discovered.

I Do ~ forever and always,
Your Dew from Heaven,
Your Misti Rains

When He

When He holds you

When His grace covers like a warm blanket on a cold night

When His love drips like the rains of heaven

When He stills your soul

When He paints you a picture in the sky

When He breathes on you

When He calls you His beloved

When He does all those things that only He can do

When His love is so consuming, so beautiful, that I have to pen poetry to try and match its sweetness

When He

Embracing Divinity

HOW CAN WE TRULY DO FOR OTHERS WHAT WE CANNOT DO for ourselves? There is a passage in the Bible that says to love others as we love ourselves. There was a key ingredient in that passage I was missing most of my life. If we are to love others as we love ourselves, how could I truly love well while being inwardly critical, comparative, and judgmental of myself? How could I teach others to do or be something I was not authentically living in my heart?

I spent most of my life having not experienced the beauty of falling in love with myself. I was not one who could declare with gratitude and deep meaning that I was fearfully and wonderfully made. Having not fully learned to love me, how could I truly know how to love others?

Is the soul of mankind not where God resides nestled within a glorious temple designed to shine forth His Light? Can we not love the Divinity and Universal Wisdom that has crafted us into being and is guiding from within our hearts? Must we separate ourselves from this Divine Beauty lying within us all? Perhaps this was why it was so important that Jesus prayed that we may be one as he and his Father were one. I needed to tear down the veil of separation that categorized me as some lesser version of God. It kept me weak and playing the role of victim most of my life.

I suppose this is why Jesus has saved me in more ways than I could ever articulate but perhaps differently than most conventional doctrine has taught. He became my Savior by teaching me how to save myself. Jesus, a man, flesh, and blood like me, awakened to his Sonship, His inheritance, and His divinity. What I love most about him was that against all odds and accusations of heresy and blasphemy, He taught others that they could do the same. He wished us all to know that as He was in this world, so are we. He wanted us to know this truth to such a degree that we could even do greater things than Him if we believed and accepted this truth. He wanted us to remove this dividing wall that separates us from our oneness with God and embrace our Sonship as a child of God, a beautiful extension of all that He is.

For lack of better verbiage, I use the pronoun Him in this book. Yet, how does one define the Breath of Life with such limiting views? He is more than just a He to me. He is the truth living within us, the Great Spirit of old, the love we all need, the home we are all searching for. He is the Father in His discipline and provision as well as the sweet Spirit of a loving and nurturing mother tenderly guiding her young. He is the Son, the Christ that is me, an extension of all that He is. When I burn with love for Him, I burn with love for me for I have acknowledged our oneness and walk in freedom forevermore.

Although I could list dozens of passages that pinpoint Christ and the Spirit of God being in us having made his abode in us, people still speak of themselves as separate from Christ. Perhaps this is why so many walk powerless, confused, and disconnected from the truth. Blindness is caused by not understanding or recognizing the Divinity nestled within us. When we don't see the power available to us, we respond to life as victims trapped beneath a pile of circumstances out of our control. This breeds insecurity, doubt, fear, anger, resentment, bitterness, jealousy, and a plethora of other emotions that lead us to make choices that ultimately hurt us and take us off course from our destined path.

When despair comes from these off-course moments, it can often serve as a catalyst and ultimate incubator for greatness. It causes heat and pressure and maturity via tremendous soul growth. Growth never comes without some level of discomfort. However, it is through this process we begin to see wings emerging from our once-crawling-upon-the-ground caterpillar state. We see things within ourselves and find strength, courage, tenacity, and a passionate fire that had we previously known was there, we would have never taken some of the paths we found ourselves upon. With this knowing, we can offer ourselves forgiveness for not knowing then what we know now. In this state of being, strength emerges, and courage arises to forgive ourselves and to forgive others wherever they are in their process of growth.

A significant piece of embracing my divinity and achieving genuine love for myself was arriving at a place of forgiving myself. I wouldn't be able to write these words had I not conquered such a daring feat. One day I was meditating on these truths when some of Jesus' final words came to mind, "Father, forgive them for they know not what they do." I had previously only exercised this principle in regard to others but had never applied it to myself. Could the Christ within me offer myself the same words? Could I forgive myself for the times in my life when I was blinded and couldn't see what I now have eyes to see?

Now we know better. Now we live better. We embrace our Divinity. We understand the strength and power within. We no longer fear. We no longer settle. We no longer eat crumbs from the floor of life's leftovers. We see ourselves as royalty. We love ourselves as royalty. Thus, we no longer allow for insecurities to evoke choices that demote our value. We also recognize the Divinity in others, no matter how much or little their actions indicate their awareness of it.

Thus, we have a yielding sword, no longer a need to fight, to argue our point, to convince another, to stew with bitterness or resentfulness for their words or actions towards us. We now know we can affect change outwardly by acknowledging, utilizing, and releasing the richness of that great power from within us. We gain strength to overcome by how much we have forgiven and by how great our capacity is to love both ourselves and others. This is when we are our most Divine, our most effective, our most like God.

Mom,
Are You Going to Die?

"*M*OM, ARE YOU GOING TO DIE?" I heard these words echoed from my older son Riley as he followed behind me, and we walked into the house. I wasn't expecting to hear a statement so grounding and gripping after a day at the lake laughing and playing together. After my brain aneurysm, the sacredness of life had become a moment by moment realization for us all.

Without a moment's hesitation I replied to my son without turning around or stopping what I was doing, "I don't want you to be concerned about that, Sweetie."

Riley quickly responded, "Well, I am."

I paused and then said to my twelve-year-old son, "There's a song the Holy Spirit is continuously singing over me. It says,

> 'The Lord has promised good to me.
> His Word my hope secures.
> He will my shield and portion be
> as long as life endures.'

"Riley, waves come and go, flowers wither and fade, but I carry the living Word written upon my heart, flowing through my soul, and released throughout my heart. That Word can never die nor can I. This Word became much more than pieces of paper for me when the Spirit of God filled me with a truth that set me free. I want you to always treasure truth when you see, hear, or read it, but your greatest joy will come when you find it within your own heart. The Word is living, breathing, and speaking to you continuously from within your heart and from within all of creation. The Bible tells us that all the animals, the plants, and the many wonders of this world are given to teach of it.

"All answers, all comfort, all healing, and everything you need is in the Word of God. I'm talking about more than a Bible or a religious book, Riley. I'm speaking of a Force that is alive and breathing and speaking right this minute. The Word is my everything. In the beginning was the Word and the Word WAS GOD and the Word became flesh and lived among us. Now that the beautiful Spirit of that Word lives IN US, our flesh is housing this magnificent Force. We are storing the Divine. We are holding heaven in our hearts. We are divinity wrapped within humanity—God with Us—God IN US.

"You are the storehouse for all that ever was and all that ever will be. With this knowing, nothing is impossible for you, absolutely nothing. Seek the kingdom of heaven. Search for this Word with all your heart. You must look within yourself to find it. It's not out there, Riley. It's in here. As I took my hand and placed it upon my son's heart, his eyes began to widen.

"You will hear it speaking through the gentle whisper. I have never found this Word, this amazing God that has always been, limited to any book, any religion, any dogma, or any governmental or personal agenda. This Word is too expansive, too glorious, too massive, and too far reaching with its unbiased mercy and loving compassion to be limited to one 'special' or 'chosen' group. Riley, this Word, this God, is in *all things*. When you come to a place in your life when you can see God in everything and everyone, you will begin to praise, you will begin to burst with gratitude, and this Word will inhabit you. If you are still separating this Word in only one book, or one people, or resting it upon one land, you may see glimpses of truth, but you will never fully be consumed by it, and you will never feel completely free.

"I have seen this Word, this God, and this Living Truth, spoken through a Buddhist Monk, a Hindu girl, a Baptist preacher, and a Japanese girl as she serves her family dinner with loving kindness and respect. I have seen it in the seashells, the clouds resting upon the mountaintops, and in the fog hovering amidst the meadows I love so dearly. I've seen it in the tears of an adulterous woman repenting without words from the cry of her heart. I've seen it in the hardened man who forgives after years of holding onto a rotting bitterness towards another. I've seen it on the cross of Calvary as the Christ of God gave His life for his friends that they may know the truth and path to salvation that spurred His passion so intently. I've seen it in the New Age community as they focus their hearts to speak life, feel gratitude, and show respect and appreciation for every facet of nature. I've seen it in the heart of an atheist who seeks so desperately to stand on what he believes are principles of truth. I've seen it in the prideful, religious man who lives in fear and self-righteous fervor yet believes wholeheartedly his pointing out the failures and mistakes of others is pleasing to God. I've seen the Light and the Word in the darkest of places and in the darkest of hearts. There is a Light so true and so brilliant that even the darkest heart cannot blacken its shine.

For there is 'One God and Father of all, who is above all, and
through all, and in you all.'
(Ephesians 4:6)

"Seeing glimpses of God in all things and all people will give you a peace you will not find believing that He only exists in a limited few. Living as if you carry the presence of God, and others do not, will keep you separated from a truth that God may have wanted you to find in places you may have otherwise never looked. Always be listening for the Word from within you and from within others. Separating yourself from people who are different from you separates you from discovering hidden truth and has caused this world much grief, division, sorrow, and death.

"So, to answer your question, 'Mom, are you going to die?' Sweetie, we are all going to die, on this physical plane, but we can live forever. You see, in a sense, I have already died. As strange as this might sound, I had been living, but I was dead. It has been appointed once for man to die; thus, how can I fear what has already been? What does this mean, you might ask? I was dead, but now I am alive in Christ. The Word is within me. As Deepak Chopra once said,

'Religion is for people who are afraid of going to hell.
Spirituality is for those who have already been there.'

"The Word of God endureth forever, Riley. Fill your heart with God, Son. It's more than a book. It's a whole kingdom. Live in paradise with me. It begins now. It exists for always. You're in my soul tribe, sweet boy. I've known you forever and I'll know you for always. Let's never die together.

"I know you may have expected a different answer, but these words are much more important for your journey. If you will absorb what I'm saying, they will become a part of you and hold us together for always."

Dedicated to my older son, Riley:

'The earth shall soon dissolve like snow
The sun forbear to shine
But God who called me here below
Will be forever mine.'

And Riley, you are forever mine.
Unending love. Amazing grace.

Words from the Father

YOU ARE DEAR TO MY HEART, AND I LOOK AFTER YOU like a good Shepherd. My glory follows you like a cloud. It rests upon your face. I long for your closeness and will give you the answers you seek. My Spirit is teaching you all the things you wish to know.

Stop your worry, impatience, and doubt. I hush your worry. I silence all fear. I bring calmness to your soul. These are gifts I have given you. You must receive them by faith. Your faith is your lens to see. Trust me.

I am still mending you to be my vessel. I am repairing every shattered piece to make it whole. I am the Potter, and you are my masterpiece, a glorious creation sculpted in my hands and formed by the love that I hold in my heart for you. You are a vessel lined with gold and draped in pearls. The outside is beautiful but from within holds the rich flavors of life. I have poured my virtues there. Flow beautifully, Darling. Quench the lips of all who are thirsty for the sweetness of the rich treasure I have placed within the container of your heart. Love my people. This is what I ask of you. There is no strife in love. Be my vessel to display my marvelous Light, to demonstrate My awesome power, to open the eyes of the blind, to stand bold against the whispering lies of the evil one, and to release the hearts of this world from their captivity.

Radiate! Illuminate! Shine your Light across the land—sparkle bright, Little Love. You are mighty for the pulling down of strongholds.

That They May Be One

THE HOLY SPIRIT ANOINTED JESUS CHRIST WITH SUCH A WONDERFUL GIFT for bridging the spiritual and physical realms so that even a small child could comprehend it. He called God His Father. Who could not relate to the term "Father" and the role through which this natural realm understands the facets of such a role? Jesus understood He was one with such a Force. He was the Son, pulsating with the same blood, the same hardwiring, the same mindset, the same "genetic code," and possessing the inheritance of the Father. It is a note-worthy feat when one realizes what Jesus discovered. He did his very best to convey this truth yet most, even those who covet the words of Christ, have yet to understand it. They continue to separate themselves from God and fail to see themselves as One with Him. They do not see themselves as a Son or Daughter of God, God in them, and them in God, one flesh, one Spirit, and one Union.

I hear people say their body is a temple of God yet speak of God as some outside force. Why would God wish to punish himself? Not heal himself? Not guide himself? Not will the best for Himself? Is He not in you? Are you not one with God? And yet, people still seem to question if it is God's will they live or heal from their infirmities. This concept must not be overlooked in the journey of one's existence. It is core to the truth and meaning of life. It was core to the message of Jesus Christ. It is core to any message I will ever speak. God does not want you to be sick. God is the life force within us all that aids our restoration and helps us grow, that helps us live, and that

You have a lower nature, and you have your Higher Self. The Higher Self is the God part of you, the one guiding you, speaking to you, and directing your steps.

helps us thrive. To love myself is to love God. To love God is to love myself. Once you realize you are God and God is you, and you are one, a shift takes place in how you view the difficult circumstances in your life. It changes how you view the concept of death.

Throughout all of nature is demonstrated the will to survive and live. Even a spider will run frantically to spare its own life when it feels a threat to its existence. However, once you realize you will never die, then when difficult circumstances come or things that in the world's eye view seem to threaten your existence, you stop running like the spider. You stop worrying or frantically panicking. You are no longer anxious. You stand firm. You realize as did the Christ that in this world you will have trouble, but you can cheer up, the world has already been overcome. And once you acknowledge you have overcome the world and will never die and once you understand that God is in you and God does not wish to harm himself, you realize that all things are working for your good. You realize that God has a plan for you, one to give you a hope and a future, and one to prosper you. You realize that you and God are one and that if God has allowed himself suffering or pain, it is only for the benefit of the soul. You mount up with the wings of an eagle and see your circumstances from a higher plane and through the lens of a more elevated Truth.

When Paul says, "I live now not I, but Christ in me," he didn't say Jesus, the historical character, in me. He said, "Christ in me." When Jesus' Jewish opponents picked up rocks to stone him, He said to them, "I have shown you many good works from the Father. For which of these do you stone me?" They replied to him, "We are not stoning you for any good work, but for blasphemy, because you, a mere man, claim to be God." To which Jesus answered them, "Is it not written in your Law, 'I have said you are "gods"? John 10:31-34

> *"I said, 'You are "gods";*
> *you are all sons of the Most High.'*
> *But you will die like mere mortals;*
> *you will fall like every other ruler."*
> (Psalm 82:6-7)

Is the historical character of Jesus Christ the only incarnation in history that has brought forth the second person of the blessed trinity? Should we not also assume such a role?

John 10:35-39 reveals a profound text when it reads,

> *"If he called them 'gods,' to whom the word of God came—and*
> *Scripture cannot be set aside—what about the one whom the*
> *Father set apart as his very own and sent into the world? Why*
> *then do you accuse me of blasphemy because I said, 'I am God's*
> *Son'? Do you not believe me unless I do the works of my Father.*
> *But if I do them, even though you do not believe me, believe the*
> *works, that you may know and understand that the Father is in*
> *me, and I in the Father.' Again they tried to seize him, but he*
> *escaped their grasp."*

My prayer is similar to that of the prayer of Jesus. My prayer is that you may know, as did Jesus, that you have been set apart as God's own son or daughter and that you have been sent into the world. My prayer is that the world may know you by your precious works. My prayer is through your life, and through your works, others would know and understand that God is in you and that you are in God. Though there will be those who try and "seize you," my prayer is that you would both mentally and physically escape their grasp. Jesus Himself emphasized,

*"My prayer is not for them alone. I pray also for those who will believe in me through their message, **that all of them may be one,** Father, just as you are in me and I am in you. May they also be in us so that the world may believe that you have sent me. **I have given the glory you gave me, that they may be one as we are one—I in them and you in me—so that they may be brought to complete unity.** Then the world will know that you sent me and have loved them even as you have loved me. Father, I want those you have given me to be with me where I am, and to see my glory, the glory you have given me because you loved me before the creation of the world. Righteous Father, though the world does not know you, I know you, and they know that you have sent me. I have made you known to them, and will continue to make you known in order that the love you have for me may be in them **and that I myself may be in them."***
(John 17:20-26)

The man Jesus Christ was consumed by the awakened fact of who He truly was. He was consumed by the Spirit of Christ that had existed before the foundation of the world. He was a mere man of flesh and bone just like us, and yet He was one with His Father. He was one with God. Jesus would often switch back and forth while speaking, at times referring to himself as the Son of Man, and at times referring to himself as the Son of God. He was a Son of Man, and He was also a Son of God. He demonstrated by the compassionate life He lived serving, healing, and forgiving others, that He was both. Is not this the mark of one who has been set apart and sent into the world by the true Father, the God of love? There is no greater love than this that He was willing to lay down his life for his friends.

Jesus was murdered, yet was willing to suffer immensely, ultimately giving His life so that He could share the discovery of what His Father had revealed to Him. He healed on the Sabbath, refused to stone adulterous women to death, and mingled with those that weren't of His faith. He wanted the world to know the path to salvation, the way to discovering this inner kingdom of heaven to be lived on this earth from within the hearts of man. He wanted what was above to be so below, the will of heaven to be found upon this earth.

The teachings of Jesus Christ are the way to salvation. The Christ of God is the door through which all other truth is expanded. If you go in search of the kingdom of heaven, the Spirit will lead you to the same truths revealed to the Christ. What is difficult for many people to understand is that with or without the Bible, the Spirit reveals these mysteries and truths to any and all who seek for them. A child without an understanding of the Bible can enter the kingdom of heaven. There are those who are men of the book, and there are those who are men of experience. If those who follow the letter of the law fail to respect those who are led by the Spirit, they will miss understanding and wisdom that is solely revealed by the Father.

Jesus replied, "Blessed are you, Simon son of Jonah,
for this was not revealed to you by flesh and blood,
but by my Father in heaven."
(Matthew 16:17)

Often people refer to God as their Higher Self. This expression is snubbed upon by the Christian community, yet without the eye of an eagle and an ability to see beyond the programming and conditioning of religious systems, I can understand why. Jesus was one with God. He was both man and God. There was His lower nature and his Higher Self, the Son of Man and the Son of God. If you are one with God, you too are exactly like Jesus. You have a lower nature, and you have your Higher Self. The Higher Self is the God part of you, the one guiding you, speaking to you, and directing your steps. Jesus depicted Him in human terms as the Heavenly Parent called the Father or the protecting and nurturing Shepherd. This "Higher Self" has the word "Self" in it, because it is a part of you. God is a part of you.

I find it interesting that the first time around, people were expecting the Christ to come in a cloud or with a majestic kingly entrance heralding a message of deliverance that would set them free from their current oppressive circumstances. That is what the current religious doctrine of the day promoted as the idea of the Christ. However, the message of the Christ was to enter as a child, live as a mere man, discover the kingdom of heaven within, and teach everyone the way to salvation and this glorious path of freedom. However, people failed to receive the idea that God was revealing Himself through flesh and bones. People failed to see deity through the human condition. Could we be missing the point again? Do we ever learn from our mistakes? Did we truly listen to the cry from the heart of the Christ? People are so focused on looking for Jesus to return upon the clouds, deliver them from their current circumstances, and blissfully carry them away to paradise that they have failed to create paradise amidst the lives they are currently living. They have failed to find the spiritual kingdom existing here and now. They have failed to create heaven on earth in their everyday circumstances, and they have failed to release it upon others.

Have we also been so busy looking for the signs in the heavens that we have failed to miss the signs within one another? Jesus was passionate about people realizing they were one with Him and with God. He wanted us to recognize a treasure that is placed in us, the earthen vessels, a place where many are not searching. Perhaps Christ is already here, within some of us? Perhaps Christ has been returning for hundreds of years. While people are busy seeking a sign or a wonder and a final act of ultimate deliverance from oppression, could we be missing the Spirit of Christ, which has returned through God's most favored and treasured possessions, His people, His creation? Could we be missing the freedom to be grasped as the will of heaven infiltrates the hearts of those upon this earth? A spirit descended upon Jesus, allowing Him to herald a greater truth than what His culture knew or understood. He was murdered for failing to adhere to their laws, to their rules, and to their religious order. Could we be overlooking a message from one who is from above, filled with the Spirit of Christ, and standing in our midst? Could we be seeking to go to heaven when all along heaven is destined to come here, to find its way into our hearts? I pray that we focus less on going to heaven but more on bringing heaven here. I pray we place our attention upon releasing it from the storehouse of our hearts. Hasn't it always been about God's will in the heavens being brought to the earth below?

> *Once, on being asked by the Pharisees when the kingdom of God would come, Jesus replied, "The coming of the kingdom of God is not something that can be observed, nor will people say, 'Here it is,' or 'There it is,' because the kingdom of God is in your midst."*
> (Luke 17:20-21)

In all that I've written today, the theme I feel the Spirit is hovering upon my heart is simple, yet most will miss it. I missed it most of my life and as a result, was still subject to fear and riddled with uncertainties. Until one day, I was sitting outside on my patio, meditating on one passage that was continually being brought to my attention. The passage was from Psalm 46:10, and it says, "Be still and know that I am God." As I began to repeat it in my thoughts over and over, the Spirit began leading me to place the emphasis on the "I". Be still and know that I am God. A burst of surging energy and Spirit power pulsated through my body and through every fiber of my being. I knew I had just

spoken truth. My lower nature resisted and questioned. The religious programming began to hurl insults at me as did the Pharisees to Jesus, "Who do you
think you are? You're not God! That's blasphemous. You are just a mere human.
You should be crucified and burned! Stone her!" And yet, I didn't care. I knew
it was true. I knew we were one. I was Him. He was me. And I began to pulsate
with a desire for everyone to know the truth that would set them free. Christ
has returned. I am no longer seeking Him nor awaiting His presence on a
cloud. I found him. I feel him. I see him every day. We are the best of friends.
We are the greatest of lovers. We are as the Christ prayed we would be, existing
in complete harmony.

Perhaps those still looking to meet Christ in the air still feel an emptiness
or lack of completion because they are still awaiting a union that is available
to them now. To these, I would say, the kingdom of God is in your midst.

When trials or situations arrive that threaten my existence, I no longer run
like the spider seeking to spare his life. I have already found life. God is in me,
and God lives forever. If I am faced with a tumor in my brainstem as is my current situation, I speak to the Highest Version of myself, and I ask, "God, what
do you want to experience through me? What do we want to learn from this?
How is my soul seeking to expand and grow?" I never doubt that God wills
something good for us. I don't see Him outside of myself wishing to punish
me, nor do I plead or beg for Him to hear my cry. I don't see myself subject to
His beckon mercy. Why would I do that? We are in love. We are married. We
are one flesh, one unit, and one being. I am Divine. I am the Daughter of God,
begotten of Him. If Christ be in me, how could I not speak as Him, and how
could I not think with His mind? We are of the same Spirit, the same mind, and
the same truth. With this knowledge, everything is counted as joy. Even death
loses its sting. What is death but a continuation of a journey?

When you truly know that you have merged with God, you lose the concept
of fear. Would God fear sickness? Would God fear a difficult circumstance?
Would it steal His joy, or would He count it all joy? Accept where you are and
express gratitude in all things. If God be for you, if God be *in you*, who or what
could ever truly be against you?

I have given them the glory you gave me,
that they may be as one as we are one,
I in them and you in me
so that they may be brought to complete unity.
(John 17: 22-23)

What If?

What if I told you I would not leave you nor forsake you?

Because I did

What if I told you I would listen and guide?

Because I did

What if I told you I forgive and cleanse?

Because I do

What if I told you my love never ends?

Because it doesn't

What if you knew my heart towards you?

Because I want to share it

What if you could see Me?

Because My glory is revealed in you

What if you could feel Me?

Because My touch is tangible and gives power, strength, comfort, and love

What if you didn't have to worry over your future?

Because you don't

What if you knew I had made all your provision?

Because My name is Provider. I am your All Supplier.

Because I AM

Because I HAVE

What if I told you I hear you and you're not alone, and that I go before you making your crooked paths straight?

What if I told you that I deliver you from evil?

What if I told you that I make a way where there is no way?

Because I do!

Are you listening to Me?

I do!

I am!

I am everything you need!

My promises are true.

I cannot lie, and I am faithful to you.

What if I could hold your hand and be your closet friend?

Because I want to

What if I could call you my son or daughter and care for you as the apple of my eye?

Because I do

Please call me your Abba Father.

You are my beautiful and perfect creation.

What if I could be your lover and romance your heart?

Because my love is intoxicating. Nothing can compare to it, and it carries the power to conquer all!

Nothing can separate you from My great love!

What if I told you I'm preparing a beautiful home for you in a land everlasting?

Because the plan laid out for you is beyond what you can think or imagine.

What if you believed all My promises to you?

And what if by faith you could obtain them all?

Because you can

Ask for Me and let Me come to you.

I sit in the seat of your soul, and I rest in the depths of your heart.

I am you, and you are me.

We are One.

Together Forever.

Release Me.

A Holy Kiss

*I'*M GOING TO LOVE YOU WHEN YOU FAIL ME. I will be there when you let the darkness in. I love you, fair child. I am not angry with you. As a Father, my love remains. I want your heart, your mind, and your soul. Merge them with mine. Press into me. All I ask is for your best. My ways and thoughts are higher. I ask you to trust me and surrender to my will and good plans for you. When you pass through the waters, I will be with you. They will not overtake you.

Where are we going?

To a place free from the bondage you face. Listen to me, and I will move you swiftly. Lay aside the distractions of ungodliness. You will find no satisfaction in them. I know what satiates the hearts of man. I know what will satisfy you. You must align to my purpose. You are not meant to seek temporal fulfillment that cannot sustain. I will go before you and remove these distractions because your heart remains to please me. I am your helper. My angels work to accomplish my purpose. They heed my instructions to guide and fight against your adversaries. They will remove and silence the lies you have allowed to penetrate your mind.

I want you to look within, go to my house, and offer your thanksgiving there. Your continuous state of gratitude is allowing me to provide you with more things to be grateful for. You are sowing good seeds. You will reap a good harvest.

A teacher of my ways is your name. Listen to my guidance. You will speak of my truth, holiness surrounding you to cast away the shadows. A heart full of love makes it pure and bright. Prepare to enter the house of one who has lost power, reconnecting them to the Light. I am making bread and water of endless supply to fill the hungry and quench the thirst of the oppressed. You are to break it, give it to them, pour it, and give them drink.

Who can compare to my affection for you? Who can rescue like me? I am your God! I am the voice within guiding you to triumph and victory. Behold the pureness and power of my great love! I have been and will always be merciful and longsuffering with you. I delight in watching your soul grow. I have redeemed your life from the pit of despair. You are an extension of me, and I am the highest version of all that we are. You are becoming more and more like me every day, the utmost version of all I designed you to be. The seed is becoming the mighty oak. I am so proud of you. I called you forth from your dark place, and I embraced you with my Light. I will shine as the Light of an angel across your face, so others will know I am with you, and I am their God. I wish to illuminate and cause all to shine with the countenance of one who has obtained authentic freedom.

Do not be impatient with me. My timing is perfection, and there are rewards and blessings for those who wait on me to make good on my promises.

Ask for it.
Believe for it.
Become it.
Feel it.
Receive it.

I love you. Now come here to me. Feel the holy kiss I place upon your cheek. My darling girl, my mind never tires of you, nor do I forget your requests before me. I see you. I see all of you. From your beginning, before I breathed life into your frame, I knew your soul. I knew you as a child. I know you now. I will know you in the days to follow, and I will know you from my Holy Hill. Trust that my plans for you are good. Receive the gift of love I offer you. I give it freely.

When Dust Becomes Divine

1 WOKE THIS MORNING THINKING ABOUT THE STORY of the blind man in the Bible. In the story, Christ reaches into the earth and with his spit made mud to cover the blind man's eyes. Then having washed with water, the blind man could see! I began to imagine what it could have looked like when God made man at the beginning. Envisioning the great Potter molding and shaping the most magnificent masterpiece of all time left me in a state of awestruck wonder. I imagined our Creator shaping us with the dirt of the earth and the saliva of his own mouth. How intimate! It was the first kiss, an eternal kiss! It was a forever life-giving exchange! With loving tenderness His hands crafted away, making mud from the dirt, creating beauty from ashes, making something from nothing, sculpting treasure to call his own.

My mind drifts back to the story of the blind man. As I imagine the Christ reaching for the dirt, I cannot help but envision Him beginning to sculpt all over again! Oh my! The Word sent among us, the God from the beginning of ages. He was sculpting again! He was creating again! He was making new eyes to see!

After Christ places the mud upon the eyes of the blind man, he sends the blind man to wash his eyes in the water. This is too good! He sends the blind man to cleanse His sight through the life-giving waters. Christ wanted to give the man so much more than natural sight. He wanted to give him spiritual eyes that had been cleansed by the Spirit and washed in the waters! Those that carry Christ within them will desire to do the same.

My mind drifts to the woman caught in adultery being stoned. The Christ of God reaches down and begins to draw in the mud. Many think Christ was writing the sins of those who wished to stone her in the dirt. But this morning, I see something so much more! I do not believe the mind of Christ was thinking of their sins. Christ didn't come into this world to condemn us but to free us! Those who are alive in Christ carrying his mind and heart will also provide a sense of liberation for all those standing in their light.

While Christ was running his fingers in the dirt, I didn't see a sentencing of sins. I saw the hand of God remembering his covenant with man, remembering His love. There is an anonymous quote that says, "If ever you feel like quitting, remember why you started." Was God in His frustration with the Pharisees and the mess of man's intent and ignorance, remembering the moment He fell in love with us, His earthen treasure, His magnificent creation?! Was the Christ of God reflecting on that blessed day as He moved His fingers through the clay?

I feel a warmth coming upon me as I hear the words God spoke at the beginning of our creation, "It is very good." I can see the atmosphere of the scene, changing as the Word of God begins to kneel down closer to the dirt. Mercy begins to be released from the soil and from the air. All of creation begins to remember and respond. Grown, angry men begin dropping their stones. Something too tender, too heart-piercing begins to happen when the Creator of every living soul begins to move his fingers in the dust of this earth! Oh, how He remembers us! How He shapes us! How He loves us! How He's forgiven and redeemed us! How He knows us! He knows every fiber, every unlocking code to the depths of our closed and so often tightened and hardened hearts. He has us etched on the palms of his hands and has our destiny written in the stars above us.

We are the dirt! It is from whence we came. This earth is our mother, and she nurtures us daily. When the God of all living things places His hand in the dust, into us, blind men begin to see, and hardened men begin to cast away stones! Masterpieces are formed! Mighty vessels are made! Then comes the cleansing by water and the purification by fire. Then the usefulness of a vessel emptied and ready for the Word of God to come and pour Himself and His life-giving power into the place where there was once nothing.

Oh, but when His breath comes!
When He intimately touches and reaches
into the fabric of our soul!
When He places the divine kiss upon our lips!
When the Word is deposited!
When His love comes!
When His mercy begins to flow within us!
When His Light floods our house!
When the Clay becomes a vessel that leaks the goodness of all that
God, the Creator, has placed within it!!
When we become God, and God becomes us!
When we become one with the Maker of our soul!

When DUST becomes DIVINE!

Selah

Always Being Your Love

YOU NEED NOT WORRY, MY DEAR CHILD. Believe and place your trust in me. My eyes are upon you working all things together for your good. I have places secured for you that you do not know, ones you cannot conceive. Delight yourself in me for I long to meet the desires of your heart.

Like fresh rain, I am pouring out my blessings over your life and upon your children. With my mouth, I speak your destiny into existence. I command and shift the elements surrounding you to align with my perfect will. On the day you were born, the stars were perfectly aligned to herald your entrance. I am the Great Shepherd who rescued your life from the pit. You looked within, and you found me. You listened to my whisperings. My voice guided you away from the cliff-hanging moments of your life, and now I have set your feet firmly on the Rock. I have given you the promises of great joy, which are yours for this day.

Receive my truth, Dear One. Do not doubt my sovereign will for your life. Did I not carve you into existence with my bare hands? Did I not breathe life into your soul before the foundations of this world? Open your eyes to see my great purpose!

I have positioned you to make my name great upon the nations.
My name is Love.
I am love.
Share me with the world.

You will complete my design as I blow the winds of the Holy Spirit. He will come upon you and fill you to speak my thoughts and portray my heart among men. I am finishing the good work that I began in you. With boldness, you will speak my heart.

Resist the ways of your past when you disobeyed my voice. Do not look back. You were not created to dwell in that desolate land. I am placing you in a land of plenty where you will flourish in obedience to my ways, in complete alignment with your highest and best good. You have the strength of a king to speak my commands. A key to my kingdom I have given you to release captives and usher freedom for those enslaved. You will cast away evil dwelling in the hearts of man with the love I have placed within you.

When you walk from place to place, feel the weight of the crown I have placed upon your head as a reminder of the authority and the inheritance I have given you. The enemy is beneath you. You bound, defeated, and silenced his whisperings in your mind. It is time now to be my word to the lost sheep. Feed them and lend to them with great love and compassion.

I have a trail paved before you. And although you will only feel the effortless task of placing one step in front of the other, you will be climbing a steep hill that leads to the highest mountaintop. You were created to soar in the high places with me, a light shining like a city on a hill that cannot be hidden, a display of my glory. Illuminate the darkness around you. Shine brightly for me.

Be full of my peace this day. Tune your ear to my voice. I am always speaking to you. I will never stop. I love you. I long for you. I am pleased with you. I am fighting for you. I provide for you. I protect you. I guide you. I position you. I hold you. I touch you. I marvel as I gaze upon you. You are beautiful to me. You are a reflection of my perfect creation. You lack nothing!

I have given you everything you need to please me. You are my Sweetheart, the apple of my eye. Dine with me ... taste, drink, consume the fullness of the pleasures I lay before you. In righteousness shall we dwell together, the beauty of my splendor on display.

Your name is constantly before me, on my hand, in my heart, on the tip of my tongue, at the forefront of my mind, and written in my sacred book. I dwell within your heart. I am consuming all your thoughts. I am the great love of your life. I have written you the greatest love story ever told, and you are my leading lady. Come away with me. I am your Prince who came from afar to rescue you. All the riches of heaven could not keep me from you! In fact, my Love, I want to share all I have with you. I have brought the abundance of my throne with me and all my inheritance. Can you feel me showering you with my very best?

I want to say again how beautiful you are. Watch and see what I do for you today. The sunset is yours, painted with colors that remind me of you. The flowers remind me of the sweetness of our love. Don't forget when you see the yellow ones to shine brightly to reflect my magnificent love for you. Let's keep talking all day long. You never have to miss me. I am here with you. I am within you.

Always being your love,
God

No Matter What It Is

No matter what it is, God is with you.

A Shepherd to guide you

A Peace to quieten you

A Wind to refresh you

A Light to illuminate you

A River to cleanse you

A Cloud to cover you

A Shield to protect you

A Rod to correct you

A Hand to touch you

A Grace to forgive you

A Living One to Resurrect you

An Ascended One to lift you

An Assurance for your concerns

A Help for your cry

A Presence for your loneliness

An Answer to your problem

An Order for your chaos

A Provision for your need

He is the wheel inside the wheel

He is All Complete

All Sufficient

He is an All Supply

He is God

He is with You

He is in the midst of You

Call upon Him

He is Everything

He is Mighty to Save

No matter what it is.

The Thawing

$\mathcal{M}$Y PEOPLE ARE LIKE FISH IN A FREEZER. They've grown cold to the sound of my voice.

Iced over

Lifeless

Waiting to be devoured

With the words I will give you, you will prophesy to their cold hearts. My breath will fill your mouth, and you will thaw them with the heat. Blow the warmth of my Holy Spirit onto their dry bones. "Receive ye the Holy Ghost," you will say. "Now awaken from your slumber! I call you forth from your dead place!"

See their bodies dance and tremble like a fish out of water. For it's the water that gives them life. They've been swimming in a river that led to death, a sea of emptiness and drought. You will give them water of a different kind. Open your mouth and cover them with your dew! You will see their souls begin to bring warmth to their inner frame. They will swim in a new river that gives life and never runs dry.

Now go! Release your net and get ready for a haul. I say, "Prepare the nets." I send you fish too many to count!

Prophesy! Prophesy! Prophesy, my love. You are my mouthpiece. I love you. I have spoken now. Listen, for I will always guide you.

Narrow Pathways

Little rooms hold large amounts in my kingdom.

They are small but mighty, rare, and full of jewels.

Never look at the size of a situation and determine its worth.

For large is often void and empty.

Small is often full and complete.

My pathways are narrow.

I place the most valuable I own on their roads.

Follow the footprints I've set before you.

This is the way.

Walk ye in it.

Steady Me

WHEN THE LIGHTNING QUAKES and the thunders roll,
When the forces of this world continuously rattle my soul,
Steady me
Steady my frame
Steady the deepest parts within
Bring your order amidst my chaos,
Your timing into my instabilities
I need you
Hem me in and bind me to your side
Merge souls with me
Let's be one
Place your angels to guard the door of my heart
I need your strength
Seek after me, Majestic One
Silence the war within
And let your peace wash me like a flood
Empty
Utterly helpless without you
You are my fill
You are my portion
Help me enter your rest
Comfort me in this place
Without you, I will fail
Without you, I will surely die
Preserve my life
Lift my Spirit from within me
Fill me with your hope to endure the darkest nights

I am coming for you, Darling Girl. Feel me rising from within you. Stop listening to the nonsense of others. Hold fast to my promises. Stop separating yourself from me. How can I leave you, Love? I am with you forever. Pull deep. Let me emerge.

Dear Christ of God

DEAR CHRIST OF GOD,

I remember you. I honor you. I feel you. I listen to you.

I am you. You are me. Forever connected. We are one.

Every day I thank you not only for the words you have spoken throughout the ages, but those your Spirit continues to speak to me now—the same Spirit abiding in you as it is in me.

Together. United. Risen.

You brought heaven to earth and placed it in my heart.
No separation. No divide.

This day and always I delight in our journey together through this gloriously delightful and spiritual kingdom where we feast as one.

With all my sincere gratitude for the flame you placed within me,
I love you. I love your mind. I love your heart.
It moves me every single day.

To the Christ of God and the same life-giving Spirit
that unites us for always,
I honor you and bless you, this day and forever.

You rose so I could rise.

Thank you for being the single greatest Trailblazer I have ever known, giving your life to show us all the way back home.

Made in the USA
Lexington, KY
28 October 2019